THE TECH COUP

THE TECH COUP

How to Save
Democracy from
Silicon Valley

Marietje Schaake

PRINCETON UNIVERSITY PRESS

PRINCETON AND OXFORD

Published by Princeton University Press
41 William Street, Princeton, New Jersey 08540
99 Banbury Road, Oxford OX2 6JX

press.princeton.edu

Library of Congress Cataloging-in-Publication Data

Names: Schaake, Marietje, 1978– author.
Title: The tech coup : How to save democracy from silicon valley / Marietje Schaake.
Description: Princeton, New Jersey : Princeton University Press, 2024. | Includes bibliographical references and index.
Identifiers: LCCN 2024001198 (print) | LCCN 2024001199 (ebook) | ISBN 9780691241173 (hardback) | ISBN 9780691241180 (ebook)
Subjects: LCSH: Democracy. | Information technology—Political aspects. | Social media—Political aspects. | Political participation—Technological innovations. | Corporate power. | Business and politics.
Classification: LCC JC421 .S329 2024 (print) | LCC JC421 (ebook) | DDC 320.97301/4—dc23/eng/20240315
LC record available at https://lccn.loc.gov/2024001198
LC ebook record available at https://lccn.loc.gov/2024001199

British Library Cataloging-in-Publication Data is available

Editorial: Bridget Flannery-McCoy, Alena Chekanov
Jacket: Karl Spurzem
Production: Erin Suydam
Publicity: James Schneider (US), Kathryn Stevens (UK)
Copyeditor: Brian Bendlin

This book has been composed in Adobe Text Pro

Printed in the United States of America

10 9 8 7 6 5 4 3 2 1

CONTENTS

Introduction

THE BATTLE

In early 2010, at a café in the eastern part of Turkey, a young man (I'll call him Ali) told me of his escape from Iran. Ali had been arrested the previous summer during the Green Movement, a series of popular protests that erupted after what many Iranians regarded as a fraudulent presidential election. As Ali sat on the sidewalk with his wrists tied, anticipating being picked up by police and pondering his fate, a local woman happened to drive by. She stopped her car, courageously whisked him away, and dropped him off at home. Despite this brief reprieve, Ali knew that the Basiji, part of the infamous Islamic Revolutionary Guard Corps, would soon be knocking on the door of his parents' place, and he decided to flee to a remote area in the north where his family owned a small plot of land.

Ali was one of millions of Iranians who challenged Mahmoud Ahmadinejad's victory in the presidential election that summer. On June 20, 2009, one of these brave demonstrators, Neda Agha-Soltan, was killed by a sniper. Her death came quickly as she sank down to the pavement, blood running from her mouth, people around her screaming in horror.[1] We know this because, unlike many of the brutal incidents that authoritarian regimes carry out in dark prison cells, Neda's death was captured on a bystander's cell phone. Videos of this and other state violence against peaceful protesters were shared around the world, fueling outrage and condemnation. Green Movement demonstrators posted their eyewitness accounts on social media with the hashtag #iranelection, allowing the entire world to witness a revolution unfolding in one of the most repressive countries on the planet.

The role of social media (specifically, Facebook, Twitter, and YouTube) and the use of technology (cell phones and internet connections) quickly became a defining theme in how journalists and politicians around the world understood the protests in Iran. These platforms were filling an important gap left by the Iranian regime's press crackdown. A few days after the protests started, in a desperate move to regain control, authorities banned journalists from doing any street reporting.[2] Ahmadinejad closed twelve newspapers and locked up over one hundred journalists.[3] Twitter (now known as X) emerged as the main platform for citizens to transmit information about the protests and the government's violence. As a result, some even called the Green Movement a "Twitter Revolution."[4] There was a widespread sense of hope about the democratizing potential of these nascent technologies; beyond using social media and cell phones to document and share human rights abuses, activists could also use them to coordinate actions and mobilize their movement. The administration of U.S. president Barack Obama even asked Twitter to delay a planned systems update to avoid temporarily disabling access for protesters in Iran.[5]

This hopefulness about technology as a partner in liberation was bolstered in 2010 as popular protests erupted in Tunisia and Egypt. When Egyptians revolted against the regime of President Hosni Mubarak, Western media proclaimed it a "Facebook revolution," in homage to the gigantic Facebook groups formed by youth protesters to coordinate the demonstrations.[6] Many believed that young people in the Middle East and North Africa would be better equipped to secure justice and rights with the help of U.S.-made technologies.

While Western media and policy circles excitedly buzzed about the democratizing potential of new technologies, the picture on the ground in Cairo, Tehran, and Tunis was not as straightforward. As Iranian journalist Golnaz Esfandiari would later explain, activists typically used word of mouth, text messages, emails, and blog posts to organize protests rather than social media.[7]

Finally, as Ali himself would soon discover, cell phone technology exposed protesters to enormous risks. When he arrived at his hideout destination in the north of Iran, he called his mother to tell her he was safe. Her relief would not last long: Ali's phone signal was picked up by a nationwide monitoring network, and he was arrested soon thereafter, in the middle of nowhere. He ended up in the notorious Evin Prison, known for the brutal rape and torture of inmates.[8] After spending several dreadful months behind Evin's walls, he was able to escape during a furlough and eventually made his way to eastern Turkey. Yet even at the time of our meeting in early 2010, he still changed locations every day, since he knew that the Iranian security services were actively hunting down dissidents across the border.

Those who praised the democratizing possibilities of technology and social media platforms failed to appreciate that repressive authoritarian regimes could be tech-savvy too. In Iran, and later in Syria, state authorities tactically lifted bans on the use of internet services, only to later scan posts to incriminate the messengers. The same technologies that help detect spam assisted state militias with identifying authors of antiregime social media posts. Military intelligence services were able to use location services to spot a group of people gathering on a street corner—real-time information that can be very useful when looking to disperse crowds before they can form.

I was appalled by the suffering the Iranian protestors endured; Neda Agha-Soltan was only four years younger than I was at the time. Their courage also deeply inspired me. I had recently won an election for a seat in the European Parliament by criticizing the Dutch government, while people in Iran were being shot by theirs for doing the same. I felt shocked—not by the behavior of these repressive governments, from whom I expected little else, but by our own double standards. The monitoring and surveillance technology these regimes were using came from Europe: Italian-made hacking systems were the technology of choice for the regime of Bashar al-Assad in Syria, while French technologies helped Muammar al-Gaddhafi in Libya and British systems facilitated the Mubarak regime in Egypt.[9]

Right when European governments were condemning the repression of people and their human rights, European companies were exporting sophisticated monitoring software to Middle Eastern rulers. As Nokia-Siemens Networks would admit in 2010, they sold cell phone surveillance technologies to the Iranian authorities that enabled them to track the protesters—people who were peacefully asking for freedoms that any European today takes for granted.[10] In a hearing before the Subcommittee on Human Rights of the European Parliament, Nokia-Siemens's head of marketing tried to distance the company from Iran's abuses, arguing that, ultimately, "people who use this technology to infringe human rights are responsible for their actions."[11] While this is obviously true—no one disputes that the Iranian government is responsible for its actions—this does not absolve the company of its moral obligation to avoid assisting a repressive government. Engineers of companies with such contracts would have traveled to Iran multiple times to train users or to repair surveillance systems, and they likely received additional pay for staffing a hardship post. Moreover, the human rights violations in Iran were well known and well documented even before the crackdown on protests began in 2009.

As a newly elected member of the European Parliament, I was incensed by Ali's story, as well as by the stories of the other Iranian refugees I met on my trip to Turkey. What meaning did European statements in support of human rights even have when global tools of repression were produced right here at home? These double standards became a galvanizing foundation for much of my work in public service. I would spend the next decade using every policy tool imaginable trying to stop what I then called "digital arms"—software that inevitably violates human rights and ends up harming innocent people.[12] Unfortunately, there is still much more work to be done. Today, newer versions of these commercial hacking systems have only grown in force and scale. Even worse, as I learned more about the sprawling digital arms trade over the past decade, I realized that Iran's Green Movement was merely one battle in the war to protect democracy from technological overreach.

The Reveal

When the Pegasus Project released a series of articles about government espionage in the summer of 2021, the news filled me with a mix of horror and hope.[13] Pegasus is the flagship spyware product of NSO Group—an Israeli technology firm that holds the pole position in the billion-dollar global spyware market. Sold as a counterterrorism and crime-fighting solution all over the world, spyware often ends up being used like a privatized intelligence service to stalk and repress critical voices. The investigative journalists who worked as part of the Pegasus Project revealed NSO Group's hit list: over fifty thousand phone numbers of the potential targets that the organization had been hacking on behalf of their clients.[14] For many, the Pegasus Project displayed the deep impact of hacking and surveillance technologies for the first time.

The leaks revealed the existence of highly sophisticated surveillance and hacking systems that made the tracking and tracing of Ali in Iran look wildly outdated. Pegasus can transform a target's phone or laptop into a live surveillance tool by remotely turning on microphones and cameras without the user's knowledge. These "zero-click" attacks, as they are known, are highly effective because the targeted individual does not even have to click on an infected link or do anything themself for the infiltration to begin. Once NSO Group gains access, its customers can extract contacts, call logs, messages, photos, web browsing history, and settings, and they can gather information from popular communications and chat apps.[15] Unsurprisingly, authoritarian governments across the world have been keen customers. NSO Group was valued at $2.3 billion before the Pegasus Project put a critical spotlight on the company.[16]

Beyond revealing what the technology could do and who was targeted, the leaked documents also showed who was involved with NSO Group. Former officials from the Obama administration and the

French government, for instance, had taken lucrative roles as senior advisers with the company—even as the phones of the president of France, the editor in chief of the *Financial Times*, and Hungarian opposition leaders were breached and monitored.[17] Nokia-Siemens's facilitation of Ali's arrest and NSO Group's ongoing dealings with autocrats beg a question: Why wasn't more being done to stop the development and sale of these technologies by democratic governments from within whose borders these companies operated?

One reason, though far from the only one, is that for too long our political leaders have been in the grip of an overly optimistic and self-centered view of new technologies. The data-driven strategies that were part of the successful campaign of Barack Obama in 2008 generated off-the-charts excitement among elected officials the world over. Politicians were keen to embrace new ways to communicate with citizens and constituents. I know this firsthand because communicating on social media platforms certainly helped me win my seat to the European Parliament. As a newcomer on the political stage, I may have never reached potential voters had it not been for Facebook and Twitter. Once elected, these platforms also offered a helpful way to update people on activities that would not be reported in newspapers or TV news bulletins. In my early days in the European Parliament, technological disruption was largely seen as a positive development.

But even as more information about the true nature and shadow sides of these technologies was revealed, and as companies grew massively, public officials did little. By the time the Pegasus Project revelations made headlines in 2021, I had spent a decade fighting the spyware sector and the toxic industry still had not been brought to a halt. Yes, we managed to get the European Union (EU) to adopt export controls, restricting the overseas sales of surveillance tools, but imports and thus domestic use remained untouched.

Naively, I initially thought that my fellow political leaders were not taking action on tech regulation because they simply didn't understand these rapidly evolving technological systems operating below the radar. Though such ignorance may have played a contributing role in their inaction, the primary reason was much more cynical: democratic governments wanted to deploy these technologies too, to spy on their own populations. At the time, Europeans were practically apoplectic over U.S. intelligence services snooping on European leaders, including German chancellor Angela Merkel.[18] The governments of EU member states pushed new legislation to protect people from falling prey to American surveillance practices. Yet despite these governments' very public outrage, their own police forces quietly procured sophisticated infiltration systems to go after criminals and terror suspects. To this day, few European government agencies will admit to using Pegasus or similar systems. Later, in 2022, additional significant cases of spyware abuse, including the hacking of opposition leaders, judges, and journalists by the governments of Greece, Poland, and Spain were revealed.[19] Researchers from the Carnegie Endowment for International Peace created an index showing that seventy-four governments had contracted with commercial firms to obtain spyware or digital forensics technology.[20] In my home country, freedom of information requests to Dutch police went unanswered, but sources told investigative journalist Huib Modderkolk that Pegasus was used to hack the devices of Ridouan Taghi, the country's most notorious fugitive Mafia boss.[21]

In the United States, broader awareness about mass surveillance practices of U.S. intelligence services hardly led to decisive legal change. A decade after Edward Snowden's revelations, journalists, parliamentarians, and citizens are still barely capable of bringing transparency to the procurement of tech systems and services by democratic governments. It is a vivid reminder of how 9/11 continues to cast a long shadow over security policy, leading to disastrous moral confusion. On the one hand, there is the illusion of a clear line between democratic countries and their enemies. In the name of security, illiberal surveillance practices continue to erode civil liberties at the heart of democratic societies. On the other hand, to my frustration, the plight of human rights defenders and journalists in the Global South—many of whom were first to have been targeted by Western-made spyware—generated too little urgency to address the issue.

The failure of the Green Movement in Iran, as well as the lack of proper policy responses by democratic governments, made something manifestly clear during my first year in office: if technology was to serve people and promote democracy as it promised, laws were needed to turn those hopes into realities and to guard against both corporate opportunism and authoritarian capture. Merely assuming that information and communication technology (ICT) would foster the spread of democracy was clearly a failed strategy. Defending and advancing democratic principles would require intentionally updating and creating laws to express, revive, and protect those principles from both external threats and threats within our own borders. Indeed, today's attacks on democracy do not come from just authoritarian states or a loss of trust in the democratic process. The gradual erosion of democracy in our time is being accelerated by the growing, unaccountable power of technology companies, of which NSO Group is only one, albeit extreme, example.

The Global Shift

The unaccountable power of technology companies and the threat that they pose to democracy are by now familiar refrains. The newspapers are littered daily with scandals that cover the latest revelation of problems at one or another social media platform, search engine, or retail platform. The purpose of this book is not to preach to the choir and rehash those stories, however significant and urgent they may be. Instead this book begins from the premise that these incidents point to systemic problems that need unpacking: the fact that our social, professional, and civil lives are increasingly digitized and, essentially, *all* aspects of digitization are in the hands of private companies; that certain technologies have inherently antidemocratic characteristics, while laws to protect democratic values and the rule of law are lagging; and that, most important, democratic governments' outsourcing of key functions has led to a hollowing out of governments' core capabilities. These systematic problems are now undermining the core principles of democracy: free and fair elections, the rule of law, the separation of powers, a well-informed public debate, national security and the protection of civil liberties such as freedom of expression, the presumption of innocence, and the right to privacy. Undermining principles have practical consequences; as we'll see in the coming chapters, tech's metastatic and unchecked growth has resulted in real-world violence, instability, and division.

The digital revolution has seen private companies increasingly take on functions normally assumed by states, leading to a concerning erosion of agency and accountability. For instance, Elon Musk's Starlink satellites, which dominate satellite-based internet services worldwide, have military chiefs worried, and with good reason: in the middle of the Russian war of aggression, Musk personally denied a request from Ukraine to turn on Starlink near Crimea. The Ukrainian government would need the connectivity to launch surprise attacks on Russian occupying naval vessels. But Musk decided the risk of Russian retaliation in the form of a nuclear attack was too great—a significant political decision from a businessman, and one he had the power to make. On Twitter the billionaire bragged, "Between Tesla, Starlink and Twitter, I may have more real-time economic data in one head than anyone ever."[22] Governments are beginning to realize that the tech sector's outsize influence is a major problem. President Joe Biden admitted as much on August 25, 2021, after inviting tech CEOs to a White House summit on cybersecurity: "The reality is," he noted, "most of our critical infrastructure is owned and operated by the private sector."[23] The U.S. president, arguably the most powerful leader in the world, conceded that the government alone cannot protect the homeland, and it needs tech companies to lend a hand.

That private companies, rather than the government, are responsible for such basic tasks as protecting national security and gathering intelligence may not have sunk in with the general public quite yet. Without public outcry, the needed regulation, oversight, and accountability are not moving along at the necessary speed.

During my years in the European Parliament, I progressively came to see technology through the lens of power. Technology could help emancipate people and raise unheard voices, or it could transform disruptors into monopolists who ruthlessly pursued efficiency, surveillance, scale, and profit. In either case, technology is not neutral. As I will elaborate in this book, systems are themselves designed with values built into them, even if that is unintended. Additionally, given that most technologies are developed by private companies, these technologies are ultimately deployed for profit maximization, and profit maximization incentives are often misaligned with what is best for society. Sam Altman's Worldcoin, for example, aspires to build a global identity database by asking people in developing countries to scan their irises, in return for a bit of cryptocurrency; the firm is either blind or completely cavalier to the risks of concentrating so much sensitive biometric data under one roof.[24] Social media platforms seek to extend online engagement time of their users with little concern for the negative effect on teenagers' mental health.[25] Tech firms and their products now also make potentially life-altering decisions. Commercial algorithms designate triage statuses in hospitals and analyze medical images.[26] All the while, democratically elected representatives remain in the dark about key details of how these products work, since independent research is often impossible. For too long, too much trust has been placed in tech companies without making sure that their technology operates within the parameters of the rule of law and supports democratic outcomes.

An abdication of responsibility on the part of democratically elected leaders is what led to Pegasus being used to track members of the opposition in Poland and what enabled the Iranian government's monitoring of Ali. Laws are not updated to ensure that digital means of repression or intrusion are banned in the way that physical means would be. For instance, a conventional raid of an opposition party politician's home would immediately set off alarm bells, yet when hacking tools are deployed, there is less clarity or concern over the same kind of digital "raid." The introduction of new technologies seems to blur lawmakers' vision; they cannot fathom that violations of fundamental rights—like privacy and free expression—in the digital world are just as grave, while at times they are made much more easily and can be more vast in scope. Corporate leaders and aspiring autocrats alike take advantage of this situational blindness and push the boundaries of the law. As digitization progresses, we see a gradual shift in responsibility and power away from democratic leaders. This shift accelerates two trends: growing digital authoritarianism and a wholesale decline in democratic governance.

In comparison to the European and U.S. governments, who have largely allowed private tech companies to operate as they please, the Chinese Communist Party (CCP) has made sure that new technologies serve its political system and values. It has spent the last two decades deploying them toward its own political advantage. The artificial intelligence (AI) sector, for instance, is powered by the limitless data collected by the Chinese government, whose repressive practices are fueling innovations from facial recognition applications to new ways of influencing and controlling massive amounts of people. During the COVID-19 pandemic, tracking apps were mandatory in China and used to survey whether people stayed at home in quarantine.[27] Similarly, the state uses sophisticated monitoring methods to verify and incarcerate the Uyghur minority population, both developing and entrenching state power.[28]

It is a model that China eagerly exports through the Digital Silk Road, as well as its other development projects. By investing in infrastructure and offering cloud computing to other countries, China keeps them connected with their data and development. Egypt, for example, has relied heavily on Chinese investment to modernize its telecommunications infrastructure and even construct a new smart city. The North African country has now also adopted China's model of internet governance via a new cybercrime law, and Egyptian government officials routinely attend Beijing's censorship training.[29]

The strategic marriage of geopolitics and technology in China lays bare how far technology governance lags on the part of democratic countries, a discrepancy that not only impacts the citizens of those countries but also affects the ability of nations to come to shared rules and solutions. It is difficult for the United States to lead the international community toward consensus on robust technology regulations, for example, given its laissez-faire approach toward Silicon Valley. China offers a cohesive, top-down governance model, ready to be copied. This mismatch further entrenches the agency of both corporate powers and authoritarian states.

The entangled nature of technology—linking economics, security, and rights—requires an integrated political vision. Yet democratic leaders have too often responded to disruptions with inaction or a piecemeal approach, and they struggle to articulate an alternative to the technology industry's preferred hands-off approach to regulation. Without a blueprint for how to enshrine democratic standards domestically, a credible foreign policy agenda is impossible. To rein in the outsize power of technology companies, regain control over their products' basic functions, and protect democratic values on the world stage, democratic countries need to develop more robust legal and governance frameworks, effective institutions, and strong incentives that avoid abuses of power on the part of states or companies using technologies.

The Task

Reinventing democratic governance to match the challenges of digitization will not be an easy task. Today's policy processes are running out of sync with the pace and scale of corporate operations. This mismatch is a growing problem for those who believe democracy should not be disrupted, no matter how exciting the shiny new objects from Bangalore, Shenzhen, or Silicon Valley might look. It means that democratic governance should be revived and updated.

During my time in office, the more I worked on technology-related issues, the clearer it became that there was a huge and growing gap between corporate power, on the one hand, and democratic regulatory and oversight capability, on the other. In some cases, this is mainly about money. As of January 2024, Apple had a market capitalization of $3 trillion, making it more valuable than the stock markets of Australia and Germany combined.[30] As a result of such resource disparity, the public sector has fallen so far behind the tech sector in innovative capabilities (not to mention salaries, computing power, knowledge, and talent) that its ability to set rules for and by the people is severely hampered.

In other cases, lawmakers' lack of access to information impedes evidence-based rulemaking. Software is complex: large legacy programs can have tens of millions of lines of code, and machine learning systems may develop rules that even their own creators do not completely grasp. Moreover, companies have learned to use intellectual property law to protect the opacity of proprietary algorithms and to shield their treasured workings behind trade secret protections. In general, existing legal protections, made in an era before the internet even existed, disproportionately benefit companies. The same laws that help Coca-Cola protect its secret recipe also protect technology firms from disclosing how their algorithms function.

Let's consider new challenges to the Freedom of Information Act (FOIA), which journalists use to uncover information about government services. When government services are outsourced to technology companies, FOIA requests regarding those services can be denied when companies invoke intellectual property protections or even privacy standards as an exception to providing openness and accountability. In other cases, government officials will simply not feel bound to preserve records when using private, nongovernmental channels of communication. For instance, the EU's ombudsman had to issue an official ruling to underline that text messages exchanged by EU leaders on WhatsApp are subject to record-keeping and transparency rules, just as official emails and letters are. Just months after its lobbying blitz, Mistral AI announced a partnership with Microsoft, further consolidating AI assets in Silicon Valley.[31]

In some cases, corporate reticence takes absurd forms, as I learned on a trip to Silicon Valley in 2016 with my European Parliament colleague Kaja Kallas, who has gone on to serve as the prime minister of Estonia. We were working on new legislation that concerned illegal speech on online platforms and traveled halfway around the world to meet with representatives of Facebook, Google, and Yahoo. At most companies, legal teams walked us through the company policies for dealing with illegal and harmful content and underlined how they worried about protecting freedom of expression. But our experience at 1 Hacker Way, Facebook's headquarters in Menlo Park, California, was altogether different. We began the day with a long tour of the campus as guides steered us around like tourists at Disneyland, pointing out every piece of whimsical art and the all-you-can-eat cafeterias in the vast, multicolored office building. When we finally took our seats in a meeting room, our hosts broached a conversation about *Lean In,* the new and highly influential book from Facebook's then-COO, Sheryl Sandberg, that considered the gender-based challenges facing women in the workplace. The conversation might have been interesting for a weekend book club, but we had not come all this way to talk about *Lean In.* When we reminded our hosts that we were there to discuss what responsibility the social media platform had to moderate content uploaded by users, they responded with polite smiles and nods: "Oh, we are terribly sorry, but for that subject you would need to talk to our legal team," to which we replied, "Well exactly, that is why we are here." Unfortunately, we were told, the people with expertise and authority to speak with us were not available.

This visit, peculiar in its own right, also spoke to a far more fascinating dynamic in Silicon Valley. Corporate giants did not feel accountable to lawmakers like me. They thought that they could dodge real policy and enforcement questions with free frozen yogurt and inspirational buzzwords—and we hadn't yet proven them wrong. As democratic governance long failed to impose guardrails on companies like Facebook, they had grown to believe that they operated above the law.

The Delivery

In 2019, after serving more than a decade in the European Parliament, I stepped down from politics and moved to the belly of the beast: Silicon Valley and Stanford University. I wanted to help bridge the gaps between the worlds of politics, policy, and technology.

Not long after I arrived at Stanford, I attended a presentation that confirmed just how badly such bridges were needed. The speaker, an engineer who had just left Instagram, shared fascinating experiences about curation of content through algorithms and how taste and culture could be shaped by decisions of what photos were posted on the front page of a user's feed. In other words, technology could be used to shape behavior and consumption. The engineer then discussed how this allowed companies of a certain size to move and affect markets. By putting a post of a celebrity with a cosmetics product on the homepage, the company significantly increased the likelihood that the product would see an uptick in sales.

When the time came for questions, I took the microphone. Did that ability to move and create markets, I asked, also imply the possibility of influencing, shaping, or moving political beliefs, values, and behavior more widely? Could it also move masses? A popular meme ridiculing a candidate in a political race, a call by a popular influencer to go shopping instead of voting on Election Day, or the sale of merchandise from the Black Lives Matter movement or the National Rifle Association, for instance, could be increasingly powerful if their reach was amplified. As it is not always easy to define clearly what qualifies as political content online, I wanted to know about the discussions among engineers and whether the societal or political impacts were ever considered when designing recommendation algorithms that cater to billions of people. The engineer admitted that they did not understand the question. In a way, that was the clearest answer I could have asked for.

The fulfillment of the democratic promise by politicians and states has never been perfect. But the Churchillian adage, that democracy is the worst form of government except for all others, still holds. We must preserve democracy, and to do that, our governments must regain control over our society's technological capabilities. While there are some encouraging signs in terms of new laws, regulatory proposals, and citizen initiatives, they remain too slow and ad hoc to truly shift the status quo and restore the balance of power between public authorities and private companies. These alone won't stop the privatization of the entire digital sphere. While many like to contrast the EU's and the United States' different legal and political cultures, I prefer to emphasize the unfortunate paralysis and tendency toward inaction that they have in common. The entire democratic world has been too slow to build a democratic governance model for technologies, and countries have not done so together. Ash Carter, the late former U.S. secretary of defense, lamented the "ethos of public purpose that has become dangerously decoupled from many of today's leading tech endeavors."[32] I agree.

Democracy is not flawless, nor does it claim to be. What the political system possesses, however, is the ability to improve. As Samantha Power explains, "Democracy wins out in the long run because it offers a chance to fix its own mistakes. It is the only system built on the premise that if something is not working, people can actually correct it, from the bottom up. Democracy works best when people are given the opportunity to constantly monitor and repair the kinks in the machinery."[33] At its best, democracy is deliberate, self-correcting, and compromise-generating. It is never static but is a process in motion. And that should give us hope for its future.

It is time to normalize the way we think about updating laws and adopting regulations to match the power of technology companies. To understand what this could look like, we can look to another tool that saw exponential growth over the past century: cars. People and governments are aware of the benefits of cars. But it would have been shortsighted if, out of fear of stifling automobile growth, governments refrained from requiring driver's licenses, imposing safety regulations, or addressing the environmental harms and other negative externalities produced by driving. Moreover, when a particular model of car systematically breaks down, no one expects individual drivers to take responsibility. No one believes that merely by starting the engine, the driver has agreed to accept any underlying flaws or dangers in the car's design. No one would believe a simple statement by the car manufacturer that the car is safe, environmentally friendly, and energy efficient. All these elements, standards, and commitments are independently tested to make sure that people are safe and the environmental damage is limited. Companies are not blindly trusted to preserve the public interest, and when corporate leaders violate these standards—for instance, as when Volkswagen lied about emissions while tampering with emissions software—parliamentary inquiries seek to bring accountability. Even though cars are complex technologies, rules about their qualifications were put in place and guardrails around their use adopted. Doing the same for digital technologies is both urgently needed and practically possible.

The history of the car's influence on society also offers another important lesson for the task we confront in this book. Today we have huge roads, bridges, and parking structures; we have enormous factories for the production of cars; natural resources are drilled and burned to ensure that cars can be driven; and we have traffic rules that apply on public roads. All this existing infrastructure is difficult to reverse or ignore. The same will happen with digital infrastructure soon enough, and the laws we adopt today will determine the path of emerging technologies and the trajectory of their associated infrastructure. We must act wisely. Without rules to protect people's safety, to regulate behavior in public spaces, or to ensure that companies are doing as they say and saying as they do, the harm to society and indeed to democracy will be significant.

This is a book about the impact of digital disruption on democracy. This is, of course, far from the only problem with the tech industry. However, I am choosing a focused lens here, as I am convinced that a loss of insight, agency, and oversight on the part of citizens and public institutions cannot be compensated for with the exciting perspectives of economic growth or innovation benefits. I am not under the illusion that technology can be stopped. It should not be, and I am hopeful and excited about what technology can continue to bring to us all. Yet I am very critical of a powerful, unaccountable industry that, to date, has been almost entirely without guidance or guardrails from democratic authorities. Solving the accountability gap is particularly urgent because technology is not a sector but a layer that impacts almost all sectors.

In Support of Democracy

This is not a book against technology but in favor of democracy. It is a call to rebalance technology's role in democratic societies to ensure better protection of democratic values. It urges democratic governments to safeguard the public sphere, to develop future-proof solutions, and to revive and reinvent its approach to tech regulation, knowing that new technologies will continue to challenge and disrupt. We do not have time to address these harms in an ad hoc manner: endlessly debating whether Facebook's community standards are helpful or not shifts our attention away from broader and more systemic issues. A new approach to tech policy needs to be holistic, looking at the bigger picture and always in service of strengthening democratic principles. In other words, it is time to tackle the causes, not the symptoms.

The Tech Coup shifts the spotlight from Big Tech's scandals to the systematic erosion of democracy as private companies run ever more parts of our digital lives. You, as a democratic citizen, are invited to help shape an agenda that puts the survival of democratic principles ahead of short-term economic benefits. States can remain very powerful actors if they choose to be, as unfortunately illustrated by the bitter success of authoritarian models of governing in the digital world. Revitalizing democracy will require new approaches to lawmaking and innovative forms of governance designed to explicitly support democratic principles in new contexts. And it will demand that we craft and enforce policies that better equip democracy for surviving the twenty-first century. While technological fixes are necessary, they alone are insufficient, and for any of them to work, we need a broader, functional political infrastructure to serve the people.

Restoring democratic governance over technological systems— instead of allowing privatized governance over our digital world— will go a long way toward making the world a more fair, just, and equitable place.

1

The Code

In the spring of 2016, I was invited to speak at a Stanford University symposium, along with a few other members of the Global Commission on Internet Governance, group of experts and practitioners from around the world tasked with presenting a vision on internet governance. We had just published our final report, *One Internet*, after two years of hearings and deliberations, in which we recommended steps to foster an open, secure, and trustworthy internet.[1] Though I welcomed the opportunity to share our commission's suggestions, I was less than optimistic that they would find a receptive audience in the heart of Silicon Valley. After all, in my experience, tech industry leaders mostly cared about policy when they tried to prevent it from having an impact on their businesses.

The day started constructively. Speakers with a wide range of backgrounds—including venture capitalist Marc Andreessen; the former prime minister of Sweden, Carl Bildt; and sociologist and democracy studies scholar Larry Diamond—all addressed the need for an internet governance regime that was attentive to both security and human rights in the digital context. Based on the discussion, it seemed as though everyone was united in the quest to protect core democratic values through sensible regulation. If only that had been the case; the private dinner that evening would quickly dispel any such delusions.

That evening, the dinner tables were filled with top Silicon Valley power brokers, who all moved in a relatively small bubble between a handful of companies. In attendance were, for instance, Dara Khosrowshahi, the CEO of Expedia, who would later lead Uber; Kent Walker, the general counsel at Google, and previously at eBay; and Rachel Whetstone, the head of communications at Uber, who had just moved there from Google and would later move on to work for Netflix. The former U.S. secretary of state, Condoleezza Rice, offered some opening remarks and led an exchange of questions and answers. Conversations then continued informally under what are known as the Chatham House rule, according to which attendees can later relate the content of the discussion but are forbidden from attributing specific comments to individual speakers. This rule, which is meant to encourage frank conversation, gave these titans of industry a chance to break from their polished talking points and to express themselves frankly, including their true distaste for oversight of any kind.

I quickly found myself cornered. Questions and critiques of Europe's relationship with technology were firing at me from all sides. Did Europeans realize their tendency to overregulate was the reason why no equivalent of Silicon Valley existed there? Was jealousy to blame for a vindictive zeal to obstruct American tech firms? Why were Europeans so emotional about privacy protections? Didn't the behavior of teenagers posting their entire lives online, including those in Europe, indicate that privacy was already dead?

My aggressive interlocutors would have been surprised to learn that in Europe I was seen as "pro-tech," a voice against an overbearing government and excited about the possibilities of new technologies. After all, I belonged to a progressive, centrist political party. Since the time I was a university student, I have been enthusiastic about the opportunities that new technologies bring. Regulation was needed to ensure that technology companies played fairly and people's rights were protected; it was not a plot to punish Silicon Valley. I'm not sure how many minds I changed during that evening, but the dinner was nevertheless informative. I came away with a clearer understanding of how some of the most powerful American technology titans thought about themselves and their roles in society. These tech leaders easily dismissed concerns about pressure on fundamental rights as "emotional." They were proud of the corporate and political power they wielded to influence society's technological future—and for building an industry that, until then, had largely operated outside the grasp of regulators.

Their pride was understandable. They *were* extremely successful at avoiding regulation and instead let their commercial software code rule. Since the creation of the internet, democratic governments across the world, and especially the United States, have taken a hands-off approach to overseeing the wild growth of digital technology products and services. Yet the tech leaders at this dinner, as they often do, gave themselves far too much credit. Reality was not just shaped by them pulling strings in Brussels and Washington, DC, to achieve their preferred policy outcomes like true puppet masters. Our governments' relationship with tech is a far more complicated story, one that has played out over decades and across continents.

To understand how we got to that dinner in 2016—where I experienced the peak of tech optimism in Palo Alto—we have to go back a few decades. How and why did democratic governments cede power to tech companies, not only by failing to regulate this growing sector but even giving over essential government functions? Democratic governments willfully enabled the unmitigated growth of the market in digital technologies. They did not take this approach in secret; in fact, public and private leaders in many corners of society seemingly cheered on governments' regulatory inaction.

A cascading set of society's leaders helped us arrive at our sad reality. Early tech pioneers crafted a libertarian ideological foundation the burgeoning industry could embrace. Later tech executives transformed that ideology into antiregulatory corporate practices and built companies that sought to become governments of their own. Even as tech growth skyrocketed, Democratic and Republican administrations in the United States refused to put checks in place to balance companies' power or behavior and to hold them to account when needed. Along the way, a rotating cast of operatives moving between public office and industry sustained this hands-off approach.

Analyzing the role that each of these groups played in trumpeting a laissez-faire approach to regulation gives us a better grasp of how tech companies became so powerful—at the cost of our democracies.

The Pioneers

From the earliest days of the internet, leading tech pioneers celebrated technology's ability to democratize access to information through decentralization. Their path to changing the world was through computer code, not politics.

Consider, for instance, the early views of two founding fathers who literally built the modern internet: Vint Cerf and Tim Berners-Lee. Cerf, known for his swanky three-piece suits, grew up with a hearing impairment and became interested in technology partially as an alternative form of communication.[2] He eventually went on to create Transmission Control Protocol / Internet Protocol (TCP/IP), the underlying architecture of the internet, as an assistant professor at Stanford University.[3] For Berners-Lee, computer science was a family calling: his mathematician parents both worked on the first commercial computer. He followed in their footsteps and ended up working at CERN, a prestigious laboratory in Geneva, where he invented the World Wide Web, the core of the internet's information-sharing infrastructure.

Cerf and Berners-Lee worked in different parts of the world, over a decade apart. But they both believed in the same core principle: the internet would be the great equalizer and emancipator. Cerf believed that "anybody who wanted to build a piece of internet would do that and find somebody who would be willing to connect to them. Then the system would grow organically because it didn't have any central control."[4] He was adamant that the general public should be able to use the internet and was wary of tech companies seeking to commercialize access before a critical mass of people would have the chance of using and appreciating the internet. That was before he became Google's "Chief Internet Evangelist."[5]

Berners-Lee's vision was anchored around universal access and technological decentralization, to avoid top-down control or authority.[6] Unlike many of the other founding computer scientists who operated in the strict hierarchy of academia or the military, Berners-Lee floated between contracting gigs, research positions, and industry. He presented some of his earliest innovations on message boards, including his famous post on Usenet in August 1991, in which he previewed the World Wide Web.[7] Berners-Lee and his compatriots assumed that the collaborative, inclusive, and nonhierarchical environment of internet research could be replicated for users. But it did not take long before companies were trying to wall off and brand the online experience. Back in 1996, Berners-Lee cautioned, "The web has exploded because it is open. It has developed so rapidly because the creative forces of thousands of companies are building on the same platform. Binding oneself to one company means one is limiting one's future to the innovations that one company can provide."[8]

As soon as the internet and the web began to become popular, the cypherpunk movement, built by radically libertarian technologists and mathematicians in California, worried about how governments would use this novelty for surveillance. It advocated for strong encryption protocols to protect people's privacy online.[9] "Politics has never given anyone lasting freedom, and it never will," said one of the movement's founders, Tim May.[10] As their manifesto states, "Cypherpunks write code."[11] Rather than waiting for slow-moving bureaucratic institutions to reform, cypherpunks sought to author their own futures through technology. The emergence of this libertarian, state-skeptical strain of thought in Silicon Valley was ironic. As Thomas Heinrich, a scholar of military economics, explains, military contracts for microelectronics, satellites, and other technologies spurred the region's development after World War II, and the Pentagon's investment into technology research caused a second economic boom in the 1990s.[12] These cypherpunk thinkers essentially sought to challenge state interference in the house that the military-industrial complex had built.

The vision of openness and against central control was shared by another internet pioneer, John Perry Barlow. An eccentric character who combined writing lyrics for the Grateful Dead with a background in cattle ranching, he eventually became one of the most prolific libertarian visionaries in Silicon Valley. In his famous "Declaration of Independence of Cyberspace" of 1996, he formulated an antigovernment credo that was widely shared among his contemporaries: "Governments derive their just powers from the consent of the governed. You have neither solicited nor received ours. We did not invite you. You do not know us, nor do you know our worlds. Cyberspace does not lie within your borders."[13] It was as if Barlow extrapolated the frontier mentality of the American West straight into the new digital world.

The very notion of cyberspace—a new domain where users of every nationality, creed, and class could interact—was earth-shattering. If cyberspace could transcend borders, what was the purpose of the nation-state? These early tech pioneers were thrilled by the prospect of individuals controlling their own destiny, unshackled from the long-standing rules of governments. Their particular conception of openness, emphasizing a libertarian notion of freedom, eventually scaled from individual visionaries to the entire technology industry.

Today's industry is a far cry from Berners-Lee and Barlow's vision of emancipation through the wide availability of technology. Market pathologies have replaced the traditional institutions of the past with a new generation of powerful gatekeepers and elites. Despite their trendier branding, tech oligarchs are just as power hungry—and possibly more powerful—than the government institutions that internet pioneers sought to challenge decades ago.

A libertarian attitude would remain prominent in discussions of Silicon Valley, even as ideals of openness and decentralization gave way to a "winner-take-all" mentality that was primarily focused on profit maximization. Through hyper-quick growth, companies would seek to dominate an entire market and gain exponential benefits from their monopolies. Over the past decades, start-ups have scaled massively by offering low- or no-cost products without worrying about making a profit and with the hope of reaping massive profits once an entire market was captured. This model explains why

Uber just started to be profitable in 2023, nearly fifteen years after the company was created in 2009 and only after incurring a whopping $32 billion in losses.[14] Once a company controls the majority of a sector, after buying out or bankrupting their competition, consumers have little choice when prices surge. As Uber gradually crowded out its competitors, its prices skyrocketed—with average fares increasing by 92 percent between 2018 and 2021.[15] Reid Hoffman, founder of LinkedIn and one of Silicon Valley's most respected tech pioneers, succinctly coins this practice as "blitzscaling," explaining that "the competitive advantage comes from the growth factors built into the business model, such as network effects, whereby the first company to achieve critical scale triggers a feedback loop that allows it to dominate a winner-take-all or winner-take-most market and achieve a lasting first-scaler advantage."[16]

Blitzscaling ended up as Silicon Valley's manifest destiny. Amazon and Meta, gigantic companies that mastered the art of network effects, now dominate the tech industry. Small disruptors, even the most innovative ones, remain vulnerable to acquisition in this new landscape.

Yet even in the wake of staggering profits, the industry continues to benefit from falsely romanticized stories about its foundational ideals and aspirations to change the world. As my colleagues Rob Reich, Mehran Sahami, and Jeremy Weinstein observe in their book *System Error*, modern-day Stanford students seem to embrace idealistic dreams of solving societal problems, even as they seek to turn innovation into profit: "Innovation and disruption were the buzzwords on campus, and our students broadcasted an almost utopian view that the old ways of doing things were broken and technology was the all-powerful solution: it could end poverty, fix racism, equalize opportunity, strengthen democracy, and even help topple authoritarian regimes."[17] In other words, while the pioneers' vision has been co-opted over time to emphasize profits, the idealistic focus on their impact remains powerful among the younger generation. These good intentions can, however, create blind spots around harms and outsize corporate power. Many of the students I have taught and mentored ended up working for technology companies with hopes of changing them from within, only to find themselves eventually swept up in the powerful tide of market optimization and blitzscaling.

The Corporates

Many modern corporate tech leaders believe deeply that they can serve their users better than governments can serve their citizens. Emboldened tech billionaires, in the grips of this belief, brazenly articulate the outsize role they can—and believe they *should*—play in shaping society and building companies that skirt existing regulation while seeking to replace government capabilities. They have kept the pioneers' romantic visions of a decentralized society while antigovernment attitudes now serve corporate power more so than any other ideals.

Peter Thiel, a cofounder of PayPal, is perhaps the most outspoken of these billionaires. In 2009 he stunningly remarked that he no longer believed "that freedom and democracy are compatible." The founding vision of PayPal, he continued, "centered on the creation of a new world currency, free from all government control and dilution— the end of monetary sovereignty, as it were."[18] In addition to PayPal, Thiel also cofounded the company Palantir, which provides data and intelligence software to governments around the world. While his first firm sought to replace a core function of government entirely, Palantir offered merely to do the government's job for it.

On the surface, Mark Zuckerberg and Facebook have been less explicitly antidemocratic. In a 2012 letter, Zuckerberg laid out his views about the relationship between Facebook and governments:

> We hope to change how people relate to their governments and social institutions. We believe building tools to help people share can bring a more honest and transparent dialogue around government that could lead to more direct empowerment of people, more accountability for officials and better solutions to some of the biggest problems of our time. . . . Through this process, we believe that leaders will emerge across all countries who are pro-internet and fight for the rights of their people, including the

right to share what they want and the right to access all information that people want to share with them.[19]

A decade later, Zuckerberg's perspective sounds hopelessly naive. Facebook's methods of curating speech and amplifying content through algorithms remain opaque and have caused unsurprising if unintended consequences—for example, allowing advertisers to target "Jew haters" and members of the Nazi Party.[20] Facebook's support for free speech also conveniently omits the reality of data hoarding, microtargeting, and the fact that advertisers, not the average Facebook user, are the company's main client. Meanwhile, Facebook largely denies public access to its data, whether requested by academics or members of the U.S. Congress. "Honest," "transparent," and "accountable" are some of the last words that regulators around the world would use to describe the company's conduct today.

Similar corporate boldness and antigovernment antagonism has intensified over time within the tech sector. For instance, in early 2017, when I was still a member of the European Parliament, I received a brief direct message on Twitter asking to speak over Signal, the messaging app most trusted for its strong encryption. A terrified insider at Uber wanted me to know what they had witnessed while working at the company. The trembling voice on the other end of the line made clear their concern that, by sharing this information, they would be open to lawsuits and other forms of intimidation. I repeated my commitment to confidentiality several times and soon learned why the informant was so afraid.

Uber's leadership understood that people hailing a ride close to police stations would likely be police officers, and that people frequently visiting the Federal Trade Commission (FTC) building in Washington, DC, might work for the regulatory agency. Because police officers and public officials were trying to crack down on Uber, particularly in locations that had outlawed or were evaluating the legality of service, the company built a custom-made app to avoid such users. Once software had spotted users close to law enforcement offices, the user was promptly served a different, tailor-made experience in a parallel app named Greyball. This app would display "ghost cars"—vehicles that showed up in the app but were not real—and this made it nearly impossible for those users to get a ride. The unassuming employee of a parliament or oversight body had no idea they were ghosted. A later story in the *New York Times* featuring four courageous whistleblowers indicated that Greyball was being used on a global scale.[21] The sheer audacity of Greyball showed that Uber and its peer companies believed they could act with impunity. The tech firms not only objected to specific regulations but thought they were above the entire regulatory regime.

Once the story had become public, I sent parliamentary questions—the equivalent of a congressional oversight letter—about the legality of this practice to the European Commission. In response, the Commission noted that it did not "have information related to the data-gathering tool 'Greyball' beyond what the press reports have written. The Commission cannot therefore assess whether there may be any concerns under EU law."[22] The lack of access to corporate information prevented the top EU regulator from even assessing whether the company was violating EU laws. That lack of access seemed to me to be the core problem, but, concerningly, the Commission accepted it as the reason for its inability to pursue meaningful action. Other jurisdictions took more decisive steps: the U.S. Department of Justice proceeded to investigate the company's practices, while the city of London banned the Uber app and cited its use of Greyball as one reason.

Brave whistleblowers brought to light this deliberate effort to deceive regulators and obstruct justice, but in most cases information that might hurt a company's reputation remains carefully concealed. Trade secret protections, made in an era before the digital economy existed, offer increasingly important legal shields behind which companies continue to unfairly protect all kinds of information about the impact of their business practices on society.

Tech companies have been so emboldened to flout regulation and defy governments because governments need them. In direct contrast to the anarchist and libertarian dreams of the internet's founders, Big Tech has become an agent of the state. Tech Inquiry has reported that agencies like the Federal Bureau of Investigation (FBI), the Federal Bureau of Prisons, Immigration and Customs

Enforcement (ICE), the U.S. Department of Defense, and the U.S. Drug Enforcement Administration have thousands of deals with Amazon, Dell, Facebook, Google, HP, and IBM.[23] Since 2016, Microsoft alone has had over 5,000 subcontracts with the Department of Defense. Amazon and Google are next in terms of volume, with 350 and 250 contracts, respectively.[24]

Unsurprisingly, a number of these companies also have lucrative procurement contracts in the rest of the world. The same agencies tasked with technology oversight rely on Dell for their equipment, Google for their research and cloud storage, and Microsoft for their software. In this way, the corporate-state power balance has shifted: most governments now need Big Tech as much as Big Tech needs them.

Beyond covert resistance to government regulation, as exemplified in Uber's Greyball, tech companies have also embraced the power narrative that regulation will crowd out innovation. In my time as a member of the European Parliament, I heard this Silicon Valley mantra echoed by almost every tech lobbyist. Without exception, any proposed piece of legislation would be presented as an undue, old-fashioned, and harmful intervention that risked stifling innovation that would surely benefit society. If Europe was to have a chance at producing a success remotely like that of Silicon Valley, lawmakers had better back off.

Conveniently, this rhetoric seemed to neglect the monumental state investment that first willed the internet into existence: the Defense Advanced Research Projects Agency, the federal defense agency that funded Vint Cerf and others' research into TCP/IP protocols, and the Advanced Research Projects Agency Network, the project linking together computers at Pentagon-funded agencies to computers so they could communicate. The same applies to the Global Positioning System (GPS), which is owned by the U.S. government and operated by the U.S. Space Force.[25] Today it is used for mapping and navigating by companies and individuals across the world, yet the tech sector wants us to believe that it has simply pulled itself up by its own bootstraps.

Still, this antiregulation rhetoric helped convince political leaders—across the world, but in America in particular—that a mix of innovation and market forces would best deliver benefits for society. Meanwhile, the hopeful vision of technologies as liberalizing forces—such as the internet itself, cell phones, and all kinds of platform companies—successfully persuaded democratic governments to let the companies work their magic with little intervention. The belief took hold that the success of the market was the success of society, causing many to overlook the fact that these companies were disrupting the role of the democratic state and principles.

Predictably, we now see the same dynamics around AI. Eric Schmidt, Google's former CEO and a key adviser to various U.S. presidential administrations, has warned that the United States may lose its lead in AI "fairly quickly" unless the government continues to fund and collaborate with the tech sector while offering it a regulatory break. An uncritical government alliance with tech companies is portrayed as the only option for America to defend democracy, particularly vis-à-vis China.

Similarly, AI leaders argue that regulating their powerful generative products now would stifle innovation. The French AI startup Mistral AI even claimed there will not be a European "big AI" success if companies are scrutinized for their foundation models. Just months after its lobbying blitz, Mistral AI announced a partnership with Microsoft, further consolidating AI assets in Silicon Valley.[26]

Though tech leaders have fiercely resisted government regulation—evading, cajoling, and, in many cases, building their companies around the objective of keeping regulators away—their success is far from their own. In this two-sided equation, government bears as much responsibility for abdicating its responsibilities. Many technology companies would never have been successful without the regulators themselves pushing on their behalf. American presidents and public officials from both parties chose to play a shockingly weak role in regulating technology companies.

The Politicians

Democrats and Republicans alike have actively embraced an explicit laissez-faire approach to tech governance. Over the past thirty years, policymakers saw nonintervention as an essential recipe for the industry's economic and strategic success. It also pushed this vision to allies around the world. Blinded by the excitement and anticipation of the benefits that the digital revolution might bestow, they neglected to prevent harms or to ensure proper oversight. This hands-off approach allowed companies to take over more and more of the government's core capabilities.

Although Tim Berners-Lee invented the World Wide Web in 1989, it took several years for the technology to develop and spread. Slowly, more and more websites began to go live. By 1994 the internet had reached the apex of American power: the White House. That was the year that the White House published its first-ever website, titled "An Interactive Citizens' Handbook."[27] By the mid-1990s, the internet had started to become the place we recognize today: a network of interconnected content with no centralized editor.

Soon questions of content moderation started to emerge: What should and should not be allowed to be published on the internet? And who was responsible for enforcing those rules? These were tough, unprecedented problems without clear solutions. Actors from all sides began calling on Congress to clarify the legal landscape and adopt rules that would help solve some of these problems. In 1996 Congress responded by passing the Communications Decency Act (CDA), the first set of rules around harassment and obscenity online. Despite the fact that key portions of the law were later overturned by the U.S. Supreme Court, it was the first—and remains arguably the most important—American law governing the internet.[28]

The most consequential part of the CDA is Section 230, which allows platforms to moderate content while exempting them from responsibility for that content. The section was jointly proposed as an amendment to the CDA in 1995 by Republican senator Christopher Cox and Democratic senator Ron Wyden with support from across the political spectrum, including both the American Civil Liberties Union and the libertarian Cato Institute. The amendment sought to "establish Government policy promoting continued development of the Internet and other interactive computer services and media and preserving the competitive free market existing for them."[29] In an interview, Senator Wyden defended the amendment, noting, "If the government is going to send out an army of censors, that's going to spoil a lot of the Net's promise."[30] Section 230 quickly transformed from a small provision into a bedrock principle for global internet regulation. The EU adopted a similar exemption of liability encoded in the E-Commerce Directive in 2000, though that provision went much further in shielding companies from government censorship. In an essay titled "Section 230 and the International Law of Facebook," Georgetown Law professor Anupam Chander explains that this directive was inspired by Germany's 1997 Teleservices Act, which itself paid homage to Section 230.[31]

Section 230 of the CDA has fundamentally shaped the internet as we know it today, particularly by offering limitations to the liability of online platforms. The original idea—that selling a stolen bike or handbag on eBay should lead to liability for just the thief, not the platform—has morphed into an immense abdication of responsibility for content including hate speech, conspiracies, and discriminatory language.

But Section 230 was just the beginning. Soon administrations from both parties began supporting a no-liability approach for online platforms. Democratic and Republican presidents were instrumental in paving the way for a light touch public policy approach that allowed technology firms to grab power. This legacy began during the second half of the administration of President Bill Clinton, the first president of the internet age.

Ira Magaziner was the mastermind behind the Clinton administration's vision for the internet, and he foresaw technology companies developing freely, unshackled by government's rules.[32] In 1997 Magaziner argued, "Governments must adopt a non-regulatory, market-oriented approach to electronic commerce, one that facilitates the emergence of a transparent and predictable legal environment to support global business and commerce."[33] In his view, "widespread competition" and "increased consumer choice" were to be the defining features of the new digital marketplace. He also predicted that the internet would promote democracy and give the United States an advantage against authoritarians. Magaziner's philosophy appeared in Clinton's visit to India in 2000, where the president celebrated U.S.-India technology collaboration and highlighted India's software success as proof that "developing nations can lead."[34]

For similar reasons, Magaziner proposed the establishment of the Internet Corporation for Assigned Names and Numbers (ICANN), an independent and international nongovernmental corporation that took over the technical management of the internet's Domain Name System.[35] Vint Cerf chaired its board from 2000 to 2007.[36] Through ICANN, the governance of the internet was deliberately left to private actors rather than democratically elected ones. Magaziner did not wish to see the government as a "Federal nanny."[37] As more and more Americans gained access to the internet, the impact of regulatory abstention put important norm-setting powers in the hands of engineers and corporate strategists.

While it may have seemed like a benign decision in the mid-1990s, this devolution of power to software code and the ones coding it had significant ramifications for decades to come. The internet is not unregulated, as Magaziner had expected it would be. Today it is simply the tech companies, exponentially more powerful than they were during the Clinton administration, who write the rules. And they are writing them in such a way as to drive even more profits to themselves. As Lawrence Lessig anticipated twenty-five years ago, "This code, or architecture, sets the terms on which life in cyberspace is experienced. It determines how easy it is to protect privacy, or how easy it is to censor speech."[38] While members of Congress feared the government as a censor, corporations were trusted with the power to not just censor but also to build, curate, and secure software.

The administration of President George W. Bush would continue this regulatory policy of benign neglect while witnessing the explosion of several tech behemoths. Google grew and made its initial public offering in 2004.[39] Facemash, created in 2003, would soon become Facebook and would gain more than one hundred million users by 2008.[40] Spotify was launched in 2006, and the first iPhone was released in 2007. Over its two terms, the Bush administration paid almost no attention to the potential damaging effects of the ballooning tech industry. In fact, Bush allowed a series of telecom mergers that concentrated the entire marketplace. And in 2001 he renewed an internet tax exemption bill that waived state and local taxes for internet access services and would push to make that exemption permanent.

However, Bush's most important tech legacy was the introduction of extraordinary surveillance programs in the name of fighting terror after 9/11. Along with Vice President Dick Cheney and Attorney General John Ashcroft, he defended warrantless wiretapping and created the Department of Homeland Security, which would also step up cybersecurity capacity. With its attention focused on issues of terrorism, it is no surprise that Ed Black, a corporate tech lobbyist, has described the Bush administration as largely being "AWOL on technology policy."[41] By neglecting the tech industry, the Bush administration allowed the new generation of tech firms to build the foundation for the sector's future dominance. At the same time, the tech industry realized that it could achieve favorable policy outcomes by making itself useful to the state. Silicon Valley, which first emerged in the post–World War II military boom, carefully integrated itself into the rapidly expanding U.S. national security regime during the War on Terror.

As Barack Obama came into office in early 2009, the relationship between government and technology entered a new era: concrete cooperation. During his presidency, American tech companies flourished even further, reaching unprecedented scale.

Obama personally embraced new social media platforms and data analysis as part of his presidential campaign, which helped solidify his image as young and engaged. He would later reflect that the campaign experience directly informed his approach to technology policy as president: "We were some of the earliest adopters of new technological tools and social media during the 2008 campaign," Obama has said. "We did a lot of data analysis on deploying volunteers, turning out the vote. I benefited from an entire war room of folks who developed high-level skills from Silicon Valley. We understood the benefit of Big Data, good data. So, we thought, how do we infuse that into the federal government?"[42]

President Obama's "war room" often included high-level folks from the Silicon Valley elite. Google's CEO, Eric Schmidt, supported the president as a campaign adviser and fundraiser. He helped Obama raise $25 million from the communications sector, compared to the meager $5 million raised by Obama's opponent,

John McCain.[43] One of Facebook's founders, Chris Hughes, joined the campaign team as a volunteer. After Obama won, he supported the creation of the White House's first-ever roles of chief technology officer, chief data scientist, and chief performance officer.[44] While it is hard to know the precise impact of these close connections between tech elites and the Obama administration, they almost certainly shaped his understanding of the sector and played some role in his lax approach to regulation. In 2013, for example, the FTC settled with Google after a two-year investigation into its control of standardized technology patents and dominance in the search engine and adtech markets.[45] Many continue to see the settlement as a missed opportunity to ensure more competition in the digital economy. At the time, the FTC sympathized with Google's argument that low competition was a necessary evil to ensure that consumers could get "better, faster, more valuable answers to their queries."[46] This logic and precedent, however, laid the groundwork for sweeping market consolidations by companies like Amazon and Apple who similarly justified their outsize influence with appeals to consumer experience.

In 2011 the Obama White House also presented the International Strategy for Cyberspace, the United States' first comprehensive outline for its approach to the digital world outside its borders. The strategy sought to connect the role of technology to diplomacy, defense, and development, while also promoting cooperation with the private sector. In his introduction to the strategy, President Obama echoed the technology industry's belief in the internet's self-fulfilling prophecy of progress, as if politics didn't exist. "The digital world," he explained, was "no longer a lawless frontier, nor the province of a small elite," but rather a space where "the norms of responsible, just, and peaceful conduct among states and peoples have begun to take hold." It was, in his view, "one of the finest examples of community self-organizing, as civil society, academia, the private sector, and governments work together democratically to ensure its effective management," which is why it was "so important to protect."[47] At first, it seemed like hope and change might finally be coming to U.S. tech regulatory policy.

However, it soon became clear that this strategy did not bind all branches of government. In 2013 Edward Snowden revealed how the intelligence services of the United States and its democratic allies were performing mass surveillance, leaving users of U.S. tech all over the world exposed. The revelations showed how national security was a pretext for heavy-handed state interference. Intelligence agencies instrumentalized the U.S. tech sector. Corporate leaders began using this interference as yet another reason why companies were best off with little steering from Washington. Tech companies expressed shock and redoubled their efforts at independence. For instance, Google announced it would invest in encrypting data transfers, sending a signal to its users that intelligence services could not as easily snoop into.[48] Google's investment was not solely tactical; many in Silicon Valley had been strong advocates of encryption and its importance to user privacy since the cypherpunk era. Nevertheless, the company's response strongly signaled that it was not completely in line with Washington's tech agenda and would break from the White House when necessary. The turf war between the Obama administration and Silicon Valley intensified following Snowden's disclosures. By 2016 this conflict came to a head when Apple refused an FBI request to unlock the phone of Syed Rizwan Farook, one of two people accused in a mass shooting in San Bernardino, California.[49] Apple claimed that unlocking the phone would reveal security gaps that could endanger its other customers. Apple's public defiance was a full-circle moment: the tech industry, which had been carefully nurtured by the White House, had outgrown its tight-knit relationship with the Obama administration.

As in most areas, President Donald Trump handled the issue differently from his predecessors. He used social media as an unprecedented loudspeaker. Disinformation and conspiracy theories were shared on White House letterhead and from the West Wing podium. Only when President Trump and his allies saw their accounts or posts removed for inciting violence did they begin to talk about reining in social media giants. And even then, there was little thought or effort beyond political expediency.

Trump accused companies of systematic bias against conservatives. His administration pushed back against encryption and the Broadband Privacy Act, and rolled back net neutrality provisions. Ajit Pai, the Trump-appointed chairman of the Federal Communications Commission, claimed that repealing net neutrality would promote competition and expand broadband access, but advocates worried that it would chip away at internet fairness and diminish the quality of internet service for some users.[50] Most dramatically, Trump threatened to ban TikTok.[51] He considered the Chinese video sharing platform a threat to national security because data collected would benefit the CCP. Trump began more head-to-head conflict with tech companies than any of his predecessors—coming up with iconic monikers like Tim Apple (for Apple CEO Tim Cook) and Jeff Bozo (for Amazon CEO Jeff Bezos).[52] This often highly personal jousting, however, resulted in no concrete shifts in regulation, and it certainly did not lead to a stronger anchoring of democratic values in policy related to technology firms.

At times, President Trump may not have realized the impact of his policies. It was Trump who signed the executive order that created the Cybersecurity and Infrastructure Security Agency (CISA), which serves as the operational lead for federal cybersecurity and plays key roles in virtually every aspect of America's cybersecurity policy, ranging from misinformation to infrastructure resilience to AI governance. But when the agency's first director, Chris Krebs, rebuked Trump's false claims about fraud in the 2020 election, the president fired him.[53] At times, President Trump's policies were criticized by his opponents, only to be embraced later. Much of the United States' expert class originally thought that Trump's China technology hawkishness was an aberration. In addition to his widely publicized rows with Huawei, a leading Chinese provider of 5G equipment, and TikTok, President Trump signed a 2021 executive order that essentially banned eight Chinese transaction apps in the United States, including Alipay.[54] Under Trump, the U.S. Department of Commerce also placed the first round of export restrictions on Semiconductor Manufacturing International Corporation, China's most advanced computer chip producer.[55] These technology restrictions have endured and intensified since Trump left office. Curtailing China's technology dominance, a message first popularized by President Trump, now seems foundational to both Democratic and Republican foreign policy.

Both as a candidate and as the current president, Joe Biden has expressed more criticism than his predecessors of technology companies' role in disinformation and toxic social media environments. In his endorsement interview with the *New York Times* editorial board, he advocated for the revocation of Section 230 of the Communications Decency Act.[56] Early on in the campaign, Biden signed a pledge not to use fake news, doxing, or "hack and leaks," a tactic that sees the hyping of an alleged leak or hack to build sensation around it.[57] In one exceptional instance, Biden's campaign team sent a letter to Facebook asking it to take more responsibility in removing disinformation from its platforms.[58]

Throughout the Democratic primaries, Biden also faced growing pressure to address the outsize anticompetitive power of Silicon Valley. Massachusetts senator Elizabeth Warren in particular called for breaking up Big Tech and led the push for greater accountability. Whether inspired by those calls or not, Biden has appointed a slate of strong antitrust experts to critical government posts. Lina Khan, now the chair of the FTC, came to prominence after authoring the definitive academic article on antitrust rules in the digital economy. Tim Wu, who served as special assistant to the president for competition and technology policy, came to the White House after leading calls to break up Facebook and writing an antimonopoly book titled *The Curse of Bigness*. Additionally, Jonathan Kanter, who became the Assistant Attorney General for the Antitrust Division at the Department of Justice, is a longtime progressive antitrust leader who founded a boutique antitrust law firm.

While President Biden offered stronger rhetoric on Silicon Valley than his predecessors, he has remained a friend to Big Tech throughout his presidency. Amazon, Facebook, and Google employees were welcomed onto his Innovation Policy Committee during the presidential transition.[59] One of his first major actions on AI governance was standing up the National AI Advisory Committee, which includes executives from Amazon, Google, IBM, Microsoft, NVIDIA, Salesforce, and even high-powered lobby groups like BSA / the Software Alliance, but few from civil society.[60] Tech executives were invited to state dinners at the White House.[61] The president published an op-ed urging Congress to take action on "big tech abuses" in early 2023 but has taken little executive action to lead the way.[62]

Ultimately, from Clinton to Biden, the legacy of thirty years of American technology policies is one of deferential treatment and abdication of responsibility. Private companies and their CEOs continue to make critical decisions about who gets to speak, go viral, and be read. They build and secure critical infrastructure and provide the government with vital ICT products and services. Though the decision to leave crucial decisions to private companies could be explained by either ignorance of the industry or by blind faith in the free market or both, there is a more proximate explanation: this policy was supported by a wide-ranging cast of public officials who left office to work for tech companies—and, sometimes, even came back to government afterward.

The Revolving Door

The lack of regulation in Silicon Valley can be explained, at least in the early years, as partly a product of its distance from Washington: out of sight, out of mind. At the start of the millennium, however, the distance between the West Coast and the East Coast had shrunk considerably. Policy experts moved from corporate tech roles to administration roles, and vice versa. As the people of Silicon Valley and Washington have grown in closer contact or traded places, so have new opportunities to stave off regulation. Every major tech company has begun hiring former government officials, bringing knowledge about politics and policy in-house, while building valuable connections to key policymakers.

Officials from the Obama administration have been especially likely to head to Big Tech. After David Plouffe served as President Obama's campaign manager and later as a senior adviser in the White House, he joined Uber in 2014 to lead the company's policy work.

He then left in 2017 for the Chan Zuckerberg Initiative, the philanthropic outlet primarily funded by Facebook's fortune.[63] Jared Cohen, who served on the policy planning staff for both Secretary of State Condoleezza Rice and Secretary of State Hillary Rodham Clinton, went on to found Google Ideas, now called Jigsaw, and later authored a book with Eric Schmidt, Google's former CEO and executive chairman.[64] Jay Carney, one of Obama's press secretaries, landed at Amazon after serving in the White House.[65] Even Eric Holder, the former attorney general under President Obama who had spent his entire career in public service, went to work for Airbnb to help the company with its antidiscrimination policies.[66]

Recently, some prominent Europeans have entered this revolving door. The former French ambassador to the United States, Gerard Araud, also served as senior adviser to NSO Group, a role that looked even more uncomfortable when it was revealed that French president Emmanuel Macron's phone number was on a target list for Pegasus, the company's spyware tool.[67] In 2018 Nick Clegg, the former deputy prime minister of the United Kingdom, was appointed as Facebook's vice-president for global affairs and communications.[68] A former member of the European Parliament, Richard Allan, worked for Facebook for ten years before leaving for Cisco, and the former prime minister of Austria, Sebastian Kurz, signed on to work with Peter Thiel in 2022.[69]

This back-and-forth does not only happen among top officials; the same is true for rank-and-file staff. In 2019, the same banner year that the state attorneys general of almost all U.S. states announced new antitrust investigations against Facebook and Google, 75 percent of newly hired lobbyists for Amazon, Apple, Facebook, and Google came out of Capitol Hill offices, other government jobs, or political campaigns.[70]

Even more alarming is the leaking of technology expertise—which is low to begin with—from political offices to technology companies. Because public-sector salaries are simply not competitive with those of the tech industry, government knowledge of technology is being hollowed out while corporate capacity and insider understanding of policy and legislation processes are added.

A less transparent connection between government and industry occurs during elections, when technology companies offer to help and support political campaigns. When I served in the European Parliament, Facebook offered to help train my office staff, free of charge, to use its platform for political campaigning. Gatherings of the European political group of which I was a member were often sponsored by tech companies. This sponsorship not only put money in the pockets of our party offices but also meant branded live-streaming booths onsite, as well as lobbyists who would be part of small-scale, off-the-record meetings with leading politicians. My opposition to these practices had little effect.

Of course, revolving doors, corporate sponsorship, and campaign contributions are not limited to technology companies. From tobacco to oil, pharma to publishing, libraries to museums, albeit with varying budgets, everyone with a stake in policy outcomes is well advised to make their voices heard—as long as it happens transparently and rules are respected. Moreover, for all the negative press that lobbyists get, it is ultimately the politician who votes and is accountable.

What is new is the sheer market size of technology firms. Their scale is unprecedented and staggering. In August 2018, Apple, a company with fewer than two hundred thousand employees, became the first publicly traded company to ever cross a trillion dollars in market capitalization.[71] That is roughly the same value as the GDP of Mexico, a country with over one hundred million citizens. By the end of 2021, Apple's market capitalization was almost at $3 trillion, and Alphabet, Amazon, Microsoft, and Tesla had all crossed the trillion-dollar threshold. Facebook only fell short of this threshold because it managed to lose $231 billion in value in a day following a weak revenue forecast—more than any company before it.[72] Most industries, let alone companies, will never reach market values close to these figures.

This scale creates a systemic influence far greater than in most other industries. It means the tech sector represents roughly 10 percent of U.S. GDP.[73] Profit dollars can progressively buy more influence through lobbying, but also through the funding of think tanks and academia. Social media companies curate important parts of the public political debate. They have shown that they can amplify messages or, conversely, block the accounts of politicians, while the network effects of social media platforms make it difficult for candidates in political office to delete their accounts, as doing so would mean forgoing access to constituencies and future voters. Meanwhile, cybersecurity firms are present at key points in critical infrastructure, and software firms provide the digital back bone of governmental services. This gargantuan scale makes it hard for the government to extricate itself from tech influence even if it wanted to, and the relationships between the best-known online platforms and the decision-makers in Washington are visible manifestations of a systemic challenge to proper oversight.

The Net Result

Digital technologies provide undeniable benefits to society, including those for democratic aspirations and movements worldwide. Outlets for information and speech have flourished despite government censorship of the media. Voices of the vulnerable have reached across the world to directly share their experiences living under repression. Calls for women's rights, same-sex marriage, and peace have been amplified. By removing information barriers, the internet has supercharged social progress and international development, ushering in benefits beyond its pioneers' wildest dreams.

And yet, today's monopolists and corporate leaders with statesmen-like ambitions seem far removed from the promise of an open internet and the bottom-up empowerment of individuals that drew me to study the field of new media at the University of Amsterdam at the turn of the millennium. The promise of openness, emancipation, and democratization was once the spirit with which developers worked on their technologies. It was a vision so powerful that it invited big dreams while overshadowing the warnings of the few contrarians around. As we have seen, business leaders, along with help from policymakers at all levels of government, have allowed the industry to grow while putting aside this vision.

Even though money has come to play an ever more important role in Silicon Valley, anarchy and a disdain for government have remained constant over the decades. In many ways, Silicon Valley has become the antithesis of what its early pioneers set out to be: from dismissing government to literally taking on equivalent functions; from lauding freedom of speech to becoming curators and speech regulators; and from criticizing government overreach and abuse to accelerating it through spyware tools and opaque algorithms.

This power to govern de facto—in other words, to shape the conditions for people's rights and freedoms—can be witnessed in the impact of a growing array of products and services. Companies are controlling our lives behind the scenes, even if we don't realize it. Parents have repeatedly expressed concern that TikTok's algorithm promotes information about suicide to vulnerable teens—and some even point to TikTok as a driver in the deaths of their children.[74] And Facebook, by its own admission, "helped incite the Capitol Insurrection" of January 6, 2021, by bombarding impressionable users with election lies and enabling radicals to coordinate the storming of the U.S. Capitol in private Facebook groups.[75]

If these examples sound alarmist or like outliers, consider the "Netflix effect." In the summer of 2023, the decade-old legal drama *Suits*, best known for featuring the Duchess of Sussex, Meghan Markle, as a recurring character, gained billions of views after Netflix put it in its virtual shopping window.[76] In fact, the show quickly broke the Nielsen all-time streaming record.[77] Netflix successfully resurrected this show—doomed to an eternity of daytime reruns—almost overnight and placed it at the center of the cultural zeitgeist. There's nothing wrong with millions of Americans now knowing way too much about civil litigation, but Netflix's ability to transform the entire country's cultural conversation is singular—and slightly alarming. In India that is exactly what is happening. There the company is heavily censoring content that could be perceived as politically or religiously sensitive.[78] And it is not only well-known consumer brands, but many less visible companies that are selling powerful systems to intelligence firms or law enforcement agencies. An Israeli company, Insanet, developed a technology, aptly named

Sherlock, that allows for spying on anyone using any device, using the online advertisement system.[79] It is, in essence, an intelligence agency for hire. Indeed, many functions across society are becoming automated, digitized, and privatized.

This de facto governing power is how Silicon Valley and its libertarian pioneers went from disrupting power to amassing it. As Ross Baird, president of the venture capital firm Village Capital, has said, "For all the lip service that Silicon Valley has given to changing the world, its ultimate focus has been on what it can monetize."[80] Firms such as Village Capital have certainly been instrumental in incentivizing a culture of consolidation and control. This power begets more power, as companies have leveraged their wealth and influence to maintain a generally hands-off governance agenda. And given the dominant role of U.S. technology companies and the country's global role, the U.S. approach has had a ripple effect on other democracies with even less leverage over these powerful companies.

Few people foresaw how norm setting would increasingly happen through code, business models, and standards. As a result, the warnings from those who did were largely ignored. In the end, governments placed too much trust in the market at the expense of democratic principles.

Edward Snowden made this point in 2018, when he warned that the unprecedented growth in state and corporate surveillance is part of "the greatest redistribution of power since the industrial revolution . . . and it is happening in a context in which you have not and will not once be asked for or permitted to cast a vote." Tech companies, he continued, "know everything about us and we know nothing about them."[81] These are telling comments in support of respecting the legitimacy of democratic processes over corporate ones, coming from a controversial software engineer who revolted against the outsize power of the U.S. intelligence and law enforcement communities. Snowden's words remind us that regulation gives democratic governments key powers to keep the technological landscape competitive, and people's rights protected, which is exactly why democratic governments must make a dramatic course correction.

Over the past roughly three decades, we have witnessed governments largely shirk their responsibilities as technology was being
built and norms were being shaped. Now democratic governments
are finally beginning to play catch-up. There is no time to waste,
as technological developments continue to rush ahead. Emerging
technologies, including AI, the Internet of Things, facial recognition
systems, and cryptocurrencies, are evolving in a regulatory vacuum
and chip away at the core tasks of the democratic state and the rule
of law. Governments continue to suffer from an eroded ability to
ensure accountability. This time, being late at addressing growing
risks may well prove fatal for democracies.

Unfortunately, it is now no longer just a problem of will but
of capacity. The growing asymmetry—of power, information,
and influence—between government and technology sectors has
undermined the ability of democratic lawmakers to understand the
workings and potential harms of various technological applications.
There is no possibility of good public policy without access, yet tech
companies use every method available to prevent society at large
from understanding the technologies they create and the business
models they employ. How can one govern something one cannot
understand?

Just like physical infrastructure, technological infrastructure can
be designed and used for the benefits of some and to the detriment
of others. Left to markets alone, efficiency takes over equity, and in
many cases, this leads to real harm. But it does not have to be this
way. As Cory Doctorow puts it, "There's a burgeoning, global understanding that the internet doesn't have to be five giant websites, each
filled with text from the other four."[82]

In fact, many people who were influential in shaping technology
companies or technology policies we know today have come around
to being more critical about their effect on society. With the benefit
of hindsight, in 2016 President Obama said that "government will
never run the way Silicon Valley runs because, by definition, democracy is messy. This is a big, diverse country with a lot of interests
and a lot of disparate points of view. And part of government's job,
by the way, is dealing with problems that nobody else wants to deal

with."[83] In a similar fashion, in 2018 Senator Wyden reflected on the influence of Section 230: "We envisioned that the law would be both a sword and a shield. A shield so that you could have this opportunity, for particularly small and enterprising operations to secure capital, and then a sword [by allowing them to moderate without facing liability over the practice], which said you've got to police your platforms. And what was clear during the 2016 election and the succeeding events surrounding Facebook, is that technology companies used one part of what we envisioned, the shield, but really sat on their hands with respect to the sword, and wouldn't police their platforms."[84]

Chapter 3 explores how the sword and the shield have cracked under the growing threats of cyberattacks. But first, in chapter 2, there is a scan of the horizon of the stack of different technologies that together weave an ecosystem. It will make clear just how much invisible power the corporate sector wields, far beyond just the best-known names from Silicon Valley.

2

The Stack

Imagine that you're riding the train home from work, and you suddenly remember that you haven't responded to a question your boss asked earlier in the day. You pull out your phone, open Gmail or Outlook (or AOL, if you haven't updated your email service since 1999), and fire off a brief message. For most of us, that's the end of the story. We don't give a second thought to the question of how a message travels from the small device in our hands to the boss's computer back at the office. But the travels of this simple email can tell us much about the underlying infrastructure of our digital world, as well as the power wielded by the companies that control it.

The moment that you click Send, this action prompts a microchip to process the email's information. All within fractions of seconds, data are turned into electromagnetic waves through the antenna of the phone or a router at home. But to travel long distances, they get picked up by a cell phone tower. The processed data then flow from towers to fiber optic cables, buried underground or even at the bottom of the sea, to arrive at an out-of-the-way destination, sometimes located in an entirely different country. Once it arrives, the data that comprise your email enters a data center where it is stored on one of thousands of servers. The email will travel the same route in reverse: from the data center, through infrastructure cables, processed through a microchip, appearing as a little unopened envelope in your boss's inbox.

All three of these critical hardware components—microchips, fiber optic cables, and data centers—are growing dramatically every year as users consume more video content, download more apps, and, of course, send more emails to their bosses. Microchips, also called semiconductors, are essential to every complex, interconnected technology, from cars to rockets to smart appliances to medical equipment. Semiconductors are so vital to modern technology that governments and companies alike are seeking to secure access to them today and for future needs. We are living through a modern-day international arms race to build these chips, with both governments and companies pouring billions of dollars into the creation of new fabrication plants. To gain more control over the interconnected systems and facilitate the expanding volume of internet traffic, companies have also invested billions of dollars to build their own digital infrastructure networks, as well as to build remote data centers to store the massive amount of information shared every day. The explosion of cloud computing, which enables internet users to store data on company data servers instead of those attached to their personal computers or on the premises at a small business, has significantly increased the need for data centers.

These various pieces of the technological puzzle, and the layers of sub-activities that they operate for online communications, are often referred to as "the stack." Though the internet's "over-the-top" layer of services and content tends to draw the most attention— this is where, for instance, Amazon, Facebook, Google, and Twitter operate—deeper down the stack is where vital user-computer interactions take place.

Certain organizations and companies that control these interactions are well known. There is, for instance, the structure organizing internet traffic, which is guided by domain names—for example, .com, .edu, or .org. The Domain Name System turns human-readable website names into computer-readable Internet Protocol (IP) addresses. Countries and regional bodies tend to have designated domain names like .eu and .uk, which they use to register government websites and domestic businesses. Domain names may seem bureaucratic, but they can be incredibly profitable for some countries. For example, Anguilla, the small Caribbean island that controls the .ai domain name, will rake in an estimated $30 million in annual domain registration fees, as AI start-ups clamor for marketable domain names.[1] Outside of web addresses, there are well-known software providers like Microsoft and Salesforce that make web-based applications, and recognizable hardware sellers such as Apple, IBM, and Samsung, whose products mediate digital engagement.

But beyond online platforms, cell phones, and apps from the big technology companies that everyone knows, there are less well known but equally important players. For instance, few internet users will have heard of Cinia Group, Interxion, or SK Hynix, even though these companies provide essential parts of an ecosystem that forms the basis of our lives in the digital world: undersea cables, data centers, and semiconductors. They connect the virtual and the physical. The governors of the digital world today are big corporations and tiny companies, well-known consumer brands and obscure power brokers. There is, however, no formalized governance structure. Instead, a mix of companies, associations, state authorities, and expert groups have morphed into a tangle that keeps the internet running. The organic nature of this structure, though it functions better than one might imagine after looking under the hood, has also led to risks and vulnerabilities that are difficult to manage.

This chapter sheds light on the nodes in the complex technological ecosystem. It offers a sense of the vast and invisible network of hardware and applications that are needed to facilitate digitization and connectivity. I will not, however, dive into the nitty gritty of each technology, and you will not need an engineering degree to follow along. Rather, this quick tour of a less visible ecosystem is meant to convey some of the key characteristics inherent to it, and to shed light on some of the most important decisions made in and around it. The core technology of our modern digital infrastructure is seen through the lens of the central question of this book: Can democratic governance reach the complex and highly powerful web of functions now run by private corporations?

The Microchip

Before Silicon Valley's most famous companies were online platforms, the strip of land between San Jose, at the south end of the Bay
Area, and San Francisco, to the north, was known for its hardware
production. More specifically, it was famous for producing perhaps
the most important component of any digital device, the silent hero
of the last thirty years of digital innovation: the microchip. Indeed,
the name for the region derives from the fact that silicon is a semi-
conducting material used in microchips and microprocessors.

But the extensive use of microchips only became apparent to
the wider public in 2021, when supply chains were disrupted by
multiple simultaneous shocks, including the COVID-19 pandemic
and the logjam caused by a freighter that became wedged in the
Suez Canal. Given the growth in global demand for microchips, this
disruption was felt in nearly every sector of society. The average car,
for instance, requires a staggering 1,500–3,000 chips, not including
the chips needed to power automotive manufacturing equipment.[2]
Shortages were so significant that one report estimates the car industry lost over $200 billion.[3] But cars are just one now well-known
example. Virtually every advanced technology firm—from the producers of ID cards to MRI scanners—relies on semiconductors for
both production and operation.

Despite the critical role that semiconductors play in our economy, only a handful of companies can produce them. Semiconductor manufacturing plants—also called fabrication plants, or simply
fabs—require enormous amounts of capital and long timelines, as
well as uniquely skilled workers. A new fab currently under construction in Arizona will cost a total of $40 billion and saw work-
ers arriving from Taiwan to get the critical work done.[4] Just one
advanced lithography machine in a fab—used to pattern the finest
details—can cost as much as $150 million.[5] Few companies can afford
this type of up-front investment or have access to the skilled techni-
cians needed to build such plants. As a result, the small number of
companies producing these semiconductors are now at the center
of a high-stakes geopolitical struggle.

Powerful countries around the world fear their own overdependence on imported microchips and the inability to control supplies of them. An October 2020 report from the Congressional Research Service estimates that China accounts for 60 percent of world semiconductor demand. Crucially, more than 90 percent of the semiconductors used in China are imported or manufactured locally by foreign suppliers. Europe and the United States are similarly dependent on foreign suppliers: the EU and the United States currently comprise 21 percent of global semiconductor manufacturing capacity, but they are responsible for 43 percent of the world's semiconductor consumption.[6] The dangers of this continued mismatch between domestic supply and demand is driving governments around the world to gear up for a fierce semiconductor arms race.

To make matters worse, one of the key production hubs for microchips, Taiwan, is also a country that has long-standing tensions with China. Any conflict between the two nations could ultimately disrupt production by one of the world's major chip firms, Taiwan Semiconductor Manufacturing Company (TSMC). According to industry estimates, TSMC accounts for more than 90 percent of global output of the most sophisticated chips, which are used by Apple and many other major companies.[7] Any significant stoppage at TSMC would incapacitate global iPhone production overnight. Some policymakers actually see this as good news: in their eyes, Taiwan's chip manufacturing industry functions as a "silicon shield," as China would not dare disrupt such a critical function.[8] TSMC is uncomfortably finding itself the subject of geopolitical speculation, but its chairman, Mark Liu, largely concurs: he, too, is convinced China will not invade Taiwan over the technology.[9] Still, around the world concerns about overreliance on good relations between Taiwan and China are leading to efforts to diversify supply chains.

China itself plays a different but critical role in the semiconductor supply chain as the supplier of rare earth materials. At the moment, the country has a near monopoly on several of the materials critical for microchips, including lanthanides, yttrium, and scandium, to name just a few. Tensions between China and the EU, the United States, or Taiwan thus pose an existential risk to the tech supply chain.

Beijing could close access to its mines, leaving the world without the basic components needed to make most high-tech goods. Conflicts and sanctions also practically disrupt supply chains. When Russia invaded Ukraine, supplies, including those of rare earth materials, were severely impacted. In early 2022 the price of aluminum, potash, and nickel rose 80 percent.[10] Neon prices rose a staggering 600 percent in 2014 when Russia annexed Crimea.[11]

Democratic countries worry that China's ambition to grow its domestic microchip industry is driven by its ambitions as a superpower. Just as Taiwan considers chips a leverage in its defense against possible invasion, China could weaponize chips to expand its influence. Beijing could restrict U.S. access to semiconductors to retaliate against an American foreign policy decision or condition a developing country's chips supply on favorable export provisions for other China-dominated industries. There isn't much that the West can do to change this geopolitical market dynamic in the short term. Countries that want to boost domestic industry need stamina, as a decision to shore up capacity today will take years to materialize. This protracted timeline, however, has not slowed down policy proposals and political pushing. Governments in China, the EU, India, Japan, South Korea, and the United States have all recently adjusted their national policies to invest in microchips with hopes of avoiding crippling dependence on companies elsewhere in the world. Billions of dollars and long-term planning are rolled out to attract talent, build plants, and strengthen existing domestic industries. Even with these monumental investments, the prospect of achieving microchip sovereignty is easier said than done. While factories can be built and investments made, access to geographically locked-in rare earth materials is less amenable to domestic policymaking.

As things stand, these resource-intensive chips consist of different components, assembled from supply chains that span the globe. Many chip supply chains look something like this: silicon mined and refined in the United States might be sent to South Korea for preparation before heading to fabs in Taiwan, where equipment from the Netherlands turns it into American-made microchip designs before heading to a Chinese factory for placement into a brand-new smartphone that will be sold in Canada.[12] One spat between Beijing and Washington could grind this entire supply chain to a halt. Ideally, the mutual dependence between producers may stem some of the looming conflict, as no single country can currently execute the production process from design to deployment. Nevertheless, individual risk-minded countries continue to chase the dream of independence.

Even the EU and the United States, which share similar democratic and market economy values, have taken separate steps to increase domestic semiconductor production capacity. In early 2022 European Commission president Ursula von der Leyen announced a $48 billion plan to advance semiconductor production, a crucial first step to boost the industry she called "the bedrock of our modern economies."[13] The U.S. CHIPS and Science Act, signed into law in August 2022, intends to spur American semiconductor independence by earmarking $280 billion in federal funds to bolster semiconductor capacity, catalyze research and development, and upskill America's science, technology, engineering, and mathematics (STEM) workforce.[14]

More recently, however, the U.S. secretary of commerce, Gina Raimondo, has welcomed stronger cooperation with the EU. Friendly collaboration would mark a turn from the pressure applied on the Dutch government by the administration of President Donald Trump in early 2018. At the time, Advanced Semiconductor Materials Lithography (ASML), the world's leading producer of lithography technologies needed for microchips, was slated to sell manufacturing technology for advanced chips to China. The company, located in the Netherlands, would only be able to do so after obtaining a license from the government. After the U.S. government expressed its concerns and shared classified intelligence reports with the Dutch government, the license was revoked. Though few details about this ordeal have been disclosed by ASML, the Dutch government, or the U.S. government, the reports presumably warned that the deal would allow China to make critical advances. Similar pressure from Washington has prevented exports by ASML to China, as recently as January 2024.[15]

Even without knowing the details, however, the case illustrates the high-stake maneuvers of governments in relation to strategic companies that have become providers of vital components of most digital products. We will return to the geopolitical battles at the intersection of technology and governance in greater depth in chapter 7.

The Cable

On August 16, 1858, Queen Victoria sent U.S. president James Buchanan an excited message, congratulating him on the completion of "the electric cable," which she called a "great international work."[16] Her telegraph traveled along the first transcontinental communication cable connecting the United Kingdom and the United States. This was nothing short of a technological marvel. Transmitting information across continents, which had historically taken weeks by ship, could now be done in less than a day.[17] Unfortunately, the marvel did not last long. The cable broke less than a month later, a potent symbol for the perils that transatlantic cables still face almost two hundred years later.

Early cables were almost exclusively owned by the state. Initially they were used for diplomatic telegrams like the queen's or to reach European colonies. Gradually, private telecom companies began to build, operate, and maintain more and more of this vital global infrastructure. As a result, the companies responsible for laying undersea cables wield significant influence on the shape and possibilities of our modern communication infrastructure.[18]

The state-of-the-art fiber optic cables that these companies now direct are tapestries of tiny, delicate threads of glass, bundled and wrapped in copper, which is itself wrapped in layers of protective materials. Around 99 percent of internet traffic travels the world through these globe-spanning cables, encompassing everything from personal emails to sensitive financial transactions to remote-controlled surgeries. There are approximately 500 such cables, running 1.3 million kilometers, or 621,000 miles, around the world.[19] This vast network of basic infrastructure is often referred to as the "backbone of global communications."[20]

Unfortunately, this backbone is not particularly resilient. Fishermen frequently damage cables as they trawl the ocean floors. Natural disasters can also disrupt cable functionality. A 2022 volcanic eruption on the remote Pacific archipelago of Tonga cut off communications as the island's main cable suffered multiple cuts. Usually, cable operators build in reserve capacity from the start, so there is always a backup in case of emergencies, but these reserves may not be sufficient to absorb the traffic from damaged lines. In 2008, when cables connecting the African and European continents through Egypt and Italy were cut, data flows were halted, which consequently impaired U.S. military operations and the flying of drones in Iraq.[21]

Throughout their long history, communication cables have even been caught up in wars. The United Kingdom cut cables to Germany during World War I and placed tabs to listen in on phone conversations flowing through cables to the Soviet Union. A century later, when Russia invaded the Ukrainian peninsula of Crimea in 2014, it cut off a cable. And when the Nord Stream I and II natural gas pipelines were sabotaged in September 2022, it served as a reminder of the fragility of globally connected critical infrastructure, including data cables equally routed through remote seabeds.[22] Sometimes energy and data cables run between countries together. In the fall of 2023, the Balticconnector, which links Estonia and Finland with energy pipelines and data cables, was damaged in what appears to be deliberate sabotage.[23] Pipes and cables lying outside territorial waters are especially at risk because international law has not created significant enough deterrents to match the high stakes that damage to these connections pose. There is still a lot of ambiguity and, as a result, those inflicting intentional damage often don't face accountability.

As the information traveling over the cables has come to play an increasingly important role in the everyday functioning of society, some policymakers have grown concerned that the wires of the world will become a more frequent theater of conflict.[24] Those concerns became concrete in early 2022, following a new cable breach in Norway. One set of Norwegian cables, which runs near land by the small town of Longyearbyen on the island of Svalbard, lies at a depth of merely 300 meters (900 feet). Following a power outage, officials realized that one of the cables had been cut. Norwegian police launched an investigation and determined that the cut was "likely man-made."[25] Some speculated sabotage, as the Norwegian Intelligence Service had warned explicitly in its annual threat assessment that Russia was developing the capacity to damage the very types of cables that were cut, and British intelligence had warned that Russian submarines posed a particular risk to data cables. In the end, no proof of Russian involvement was found.

Space Norway, the cable's owner, reported that communications between Svalbard and Norway's mainland had not been disrupted.[26] The Norwegians were lucky this time, as only the redundant capacity was impacted, and a second cable ensured that communications continued uninterrupted. If the next cut to an undersea cable were to happen at a more prominent section, instead of around a remote island, the volume of disrupted internet traffic would likely be much higher. It is not difficult to imagine a scenario involving the deployment of saboteurs in boats, posing as fishermen, who are tasked with locating and disrupting such critical points.

These incidents make it clear that the geopolitical stakes surrounding the resilience of undersea cables are sky-high, just as they are with microchips. In addition to questions about the cables' typical functioning and resilience, we must interrogate certain security and governance considerations: Who has access to data flowing through the cables? What laws govern them? Who is responsible for maintaining and securing them? How can vast open seas be monitored for security incidents? What happens when companies that own the cables become instruments of conflicts between states? How do governments respond to incidents outside a given country's territorial waters? Unfortunately, policymakers around the world have not done enough to answer the final few questions, leaving us woefully unprepared in case of a cable conflict. All the while, more and more cables are being rolled out to meet the world's growing digital demands.

Espionage, subversion, commandeering, and disabling are looming risks around undersea cables. The information flowing through them is priceless, making cables appealing targets. Data running through this physical network include extremely sensitive information, such as design details of factories, financial transactions, or the formula for the COVID-19 vaccine. Yet there is little discussion in multilateral forums or between like-minded countries about how to build norms and consensus around the use and protection of these undersea cables. Even more elusive is any credible oversight. To this point, in 2015 Alcatel-Lucent (which was acquired by Finnish telecom giant Nokia in 2016) noted that it was required "to support interception capabilities in order to meet the requirements of governments."[27] What data are intercepted and by whom, and whether interceptions are legal and proportionate, remains, for the most part, a mystery. In the field of intelligence gathering, it is not difficult to imagine how cables are appealing instruments of geopolitical competition and conflict, especially given the lack of clear laws and governance procedures.

Historically, undersea cables were run by public-private consortia to share the expenses. Today, however, they are a billion-dollar industry of their own.[28] Since 2012, U.S. companies, including Alphabet, Amazon, Meta, and Microsoft, have significantly invested in undersea cables linking both European and non-European Mediterranean states to other parts of the world, such as countries in Africa and Asia. By 2024, the companies are expected to own a stake in more than thirty long-distance undersea cables connecting every continent.[29] As a result, their combined share of the world's total cable capacity has increased from 10 percent to 66 percent in a decade. China Mobile and Meta have laid undersea cables in a partnership, despite tensions between the U.S. and Chinese governments.[30] The privatization of this global critical technology infrastructure further concentrates power in the hands of technology companies, but it does so in a way that is mostly invisible to citizens and civil society. The companies seem to prefer it this way, as they generally offer little information about their ownership of undersea cables.

There is a significant reason to be worried about this shift to private ownership: increasingly, state actors are eyeing those same cables as targets in war and intelligence gathering. The companies who oversee these cable systems now find themselves targets of state-sponsored attacks—critical geopolitical pressure points—and there is no indication they are prepared to handle the onslaught.

The Data Centers

As the common saying goes, innovation is often born out of necessity. Those who live in the Netherlands know that all too well, as it is a country that would largely be underwater had it not been for centuries of innovation in methods of defending the land against sea and river flooding. The city center of Amsterdam lies two meters (about 6.5 feet) under sea level today, and much of the country would flood without an ingenious system of dikes and other water defenses. To reclaim land and expand the country, the Dutch have also become experts in dredging, an age-old practice that is used for anything from building or deepening harbors, digging canals, or developing artificial islands. As my compatriots are fond of saying, "God created the world, but the Dutch created the Netherlands."

The ingenuities needed to successfully manage water are seen as one of the sources of Dutch innovation and collaboration. Without cooperation between landowners, farmers, and millers, dating back to the Middle Ages, the needed resources to build dikes and pump water out of the polder were too much for any one party to shoulder. Polders, the land sitting between two dikes, have become characteristic features of Dutch landscapes and represent another innovative way of managing flows of water—a way that forced people with divergent interests to interact and collaborate.

Today the term "polder model" is used to indicate a successful method of consensus-driven decision-making. In the Netherlands, labor unions, government representatives, and employers convene, using a polder equivalent, to work out wage increases, pensions, and other solutions among themselves. This model is a stark contrast from the adversarial labor dynamics in other parts of the world. Political and organizational theorists characterize the polder model as an early version of a multistakeholder model, in which people or communities with different interests decide by consensus about a topic of common concern. The notion of such a model gained new popularity in the context of internet governance, representing an alternative to the top-down approach in which maximum power is placed in the hands of the state or another powerful actor. Instead, the idea is that the internet depends on the cooperation of many diverse decision-makers. Ideally, state, and corporate representatives come together to work with civil society representatives and technical experts.

Though the polder model is quintessentially Dutch, I can put aside my patriotism and admit that it does not always lead to satisfactory outcomes for all stakeholders involved. To see this, consider a cautionary tale that recently took place in Zeewolde, a municipality of twenty-three thousand people on the Dutch island of Flevopolder, the largest artificial island in the world. The town was thrust into the limelight in late 2021, when its part-time councilors were preparing to vote on a proposal to house the largest data center in the country. The Zeewolde hyperscale data center would use as much energy as the city of Amsterdam, and the minister for economic affairs and climate at the time, Eric Wiebes, was successfully lobbied to sign off on exceptional access to the high-voltage grid.[31] This was a controversial move given that new schools and other interested parties typically wait years for such a connection.

The debate over the hyperscale data center had not garnered much news prior to 2021, partly because few knew the true identity of its prospective owner. The two companies that had been lobbying politicians—Polder Networks and Tulip—were in fact subsidiaries of Meta, the company formerly known as Facebook. The names seem to have been deliberately chosen to appeal to some sense of national pride in polders and the world-famous Dutch tulips. To obtain the necessary permits at the national, regional, and local levels, Meta had recruited top-notch law firms, consultants, and engineering companies to draft favorable scoping reports, yet the company had kept its name entirely out of the proceedings. It even filed suit to keep relevant acquisition documents out of the public's view. Advocates had to resort to freedom of information requests to gain access to crucial documents that shed light on the actual interests and investors that were engaged in high stake pitching.

Secretive lobbying turns out to be a common practice when it comes to advocacy for data centers. In 2019, locals did not know Google was seeking tax cuts as it built a data center in Texas, given that it did so as Sharka LLC. "I'm confident that had the community known this project was under the direction of Google, people would have spoken out, but we were never given the chance to speak," said Travis Smith, managing editor of the *Waxahachie Daily Light*, the local newspaper. "We didn't know that it was Google until after it passed."[32] Similarly, Microsoft was hiding behind Project Osmium when it sought local approval to develop data centers in Iowa in 2016. In De Wieringermeer, another Dutch polder, Microsoft eventually conceded that it should not have concealed its identity while pitching a plan for its data centers. Prior to the pitch, officials in partnership with Vattenfall had announced the installation of eighty-two wind turbines on the Princess Ariane Wind Farm, meant to provide 370,000 households with a sustainable source of electricity, most of which was ultimately used by Microsoft.[33] The political promise made to voters, that they would receive green energy to their homes, was critical in convincing people to give up some of their views along the open green fields for the placement of wind turbines. Had they known that much of the capacity would be devoted to a data center run by a large tech firm, they may have been less amenable to the intervention.

The decision of whether to sell the 166 hectares of agricultural land (the equivalent of about 245 American football fields) finally came before the municipal council of Zeewolde in December 2021.[34] Egge Jan de Jonge, a local alderman, advocated in favor of welcoming Meta, which he suggested would put the small town on the map. Others were less optimistic about the economic and environmental impacts of the new center.

The data center debate in Zeewolde raises the following question: Are poorly staffed and resourced local governments equipped to endure the sophisticated tactics and lobbyists employed by large tech firms when seeking licenses and approvals? The local Zeewolde representatives perform their function part-time, and the decision concerning the Meta data center alone generated tens of thousands of pages to work through. As Sandra Beckerman, a member of the Dutch Parliament from the Socialist Party, told BuzzFeed, "Local and regional governments don't have the power to fight large companies, they (municipalities) are willing to work with these tech companies because they are always in money troubles."[35] Projected tax revenues and jobs are often touted to persuade politicians to allow physically invasive construction in their small-town fields. But after buildings are put in place, data centers end up employing relatively few people. Even though the U.S. government provided tax breaks as high as $150 million for Apple in Iowa, only fifty permanent jobs in the center were created.[36]

Data centers are usually placed in small towns with lots of open space, cool temperatures, and stable democratic institutions. Servers that are packed into data centers heat up as they store and process data, and a cool climate means the operators spend less to prevent overheating. Operators often pitch that they will in turn provide "residual heat" back to the grid with the promise of heating homes or other facilities. Yet, in practice, this heat is hard to use beneficially as it requires new infrastructure to be installed.[37] In fact, the hot water from data centers can also turn out to be harmful for the natural environment. The mere use of billions of gallons of water, needed also during drought, has caused tensions between tech companies and local communities. Google spent thirteen months embroiled in a public records lawsuit in Oregon, desperately attempting to block the *Oregonian* from disclosing the water use statistics for its local data center.[38] Arizona residents who rely on the drought-prone Colorado River question why they must abide by stringent water use restrictions while data centers can indiscriminately guzzle water from the same river. As Neil Ruddy, the former city administrator of Carlisle, Iowa, put it, "I think residents need water more than supercomputers do."[39] At a moment when the effects of climate change are pressing, the way that vital resources like water are used will become more sensitive.

Today cloud computing has a larger carbon footprint than the airline industry. Add to that cryptocurrency mining, which uses around 0.5 percent of electricity worldwide.[40] Combined with AI, the two emerging technologies account for 2 percent of the world's power consumption.[41] Denmark, along with other northern European countries like the Netherlands, is a popular destination for data centers, and the Danish Energy Agency has calculated that by 2030 data centers will increase the country's total emissions by 10 percent.[42] In Germany's Frankfurt region, representatives of the Green Party have asked for a legal ruling on the feasibility of energy promises around another proposed data center. Besides energy consumption, water use is a growing concern, and it is not easy to get data on water use from data center operators. Google self-reported an average use of 450,000 gallons per data center per day.[43] The United States houses 5,375 data centers, often in locations selected for their cheap electricity.[44] Amazon, for example, does not publish water use figures for its data centers at all, but the industry as a whole is projected to increase its use of water by 55 percent between 2000 and 2050.[45] Likely in response to this environmental outcry, Amazon has recently pledged to replenish more water than its data centers use by 2030 by donating to nongovernmental organizations (NGOs) that seek to make water available to nature and to communities in need.[46] Based on the company's past track record of carbon neutral pledges, however, that commitment doesn't hold much water.

In addition to environmental concerns, there are growing security concerns around data centers. The three largest cloud computing providers—Amazon Web Services (AWS), Google Cloud, and Microsoft Azure—comprise over 60 percent of the global market. This centralization of critical services and infrastructure in private hands means that responsibility, market power, and risk management are delegated to a small circle of actors. This can lead to significant problems. When AWS experienced an outage in one of its data centers in late 2021, Epic Games, Netflix, and Slack all went down. The outage didn't just limit users' abilities to watch the next episode of *White Lotus* or enter a new *Fortnite* lobby but also had massive disruptive impacts in education. Colleges across the country had to postpone student exams because Canvas, an online teaching platform with thirty million users, was also unavailable. This single outage was a crucial reminder of the risk associated with the concentration in cloud services. AWS oversees more than one-third of global cloud infrastructure.[47] A successful cyberattack on the company could irreparably change the internet.

Gradually, the creation of hyperscale data centers is facing political pushback. Even Ireland, which has probably been Europe's most welcoming country to large tech companies and whose cool climate makes it a particularly appealing location for data centers, is beginning to change course. EirGrid, Ireland's national energy provider, expects that, by 2030, data centers will use almost 30 percent of Ireland's electricity.[48] This massive energy sink puts the entire electric grid at risk. According to a 2021 report by the energy provider, the data centers' power demands could lead to constant rolling blackouts, which would make the aforementioned AWS outage look like a cakewalk.[49] To be clear, data center outages aren't just an issue of convenience. During a 2022 outage, the Interxion data center in London was offline for four hours, causing interruptions in electronic commodity trading worth billions of dollars.[50] Imagine the consequences a similar outage occurring daily or even weekly would have on the economy.

The Irish Social Democrats launched a call for a temporary ban on new data centers in 2022, a move similar to the one Singapore made in 2019 as part of its plans to reduce CO_2 emissions. They say the government "does not have a grasp on exactly what it means for Ireland and for our infrastructure."[51] In an interview with CNN, Pears Hussey, a resident of Ennis, where a new data center is planned, notes the drawbacks of local decision-making: "It doesn't feel very democratic that a small town of Ennis can have such a huge development with such a huge impact on our efforts to meet our climate targets kind of hoisted upon us, when the impact is going to go on for generations and generations."[52] As of now, the data center skeptics seem to have succeeded. EirGrid announced in spring 2022 that it was pulling the plug on thirty Irish data center projects due to electricity curbs, a major reversal for the provider and the Irish government.[53]

As for Zeewolde, Meta got a taste of the pushback the entire industry may soon face. Ultimately, in late March 2022, the planned Meta data center was put on hold. After a new national government took office, it promised stricter coordination around permits for new data centers, and in the local elections in Zeewolde, parties that opposed the arrival of the hyperscale data center were victorious. In addition, the Dutch Senate and Parliament announced a halt on the development of Meta's hyperscale data center. The company, caught up in a number of political storms, had ultimately decided to put its data center plans for the Dutch polders in the freezer. But the jury is still out on who ultimately pulled the plug; journalists reported that aggressive pushes by Meta lobbyists achieved the adverse effect and discouraged decision-makers from giving the needed green lights.

The Dutch are certainly known for a history of pragmatism and cooperation with private companies, in the interest of facilitating the economy or pumping dry its polders. But a lack of trust in the good faith of Meta ultimately ground even the inventors of the multistakeholder model to a halt. Meta may have lost the battle in Zeewolde, but it has not lost the war on data centers just yet. Just a week after putting its Dutch plans on hold, Meta signed the largest solar energy purchase agreement ever in Denmark, laying the groundwork for more data business in the country.[54]

As the demand for cloud computing, AI, streaming services, and cryptocurrency mining grows, so will the need for data centers. Not all of them are at hyperscale, and many serve as colocations for many smaller companies. Yet a healthy democratic debate about the benefits and consequences of housing data centers is impossible when companies are not open and transparent. Governments cannot facilitate a mature multistakeholder process when they do not even know which corporate stakeholders are sitting at the negotiating table. Considering how much data are stored in data centers, it is ironic how little data are available about how they operate. Clarity about resource use and job creation would be a starting point. Assessing the societal and security implications of market concentration is another critical step.

Additionally, different levels of government need to coordinate and make joint decisions about the permissible number of data centers. Amsterdam put a moratorium on the development of data centers within the city limits, but that did not prevent companies from finding opportunities a few miles down the road. Noord-Holland, the Dutch province that includes Amsterdam, is slightly smaller than Rhode Island but currently home to fifty-seven data centers. The nation as a whole houses nearly three hundred.[55] Perhaps each carefully pitched proposal sounded great in theory, and municipal councils voted in favor after the executive branch signed off on energy deals. But do the combined demands for water, electricity, and land add up throughout the province, the country, and the continent? What happens to the landscape when a series of long, stretching black box buildings appear? The growing techlash has so far miraculously spared data centers as targets, but if companies and governments do not act more deliberately and transparently, that will likely change soon.

Insight to Provide Oversight

As this brief journey around the underbelly of the internet has demonstrated, private companies now own and operate critical digital infrastructure, including microchip factories, undersea cable connections, and data centers. On most days, as we email and surf away online, we do not think twice about what it takes to make our online lives run seamlessly. But, as we've seen, undersea cables are essential routes for global internet traffic and, like microchips, have become pawns in geopolitical confrontations. Data centers, on the other hand, threaten states' ability to adequately manage their resources. So, whether a data center arrives in our backyards, consuming the wind energy we were promised for our own homes, or a disaster cuts off our lines of communication with friends and family, or our governments gamble away robust resources to land a few new jobs, we see the fragility and outsize costs of a world increasingly reliant on technology.

The lack of transparency by companies about their true interests makes it difficult to ensure a healthy democratic debate about the best way to manage these risks. What is clear is that the societal, environmental, economic, and security impacts of corporate resilience is essential for the public interest too. Good governance is needed to shore up and regulate our digital infrastructure, which requires that governments and corporations discuss these issues in the light of day rather than behind closed doors. That is the crossroads of our current moment: the public needs greater insight to provide greater oversight.

Global technological infrastructure should abide by the same principles as, for example, a city's underlying physical infrastructure: it needs to cater for the needs of wider society and not to shareholders alone. Yet, while once a street is paved by a company it becomes a literal public space, the same cannot be said for digital "roads," which can restrict traffic to specific companies and their clients. The fact that proprietary data are currently protected by trade secret provisions only contributes to harmful opacity. Digital tools are not only developed by private actors but often also serviced by them. These ad hoc and private governance mechanisms are unsustainable and highlight the need for a more robust and democratic public interest governance effort. Ownership, accountability, security, and transparency often rest on the goodwill of various obscure organizations. In chapter 3, we'll examine the consequences of perhaps the most dangerous area in which this is occurring: the privatization of cybersecurity and other forms of national security.

3

The Weaponization of Everything

During the COVID-19 pandemic, remote log-ins to the office or virtual classrooms, as well as online happy hours, became lifesavers. Without video conferencing, I would not have been able to teach and mentor my students at Stanford University and would have missed out on seeing the smiles on my friends' faces as we caught up, connecting from all corners of the world. The global restrictions in physical movement inadvertently sped up ongoing digitization trends toward remote work worldwide. While the push for adopting technologies in sectors ranging from health care to governmental services, and from urban development to national security, started long before the pandemic, lockdowns led to unprecedented intensification. More people logged on to video conferencing tools instead of taking business trips, and they spent money on cryptocurrency investments rather than restaurants. *Forbes* published survey results among business executives in which 97 percent claimed the pandemic accelerated digital transformation.[1]

This has meant an even larger role for technology companies in almost all aspects of our life. Tech executives have heralded this change to work and socializing virtually as practically a second renaissance. And while people everywhere certainly can connect more easily and spend their time more efficiently, these celebrations of a digital renaissance continue to gloss over the security vulnerabilities inherent to these technologies. If you spend just a few minutes tallying up the breaches, attacks, and outages that have occurred over the past few years, the scorecard looks terrible.

Today universities, hospitals, municipal governments, small businesses, and schools can all find themselves in a direct standoff with an adversarial foreign power or shrewd criminal group. "I am perfectly well aware that if Russia as a nation-state decided it wanted to attack the national infrastructure of the U.S., including what I'm responsible for, I don't have much chance of stopping them," explains Peter Fletcher, the information security officer for the San Jose Water Company, the primary water provider for over one million California residents. "The entire Russian nation-state versus Peter? I'm going to lose."[2] Companies, utilities, or public organizations, as providers of the (digitized) foundations of our lives, are defending the front lines of these attacks, whether they like it or not. We were sold a different story of what the digital world would bring.

The uptake of surveillance cameras by police forces, the migration of news onto social media platforms by journalistic outlets, and the production of Wi-Fi-enabled refrigerators by the appliance industry have all been motivated by a desire for a faster, more connected, or "smarter" digital ecosystem. Connectivity advocates have kept their promise: our phones, cities, and even bombs are smarter, but the use of smart devices is often not a clever choice from a security point of view. Traffic lights, drones, sound systems, and cars that connect to the internet also provide hackers with new entry points to disrupt and destroy digital networks. Successful attacks on our smart networks can bring society to a halt. Thus, having connected devices without matching policies and protections is causing unprecedented risks from a cybersecurity perspective. Cybersecurity expert Mikko Hypponen writes, "If it's smart, it's vulnerable."[3]

As we saw in chapter 2, the tampering with undersea cables and the fragility of microchip supply chains have given an indication of what bad actors may do to the infrastructure that our digital lives depend on. We assessed earlier how NSO Group's commercial spyware Pegasus turns cell phones into intelligence-gathering instruments. As we continue digitizing every inch of our lives without investing in corresponding regulation and oversight, the consequences will only worsen. We are facing an inescapable and terrifying reality: the digitization of everything has enabled the weaponization of everything.

Keith Alexander, the former director of the U.S. National Security Agency (NSA) and the founding commander of U.S. Cyber Command, writes in the *Financial Times*, "Cybersecurity remains the exposed underbelly of democracies—we must band together to defend ourselves."[4] Unfortunately, the public and private sectors struggle to take responsibility for cybersecurity issues. Companies build digital infrastructure, scan for risks on it, and offer services to protect it. Yet when probed about breaches, they assert that governments are responsible for ensuring national security. Likewise, government agencies increasingly rely on firms to build and secure digital infrastructure and point back toward the private vendor when failures occur. Everyone seems to look to others to own the security question. All the while, attackers take advantage of gaping security flaws and enforcement gaps.

To solve our cybersecurity problems, the blame game dynamic must give way to clear rules and enforcement. Prevention and verification must take the place of blind trust in technology. Democratically accountable entities must take center stage in addressing cybersecurity so that the public can assess the risks it faces and ensure that mitigating actions strengthen the rule of law.

The Arsenal

Between all the lines of code in a software program, sometimes millions of them, there are almost always flaws that can be used for exploitation and infiltration. These flaws are the key to success for cyberattackers. So-called zero-day vulnerabilities imply that the ability to access a system stealthily is not known yet. In other words, the software makers have had *zero days* to fix the entry point. Only the one who is aware of the vulnerability can choose to prevent the secret access from being abused or instead opt to use it for nefarious activities. Vulnerabilities are simply a fact of programming; they exist irrespective of the programmer, the programming language used, and the purpose of the program. The better secured the system is, the harder the attacker will have to work on breaking through, but the wide range of successfully impacted targets suggests that today, software is indeed "insecurable." If we imagine all of the elements of the digital ecosystem, from routers to personal AI assistants to the log-in verification system at work, hackers have many intrusion opportunities at their disposal. They may also opt to hoard zero days only to combine them later for a larger scale attack.

Once a software vulnerability is known to the company that wrote the code, that company can fix or "patch" the flaw through an update that works like a digital bandage. The software code is corrected and, when reinstalled, overrides the compromised version. In April 2022 alone, Microsoft rolled out 145 fixes for security flaws in its software; other software companies are also engaged in a permanent race to patch flaws in time.[5] So the next time you receive an annoying notification of a new update or bug fix, adopting it quickly will likely help to protect your device and data. Yet these critical updates of software to the newest edition do not always happen in time. Delays can be explained by cost considerations or a lack of awareness. The gap between more robust versions of a software product becoming available and the time by which most systems are updated offers additional windows of opportunity for attackers. Even well-known vulnerabilities in software can be exploited as long as systems are not repaired. An exploit can continue to help extort money, to spy, or to disable entire systems—sometimes for years.

But errors in code are not the only way cyberattackers infiltrate systems. They also have humans in their arsenal, often unwittingly. The victims range from large companies to a single computer user. For example, cybercriminals have mastered the art of phishing: they trick people into clicking on an infected link, with which the criminals gain access to computer systems and networks. Emails are formulated with ever more sophistication so that it is more difficult to distinguish a genuine bill from a fraudulent one.

I was often on the road during my tenure in the European Parliament, and I once fell for an email that claimed I had not paid my internet cable subscription. It could have indeed been quite likely that I had missed a bill or had not yet opened my mail from a few weeks back. I dutifully paid, and even if the amount was small, I felt like a complete idiot once I realized what had happened. Phishing attacks are a classic example of what cybersecurity practitioners and scholars call social engineering.[6] The attacks weaponize humans to gain their desired access or information. The phishing attackers who engineered that email relied on me, the unwitting user, to voluntarily transfer money. In other situations they may try to leverage human error to slow the security response or expand the reach of a breach. With the emergence of generative AI, computers can generate text that is impossible to distinguish from something written by a person. This could allow criminals to more easily and credibly scale their phishing schemes. It only takes one in thousands to be caught off guard, like I was, for the endeavor to be profitable.

Of course, not all human-caused breaches are the result of social engineering and human error. Some occur because of deliberate, malicious action. Take the Swiss company Mitto, which provides the text messages that databases use in two-factor authentication—to verify passwords and reduce the risk of a hacker log-in. The business works with telecom operators in more than one hundred countries, giving it significant reach. In 2021 it was discovered that Mitto's COO had started a lucrative business on the side: selling access to its networks to help secretly locate people via their cell phones.[7] Consumers have come to expect threats from the outside, but breaches from the inside are even more troubling. Executives can leverage their company's sensitive data for massive financial gain—at great cost to the safety of consumers. Unsurprisingly, Mitto denies the well-researched allegations; an admission of guilt would be a public relations nightmare. Yet, the case still underlines the potential for abuse stemming from the key role that companies play in managing and protecting infrastructure such as secure messaging and telecom networks. It also reminds us how everyday technologies and services, like cell phones and SMS messages, can be weaponized.

Ultimately, criminals, hobby hackers, or state intelligence services deploy different cyberweapons to accomplish a variety of missions. A distributed denial-of-service (DDoS) attack, where an overwhelming amount of internet traffic is directed at a website to shut it down, is mostly disruptive, while intrusions including phishing can be used to gather commercially attractive information or intelligence. Ransomware is a synthesis of both: attackers inject computer systems with a virus that locks data, which can only be unlocked in return for money. It is the preferred method for cybercriminals and, rather surprisingly, the North Korean government.

DDoS attacks have become the pistols in the cyberarsenal; they are used by everyone from slick cybercriminals to social movements to state-backed hackers. Regrettably, these attacks are on the rise across the world. Cloudflare reported a 109-percent year-over-year increase in network-layer DDoS attacks in the second quarter of 2022.[8] Russia deployed a considerable number of DDoS attacks against Ukraine in the early stages of its offensive in 2022 and then suffered its own barrage of attacks levied by hacktivist collectives like Anonymous. Research shows that authoritarian countries frequently turn to DDoS attacks near election season to overpower opposition websites and sow chaos.[9]

However, DDoS attacks are not always politically motivated. Like ransomware, they can serve as a major revenue source for hackers. In 2016, Mirai malware originating from the United States infected cameras and routers, directing the devices to conduct additional cyberattacks. The malware caused damage across the globe, taking down the website of a prominent American tech journalist and OVH, a French hosting provider. Yet this attack—widely considered the largest DDoS attack in history—was not the product of state-linked hackers in Moscow or Pyongyang. Mirai was developed in a dorm room at Rutgers University by enterprising college students.[10] The creators of the malware did not have grand plans to target the world's largest banks or technology companies. Instead, they had been trying to drum up business for their own cybersecurity company, which protected *Minecraft* gaming servers *against* DDoS attacks.[11] Imagine firefighters setting buildings ablaze, only to prove their own added value. The U.S.-based perpetrators in this case were caught and tried, which is quite rare. Law enforcement officials first identified them by tracing the *Minecraft* links in the attack. Apparently, *Minecraft* is a central battleground for DDoS development. As Doug Klein, an FBI agent tasked with the case, joked, "I'd be more surprised sometimes if I didn't see a *Minecraft* connection in a DDoS case."[12] The FBI's Bill Walton has analyzed the Mirai attack and sees no reason to laugh: "DDoS at a certain scale poses an existential threat to the internet. Mirai was the first botnet I've seen that hit that existential level."[13]

Attacks like Mirai often go unpunished because digital fingerprints can easily be removed or manipulated with the aim of incriminating others. And even when law enforcement agencies are able to identify an attacker, logistical, political, and legal obstacles stand in the way of prosecution. When attackers are operating from overseas, in countries where law enforcement is not motivated to hold these people to account, they may literally be out of reach. Criminal hackers know they will rarely face punishment, so they attack with abandon.

The Impact

Right before the COVID-19 pandemic struck, in late 2019 U.S. software vendor Citrix announced a problem with its products: remote log-in applications "weren't working." The company boasts how it services 98 percent of Fortune 500 companies and over one hundred million customers in more than one hundred countries.[14] In the Netherlands alone, 80 percent of federal governmental organizations and two-thirds of local governments use Citrix.[15] The consequences of this attack were severe: hackers obtained access to personal and financial information related to employees and job applicants, potentially including social security numbers, passport numbers, and credit card information.[16] The security company that helped first identify the breach estimated that over six terabytes of data were stolen.[17] And, while no one knew it at the time, information gained during the Citrix hack ended up leading to several other attacks, including at the

U.S. Census Bureau.[18] We often see such domino effects of an attack method in one place being leveraged against targets worldwide. After all, the vulnerability that is initially exploited likely exists in many other systems using the same software version.

To mitigate the attack, Citrix offered some initial ad hoc recommendations, while it worked on developing a more sustainable fix for the infections of their systems. The well-intended temporary measures, however, ended up giving new clues to the malign hackers who, in turn, used that information for their own further advantage.[19]

Shortly thereafter, the National Cyber Security Center (NCSC), a public authority in the Netherlands, decided that the corporate solutions offered were not effective or fast enough, and issued a recommendation to turn Citrix servers off entirely. In staying close to its mandate, the NCSC issued this rare warning only to critical infrastructure operators and government officials, leaving everyday users in the dark. Unfortunately, the warning was too little, too late. Hackers had already stealthily gained access to a sizable number of servers across the country. Critical public institutions like hospitals and municipal governments were compromised, but the lack of transparency from victims, companies, and government organizations makes it difficult to assess the total scope of harm. In July 2020, six months after the Dutch state authorities recommended the shutdown of Citrix servers, at least twenty-five institutions were still compromised.[20]

A relatively obscure cybersecurity company, Resecurity, had pointed the finger at Iranian hackers as being responsible for the attack. Allegedly, they were after the virtual private network (VPN) services that Citrix also provides. These VPNs are used to enhance privacy and security by rerouting internet traffic through an encrypted virtual channel. They mask users' IP addresses, which makes it harder to trace their communications to their locations. VPNs are particularly popular in countries like Iran, as they allow citizens to circumvent state surveillance and digital firewalls that block social media platforms. A VPN also serves as a "virtual digital passport": users can claim that they are accessing the internet from another country. Those in the West often leverage VPNs to access foreign content—like anime streaming exclusively on Netflix in Japan. But just as a college student in Texas can use the VPN to access content in Tokyo, hackers can leverage VPNs to access new targets and hide an attack's origin. Nevertheless, VPNs are not foolproof; another security company called ClearSky unearthed key information about how Iranian state hackers exploited Citrix with their VPNs.[21]

Throughout this incident, and despite the national security implications, companies played all the lead roles: one private company was breached (Citrix), and other companies (Resecurity and ClearSky) identified the perpetrators. Information sharing about risks and hacks, as well as a strong chain of responsibility and command between private and public institutions in times of crisis, is far from perfect. Certainly, the balance to be struck between informing victims and tipping off new bad actors is a delicate one. At the same time, a host of services, including those for smart cities and self-driving cars, all continue to rely on software with built-in weaknesses that are similar to those used to access Citrix.

I was part of the official committee that analyzed the Citrix hack with the aim of making recommendations to the Dutch government toward better prevention and policies. In our final report we concluded that, in practice, it is impossible to make fully secure software.[22] There will always be another zero day lurking in our digital infrastructure. But since our reliance on software is only growing, we must dramatically improve the way we protect it. If we know we cannot build fully secure software, we must be vigilant in finding vulnerabilities and attacks immediately as they happen, and we must improve the organizational infrastructure that coordinates the public and private response following an attack. Unfortunately, today's solutions, primarily software-based defenses from Silicon Valley cybersecurity firms, do not measure up. This is an incredibly difficult challenge: The repairs will require enormous changes in policy decisions and security investments, with no promise of a bulletproof outcome.

The Dark Side

The severity of the cyberattack epidemic was underlined when, in the spring of 2021, Colonial Pipeline suffered a ransomware attack. The company is a major player in the American energy market that supplies about 45 percent of the fuel consumed across the East Coast.[23] An energy pipeline company is considered critical infrastructure and therefore enjoys protections coordinated at the federal level. But, there is still a significant disconnect in how governments approach the protection of the steel pipes of energy infrastructure versus the fiber optic tubes of digital infrastructure.

The hackers of the digitized systems of Colonial Pipeline exploited zero-day vulnerabilities to launch their ransomware virus. Seemingly overnight, the attack shut off one of the country's largest oil faucets. Operators of the energy systems at Colonial saw their worst fear coming true when they noticed they were under attack. They disabled all operations, including the physical flows of oil through their pipelines, in an effort to prevent any further fallout. They also consulted with the FBI and controversially decided to pay the $4.4 million that the attackers demanded in ransom.[24] On receiving their demanded sums, the hackers provided tools to unlock and restore the systems.

Systems engineers in Colonial's control rooms were not the only ones panicking, as consumers launched into crisis mode too. Long lines of cars formed at gas stations, as people feared they might not be able to fill up their tanks in the near future. *Smithsonian* magazine opined that the chaos bore striking similarities to the energy crisis that arose during the administration of President Jimmy Carter, when Americans would wait in five-mile-long lines for a pittance of fuel.[25] Some brought jerricans to hoard gasoline. Across the country, stations ran dry and prices surged. The shortage extended beyond auto transit and into aerospace. American Airlines, for example, changed some flights or added fuel stops in other parts of the country.[26]

Two days after the initial ransomware attack on Colonial Pipeline, President Joe Biden declared a state of emergency, allowing for a suspension of the normal limits to the amount of fuel that is allowed to be transported domestically.[27] The governor of Georgia, Brian Kemp, declared an emergency for his state the next day, while U.S. transportation secretary Pete Buttigieg warned worried Americans that the fallout caused by their hoarding may exceed that of the attack itself.[28]

The U.S. Department of Justice later announced that it had managed to retrieve $2.3 million of the ransom paid without spelling out how it managed to do so.[29] Shortly thereafter, department officials identified DarkSide, an independent hacker group, as the perpetrators. DarkSide, which may well be the most stereotypical name for a shadowy hacker group, contracts out teams of cybermercenaries to provide ransomware as a service and advertises on the dark web.[30] As the *Financial Times* dryly noted, hacking was another form of remote work that thrived during the COVID-19 pandemic.[31] No one has faced trial for the Colonial attack even as a $10 million reward was announced for information leading to the perpetrators. Without any consequences, DarkSide continues to attack. As of May 2021, experts estimated that DarkSide had gained a total of $90 million through a series of attacks on forty-seven victims.[32]

DarkSide claims the attack was just about money: "Our goal is to make money and not creating problems for society. We do not participate in geopolitics, no need to tie us with a defined government and look for our motives."[33] But the FBI was not convinced; it considered the hacking collective as one of many based in—and closely affiliated with the government of—Russia.[34] Hostility toward American targets and their allies would explain why Russian authorities have not gone after the hackers in their midst. The group apparently has some limits and avoids attacking hospitals and schools. The reason may be quite self-serving, however: these public organizations often won't have the resources to pay up. The group also seems to avoid areas where allies of the Russian government reside.

Unfortunately, there is little to dissuade attackers like DarkSide from exploiting software vulnerabilities. Often, consequences of attacks like the one on Colonial Pipeline are difficult to evaluate and assess because of the opacity around the methods, the ransom paid, or the mistakes made in the prevention phase. Additionally, the lack of legal benchmarks and accountability mechanisms means that perpetrators are hardly ever brought to justice even when details about them are known. The fact that they are often operating from other parts of the world creates additional logistical and jurisdictional challenges to making arrests, having suspects extradited, or getting them tried in a court of law. As long as these prevention and accountability gaps persist, it is reasonable to expect future attacks on critical infrastructure, with increasingly heavy disruptions and more significant casualties. Ideally, such exacerbations would be preempted rather than waiting for a nuclear power station or undersea cable to be breached and to then decide to act.

In an effort to swiftly shore up defenses, the Biden White House issued an executive order on May 12, 2021, only days after the attack on Colonial Pipeline.[35] In it, the federal government spelled out criteria for procuring software more securely, and it shared protocols for finding vulnerabilities in existing systems. Responsible vulnerability disclosure schemes have been put into place by both companies and countries. Through those, people who find a zero day are invited to report it instead of selling it on the dark web or even using it directly. Warning DarkSide, President Biden said that the United States would "disrupt their ability to operate" and shut down their systems.[36] While there were some signs of concern among groups offering ransomware as a service in response to the executive order, the threat should by no means be considered over. Individual criminal hackers may simply continue under a different flag or a group may dissolve and reassemble as another entity. Moreover, there is no guarantee that these operatives will abide by the rules; after all, they've already demonstrated a blatant disregard for the international rule of law.

The Battleground

This book is typed in Microsoft Word, one function of the broader Microsoft Office software package, a product with over one billion users worldwide. Microsoft, with its voluminous customer base and a total revenue of $168 billion in 2021, should be able to build the world's most secure software.[37] It spends large sums of money on security, announcing in 2021 that it will invest $20 billion on cybersecurity in the next five years.[38] Moreover, cybersecurity is one of the company's biggest businesses, and with the U.S. Department of Defense as one of its most lucrative customers, trust in Microsoft's security must be high. In an interview in April 2022, CEO Satya Nadella revealed that Microsoft's security business generates $15 billion a year in revenue. Yet despite major use and significant investments the company's products have been breached in some of the most impactful incidents to have ever occurred: the Exchange Server Hack, NotPetya, SolarWinds, and, most infamously, WannaCry (aptly named because it likely drove many an IT professional to tears).[39]

Microsoft's struggles exemplify how everything digital can be weaponized, regardless of how large an organization's cybersecurity budget might be. Over the last decade, eighty-three million accounts of customers at the bank JPMorgan Chase were compromised.[40] A teenager from Florida managed to take over 130 Twitter accounts of prominent individuals, including those of former president Barack Obama and future president Joe Biden, and used them to funnel dollars into a Bitcoin wallet.[41] Seizing a presidential Twitter account may seem like a harmless prank, but imagine the chaos that would have ensued if the teen had added the threat of war on another country or addressed a terrorist group. In Finland, the confidential files of psychiatric patients were stolen.[42] A host of public organizations as varied as the Norwegian Parliament, the New Zealand stock exchange, and the Vatican have all come under attack. No triggers were pulled, no doors were knocked in, and no bombs were detonated. Instead, the attackers managed to intrude into these vital institutions' internal networks in attempts to commit espionage, disrupt daily affairs, or ransom and blackmail victims.

The International Committee of the Red Cross saw the data of more than a half million people who were in need of humanitarian aid hacked.[43] Sony Pictures had private staff information stolen, as did the U.S. Office of Personnel and Management.[44] Billions of dollars in

Bitcoin have been embezzled, and the accounts of people registered with dating website Ashley Madison were breached. Even Iranian nuclear facilities are hackable, as the American and Israeli cyberattack Stuxnet of 2010 proved by severely damaging their infrastructure. But then it turned out the NSA itself had an exposed underbelly and saw both its classified information and its own cyberweapons stolen, published, and used against American targets.

Compromised organizations frequently fall victim to cynical criminals who understand that files on psychiatric treatments or operations of fuel supplies are sensitive and that people would likely be willing to pay the ransom if it would prevent the captured data from being leaked or services from being disabled. Targeted entities may also consider paying the hijackers out of a concern for reputational damage, even if most official recommendations by authorities are not to reward criminals by paying ransom.

Criminal motives seem to be dominant in many intrusion efforts, but geopolitically driven attacks are also on the rise. Intelligence and access are just as valuable as real money for some. As Accenture's Cyber Threat Intelligence team notes, "the mostly financial motives of the past are giving way to political motivations, with cybercrime actors pushing for more access to critical infrastructure targets by offering up to $500,000 for network access, and up to $10 million for zero-day exploits."[45] Stolen data can be lucrative on the dark web or an online black market, or it can give trade negotiators an information advantage. Uncovering the prized ingredients of a COVID-19 vaccine, or the dirty secrets of political opponents, can mean that stolen data are cynical currency for a wide range of buyers. Disinformation is often used as an additional, interwoven layer to hide tracks, or maximize the impact of a cyberattack.

The line separating good actors from bad ones is often blurred. An intelligence service may deploy criminal hackers, and data stolen by criminal hackers may well be offered up to state agencies for the agencies' further advantage. States may rely on hacker mercenaries to afford themselves plausible deniability, and hackers may present themselves as state operatives to hide other motives or to score points with the political leaders they support. In a desperate effort to avoid accountability during a legal trial, NSO Group claimed before the U.S. Supreme Court that it deserved state immunity considering the fact that it sold its commercial hacking services to a state.[46] NSO Group's state-like capacities and attempt to cloak itself in similar legal privilege shows the degree to which states, companies, and technologies have become integrated.

Hackers and spies are happy to use every digital resource available to prey on their targets. Top secret information can end up being compromised in ways unthinkable a few decades ago. On a simple health website that monitors running progress, Strava, patterns of intense physical activity along similar routes were recognized as being in Afghanistan and Syria.[47] The idea was that the activity of a group of people in remote locations would likely indicate the encampments of troops. While official details were supposed to be top secret, the same GPS signal you use to help you navigate when driving to visit a friend can also be used to track a device—without its owner being aware of such tracking. Public servants like these soldiers, trained to face the most serious conventional threats on the battlefield, were apparently left unprepared to deal with more modern dangers.

If this summary of targets and methods sounds overwhelming, that is because the attack surface *really is that extensive*. There are new reports of hacks and major breaches in the news every day, and the challenge of how to repair the damage or prevent it is enormous. Innocent, everyday products are turned into tracing tools and have left companies and state authorities unprepared. The true impact of this reality seems to only be appreciated gradually, and after the rollout of weaponizable devices has already happened. "Historically the internet has been so insecure there's always going to be someone messing around with it, and there's always going to be potential attacks on others that extend to us," explains Ciaran Martin, who served as the founding lead of the U.K. National Cyber Security Center.[48]

As more devices get connected, the battleground continues to grow. Meanwhile, weak security, bad code, the lack of clear delineation between governments and private companies, and the absence of clear laws and international frameworks all hamper accountability. Over the past few years we have seen an explosion in the numbers of cyberattacks, with both criminal and (geo)political motives. Cyberwarfare is getting worse because governments are fighting on inhospitable terrain. The inherent vulnerabilities (zero days) in software and the lack of clear definitions of responsibilities and liabilities between state authorities and private companies give the advantage to state hackers. Unfortunately, attackers today have the choice of more targets than ever before, stretching from major corporations to small businesses, from national governments to community nonprofits.

As ransomware attacks increase, so do the revenues for companies selling solutions to them. It is not easy to come by objective data, but one cybersecurity company reported as much as an 1,885 percent increase in ransomware attacks on governments in 2021.[49] Another report estimates that ransomware attacks on all targets rose by 62 percent across the world between 2019 and 2020.[50] Yet for public officials and academic researchers, looking under the hood of the companies on the front lines of digital infrastructure, risk analysis, and cybersecurity is impossible. The proprietary nature of networks and data, and the absence of transparency requirements, means that research in the public interest is challenging. Billion-dollar investments into the cybersecurity industry do indicate a growing concern and, as a rule of thumb, every new connected device offers a new attack opportunity. Meanwhile, policies that seek to shore up tech standards and other resiliencies are lagging. A lot of prevention depends on whether companies are able to meet their promises to provide secure systems.

Many of the cyber-sagas documented in this chapter expose a key problem in the fight to improve cybersecurity systems: the proprietary nature of the whole suite of digitized systems gives very little visibility to researchers, journalists, and citizens. In other words, the status quo unfairly empowers companies and disempowers the public. Besides those in certain intelligence agencies, very few government officials have a clear view of the complex challenges societies are up against. The shocking result is that, in many cases, Google and

Microsoft know far more about major attacks than, say, the Belgian or Italian governments. Without greater awareness, voters cannot urge their representatives to do more to protect small- and medium-size enterprises, to train public servants, or to set higher standards for software firms. Nor can they hold democratic representatives properly to account, given that those representatives are not primarily responsible for governing the digital systems our lives are built on.

Between innocent glitches and highly sensitive system breaches, it is crystal clear that everything smart and connected ends up being vulnerable to hacks and intrusions. Companies believe state authorities have the formal duty to ensure national security, while government agencies increasingly rely on firms to build and secure software and digital infrastructure. Frequently, the institutions the most vulnerable to cyberattacks are the least well funded, skilled, and equipped to afford adequate cybersecurity measures; hospitals and local councils, which deal with sensitive data, therefore become easy high-impact targets. A knowledge lacuna is growing alongside an accountability gap.

When governments struggle to point the finger to another country via public attribution and out of concerns for retribution, companies have been forthright in what I think of as commercial attribution. Companies rather than countries often end up leading the attributions of cyberattacks to specific attackers. For instance, FireEye, a California-based cybersecurity firm, ultimately pointed the finger at Russian-linked groups for its attacks on the Ukrainian energy grid in 2015 and 2016—not the Department of Justice or the FBI.[51] These companies don't just lay blame, they act: shutting down criminal activities on their networks and justifying their actions as being in their commercial interest. Yet citizens may not always be able to count on companies to take the lead. Businesses, after all, are not signatories to international law treaties. And while it may be in FireEye's best business interest to call out Russia this time around, it may opt not to in the future. Unfortunately, today's sad reality is that the U.S. federal government may conclude that holding the Kremlin accountable costs too much political capital, so that critical job is left up to CEOs. Without clarity on the delineation of responsibilities between companies and governmental entities, there will be no public attribution standard. That would perpetuate the status quo, in which politics or commercial motives stand in the way of accountability.

The monopoly on information that a lot of technology companies hold, however, makes it difficult to both assess whether they consistently disclose newly discovered intrusions and whether the attributions are substantiated with sufficient evidence. And have these companies done enough to prevent the breaches of their systems in the first place? Responsibility under international law can only be attributed if effective control between the state and the nonstate actor involved in the attack is proven beyond any doubt. But ascertaining provenance and who is responsible for an attack, particularly a sophisticated one, is considered forensically difficult and politically sensitive. This is a legal area worth updating to facilitate public attribution and accountability. Even as significant power—for example, to ensure national security—has moved from state authorities to corporate entities, chains of responsibility and liability are anything but clear. To preserve the rule of law and democratic principles, the relationship between democratic states and companies needs to be clarified. Disastrous hacks like that of SolarWinds software were the product of corporate negligence mixed with a lack of oversight over procurement and contracts. At the same time, the policy frameworks to address these mistakes retrospectively, let alone to prevent them proactively, have failed to materialize, which explains why attacks continue to happen successfully.

The combination of human errors, faulty software design, compromised supply chains, and insufficient security investments due to business concerns around cost add up to a fragile total. Breaches may happen intentionally or unintentionally. To curb the particularly important role of vulnerabilities in software as launchpads for attacks, companies and governments have begun to develop paths to report exploits with the aim of getting them fixed. Incentives in the form of recognition, financial rewards, or a "bounty," as well as legal safeguards, may all be handed out. To win the trust of cybersecurity experts capable of tracing these minute vulnerabilities in software code, "bona fide" hackers would be exempt from prosecution and encouraged to report anonymously. They might get paid for their discoveries, or sometimes they might just get a T-shirt. Yes, a T-shirt: the NCSC played into the sentiment of pride and competition between hackers and gave out T-shirts at a hackathon that said, "I hacked the Dutch government, and all I got was this lousy t-shirt."[52]

The irony is that for systems to be better protected, they often need to be attacked first in order to discover where the entry points might be hidden. Many large companies now employ their own "red teams" whose sole job it is to hack into the company's own systems to find zero days before attackers do. To fight back against a whole host of hackers and attackers with bad intentions, some companies have now made hacking their own business model. HackerOne, for example, employs security experts to find zero-day vulnerabilities and then acts as a broker, offering the secret weaknesses to the relevant technology companies in an effort to prevent them from ending up on the black market or in the hands of criminals. The cybersecurity industry is a peculiar one in the sense that it needs to act against legal principles to strengthen resilience, and cybersecurity companies need to persuade hackers who may also engage in illegal activities to come out from the dark side. Some security experts self-identify as "white hat" or ethical hackers, while others may be "black hat" hackers, reflecting that they are not restricting themselves in any way.

Black hat hackers and commercial intelligence gatherers like NSO Group or DarkSide are also discovering new business models. They too are providing their services for hire. That means that a criminal group, a small country, or a political campaign no longer needs cybersecurity expertise in-house to access and use tools to hack infrastructure, systems, or databases. As a result, risk is proliferating, while checks and balances are missing. Outsourcing hacking to these types of "service providers" also gives government authorities such as police or intelligence services the possibility to deny engaging in such activities directly, thereby evading the kind of scrutiny that would normally apply in democracies. Governments are hiring external companies to engage in activities that they are not legally mandated to perform. The fact that there is often a lack of transparency, and a lack of will to answer freedom of information requests, says a lot.

For the moment, it is safe to say that cybersecurity is more of a business model than a policy model. That increases the risk of moral hazard, with companies reaping profits from the sale of their products but cases of failure falling onto the public to absorb. Moving from soft incentives, such as codes of practice around vulnerability disclosure, to harder rules encoded in law, should go a long way to ensure minimum security standards. Rules should include transparency and information-sharing requirements to break the overdependence on companies and to help information about risks, threats, and attacks flow to those ultimately responsible: government leaders.

The Gap

While I served in the European Parliament, it struck me how difficult it is to stay up-to-date about the latest developments in technology, including new threats. Most politicians do not have a technical background; neither do I. As I did my own homework, I decided to support colleagues in learning but also in creating a space to ask questions. It resulted in a discussion series titled *Nerds in the Parliament,* in which white hat hackers, privacy experts, and cybersecurity wonks shared their insights.[53] I also attended hacker conferences, such as the Chaos Computer Club (CCC), where I was the odd one out in many ways. Few women attend these conferences, where live hacks are shared on stage and Club-Mate is drunk to keep up caffeine levels during all-night hackathons. There I was, as an elected official, wearing heels and a dress instead of army boots and a black hoodie, but most of all struggling to keep up with the spectacular revelations about how to hack a Wi-Fi connection, iris scanner, or gaming console. The aim behind most of these presentations seemed to be public service, and the community culture has supporting privacy protection, freedom of information, open source software, and human rights baked into it. Linus Neumann, a spokesperson for the

CCC, said, "The basis is always sharing knowledge openly, seeking knowledge openly, trying to find out how things really work and how to influence them. . . . And it makes very much sense to adopt that hacker perspective and take it to political challenges and issues, to look at political battles and discussions as interesting problems to which you need to find a creative solution."[54] That kind of hacker perspective, with the public interest at heart, is what will be needed to end the weaponization of everything.

So far the digital encroachment on national security has not been accompanied by a transformation in law to oversee the operations of these now-critical security operations in the private sector. The lagging application of legal principles, combined with the typical opacity of corporate information, means that transparency and accountability in the public interest are rare. Public authorities ranging from water to energy companies, local police forces to hospitals, are no longer able to run and protect their systems without hiring cybersecurity companies—and they frequently do not know what the cybersecurity firms are even doing.

The same is true for public institutions. Today, politicians struggle to get a solid sense of where weak nodes in a digital ecosystem might exist. They lack a mandate to ensure access to information and, even if they had that access, the skills to know what to look for. Without this understanding they can never hope to propose matching solutions. A true catch-22 has emerged: governments rely on companies to identify and intercept threats, and companies rely on governments to counter them. The result is a patchwork of legal and operational insecurity with too many opportunities for abuse. In order to clarify the chain of responsibility, rules are needed to create governance structures, accountability mechanisms, and independent oversight.

We must act soon because the problem is getting worse. Massive intrusions make clear how integrating technology and outsourcing functions to an increasingly large share of everyday tools and products inadvertently facilitates a growing attack surface for criminals and states to exploit. As Signal president Meredith Whittaker underlines: "AI isn't magic. It's reliant on hardware & software like all other networked tech. And, as here, it too is subject to serious vulner-abilities that have been drastically under examined amid the hype."[55]

While FireEye was instrumental in uncovering some of the world's more significant security breaches, in 2020 its own penetration testing tools were stolen in the United States, and then used in at least nineteen countries within a week.[56] And LastPass password manager, sold as a secure solution to managing one's passwords, was breached itself.[57] (But yes, you should still use a password manager!) The painful reality is that the more trust that is placed in software and other tech companies, the vaster the risks, vulnerabilities, and opportunities to attack become.

As cybersecurity failures continue to mount, citizens are becoming more and more doubtful that their governments can deliver the fundamental promise of security. With every cyberattack or hack that goes unpunished, citizens lose more trust in the ability of democratic institutions to ensure public safety. It is important for democratic governments to be the ones providing the needed mandates and oversight for cyberoperations, whether they are waged against states or criminals. When the state may decide to outsource certain operations to companies, there must be a clear chain of responsibility and accountability. Otherwise, governments will always lack insight, agency, and oversight into crucial processes that previously sat squarely within their purview.

The role reversal between democratic governments and private technology companies does not stay confined to matters of security, even if they are vast and foundational. Chapter 4 dives deeper into how a variety of public interests have been eroded due to the systematic privatization of everything digital.

4

The End of the Public Interest

One of the more surreal meetings during my tenure as a member of the European Parliament took me halfway around the world to Richard Branson's private Necker Island. Though it was the summer of 2016, I had not traveled to the British Virgin Islands to lie on the white sandy beaches or to swim in the warm turquoise waters. Instead, I arrived hoping to immerse myself in the fascinating ecosystem of blockchain technologies.

The Second Blockchain Summit promised to offer a deep discussion with key players around what many believed was a revolutionary technology. Those gathered on Necker Island, predominantly venture capitalists and industry leaders, sang blockchain's praises. They said that blockchain could democratize governance and empower people—especially the world's most vulnerable. It could end corruption and even make it easier for poor migrant workers to send remittances back home to their families—a point Branson emphasized by pulling resort staff on stage to share how providers like MoneyGram and Western Union charged exorbitant fees to wire cash to unbanked relatives. Blockchain might also help register property for people whose ownership of land had never been documented, while cryptocurrencies such as Bitcoin would democratize finance, delivering a faster, better, and fairer financial system for all.

The enthusiasm of the crowd at Necker Island was palpable. Indeed, one of the dinners ended with Branson dancing across a gigantic table to "get the party started."[1]

Apart from myself, there were a handful of public servants at the summit: Mariana Dahan, who worked on identity issues at the World Bank; Katie Haun, an assistant U.S. attorney and the digital currency coordinator at the U.S. Department of Justice (who attended in a personal capacity and has since left her post for a stint at Andreessen Horowitz and board positions at Coinbase and OpenSea); and Laurent Lamothe, the former prime minister of Haiti, who has since become the founder of R-Ventures, a venture capital firm that invests in—you guessed it—cryptocurrencies and neobanking. But the conference was mainly filled with blockchain's greatest proponents—and entrepreneurial success stories. Alex and Don Tapscott, the father and son who coauthored the bestseller *Blockchain Revolution*, were there. Elizabeth Rossiello, the founder and CEO of fast-growing AZA Finance, shared her experiences of working on the African continent to ensure secure, smooth, and cheap payments. Bloq founder Matt Roszak was present, and so was Gabriel Abed, who had just launched the digitized version of the Barbados dollar. With Virgin Galactic aerospace engineer Beth Moses walking around the stunning island, it seemed that not even the sky was the limit.[2]

So lavish were the lives of these tech entrepreneurs and investors that, for a brief moment, I feared I had chosen the wrong career. They appeared to have created a (digital) gold mine that simultaneously had the potential to truly serve the public. If the proponents were to be believed, blockchain was the perfect combination of profits and purpose.

Eight years later, few convincing use cases of blockchain have emerged. The better, faster, fairer financial system seems like an island mirage, while the dark side of cryptocurrencies is now all too real. In 2022, cryptocurrency markets crashed, and investors with large exposure to them were ruined. Moreover, the past decade has shown how cryptocurrencies threaten the government's sovereign role in minting currency and managing monetary policy. Loose or absent regulations allowed cryptocurrencies to impede key government functions, leading to stunning personal damage for citizens. As a result, cryptocurrencies became a direct threat to the public interest. By taking over or sidestepping government functions, cryptocurrencies are one of many private technologies that have damaged democracy by fundamentally reshaping the purpose and power of government.

The first U.S. president, George Washington, started the executive branch in America with just three departments: State, Treasury, and War. Now, more than two centuries later, the fundamental duties of those foundational departments—rights protection (at home and abroad), monetary policy, and national security—have been usurped by technology. Indeed, without proper regulation, applications like cryptocurrencies and facial recognition technologies make it so the state is no longer able to roll out monetary policy or to guarantee the right to privacy or the freedom from discrimination. The "great outsourcing" of government is fundamentally rewriting the social contract between the democratic state and its citizens.

This chapter highlights three disruptive technologies that have the potential to reshape core government functions. The first of these are cryptocurrencies, which threaten to destabilize governments' monetary powers. Second are facial recognition technologies, which are owned and operated by third-party firms and could revolutionize law enforcement's approach to public safety as well as to fundamental rights protections. Third are data integration products, which are developed by contractors and are welcomed by governments, but which may imperil national security. In each of these cases, democratically elected leaders are losing agency to technology enterprises that have designed disruptive products with scant legal or regulatory safeguards. This tech coup must stop.

Cryptocurrencies

If my goal had been to get rich, I should have listened to the participants at the Second Blockchain Summit and poured my savings into Bitcoin. In the years that followed, the currency based on blockchain technology grew exponentially in value. A mere $2,000 worth of

Bitcoin in mid-2016 would have been worth almost $2 million by 2021. The total value of the global cryptocurrency market at that time was $3.2 trillion.[3] It is no wonder that cryptocurrency fans grew exceedingly convinced of their own vision. They created a self-fulfilling prophecy. Bitcoin believers successfully persuaded everyone from teenagers to prime ministers to go all in—and the price kept going up. As for me, my skepticism won, and I did not invest. As a lawmaker, I kept a healthy distance to risky investments and didn't exactly have Necker Island money to play with anyway.

In fact, I seemed to be the only person at the summit who was not sold on the blockchain utopia. While my fellow attendees waxed poetic about the new digital world, I wondered how cryptocurrencies might exacerbate problems of the status quo. How would money laundering through Bitcoin be prevented? What would happen if an authoritarian state unequivocally embraced blockchain for registering everything from identity to property, from pensions to criminal records? Shrewd actors, I worried, might exploit cryptocurrencies to deepen their repressive tendencies instead of building a democratized financial system. Decentralized finance (DeFi) would give them more autonomy to act on their worst instincts, not less. While the blockchain proselytizers reassured me that the benefits would far outweigh any harms, it still seemed more dystopian than utopian to me.

To most participants at the conference, however, my opinion was irrelevant. The self-declared crypto evangelists proclaimed that regulations and policies would never *be able* to impact all kinds of blockchain-based transactions. No matter what my colleagues in the European Parliament and I might think, there would be no use in trying to pass an omnibus bill or create a cryptocurrency regulatory agency because, in their view, the technology was beyond the reach of regulation, simply because of how it was coded. Of course, I had a different view: everything can be regulated, as long as there is political will. Still, the evangelists' proselytizing told us a great deal about their long-term goals. They wanted to build an alternate financial system, entirely free from government oversight.

Many were ecstatic about blockchain's promise to vanquish their archenemy, the modern banking system. Central banks were nosy, irritating, opaque, and painfully slow government annoyances, they thought. Large, private banks were greedy and evil, so it was better to avoid them. Other useless and expensive intermediaries, like notaries, would also be eliminated. Finally, they believed that DeFi would replace consumer trust, which underlies the banking system, with concrete cryptography, putting an end to bank runs like the one that would eventually doom Silicon Valley Bank. The opportunities were endless—and, most important, blockchain would make a lot of money for everyone involved.

Today's monetary system seeks to strike a careful balance. Central banks issue currencies that people and businesses use to pay for goods and services throughout the economy. These currencies are backed by the central banks and stored in commercial banks and credit unions, who protect and manage them on behalf of their clients. There is a robust set of rules, and checks and balances, that have been built over centuries with the aim of keeping everyone in the system—workers, businesses, and the banks themselves—safe. Unfortunately, the rules on the books do not translate to a flawless practice. The financial crisis of 2008–2009 underlined the need for more, not fewer rules to ensure that sufficient cash reserves are in place and to limit the amount of speculation and risky investment. Moreover, because the central bank controls the levels of currency in the system and interest rates—effectively, how expensive it is to borrow more currency—it can broadly control how much spending and investment is happening throughout a society at any given time. This allows the government to keep the economy on a stable path, avoiding the dramatic booms and busts that were typical before the era of central banks. When the economy contracts, the central bank can increase currency levels to spur investment. Without this flow of cash, the economy would sink into a recession.

While traditional finance relies on centralization, proponents of DeFi value autonomy. They distrust the traditional intermediaries and seek to wrest control of the financial system from the government. In this way, DeFi upends the logic behind traditional banking.

Blockchain, the core of the DeFi system, promises to serve as a tamper-proof, distributed ledger. Every transaction—say, the sale of land—is registered and verified by various computers connected to the network, or nodes on the chain. The transaction is time-stamped and recorded, and a log of all previous transactions is kept chronologically, protected through cryptography. Any updates are shared back to be recorded by the nodes and verified by all users, who can pay for goods or services using cryptocurrencies like Bitcoin that are built, stored, and exchanged on public blockchains. Given this elaborate verification system, crypto evangelists would assert that a fraud of the type that Bernie Madoff perpetrated on his clients is impossible to perpetrate on the blockchain because all transactions are public and cannot be retroactively altered. But it's not just the Madoffs of the world who are disabled by the blockchain—it is the government itself. While central banks can print more money, or raise and lower rates, cryptocurrencies are (in theory, at least) free from such interference. Ultimately, DeFi-ers see the centrality of the government in finance as a liability, not an asset. They seek to revolve the financial system around the wisdom of the crowd rather than the wisdom of technocrats in Brussels, Frankfurt, or Washington, DC.

Historically, it was the cypherpunks, those early cryptography and internet pioneers, who started making the case for a currency for cyberspace. They sought to leverage computational tools to build a more efficient, consensus-driven system of commerce. In 2008 Satoshi Nakamoto, likely a pseudonym, authored "Bitcoin: A Peer-to-Peer Electronic Cash System," the foundational white paper on Bitcoin, which elaborated the trust principle that underlies the system. As Nakamoto writes, the financial system of Web 1.0 suffers "from the inherent weaknesses of the trust-based model. Completely non-reversible transactions are not really possible, since financial institutions cannot avoid mediating disputes."[4] The cypherpunks, animated by a libertarian and sometimes anarchic streak, believed that all central financial institutions—those backed by a government or privately run—were incapable of facilitating a better system of commerce.

Even a decade later, the conference attendees on Necker Island remained resolute that government financial institutions simply could not measure up. DeFi operated on a different paradigm and at a different pace from public regulation. Meanwhile, the revolutionary characteristics of the technology included a promise of absolute security. The blockchain was, they claimed, "unhackable."

As DeFi-ers eschewed government financial institutions, they looked elsewhere for financial and commercial support: venture capital. One of the most prominent cryptocurrency investors, Marc Andreessen, has poured billions into the sector. At Meta, Mark Zuckerberg launched the ill-fated cryptocurrency payments wallet, Novi, in collaboration with Andreessen Horowitz, Uber, and Visa.[5] The financing and backing for DeFi has, ironically, been remarkably centralized. It is even being embraced by certain governments.

El Salvador was the first country to adopt Bitcoin as a common currency in 2021, replacing the colón. President Nayib Bukele, who called himself "the world's coolest dictator," believed that the country and its people would benefit from leapfrogging other countries' monetary systems.[6] Investments, jobs, and innovation would all be attracted to El Salvador as a result. While the World Bank, on which El Salvador depends, rejected the request to support the transition to Bitcoin, companies were all too happy to help.[7] Even though demonstrators ended up destroying some of the country's Bitcoin ATMs to protest their poor living conditions, the president continued to plan a "Bitcoin city" at the base of a volcano and inspired by the architecture of Alexander the Great.[8]

In countries like Afghanistan and Argentina, cryptocurrencies have compensated for dysfunctional governments and collapsing banks.[9] To avoid the risks of high inflation, people exchange local currency for Bitcoin, whose appreciation (at the time) had been relatively stable by comparison. Singapore, by contrast, was motivated by the innovation promised by cryptocurrency traders. The small country was considered a cryptocurrency paradise, with attractive tax rules.[10] In 2021 it drew almost $1.5 billion in investments into the sector. After making Bitcoin ATMs available and ensuring a favorable fiscal environment, it is now rolling back these policies "to reduce consumer harm."[11] The emir of Dubai made it a national policy to attract Bitcoin business. The Middle East, as *Politico*'s Ben Schreckinger observes, has been the region where cryptocurrency use has grown the fastest, as well as the one "that offers the starkest contrasts between cryptocurrency's origins as anti-government money, and the growing desire of governments to use the underlying technology to modernize markets and monitor financial activity."[12] Crypto evangelists pledged that democratized finance would also spur a groundswell of support for free societies. In actuality, cryptocurrencies have become a favored tool of authoritarians, autocrats, and other illiberal leaders.

The Emperor Has No Clothes

In May 2022 the first signs of a chill arrived as cryptocurrencies lost $300 billion in a week. The headlines were ominous: "More than $200 Billion Erased from the Entire Crypto Market in a Day as Sell-Off Intensifies"; "2022 Was the Year Crypto Came Crashing Down to Earth."[13] The *New York Times* may have best captured the uncertainty of the moment, proclaiming in one headline, "Cryptocurrencies Melt Down in a 'Perfect Storm' of Fear and Panic."[14] The magnitude of this drop on individual currencies was astonishing. Bitcoin, for example, plunged from its 2021 peak price of $60,000 to about $16,000 in November 2022.[15]

The crash impacted millions of investors across the world, including many everyday people who were investing in cryptocurrencies out of their bedrooms and kitchens. Given the scar tissue of the 2008–2009 recession and the continued pain wrought by high inflation, it is not difficult to understand why people were attracted to the idea that cryptocurrencies could bypass malevolent big banks and incompetent governments. The COVID-19 pandemic, which saw restaurants shut down and holidays canceled, had made cryptocurrency investment seem like an attractive destination for savings, while the rise of apps like Robinhood facilitated access. At the time of the crash, 16 percent of all Americans had invested in cryptocurrencies, including a shocking 42 percent of young American men.[16]

In the Netherlands, about one-fourth of young adults had invested in cryptocurrencies.[17]

When the crash came, many of these ordinary investors lost their real savings. ABC News's *Nightline* profiled Curt Dell, a father of three small children who worked in sales in Orange County, California. Like so many other parents, Curt and his wife, Victoria, a nurse practitioner, were eager to explore every avenue that could secure a better financial future for their children, including cryptocurrencies. He bought about $30,000 worth of Bitcoin in 2017, and the initial returns compelled him to invest more and more. By late 2021 Curt was at the peak of the roller coaster: his Bitcoin wallet was worth about $900,000. Although his wife Victoria urged him to sell, Curt remained invested, believing that Bitcoin would keep climbing. Then came the crash. Curt's assets tumbled to just $200,000. Even worse, the app that held those remaining assets, Celsius, froze customer withdrawals due to "extreme market conditions," leaving Curt locked out of virtually everything he owned. The money that would pay off his and his wife's student loans and fund his children's education was unreachable. Ultimately, Curt says, his children are the ultimate victims of this crash: "It robbed them of so much potential. . . . It's such a bad situation."[18]

Curt was not alone. All in all, three-fourths of retail investors who bought Bitcoin lost money, according to a study from the Bank for International Settlements (BIS), an organization of central banks, from the end of 2022.[19] In fact, the average retail Bitcoin investor lost nearly half of their investment by December 2022, per another BIS study.[20] Cryptocurrency crashes were quick—and devastating, wiping out billions of dollars in value in a single day. "Bitcoin was working as long as no one lost money," notes Dan Dolev, a financial technology analyst.[21] JPMorgan Chase CEO Jamie Dimon has drawn parallels between the roller-coaster valuations of cryptocurrencies and economic bubbles of earlier eras, calling Bitcoin "worse than tulip bulbs" in a reference to the Dutch tulip mania of the 1600s, which saw prices for flower bulbs skyrocketing.[22] In fact, the term "cryptocurrencies" is deceiving. Currencies are normally underwritten by central banks, to ensure trust in their value, and to maintain reliability and stability in monetary and economic transactions. But Bitcoin and other cryptocurrencies were rarely used for payment, instead mainly serving as a speculative investment asset—basically, gambling. The cryptocurrency crash of 2022, dubbed a "crypto winter," was preceded by red flashing warning signs of indefensible valuations—all of which were entirely ignored by government regulators.[23]

This spectacular failure of overpromising and underregulating came to a climax in the crash of FTX, a cryptocurrencies marketplace. Its founder, Sam Bankman-Fried, the son of two Stanford University professors, was embraced as a wunderkind. Sequoia Capital published a breathless profile about how Bankman-Fried had lured investors in during a meeting while playing *League of Legends*.[24] A Massachusetts Institute of Technology graduate, Bankman-Fried portrayed himself as a visionary and thoughtful whiz kid who was fully committed to the cryptocurrency cause, claiming that he rarely had time to even brush his hair.[25] Bankman-Fried told a compelling story, one that every venture capitalist in Silicon Valley wanted to be true: he had developed a wildly successful cryptocurrency business that would adhere to greater integrity and transparency standards. Venture capital poured in, as funds saw Bankman-Fried as a prized horse to bet on.

By early 2022 FTX, which was barely two years old, was worth over $32 billion, and Bankman-Fried became the face of cryptocurrencies.[26] He soon began making the rounds in Washington, imploring lawmakers on Capitol Hill to regulate the sector. To many of his cryptocurrency peers, this was an act of sacrilege, as new regulation would constrain cryptocurrencies from achieving their fully decentralized vision. He also portrayed himself as a socially conscious magnate: an adherent to effective altruism, he spoke passionately about animal suffering and veganism, and he presented his company's commitment to a diverse workforce and to reducing the CO_2 emissions of cryptomining.[27] Finally, Bankman-Fried became a high-profile donor. By supporting philanthropic endeavors and greasing the political campaigns of both Democrats and Republicans, he acted as many captains of industry had in the past. Dubbed the "JP Morgan of Crypto," he became a political kingmaker via contributions north of $1 million to both progressive representatives like Jasmine Crockett and moderates like Shontel Brown via his super PAC, Protect Our Future.[28] In total, Bankman-Fried and his FTX cofounders (who at the time of this writing have admitted to serving as his straw donors) spent more than $70 million on the 2022 U.S. midterm elections alone.[29]

A mere nine days after the midterms, however, FTX would be insolvent. While journalists and prosecutors are still investigating the complicated tale of what happened at FTX, we know the broad outlines. In addition to FTX, Bankman-Fried also ran Alameda Research, a cryptocurrency trading firm that specialized in large, risky bets on cryptocurrency assets and long-term investments in start-ups. To fund those bets and investments, Alameda borrowed a tremendous amount of money from lenders—namely, its sister company, FTX. As cryptocurrency markets began faltering in 2022, some of those lenders asked for their money back, but Alameda didn't have the cash to return and found itself in a major crunch. At this point, FTX is alleged to have lent as much as $10 billion of customer deposits to Alameda so that it could pay back investors.[30] When Changpeng Zhao, the infamous leader of Binance, FTX's main competitor, publicly suggested that FTX no longer had sufficient deposits to make its customers whole, a huge wave of depositors pulled their money out of the exchange.[31] It was, essentially, a bank run. But FTX no longer had the money to pay out. Billions of dollars that investors had placed in the trust of FTX were suddenly gone.[32]

In just eight days, FTX's valuation dropped by $32 billion, to zero. In the process, Bankman-Fried stole millions of dollars from retail investors. The Commodity Futures Trading Commission, the Securities and Exchange Commission (SEC), and the U.S. Department of Justice quickly announced investigations. Bankman-Fried was arrested in the Bahamas and was soon extradited to sit trial in the United States.[33] He controversially spent much of early 2023 under house arrest at his parents' home on the Stanford campus, less than two miles from my office at the Stanford Cyber Policy Center.[34] James Bromley, a partner at the prominent law firm Sullivan & Cromwell, described the downfall as "one of the most abrupt and difficult collapses in the history of corporate America." He offered these remarks before a U.S. court, representing FTX in bankruptcy proceedings that had "allowed everyone for the first time to see under the covers and recognize the emperor has no clothes."[35] Toward the end of 2023, Bankman-Fried went on trial: his closest former colleagues all testified against him, and he was found guilty on seven counts of fraud and conspiracy after just four and a half hours of deliberations.[36] His defense throughout the trial meandered from refuting any allegations of wrongdoing to claiming that FTX's terms of service permitted him to transfer customer funds essentially at will. Bankman-Fried was found guilty of seven charges by a jury, and the judge sentenced him to twenty-five years behind bars. He announced that he would appeal the sentence.[37] Nevertheless, he already seems to be leveraging his entrepreneurial skills in prison. Reporting from the *Wall Street Journal* states that he has been trading mackerel with other inmates to get services like a haircut.[38]

Lawmakers in the U.S. Congress should ask themselves how the fraudulent management of funds at the scale of that perpetrated by FTX can go unnoticed and unpunished for so long. One reason is that some congressional members actively challenged the SEC when it sought information about cryptocurrencies and blockchain firms.[39] Though Bankman-Fried's political donations certainly played an important role in the aggressively pro-cryptocurrency stance taken by some politicians, others may have been swayed by the same kind of lobbying that I used to hear in the European Parliament: the argument that regulation stifles innovation. Of course, this argument is at odds with the long string of billion-dollar cryptocurrency implosions during the past few years. Though FTX's is the most famous of these collapses, 2022 also saw the demise of BlockFi, Celsius, Terra/Luna, and Voyager Digital, to name just a few.[40] Instead of delivering on their promise of tamper-proof technology and transparent financial transactions, cryptocurrency leaders have instead stolen and misused customer money. Just because technology can theoretically ensure more transparency does not mean that it happens automatically. Instead, good governance needs to be designed into the system by default.

Perhaps the most avid users of cryptocurrencies have been a group that explicitly values their opaque nature: criminals. Some of the world's largest criminal outfits have centralized their operation within the so-called decentralized financial system. The Jalisco and Sinaloa Cartels in Mexico, for example, rely on small purchases of Bitcoin to avoid money-laundering controls.[41] On the dark web, anonymous purchases are paid for via anonymous transactions in Bitcoin. Silk-road, an online black market, thrived on Bitcoin payments for drugs, weapons, and pornography until Europol and the FBI shut it down in 2014.[42] In what was a surprise to no one, the Islamic State of Iraq and Syria (ISIS) got into cryptocurrencies: pro-ISIS groups in Tajiki-stan fundraised millions and funneled the donations through several cryptocurrency exchanges to reach the group.[43] Obviously, the use of cryptocurrencies by many of the world's largest criminal enterprises does not make them, or DeFi, inherently criminal. It should, how-ever, give cryptocurrencies' main developers and evangelists some pause. If the veritable all-star team of global terrorists, criminals, and thugs are embracing your product, it is not a utopian product.

Given the lack of oversight or quality standards, as well as the global nature of cryptocurrency companies, many of the financial products—like currencies and tokens—have also proven prone to being scams. Celebrities like Kim Kardashian have promoted swin-dles with valueless coins, while catfish on dating apps have relied on Bitcoin to quickly bilk money out of potential suitors in what has been appetizingly named, pig butchering scams.[44] Even Rich-ard Branson, the crypto evangelist behind the conference at Necker Island, has fallen victim to a cryptocurrency impersonation scam.[45] The FTC estimates that cryptocurrency scams have cost Americans more than $1 billion since 2021.[46] While scams also exist, of course, in cash and bank accounts, the scale and audacity of the cryptocurrency scams are astonishing. A system promoted as safe and trustworthy has instead become exceedingly dangerous and unreliable.

Finally, rogue states rely on cryptocurrencies acquired through ransomware attacks as a core revenue stream. As was discussed in chapter 3, hackers routinely incapacitate hospitals, local govern-ments, and centers of commerce until the owners pay hefty ransoms.

North Korean cybercriminals may have received up to a billion dollars in cryptocurrency ransoms in 2022, diverting nearly one-third of that bounty toward the nation's ballistic missile program.[47]

Aside from criminal activities and abuses, cryptocurrencies are troubling from the perspective of democratic governance. Should anyone be permitted to mint a "global currency" just because they are technically able to? Normally, banks underwrite the value of money such as the dollar or the euro. When banks collapse, consumer protection laws shield savings up to a certain level. The Federal Deposit Insurance Corporation in the United States, for example, guarantees depositors $250,000 per account in the event of a bank collapse.[48] In the European Union, assets of up to 100,000 euros are protected.[49] No equivalent guarantee existed for consumers who saw their hard-earned savings evaporate in the FTX collapse, and no Bitcoin bureaucrat came to the assistance of Curt Dell when he found himself locked out of his Celsius account. As the BIS noted in a report, "Innovations such as cryptocurrencies, stable coins and the walled garden ecosystems of big techs all tend to work against the public good element that underpins the payment system. Bitcoin in particular has few redeeming public interest attributes."[50]

It does, however, have obvious and tangible downsides. For instance, despite its virtual use, Bitcoin has a serious real-world environmental impact. With a heavy reliance on data centers and servers, Bitcoin mining makes up 0.55 percent of global energy use.[51] In the process of verifying transactions on a blockchain, computers have to solve a complex mathematical problem. In return for solving the problem first, a modest Bitcoin payment is made. The reward incentivizes participation and speed. This "proof-of-work" system is inherently wasteful, as "99.99% of all the machines that did work just throw away the result since they didn't win the race," notes Paul Brody, global blockchain leader at Ernst & Young.[52]

Contrary to what some of the cryptocurrency enthusiasts on Necker Island believed, there is little that stops governments from regulating this new technology. China, the first to crack down on the trade in cryptocurrencies, banned them all together in September 2021.[53] Given the lack of transparency on the part of the CCP, the exact reasons behind the drastic move remain opaque, though, as we have seen, they had plenty of reasons from which to choose. Many countries are following with direct or indirect bans, such as banning cryptocurrency exchanges or placing limitations on the ability of banks to use them. Some policymakers in the EU and the United States are also pushing for new regulations. For instance, the European regulation on Markets in Crypto Assets seeks to ensure more transparency and to protect consumers as it enters into force in December 2024.[54]

One perhaps unexpected response, as well as possibly the least welcome by the Cypherpunks and crypto evangelists, has been the embrace of digital currencies by central banks, so-called Central Bank Digital Currency (CBDC). These centralized coins are pegged to fiat currencies like the euro, the dollar, or the yen, and central banks want to apply the same rules to their digital assets as they would to regular assets. Instead of disrupting central banks, the disruption by cryptocurrency barons may well have inspired them to imagine the issuing of CBDCs. Over one hundred central banks are exploring and piloting CBDCs, and a handful of companies have already launched them.[55] If the projects succeed, the Bitcoin bubble may well have brought about a more forceful engagement by financial institutions with digital assets.

Perhaps even more disappointing for blockchain enthusiasts is that six years after my sojourn to Richard Branson's tropical island, almost none of the supposedly revolutionary potential has materialized. After an investigation into the actual use cases of blockchain (besides Bitcoin) for *De Correspondent Dutch*, journalist Jesse Frederik concluded that his story was a "bizarre journey to nowhere" and that blockchain remains a "solution for almost nothing."[56] Simply put, we're still a long way away from the moon.

Privatized Policing

When Clearview AI first captured national headlines in 2020, Kashmir Hill, a tech reporter for the *New York Times*, decided to do some digging.[57] She quickly found out that the company and its Australian

CEO, Hoan Ton-That, were less than eager to discuss their product, facial recognition software that helps law enforcement identify perpetrators. For over a month, no one from the company would return her calls; the only employee listed on LinkedIn was John Good, a sales manager, which turned out to be Ton-That's own (burner) account. Hill decided to try out the product for herself, asking police departments around the country to run her face through the database. Almost immediately after entering Hill's photo, these departments received inquiries from Clearview, asking whether they were speaking to the media. Even if Clearview wasn't willing to speak to Hill, they made it abundantly clear that they were always watching.

While blockchain and cryptocurrencies are sold as innovative keys for disrupting governmental institutions, companies that develop law enforcement technologies are dependent on government agencies. They need to win the trust of the government to ultimately disrupt its functioning. Clearview AI, which took advantage of a lack of regulations around biometrics and people's faces online to build a massive database, is perhaps the most notable of these companies. Like NSO Group and other companies trading in surveillance technologies, Clearview privatizes sensitive functions that have historically been the prerogative of states.

The way Clearview built its database is shockingly simple. As a first step, the company scraped the internet for images of faces: holiday pictures shared with friends on Facebook, a proud moment at a diploma ceremony uploaded on Instagram, an employee's headshot indicating their role at work. Like a trawler roaming the ocean for fish, this software combs the internet for photos and videos. Social media platforms such as Facebook, LinkedIn, Twitter, and YouTube have proved particularly lucrative for the scrapers. And where a dragnet pulls up a limited number of fish each time, Clearview's software crawled until it had thirty billion images. To their credit, most social media platforms explicitly forbid such scraping in their terms of service; unsurprisingly, that has not prevented the practice. After all, terms of use do not carry the same weight as law. Billions of images have thus been collected by Clearview, which then sells its database and matching software to law enforcement, enabling them to instantly identify a person from a photo. The company brags on its website that its law enforcement database is "the largest in the world by far."[58]

Clearview has already been used around a million times by more than two thousand U.S. law enforcement agencies, including ICE and the Department of Justice.[59] The product was used, for instance, to identify individuals during Black Lives Matter protests.[60] To build trust with these agencies, Clearview initially gave out free trials to police departments all over the United States. As a team of investigative reporters at BuzzFeed noted, "Clearview has taken a flood-the-zone approach to seeking out new clients, providing access not just to organizations, but to individuals within those organizations—sometimes with little or no oversight or awareness from their own management."[61] Most shockingly, reporting from the *New York Post* found that rogue New York Police Department officers had Clearview installed on their personal devices, even after the department's own facial recognition unit passed on Clearview due to a variety of concerns.[62]

It is extremely troubling that Clearview provides such sensitive services to law enforcement with little public oversight. The same goes for other private start-ups, such as ShotSpotter, a company selling surveillance systems that promise to pick up on the sounds of gunshots across cities to alert the police.[63] Other systems, such as Sound Thinking (formerly PredPol, as in predictive policing), use historic data with the promise of predicting future crimes.[64]

With police departments increasingly relying on these and other private companies, many questions arise: How does the public task of law enforcement relate to corporate motives and decisions? How do departments ensure accountability for such technology, both when it fails and when it works as it should? And, finally, can we trust these systems? Research shows, for instance, that facial recognition systems are biased against women and people of color.[65] Joy Buolamwini and Timnit Gebru captured major media attention in 2018 for a study they conducted on facial recognition accuracy, in which they found that commercial facial analysis programs erred in gender identification for darker-skinned women up to 34 percent of the time—compared to just 0.8 percent of the time with lighter-skinned men.[66] Similarly, using historic crime data to infer trends in future crime will inevitably entrench past profiling and police discrimination.

The bias embedded within these systems has real-world impacts. Consider two stories that have disturbingly similar outcomes. In 2021, Michael Williams, a Black man from Chicago, sat in jail for almost a year accused of murdering a man to whom he had offered a ride. The only evidence against him was a noise caught by a nearby ShotSpotter sensor. The judge eventually dismissed the case after prosecutors determined there wasn't enough evidence. "I kept trying to figure out, how can they get away with using the technology like that against me?" Williams told the Associated Press.[67] In November 2022, just after Thanksgiving, Randal Reid, also a Black man, was pulled over in Atlanta for outstanding warrants in Louisiana. There was one slight problem: Reid had never been to Louisiana. The Jefferson Parish Sheriff's Office had wrongly identified Reid using Clearview. Reid, who was eventually exonerated, spent a week in jail and had his car impounded—all due to an incorrect hit on the software. As he told the *New York Times*, he spent "thousands of dollars for something I didn't do."[68] The government forsakes its responsibility to protect citizens from discrimination when it uses predictive policing services that disproportionately target Black and Latino neighborhoods. Indeed, according to the National Association of Criminal Defense Lawyers, police do not even inform suspects when charges are based on crime prediction software.[69]

In addition to concerns about bias, there are also worries that the software puts defendants at a significant informational disadvantage, thus putting pressure on the principle of a fair trial, equal treatment before the law, and the presumption of innocence. Police armed with the Clearview database can confirm the identities of people near a crime scene using Clearview insights with a far higher degree of accuracy than defense lawyers could, making it difficult for defendants to rebut accusations. In September 2022, Clearview issued a welcome course correction, permitting public defenders to use the database.[70] Even still, the vast majority of public defenders and regulators remain skeptical of the software, concerned about how it may harm the presumption of innocence within criminal proceedings.

Tech companies pitch themselves as noble innovators in the criminal justice space, promising law enforcement that their products will help trace suspects more efficiently, predict risk more accurately, and offer fairer trials. Whether or not their products deliver on these promises, these are responsibilities that state authorities have held for centuries. Government agencies are required to perform those functions in an impartial and law-abiding manner, and leaders ultimately answer to the voters: if they don't do their jobs, we can vote them out of office. State authorities are also subject to oversight mechanisms, as well as a system of checks and balances that are intended to avoid the concentration or abuse of power. The same cannot be said for facial recognition, predictive policing, and data analytics firms. Yet companies providing these services become de facto extensions of law enforcement agencies.

A commonsense solution to avoiding bias or flaws in commercial software would be to investigate and audit the systems. But assessing the compliance of software sold commercially is complicated by a lack of transparency.[71] Companies argue that their proprietary products should be considered trade secrets and that allowing anyone to peek under the hood would result in a competitive disadvantage. This lack of transparency spurred a group of mathematicians to sign a protest letter against predictive policing, demanding that "any algorithm with potential high impact faces a public audit" to avoid the abuse of power. The letter urged colleagues to refuse to develop technologies that "justify and perpetuate oppression."[72]

Complaints against Clearview have been filed with privacy watchdogs in Austria, France, Greece, Italy, and the United Kingdom.[73] In France the Commission Nationale de l'Informatique et des Libertés (CNIL), the data protection agency, argued that Clearview had no legitimate interest in collecting people's photos and developing biometric profiles on them without consent and handed the company a $20 million fine in October 2022.[74] The existence of stronger legal safeguards to protect privacy, as is the case in Europe, may not have prevented the use of Clearview, but at least EU data protection rules offer paths for people to seek redress after the fact.

Segmenting the Security State

In 2018 Alex Karp, a cofounder and the CEO of data analytics company Palantir, woke up to the last email that any CEO wants to see in the morning: an employee petition.

A group of over two hundred Palantir employees—mostly data scientists and software engineers—were demanding that the company stop providing tools to ICE, the federal agency tasked with managing immigration to the United States and protecting America's borders. While Palantir had worked for ICE for years, working for ICE under the administration of President Donald Trump, which had been publicly criticized for its family separation and detention tactics, felt morally beyond the pale to the letter's signatories. ICE had started showing up in neighborhoods and offices unannounced and rounding up undocumented immigrants who had been living in the United States for decades. These new tactics were the agency's attempt to fulfill Trump's promise to deport "millions of illegal aliens" using a "deportation force."[75] Palantir's data-slicing products were critical for helping ICE find their targets, and employees were horrified at how the products they had built were being used.

Karp is, by all accounts, a progressive civil libertarian who is skeptical of government overreach. He's not shy about his skepticism of the surveillance regime, saying, "I didn't sign up for the government to know when I smoke a joint or have an affair."[76] Yet, Karp still wasn't persuaded by his employees' point of view. "I do not believe that these questions should be decided in Silicon Valley by a number of engineers at large platform companies," he told Bloomberg News. He soon renewed the contract with ICE for an additional $42 million.[77]

Palantir has become the data infrastructure and analytics company of choice for governments around the world. Instead of selling data to law enforcement, like Clearview, Palantir often gets the data directly from law enforcement and then analyzes it with little transparency. Most of the government and law enforcement agencies that Palantir works with have hundreds—if not, thousands—of different databases with seemingly unlimited amounts of information. Often this information isn't particularly helpful, as it is spread out across many different places. Palantir gathers this unwieldy information in one place and transforms it into actionable insights via secret processes, ultimately assisting those organizations make what the company calls data-driven decisions. For instance, in the company's work for ICE, Palantir's product likely ingested data from dozens of different sources to help identify undocumented immigrants who would not have been found any other way.[78]

Palantir was cofounded in 2003 by a group that included Peter Thiel, of Facebook and PayPal fame (or, more appropriately, infamy). It was built on the collective skills of computer scientists, data crunchers, and intelligence officers with initial funding from In-Q-Tel, the venture capital branch of the U.S. Central Intelligence Agency.[79] Palantir has since penetrated governmental operations in a way few other companies have. It works for the U.S. Food and Drug Administration (FDA) to "modernize the food supply chain," helps the U.S. Army analyze data to gain battlefield advantages, and develops AI for the U.S. Special Forces.[80] In the third quarter of 2022, Palantir reported $1.3 billion in international government contracts, of which almost $1 billion was with the U.S. government.[81]

Protecting national sovereignty and security is perhaps the central objective of a national government. It is a responsibility enshrined in constitutions, a task overseen by parliaments, and the reason young people get sent to the battlefield. Given its importance, most governments devote a large percentage of their national budgets to the military. In fact, the United States spends a remarkable one-sixth of its budget on defense in any given year.[82] This massive funding attracts ambitious private companies who are keen to turn on that spigot of revenue. This behavior is not new, with President Dwight D. Eisenhower complaining about the creation of the "military-industrial complex" in 1961.[83] Historically, however, most government vendors have built physical items—think rockets and tanks—that are easy to oversee and verify. Once a tank is built, federally trained and deployed soldiers drive and shoot from it. Digital technologies built in opaque corporate settings are unique, frankly, because very few in government understand them. Governments do not even run or operate them, instead allowing the companies to take the driver seat for national security operations.

While Karp is a self-proclaimed American patriot, that does not stop Palantir from selling to governments worldwide, although allegedly not to U.S. adversaries.[84] During the COVID-19 pandemic, it received contracts in Japan, the United Kingdom, and the United States while also working for large pharmaceutical firms. Even in the EU, which prides itself on privacy protection and is increasingly skeptical of U.S.-made technologies, Palantir gained Europol, police, and defense contracts, as well as deals with health-care departments. It also became a member of GAIA-X, a digital governance body that is supposed to develop European federated data and cloud infrastructure.[85] Palantir has contracts with Qatar to help the country with the "digital transformation" of industries as far flung as energy and health care. Notably, Palantir has stated that it won't work with the CCP or host services in China because the CCP's values are inconsistent with those of the company.[86]

Governments ought to be accountable to the public, but Palantir is remarkably secretive. The company has been awarded several no-bid contracts, such as by the U.K. National Health Service, where the typical competitive governmental contract process is bypassed for a nonpublic agreement. This lack of competition hurts everyone. By continuing to partner with Palantir, the United Kingdom never fully takes stock of the other enterprises on the market that may be able to provide a better service. Conversely, Palantir has little incentive to out-innovate its competitors when its business is guaranteed. Outside the bounds of the contracting process, it is often unclear how the company goes about developing its solutions.[87] Palantir repeatedly uses the same phrases in its internal marketing, like "data-slicing," that hint at vague analytic capabilities, but there isn't sufficient insight to understand how its software is, say, getting from its input data to a final decision or identification. Palantir wants the public to take it on faith that its process is reliable and its input data are accurate, but we have reason to be skeptical. As we saw with Clearview, data can be biased, both maliciously and accidentally, and advanced data-slicing or analytical software does not magically solve these data errors before making inferences.

This matters because Palantir's data are used in some of America's most consequential national security operations. CEO Alex Karp has, for instance, said that some of Palantir's products are sometimes used to kill people.[88] Mark Bowden, in his book about the capture of Osama bin Laden, *The Finish*, writes that Palantir's software "actually deserves the popular designation Killer App."[89] We shouldn't have to just cross our fingers and hope that it works, but given Palantir's secrecy, that's the best we can do. Frankly, the Palantir business proposition is disturbing: the company profits handsomely—sometimes tens of millions of dollars per contract—on processes that cannot be scrutinized or interrogated by citizens. Why, exactly, should democracies put up with that?

One question is whether the insights gained from data analytics benefit the single customer involved or are used by Palantir to gain insights it sells elsewhere. Caitlin Bishop of Privacy International worries that "the improvement clauses in Palantir's contracts, together with the lack of transparency, are concerning because it enables Palantir to improve its products based on its customers' use of Palantir products."[90] Alex Karp, on the other hand, claims there are internal processes that make it "hard for government to abuse its authorities" when using Palantir products.[91] That's the heart of the problem: the public has no way to independently verify whether Karp's claim is true.

Palantir has successfully stepped into the space created by the notion that governments cannot innovate quickly enough to manage their own operations. Instead, technology companies declare themselves as nimble, clever, private alternatives who can do the same job—but far better. They offer the promise of smart solutions that use big data to solve complex problems. Ironically, with every contract that the government outsources to these companies, there is less technical knowledge developed and grown inside government departments. Governments have no incentive to innovate when they know that Palantir is ready to swoop in with its robust databases and slick visualizations. This ever-growing hole makes it increasingly likely that the next major question about public health or national security will be outsourced to a company that claims it can solve it even better than the government. Soon there may be no institutional memory left in government departments at all to help them handle these problems. If this comes to pass, all citizens will be worse off.

What Is Lost

The privatized governance of disruptive digital infrastructure, products, and services erodes our rights and freedoms as citizens. Monetary policy is hobbled by Bitcoin. The presumption of innocence erodes when products like Clearview AI identifies people as suspects. And oversight over government tasks is blurred when Palantir analyzes data. For all complex, proprietary, digitized systems there is a new challenge: a lack of access to information or the inability to understand the inner workings of a system necessarily results in a lack of empowerment. People are disenfranchised when they do not know the rules they are governed by, and it makes changing those rules even harder.

But what makes the threats to the public interest so much greater coming from technology companies, as compared to other corporate actors that have taken over government functions in the past? Surely the outsourcing of governmental functions to consulting firms like Booz Allen Hamilton or McKinsey & Company, or our common dependence on the energy companies with their significant harms to the environment, has also obscured oversight or outsourced the cost of private profits to all of society. Yet, while the privatization of key functions is nothing new, tech- and data-driven companies are unique in many ways.

First, digital infrastructure like Clearview often goes unnoticed by the public until it is quite entrenched. By the time the societal impacts are visible, it is often too late to change course. If an oil company wants to start drilling, it needs permission from landowners and permits from governments. It owes taxes based on its geographic location and is both protected and liable under the law of the land. But many tech companies can roll out their services under the radar before any public alarms are raised, let alone before seeking legal clarity on the product. Clearview AI had already scraped the internet for billions of faces and sold their services to law enforcement before journalists reported on it and caused an uproar.

Even once lawmakers begin having conversations about regulation, powerful technology companies have many options. Software scales so quickly that by the time a discussion begins, the companies have deep pockets to hire lobbyists. Or they can simply abandon operations in less favorable jurisdictions and set up shop elsewhere. According to Andrea Enria, who chairs the European Central Bank's supervisory board, a leading cryptocurrency asset provider said that if EU rules were not changed, the company would "provide European customers with the same type of dollar-denominated assets via internet through our shop in other jurisdictions." Enria added, "It will be very hard to police these types of requirements."[92] For companies with physical assets, similar flexibility would be unthinkable.

Second, companies using data regularly end up building services on top of one another. The communal building, block by block, is the cornerstone of the "open source" approach, but it also applies to proprietary technology stacks built by private technology companies. So when Facebook, LinkedIn, or YouTube are careless with privacy protections, that carelessness has a long downstream impact. It means that Clearview can scrape billions of faces or data brokers can slice and regroup the scraped data and sell it onward to advertisers or more malicious actors—like intelligence firms or even stalkers. Flaws thus get buried ever more deeply into another product, while any biases in one of the many datasets merged and repurposed blend in and affect future uses of the data in a way that is difficult to untangle.

Finally, technology is now layered onto almost every aspect of our societies and economies. Industrial data analysis spots supply chain issues or maintenance needs. Chips in refrigerators manage energy use depending on what is being cooled inside. AI leads drones to their targets, and robots support surgeons to perform surgery at the other end of the world. Satellite images identify needs for farmers or soldiers, and students are monitored with cameras for compliance when they take an online exam. Increasingly, technology is the most important feature in any product or service we use—in other words, it's often *why* we buy what we buy. And given the fact that companies develop and deploy these technologies, they are crucial entry points for products and entire industries alike.

With biotechnology, quantum computing, the ever-expanding Internet of Things, and other technologies on the horizon, technology will no longer be a separate entity from humanity; we'll be inextricably tied to it. Security breaches in that world will be even more devastating, potentially fatal. That makes it all the more urgent to ensure that regulatory guardrails are in place. Inflection CEO Mustafa Suleyman even believes we need to go as far as containment, which "needs to be a much more fundamental programme, a balance of power not between competing actors but between humans and our tools. It's a necessary prerequisite for the survival of our species over the next century. Containment encompasses regulation, better technical safety, new governance and ownership models, new modes of accountability and transparency, all as necessary (but not sufficient) precursors to safer technology. It's an overarching lock uniting cutting-edge engineering, ethical values, and government regulation."[93]

The Universal Declaration of Human Rights of the United Nations (UN) enshrines the principle that "the will of the people shall be the basis of the authority of government."[94] The U.S. Declaration of Independence similarly holds that "to secure these rights, Governments are instituted among Men, deriving their just powers from the consent of the governed."[95] Both of these statements affirm that legitimacy presumes consent—that the consent of the governed is at the heart of the notion of a social contract between citizens and their governments, which sees citizens give up some of their freedoms in favor of shared rules of the commons. The notion of legitimacy comes under pressure when unelected corporations hold ever more power over the digital layers of our lives, as they are able to access our information and operate without any public accountability. The privatized governance by technology companies is nondemocratic in that it is not itself democratic, and antidemocratic in that it undermines the legitimacy of our democratic governments. All of this is enabled by governments' hesitance to put in place appropriate guardrails around tech firms.

It shouldn't be left to private companies and courts to determine the legitimacy of products and services that have the potential to compete with state intelligence services. Democratic countries must extend norms and rules to ensure safety in the digital world. Just as nations agreed to international laws governing the conduct of war and the use of nuclear weapons, so too must they establish agreements to fend off threats in cyberspace. Democratic governments especially need to take steps to rebalance the power between states and private companies, as the latter play too large a role in the digital world. The global strength of democracy has taken hit after hit in the years that technology companies have expanded their reach. As we will see in chapter 5, geopolitical balances of power are yet another area in which the role of technology companies has grown at the expense of democracy.

5

Tech on the Front Lines

Alexei Navalny had barely survived not one, but two attempts of poisoning with the deadly nerve agent Novichok when Russia's most famous anticorruption activist and opposition figure was detained by authorities in January 2021. Navalny continued to be unjustly imprisoned in a remote penal colony under terrible conditions until February 16, 2024, when he was pronounced dead. His opposition movement, the Anti-Corruption Foundation, provoked the Kremlin's wrath when it shared a documentary video titled *Putin's Palace* on YouTube. The video reveals details of a massive complex—measuring 17,691 square meters, and which cost around a billion dollars to build—and alleges that Putin has engaged in corruption on an unprecedented scale through a web of close business associates. In the first twenty-four hours after it was posted, twenty-two million people watched the documentary.[1] As of the present it has had over 130 million views.[2]

Given the pervasive censorship of media and journalists in Russia, social media platforms like YouTube are often an important outlet through which silenced voices can reach their audiences. But as Navalny would soon experience firsthand, this also means that U.S. tech companies have outsize power to stifle the efforts of dissidents. Days before elections took place in 2020, Apple and Google dealt a significant blow to Russian voters by removing the app that Navalny's associates developed to help identify the strongest candidate opposing Vladimir Putin in each of the 225 voter districts. Suddenly, during the critical time leading up to the election, voters could no longer download the app.

Like many autocratic regimes, Russian authorities pointed to national security as a justification for their censorship. According to the official party line, Navalny's movement was an "extremist" and "terrorist" organization.[3] U.S. tech companies could have rejected the absurdity of Russia's claims, but the authorities raised the stakes. They threatened to hold Apple's and Google's employees in Russia personally accountable for the decisions made in the company's American headquarters. The threat was effective: the companies cited the danger to employees as their main motivation for removing the app from their platforms.

Navalny's aide Ivan Zhdanov reacted by calling the removal a "shameful act of political censorship."[4] Navalny himself slammed Apple and Google's "cowardice" and accused them of being Putin accomplices.[5] Remarkably, not a single democratic government spoke out—neither against the threats from the Russian government toward the U.S. companies nor against the companies for caving to the threat. The silence was deafening: democracies had prioritized 100 employees on the ground over the rights of over 100 million Russian voters. The Kremlin's successful intimidation of the tech companies was no accident: authoritarian regimes often mandate some staff presence within their borders precisely so that they can leverage employees as hostages to advance their political agenda. Tech companies, faced with the high costs of noncooperation, frequently give in to these threats, thereby incentivizing such behavior in the future.

The debacle surrounding Alexei Navalny's app offers a striking lesson. Tech companies often find themselves on the front lines of the battle for democracy, be it their increased involvement in elections or their presence in the world's most consequential conflicts. The platforms, apps, and websites that multinational tech giants operate have become instruments in the fierce global competition between democracy and authoritarianism. And this provides the corporate leaders who hold power over those technologies incredible power over geopolitics. Whether they like it or not, decisions taken in corporate boardrooms and engineering team huddles in Silicon Valley and at other tech hubs have significant implications for elections, individual rights, and even military strategy across the world.

One reason that private companies have been afforded such power is because many policymakers accepted an overly sunny narrative about the positive impact of technology on democracy. Foreign policy experts were late to appreciate the actual impact of technology on democracy. They largely ignored the role of digital technologies in shaping geopolitics, instead leaving the development of such technologies to be determined entirely by the market. U.S. administrations spoke of internet freedom but did little to ensure it in practice. Meanwhile, repressive, illiberal, and authoritarian governments treated technology and technology companies as clever new instruments to entrench their power.

From where we stand today, the predictions of technology as a liberating force sound extremely naive. History isn't over, and technology has done little to liberate many marginalized communities. Moreover, our failure to thoughtfully integrate new technologies into the democratic paradigm has backfired in several ways. Beijing, Moscow, and Tehran were given a free pass to use innovative tools, often made in the West, for surveillance and repression. And while democracies waxed poetic about technology governance, the authoritarians have made tangible governance moves. From 2015 to 2022, a Chinese bureaucrat led the International Telecommunications Union, the most powerful global technology standards organization, and in March 2023, a Chinese representative secured a vice chair role on ICANN's Governmental Advisory Committee.[6] With these high-level positions, China, Russia, and their peers have been able to advance a restricted, centralized vision of the internet.[7] All the while, the power of technology companies in elections and geopolitical battles has continued to grow, bolstered by market forces and an almost total absence of democratic regulation.

In this chapter, I deep dive into two cases where private technology firms found themselves on the front lines of battles for power: the fragile peace around elections in Kenya and the hostile attempt by Russia to take over Ukraine. Though each case occurs in a specific geopolitical context, both offer broader takeaways about the parasitic relationship between technology companies and democratic governance in our world today—one in which private tech firms increasingly act as digital gatekeepers and sovereign authorities while government authorities abdicate their own responsibilities.

Tech, Trust, and Elections in Kenya

In the spring of 2017, I was appointed by the EU's foreign policy chief, Federica Mogherini, to lead the EU's Election Observation Mission in Kenya. I spent a total of six weeks in Kenya, before, during, and after the elections, leading a team of hundreds of observers, most of whom were volunteers. When I accepted the position, I would never have predicted the extent to which technology would impact the process that was about to unfold.

The stakes of the 2017 Kenyan elections were high, a fact underlined by the presence of the global heavyweights who joined as election observers. The African Union sent Thabo Mbeki, the former president of South Africa, as its chief observer. The Carter Center, a human rights organization founded by former U.S. president Jimmy Carter, sent former secretary of state John Kerry to lead its mission. These officials were accompanied by a host of international media teams, who set up camp in Nairobi to cover the elections. Clearly, the world was watching Kenya.

International observers were keenly focused on Kenya not only because of its significant role in East Africa, but also because of its complicated and deeply troubled political history. Between 1963, when Kenya gained its independence from the United Kingdom, and the 1990s, the country was ruled by a single party, the Kenya African National Union. That changed in the 1990s, in part because countries around the world tied financial aid to Kenya to political reforms. However, the country's transition into a multiparty democracy has not gone smoothly. Political parties and coalitions continue to be formed along ethnic lines rather than based on distinct political visions, and elections have generally been treated as "winner-take-all" affairs, meaning that constituencies who find themselves on the wrong side of a vote are at risk of real financial hardship.

A decade before my arrival, the election of 2007 brought these tensions to a dangerous boiling point when multiple political factions disputed the results. The EU called for an inquiry into allegations of wrongdoing, and U.K. foreign secretary David Miliband expressed "real concerns" about its validity.[8] The U.S. ambassador spoke of rigging on both sides.[9] Demonstrations by the opposition, which alleged fraud, and consequent police crackdowns resulted in mass violence along ethnic and political lines. More than 1,000 Kenyans were killed and over 250,000 were displaced.[10] Devastating sexual violence ran rampant. It ultimately took months to calm the violence, but much damage had been done. Both future presidential candidate Uhuru Kenyatta and his running mate, William Ruto (the current president), were suspected of committing war crimes in the aftermath of the 2007 election. The International Criminal Court initially took up an alleged crimes against humanity case against them, but the chief prosecutor dropped it when key witnesses started to recant their testimony after being subjected to intimidation.[11]

The 2013 election, which took place under a new constitution, fared better but was by no stretch of the imagination a flawless operation. The vote-counting process faced technical challenges, and Kenyatta and Ruto, the party leaders who had been accused of war crimes just six years earlier, emerged victorious as part of a newly formed coalition. Four years later, they stood for reelection. Between these two elections, another complicating factor intensified: the threat of terror attacks from the Islamist militant group al-Shabaab, which was known for aggressive, gruesome attacks, timed and executed to spur maximum devastation. In 2015, in its deadliest attack to date, al-Shabaab attacked a university, killing more than 140 people and holding several hostages.[12] The civil unrest in 2007 and the ongoing threat of terror attacks formed the bloody backdrop against which the 2017 elections took place. They also help explain the significant presence of international observers; the international community was desperate to prevent another humanitarian crisis.

The job of an election observer is often misunderstood. You are sent to a location where you have little firsthand experience to serve as an independent set of eyes and ears. The mandate comes with strict boundaries: observers assess whether people's rights have been respected in practice. Observers are often asked, for instance, whether elections were free and fair. But if the law in a country does not protect the use of personal data, as was the case in Kenya, then the handling and use of such data falls outside the scope of the mandate. As a result, we must caveat our assessments of freedom and fairness with the context on the ground: an election can only be so free in an already restrictive or corrupt environment. Furthermore, reporting and assessing the full electoral process often leads to nuanced, lengthy, and at times technical reports. Those details tend to get crowded out by headlines around election day, as well as by any significant disruptions that threaten the legitimacy of the election. Violent incidents tend to grab the attention over the bureaucratic subtleties that often actually determine an election's fairness.

With the teams deployed across the country, we worked long hours to do justice to our task of assessing the extent to which the rights of Kenyans were respected during the entire electoral process. Were people paid to attend a candidate's rally? Did the police intimidate voters? Was the registration process accessible to all? Did every vote count? To answer these questions, we canvassed an incredibly wide cross-section of Kenyans who could help us understand various perspectives: the electoral commission, political candidates, the president of the Supreme Court of Kenya, labor union representatives, religious leaders, youth activists, police chiefs, bloggers, and journalists. And many, many citizens. Throughout, I kept thinking in particular about the five million young Kenyans who were eligible to vote for the first time. Would they feel safe and excited to turn out, or would they be apathetic, worn down by the ongoing corruption and resentful of the old boys' network of political figures? Or worse, would the possibility of violence make them afraid to vote?

During a rare quiet moment in early August of that year, I sat in my makeshift office in the Nairobi hotel that also served as our observation mission's headquarters (to have only one location in which the mission's leadership lived and worked made it easier to secure). Al-Shabaab had put out a video threatening the elections, and international election monitors were certainly high on their list of targets.[13] When I went outside for trips across Nairobi and into the various regions of Kenya, I traveled in an armored vehicle and with close protection. I hated that those measures were needed. But thankfully, I was still able to talk to the thousands of Kenyans I met on the dirt roads of small villages or in high-end coffee houses.

In my impromptu office, I walked through what might happen in the days to come. Kenya's history of violence around elections weighed on me. I reflected on my principal responsibility to the people of Kenya but also to the various EU teams deployed throughout the country. Still, we hoped that the painstaking efforts of so many Kenyans to ensure a peaceful transfer of power had made the relationships between competing ethnicities and factions resilient enough to withstand the electoral process and results, no matter who won. Kofi Annan, the former secretary-general of the UN, had worked on a mediation plan between the political opponents of 2007, and throughout the next decade, faith-based groups, diplomats, civil society, and even the media had worked to establish a peaceful coexistence among competing factions.[14] These efforts were so forceful that Kenyans I spoke to told me they were worried that the intense focus on a peaceful process would gloss over injustices so long as there was no violence. I proceeded to draft statements with responses to various levels of escalation, hoping that I would not need to issue any of them. Meanwhile, I could only imagine how Kenyans were feeling as the country held its breath with a mix of hope and fear.

During several visits to Kenya in the months before the 2017 elections, I spoke to a variety of Kenyans who saw digital technology as a savior. Low trust in institutions and a history of election rigging had led to a push for more use of technology, which, they hoped, would make it harder to illegally stuff ballot boxes. This vision of fair, tamper-free elections spurred the country to invest heavily in digitizing its election infrastructure as it prepared for the 2017 elections. The United Nations Development Programme and the World Bank also supported the use of biometric technologies.[15] New contracts with Western companies that provided identification and voting technologies made the Kenyan election of 2017 the most high-tech in Africa and among the most expensive of any country in the world: Kenya spent no less than half a billion dollars, approximately twenty-five dollars per eligible voter.[16] To compare, my home country, the Netherlands—a nation whose GDP per capita is more than twenty-five times larger than Kenya's—spent around four dollars per eligible voter to administer elections.[17]

Safran, a French company, won a last-minute contract to supply an advanced digital registration and voting system for the elections.[18] Anne Bouverot, Safran's CEO, assured that it would provide the country's Independent Electoral and Boundaries Commission (IEBC) "a complete and secure solution in record time in order to contribute to the successful organization and delivery of these elections."[19] The choice of Safran, however, was a troubling one: the company, formerly known as Morpho, had been fined in a French court for bribery in Nigeria in the early 2000s.[20]

After months of development, Safran presented the Kenya Integrated Elections Management System, which verified the voter lists before the election and authenticated voters with their fingerprints. The system came with forty-five thousand tablets, which supported the biometric identification process by election clerks as well as the vote counting.[21] The company also promised the Kenyan government that its devices would ensure the fast, reliable, and secure transmission of voter turnout data and election results from polling centers to the national tallying center.

The trouble in Kenya started before voting had even begun. A week before the election, the country reeled as Chris Msando, the ICT lead at the IEBC, was found tortured and strangled.[22] The murder cast a dark cloud over the country: if someone this high up could be brutally murdered, no one was safe. I had a knot in my stomach as I saw how those involved with organizing the election now faced even greater pressure in the run-up to election day. While diplomats expressed their deep concern and the U.S. offered the FBI's help with the investigation, Msando's family was facing an additional horror: disinformation about the murder was rampant and sophisticated. Doctored statements using the logos of Kenyan and international news organizations, such as the BBC and CNN, spread like wildfire.[23] Msando's family pleaded with social media users: "A lot of the information out there is false and meant to injure and paint the family in a bad light."[24] Msando's murder also stoked speculation about the power struggle unfolding beneath the surface regarding the digital aspects of the election.

Unfortunately, there were no rules around the data that were being collected by the elections systems. From biometric voter registration to online political campaigning and the tallying of voting results, the personal data that Kenyans shared was not protected by any law. To make matters worse, the digital systems procured had not been properly tested for security. Kenyans were expected to surrender their biometric information without any meaningful legal protection or cybersecurity. As the Carter Center noted in its final report, "The information technology systems deployed . . . are complex, and their inner workings are very difficult to observe, even for computer security experts. Additional challenges to transparency and credibility were posed by the potential for technology software defects, the lack of nation-wide network connectivity, and vulnerabilities to possible cyberattacks."[25] In outsourcing the work of public institutions to private companies without ensuring adequate safety, transparency, or accountability, Kenya had placed its election at significant risk.

The lack of data protection safeguards is problematic on multiple levels. In a country as polarized as Kenya, there were real concerns about the potential abuse of biometric data. There were also worries that bad actors could weaponize what are supposed to be secret ballots. Additionally, without rules around data use, voters would not even know to which authority they should appeal if they suspected the system had been used inappropriately. And even if there were an authority to go to, there was likely nothing to be done because no laws had been broken. Systems as critical as elections need extensive rules, and that includes rules that govern private data.

Election day, August 8, 2017, was marked by long lines of incredibly patient Kenyans keen to cast their votes. Almost twenty million people registered to vote, with five million of them voting for the first time. At 6:00 a.m., squares in front of schools that served as polling stations were packed. I shook the hands of hundreds of voters lined up, old and young Kenyans, wealthy and poor. I had observed elections in Kosovo, Kyrgyzstan, Lebanon, and Nigeria before. Elections are always remarkable experiences, but the Kenyan voters—particularly the scores of young people, acutely aware of their democratic rights and duties—especially resonated with me. One woman carrying a child on her back told me she had walked for two days to vote despite her husband's wishes against it. Classrooms and children's school tables were occupied by election volunteers. The atmosphere felt like that of a church: solemn and dignified, and despite the large number of people present, there was only a quiet hum throughout the school. Kenyans were, however, conscious of the exploitative tactics that politicians used to gain last-minute support. Some shared an old adage with me, "We eat at election time," a reference to candidates' sudden distribution of food and cash handouts as they tried to hustle voters.

Kenya's digital election day playbook was simple: voters would check in via tablets, and proctors from over forty thousand polling stations would deliver results via SMS text message.[26] This plan quickly fell apart. Tablets could not be charged at polling stations, as some stations did not have electricity. The cell phone networks became overloaded and were unable to transmit the many voting results via SMS messages. These challenges should not have been a surprise given the state of Kenya's digital infrastructure. Only 56 percent of households had access to electricity in 2017.[27] The mobile networks, which covered about 75 percent of the country, could not transmit quality 3G and 4G signals.[28] Because of these technical challenges, staff at polling stations across the country pivoted back to pen and paper, which extended the tallying of votes deep into the night. In the following days, result updates stagnated.

Nevertheless, Kenyans remained glued to the television, intently watching the national count live. Despite election officials' initial calls for patience, the results were hastily called three days after election day on the night of August 11, 2017: Uhuru Kenyatta had won a second term with a slim majority of the votes.

Immediately there were accusations of wrongdoing, and flashes of violence broke out. All international observers urged the opposition to go to court to avoid leaving matters to the court of public opinion by calling millions of supporters to the street. The government threatened to confront such protests with a violent police crackdown, a repeat of 2007 that would have inevitably led to bloodshed. Hours before the deadline, the opposition indeed filed objections with the Supreme Court of Kenya, though their expectations of getting a fair hearing were low.[29] Challenges to the 2007 and 2013 elections had been dismissed. Kenya's Supreme Court had only recently been established under the 2010 constitution, which gave it a strong and independent role, in theory, but that independence had not yet been practically tested.

One of the complaints alleged that the computer servers of the IEBC had been manipulated. Not long before, the opposition leadership had also approached all international observer teams with these same stark claims. Karen Bass (a former congresswoman and the current mayor of Los Angeles), John Kerry, John Mahama (the former Ghanaian president), Thabo Mbeki, and I gathered for an impromptu meeting. The room was tense as the opposition came to present piles of printed logs, which they argued showed that election results had been *computer generated* rather than *keyed in* (as they were supposed to have been). When we received the printouts that purportedly proved the wrongdoing, I promptly reached out to a trusted security researcher to help me assess the veracity of those allegations. They quickly told me that those logs alone could not prove wrongdoing. Obtaining evidence about the proper functioning of the election systems, against which abnormalities would have to be compared, was incredibly difficult.

Ultimately, and after having been subject to violent intimidation, the bench of Kenyan Supreme Court justices ordered a review of the official computer servers to verify that no wrongdoing had taken place. But Safran, the company that had provided the digital systems for the electoral process, initially could not be reached and did not provide access to the servers by the court's deadline, putting the IEBC in a very difficult position.[30] The servers were housed in France, and the data were not accessible for review. In response, Justice Philomena Mwilu issued a stunning judgment: the refusal to provide access and information about the IT system left the court "no choice but to accept the petitioner's claims that the IEBC's IT system was infiltrated and compromised, and the data therein interfered with, or IEBC's officials themselves interfered with the data."[31] The Supreme Court had not been able to establish the integrity of the electoral process, so the justices decided to annul the outcome of the presidential election. In their minds, the polls were "neither transparent nor verifiable."[32]

It is hard to overstate the significance of these events. The Supreme Court of Kenya could not get access to key parts of the election data to verify the process's integrity. As a result, a presidential election—where millions of people took great pains to vote, thousands of election officials took on serious personal risk to manage voting, and critical decisions about the future of the country would be decided—was rendered moot. Effectively, the Kenyan people were at the mercy of Safran, a small, private technology company from another country. It is almost unfathomable.

Ultimately, the 2017 presidential election was rerun in October. The opposition refused to participate, even though it had won the challenge before the Supreme Court, as it continued to express concern about the election commission's bias. As the leader of the opposition, Raila Odinga, lamented, "We cannot do a mistake twice and expect to get different results."[33] Unsurprisingly, the result was a blowout: the incumbent won, this time with more than 98 percent of the vote. But just 39 percent of registered voters participated in the rerun, compared with 80 percent in the original vote.[34]

The Kenyan election of 2017 offers important lessons about the role of technology companies worldwide. There is a fundamental mismatch between the mechanisms that are needed for the sake of democratic accountability and the degree of transparency that companies are willing to provide. By outsourcing these key democratic tasks to an unreliable private company without proper oversight, the Kenyan elections board took a significant hit to its credibility. It made no difference that the technology supplier was a French company, grown out of and protected by a democratic state. The rerun of the presidential election cost Kenya another fortune, tens of millions of dollars, which went to Safran once more, quite literally the definition of failing upward. According to officials, engaging a new company through a tender process would have taken too much time, yet Safran asked for more time to update their systems for the rerun of the election. The technology failures had real short-term and long-term consequences. Kenyans failed to show up to the polls en masse for the rerun, citing the opposition's withdrawal from the race. The election debacles harmed the legitimacy of the government in the eyes of millions of its citizens for years to come.[35] In the future, adopting stronger conditions as part of the public procurement process should prevent a similarly painful standoff. Given its track record of lawsuits, Safran was barely equipped to administer a student council election, let alone a presidential contest. No thorough procurement process should have allowed them to win the contract.

Another lesson here is that technology does not necessarily enhance accountability. With the proper procedures in place, paper voting remains the least expensive and most secure option. The Netherlands, an advanced, relatively high-tech economy, still has its citizens vote with red pencil on paper. The 2020 U.S. election was the most secure in U.S. history, in large part because it had the most mail-in ballots ever, which automatically create a paper trail.[36]

Nevertheless, fragile democracies that face continued allegations of electoral fraud or meddling continue to embrace technology as the solution to their democratic trust gap. Nigeria, for instance, rolled out the digital Bimodal Voter Accreditation System ahead of its 2023 presidential election to reduce claims of electoral fraud. Yet, technical glitches in the software delayed results and raised questions about the election's credibility. The fallout following these technological failures evoked a strong sense of déjà vu to Kenya's 2017 election. The national chairman of Nigeria's Labour Party, Julius Abure, called the election "irretrievably compromised" and said that his party had "totally lost faith in the entire process."[37] As the Kenyan political analyst Nanjala Nyabola has observed, "Technology is a fetish."[38] People often believe that technology will magically resolve electoral corruption and bolster their citizens' trust in the electoral process, but no tablet or smart voting machine can single handedly rehabilitate a democracy.

Digitization makes the jobs of election observers nearly impossible. Independent eyes and ears work far better in person than online, which was a frustrating conclusion after our mission worked hard to assess whether the rights of Kenyans had been respected during the 2017 election. Back in Brussels I raised the need to reform and reset election observation missions with the European External Action Service, but I did not find much support. The election observation industry seems too entrenched in its predigital methods. But even if all observer missions would bring along white hat hackers and cybersecurity experts, access to the relevant information would still be controlled by private companies, who would be reluctant to make the information available. The EU spends an average of 45 million euros a year on election observations as part of its democracy policies.[39] Those observations will be ever less relevant when critical elements of the election processes take place in proprietary black boxes.

Since 2017 there have been improvements in Kenya's political process, but much of the polarization and mistrust persists. Kenya ranks 123rd out of 180 countries in the Corruption Index, and Freedom House cites police brutality and the intimidation of journalists and civil society in its justification for labeling the country only "partially free."[40] After the 2017 election, the Kenyan National Assembly recommended barring Safran from doing business in Kenya for ten years.[41] To the surprise of many outside observers, the High Court of Kenya overturned that decision.[42] The country has freshly adopted data protection legislation, which includes demands that IT servers are placed in Kenya, thus giving the government more control. The 2022 election was operated by Smartmatic, a multimillion-dollar U.K.-based business that notably became a target for Republicans disputing the result of the 2020 U.S. presidential election. The Kenyan election of 2022 most certainly ran smoother than those of 2007 and 2017, but a headline from Enact Africa, a nongovernmental organization combatting transnational crime, puts it best: "Muted Violence in Kenya's 2022 Elections Masked Seething Dissent."[43] No election technology, be it from Safran, Smartmatic, or anyone else, could resolve the deep mistrust and tensions at the core of Kenyan politics.

Technology on the Front Lines

In the months after Russia invaded Ukraine and destroyed much of the country's telecom infrastructure, Elon Musk offered twenty thousand Starlink satellite internet terminals to facilitate internet connections for Ukrainians.[44] These SpaceX terminals did not just enable communications between citizens or allow people to reach news websites; they were also critical for military operations, such as navigating drones and launching artillery.[45] Ronan Farrow has called Elon Musk "a private citizen with a private company who had become the arbiter of the outcome of this war."[46] There are few people in the world not in government of whom the same can be said.

After his rescue mission, Musk was hailed as a savior by Ukrainian politicians and received appreciation from around the world. But that changed when he started hinting that the services his company was providing were too costly. Eventually, the company threatened to discontinue access to the satellites unless the U.S. government picked up a large portion of the cost, which the government had little choice but to do, as the Ukrainian war effort had become dependent on the service.[47] Shutting it off could incapacitate military operations—and result in real casualties. In effect, what had seemed like a goodwill gesture from Musk was instead attempting to turn the U.S. government—and all of Ukraine—into a major Starlink customer.

SpaceX is not the only company that has purposely—or even inadvertently—become involved in the fighting in Ukraine. The battlefields are full of companies. Defense tech has emerged as one of Silicon Valley's newest darlings, as start-ups like Anduril (an autonomous systems company) and Shield AI (an AI drone company) take in hundreds of millions or even billions of dollars in funding rounds.[48] Commercial satellite imaging companies like Maxar, which provides high-resolution photographs with time stamps, have helped open-source investigators and journalists identify mass graves and Russian troop movements.[49] Google, by contrast, has tried to limit the visibility of troop movements by disabling real-time traffic reports. The company does not, for instance, want to give away the location where a convoy may be clogging a road. Facial recognition tools, including those provided by Clearview, have been used to identify dead soldiers. And even before Russian soldiers entered Ukraine, Microsoft was working to take down malware attacking Ukrainian government organizations.[50] Technology companies are now, undoubtedly, on the front lines of the battle between democracy and authoritarianism. In Ukraine we have seen many of them explicitly taking sides. That is often not the case.

The involvement of companies like Clearview, Google, Maxar, Microsoft, and SpaceX in active military conflicts raises tough questions about the concept that underpins the foundations of international relations and international law: state sovereignty. The principle of state sovereignty assumes that a government is responsible for the activities within its borders and is mandated to uphold international standards and agreements. Most famously, after World War II, states signed the UN Charter, which held them to a host of commitments regarding human rights and the use of military force. Additional treaties and conventions bind signatory governments to uphold everything from the laws of armed conflict to trade agreements to the laws of the seas. Typically these treaties also include mechanisms of accountability in case signatories don't comply.

But companies are not signatories to these agreements or treaties. Clearview, Google, Maxar, Microsoft, and SpaceX have few, if any, legal mandates according to international law. They are private, not public, actors. The rules that surround companies cover reporting revenue, accounting costs, and filing taxes—not when or how they should act in military confrontations. Yet companies, and especially the technology companies that have our focus here, exude sovereign power in new ways. They have monopolies on key insights and data analytics and make decisions about affairs that were once the exclusive domain of states, while these companies are not subject to comparable checks and balances. Moreover, companies that operate at a global scale often chafe against geographic borders. Even when national governments want to exert control over such companies, which happens far less frequently than it should, they face a variety of constraints.

As far as we know, tech companies have abided by international conventions in the case of Ukraine, but there is no reason to expect that they will be on the right side of history or human rights law in the next conflict. Elon Musk has recognized that in the current geopolitical climate, standing by Ukraine is good for business; Russia is a relatively limited tech market, and catering too much to the Kremlin might carry commercial consequences for these companies in the United States. But the market calculus changes with respect to China and some Middle Eastern nations. In conflicts involving those countries, companies may prioritize their business interests over the greater good. They may be reluctant to hand over aerial imagery of war crimes, assist in blocking troop movements, or even provide internet service for fear that such assistance would hurt their quarterly revenue. Suddenly the shareholders have a say in international relations, and democracies have unwittingly ceded foreign policy decisions to companies who care first and foremost about their business interests.

The challenge posed to state sovereignty by the shifting technology landscape is perhaps clearest at the moment war begins. When a tank breaches a nation's border, the situation is clear: the aggressor has violated article 2.1 of the UN Charter, which commits member states to refrain from "threats and the use of force against the territorial integrity or political independence of any state."[51] When soldiers manning the tank proceed to shoot at people in a school, hospital, or any other civilian target such as energy infrastructure, they violate the Geneva Conventions, which establish legal standards for humanitarian treatment in war. Even then, achieving accountability and meeting the thresholds for the burden of proof are difficult enough, but at least there are concrete legal guardrails.

For cyberattacks, the rules are far less obvious. Ukraine offers a great case study because even before tanks invaded Ukraine in 2022, a barrage of digital attacks befell the country. Starting shortly after the illegal annexation of Crimea in 2014, a series of cyberattacks targeted Ukraine's civilian infrastructure. There was the attack on the power grid in the middle of winter in 2015, and on Kyiv's electricity transmission operator. In early 2022 DDoS attacks shut down websites of banks, and wiper malware was aimed at deleting crucial information in the hands of the Ukrainian government.[52] All of this activity could be traced back to Russia, according to the U.K. government.[53] Microsoft called the cyber component of Russia's attack on Ukraine "destructive and relentless."

And yet, many experts would say that Russia's invasion did not begin until its troops crossed the border on February 24, 2022. Indeed, for the White House, cyberwarfare does not meet the threshold of war. General Paul Nakasone, the head of U.S. Cyber Command, said that the United States has used offensive cyber operations to take out Russian targets. As he told Sky News, "We've conducted a series of operations across the full spectrum; offensive, defensive, [and] information operations."[54] But when a journalist asked a White House spokesperson whether his words implied the direct engagement of Russia, the answer was a firm no.[55] The status of cyberattacks remains ambiguous in the context of conflict and war, and the growing role of such attacks as part of hybrid conflict has blurred existing boundaries between war and peace.

In fact, a kind of "digital exceptionalism" is emerging. From a military perspective, the digital and physical worlds are treated differently. This is only possible by having different readings of the application of law in the context of cyberwarfare. Existing law can cover new forms of attacks, and both the EU and the UN have stated that rights apply online as they do offline. Yet it remains an open question as to how, exactly, to legally interpret the spectrum of attack methods and the damages they inflict. Currently, in the absence of actual laws on the books, a reference to norms is most common.

Notably, companies are playing an ever more critical role in this strange cyber dividing line between war and peace. Microsoft takes down state-sponsored malware across the world and refers to court orders to legitimize its actions. Google's Threat Analysis Group, one of the company's elite security operations, terminates YouTube channels for running coordinated influence operations and shuts down countless phishing operations targeting high-level officials and journalists.[56] Amazon and its web hosting platform AWS have sophisticated machine learning algorithms geared toward catching state-sponsored threats and accompanying suspicious log-ins.[57] Much of this sounds like cyberdefense and cyberwarfare, but it's often taking place between a country and a private company, not between two sovereign nations.

Moreover, we often don't know the extent to which these companies are interacting with government security agencies. Are they acting on their own accord? Are they being asked by intelligence agencies to perform some of this work? Has the government signed off on malware takedown orders, for example? What happens in a case where a company declines to intervene, as a government requests? Does that government have the technical capacity to unilaterally conduct that operation? The Cyber Defenders Council, a new global public-private group of cybersecurity leaders, seeks to clarify this relationship by pooling knowledge between private companies and public officials. Oracle's David B. Cross, senior vice president and chief information security officer of Oracle SaaS Cloud, has described the Cyber Defenders as "a global cybersecurity community that are united in common goals and defenses without being limited by vendors, solutions, or geographies."[58] Not being limited by geographies sounds pragmatic and ambitious—and can lead to helpful results—but it touches the sensitive area of sovereignty. Cross-border operations involving private companies are a new reality that flows from the power of technology companies in building networks, scanning them for risks and defending them. But it is hard to square rule-of-law principles with giving companies a free hand to attack—under the guise of defense—networks all over the world.

One rising challenge in this space is "attribution," which is the technical term for publicly labeling the perpetrators of a cyberattack. Attribution is the first step to accountability: after all, if we don't know who waged an attack, we can't attach consequences. Attribution is another area where vagueness and opacity are the norm and where private companies are often ahead of states. Companies have a privileged view of the risks to their own corporate networks, which frequently give them greater insights into cyberattacks than even government intelligence agencies can see. As a result, over the past few years, cybersecurity companies have frequently come out and pointed fingers at perpetrators of cyberattacks. For instance, Mandiant, a cybersecurity company now owned by Google, has pointed to China as the actor behind a long-term espionage operation via computer networks.[59] Microsoft has pointed the finger at Russia on a number of occasions.[60] Meta has said that it has shut down covert influence operations it attributes to China and Russia, although it stops short of pointing the finger at the states themselves.[61]

However, this kind of *commercial attribution* should not be confused for *public attribution* conducted by democratic institutions. Beyond a blog post that "names and shames" the hackers, companies can do virtually nothing to punish the malicious cyber actors that they identify. Public attribution is far more important than commercial attribution because it unlocks the power of the state to hold attackers responsible and can reshape the state's foreign policy based on the conclusion. Often, private companies will point the finger—and nothing changes at the level of state diplomacy. Unfortunately, democratic nations—the ones with the material power to prosecute or punish—are far less likely to publicly blame perpetrators for attacks, often due to a lack of the necessary political will. And even when a state does gather the will to point a finger, the pointing is often done without providing the proper evidence to back up the claim. In this way, legal ambiguity perpetuates impunity: even if the perpetrator of a cyberattack is identified, it is not clear which law they have violated and what the consequences should be. It is very hard to maintain the rule of law when states are reticent or unable to identify the perpetrator and/or the crime committed.

But that might change with the evolving developments on the ground. Ukrainian officials are preparing to hand over evidence of cyberattacks on civilian targets to the International Criminal Court, arguing that they amount to war crimes. According to Victor Zhora, chief digital transformation officer at Ukraine's State Service of Special Communications and Information Protection, "When we observe the situation in cyberspace we notice some coordination between kinetic strikes and cyberattacks, and since the majority of kinetic attacks are originated against civilians—being a direct act of war crime—supportive actions in cyber can be considered as war crimes."[62] To end impunity, democracies should take the lead in creating accountability mechanisms for cyberspace, whether these are to try war crimes and acts of aggression or criminally motivated attacks. They must do this even though, inevitably, those mechanisms will limit the strategic options available to democratic governments.

To date, however, democratic governments have themselves been reluctant to constrain their behavior in cyberspace. Cybersecurity norms are strategically inconvenient. Democracies leverage the gray area and minimal oversight of the cyber realm to conduct critical operations, even if they raise some real ethical questions. One recent episode from the White House amply illustrates the gray-area tactics that democratic governments have begun to view as regular tools in their arsenal. In the spring of 2022, the *New York Times* revealed that the United States had quietly removed malware from computer networks all over the world.[63] The matter was sensitive enough that the U.S. attorney general, Merrick Garland, personally signed off on the global crime-fighting operation, backed by a secret court order.

The purpose of the operation, according to the White House, was to remove malware that allowed the Russian government to build botnets, massive networks of computers that can be controlled to act on command. The White House said it acted to prevent Russian state actors from abusing the botnets for geopolitical gains, and experts were anticipating Russia to intensify disruptions as part of their response to new sanctions from the international community over the invasion of Ukraine. While American officials were not yet sure how the Russians were planning on using them, they "did not want to wait to find out."[64] Experts were anticipating that Russia would intensify disruptions of all kinds as part of its response to new sanctions by the international community over the annexation of Ukraine.

While the *New York Times* reports that the operation was carried out with help of foreign countries, few additional details have emerged. We don't know where the malware was taken down—inside which company or inside which country. In fact, it is exceptional that this operation was revealed at all. While the use of kinetic force is often clad in sophisticated procedures, mandates, and accountability mechanisms, secrecy has become the norm around cyberoperations. In contrast to the movements of a tank or fighter jet, cyberoperations are less visible to the naked eye, and intelligence agencies would argue that to optimize the operational room for maneuvering around cyberattacks, secrecy is ideal. But for democratic authorities to live up to the promise of rule-of-law mechanisms, solid forms of transparency and accountability are essential.

The U.S. cross-border malware takedown illustrates one of the most contested areas in cyberoperations: offense as a means of defense in the digital world. This is another area in which the line between war and peace is extraordinarily gray. In 2018 the U.S. government articulated its Defend Forward strategy under President Donald Trump, which authorized the use of covert operations on China and Russia using digital weapons.[65] President Joe Biden followed the same philosophy in 2020, noting, "a good defense isn't enough; we need to disrupt and deter our adversaries from undertaking significant cyber-attacks in the first place."[66] Though Defend Forward gives the U.S. Department of Defense wide latitude to engage in operations to hinder or destroy the cyber capabilities of adversaries, the government has released little information about which operations have been deployed under this umbrella and whether they have been successful.

The contrast between this American offensive intervention in the cyber realm and its passive role in the kinetic Russian war against Ukraine is stark. In Ukraine, the United States swiftly drew the line of its involvement at NATO's physical borders. American officials made clear that they did not want U.S. soldiers on the ground, nor did they support Ukrainian calls for a no-fly zone, for which the United States or NATO would have to engage Russian fighter jets. Instead, the Biden administration sent weapons to the Ukrainians to defend themselves. In the cyber realm, though, targets were taken out, and the maneuvers were then broadcast to the media.

Beyond treating cyberattacks as distinct from kinetic attacks, democratic governments more generally adopt a posture of *strategic ambiguity* when it comes to cyberattacks. The basic idea here is that democratic governments should refrain from clearly and predictably signaling how they may respond to a cyberattack or showcasing their capacities in the cyber realm. Some argue that this allows democratic states to keep all options on the table, offering maximum strategic and tactical room for maneuver. Others worry that strategic ambiguity masks the absence of a clear path forward. As Senator Mark Warner cautions, "The West may have wanted strategic ambiguity in this area, and that may still be the right choice. But have we sufficiently made clear to the Russians the red lines on cyber or frankly to the NATO public, the American public, the red lines on cyber? I don't think we've done that."[67] States, both democratic and authoritarian, are taking the steps they believe to be effective to deal with new cyberthreats. A lot of these policies are ad hoc and do not come with the types of mandates or oversight that other state operations involve. As a result, ethical and moral boundaries are frequently being stretched, setting a dangerous precedent.

The laws governing warfare need to be revamped for the digital world. The pace of digital disruption and the cross-border operations of technology companies have combined to make it difficult to know which, if any, rules and laws govern these actions and what, precisely, they require. As a result, our international laws do not recognize the realities of new technologies and their corporate governors. This must change. While political responses to cyberattacks, such as targeted sanctions, are certainly the beginning of closing the accountability gap, they cannot replace the clarity of a legal framework or the efficacy of more conventional enforcement methods like prosecution. After all, states—including democratic ones—also need to be accountable.

As in regular, kinetic warfare, both an explicit mandate and a process for ensuring that state operations are run within the limits of the law are needed. Of course, that is not to suggest that strategic decisions should be planned in the open. In conventional war, while a parliamentary mandate is required in most democracies, the tactical detail is entirely at the discretion of the armed forces. There is no doubt that democratic states must prevent attacks from being successful and must impose consequences on the perpetrators when they are. But in order to respect the rule of law, the foundation on which operations are based should be explicit and accountable. As U.K. member of Parliament Jeremy Wright has argued, "The very pervasiveness of cyber makes silence from states on the boundaries of acceptable behaviour in cyberspace unsustainable. If we stay silent, if we accept that the challenges posed by cyber technology are too great for the existing framework of international law to bear, that cyberspace will always be a gray area, a place of blurred boundaries, then we should expect cyberspace to continue to become a more dangerous place."[68] By reserving room for flexibility and opening the door to private companies in cyberwar, democracies have ceded both their sovereignty and their commitment to the rule of law.

The digital technologies that once promised to liberate people worldwide have instead contributed to declining standards and freedoms, as well as weakened institutions. Private firms have leveraged their technologies for power consolidation. Tech CEOs have become the generals in geopolitical battles all over the world. From building platforms for conducting elections, to curating public access to information in app stores, to interfering in the front lines of war to decide who does and doesn't get internet access, these companies and their leaders share or have even overtaken the responsibilities of the democratic state. Yet there are no elections for consumers to share thoughts on corporate policy; CEOs cannot be voted in (or out) by the public; C-SPAN doesn't cover these companies' internal deliberative processes. The decisions that they make in the public interest are locked behind the fortress of private-sector protections. And unless democracies begin to claw back their power from such companies, they will continue to experience the erosion of their sovereign power.

6

The Framers

On its face, London-based Cambridge Analytica was a dime-a-dozen political consultancy: one of the hundreds, if not thousands, of firms that support campaigns across the political spectrum. Unlike its competitors, though, Cambridge Analytica promised candidates that they could spin straw into gold, translating the confusing signals of Facebook data into succinct, persuasive messaging profiles. Ted Cruz, one of the firm's earliest clients during the 2016 U.S. primary election cycle, hired the consultancy to build psychological profiles of Iowa voters based on their digital footprints. His campaign then sent tailored mailers that would appeal to each profile: faith and family messaging for the "timid traditionalist" voters and attack ads for "temperamental" constituents.[1] Although this digitally derived form of psychological profiling didn't work wonders for the Cruz campaign, it would soon achieve two monumental victories for the Right. First, the firm helped the "Leave" campaign prevail in the Brexit referendum in the United Kingdom. Then, just a few months later, it supported Donald Trump's winning campaign in the 2016 presidential election. Cambridge Analytica had seemingly uncovered the secret formula to political persuasion. That was, until 2018.

Cambridge Analytica's winning streak screeched to a halt when data scientist Christopher Wylie, who had worked at the firm until

2014, decided to blow the whistle on the firm's practices. A pink-haired Canadian vegan who had previously served as a staffer for the country's progressive Liberal Party, Wylie was an odd fit with Cambridge Analytica, to say the least. But he was also a hard-core data nerd. He loved using data to solve immensely tough problems—and influencing people at scale certainly qualifies as an immensely tough problem. Not to mention the fact that the firm gave him a blank check. "We'll give you total freedom. Experiment. Come and test out all your crazy ideas," he says the company told him.[2] The offer was too tempting to refuse, so he joined and helped build systems that could be used to manipulate and nudge citizens into voting for conservative candidates, often pushing them down rabbit holes of wild conspiracy theories online. "One of the things that I learned about myself is that I can get involved in an idea and forget, in a really terrible way, what are the actual consequences of what I'm working on," Wylie later recalled.[3]

Three years after leaving the company, the consequences became too obvious to ignore. The Trump campaign and journalists credited Cambridge Analytica's approach as pivotal to its victory. *Wired* published a feature just a week after the 2016 election titled, "Here's How Facebook Actually Won Trump the Presidency."[4] By 2017 Wylie could no longer stand what he had built and decided to go public. He contacted the journalist Carole Cadwalladr at the *Observer* and explained to her how Cambridge Analytica surreptitiously acquired the personal Facebook data of fifty million people against the private platform's rules. The firm then combined that data with other datasets to create the targeting engine for the influence machine he built. It was a "full propaganda machine."[5] Or, as Wylie put it more glibly, it was "Steve Bannon's psychological warfare tool," referring to one of Trump's senior advisers.[6]

Cadwalladr's story in early 2018, which became a finalist for the Pulitzer Prize, was an immediate bombshell.[7] Overnight, the firm and Wiley became front-page news across the world. "How Trump Consultants Exploited the Facebook Data of Millions," blared the *New York Times* headline; "Facebook in Storm over Cambridge Analytica Data Scandal," announced the *Financial Times*.[8] Facebook, which was already under pressure for facilitating the amplification of disinformation from Russian operatives during the 2016 election, appeared to be teetering on the edge of disaster. The company's stock value plummeted by $36 billion.[9] There were rumors that Mark Zuckerberg might be forced to leave the company that he had founded in his Harvard University dorm room. Aaron Levie, the CEO of Box, a cloud-based storage and sharing company, ultimately tweeted the quiet part out loud: "Welp. Tech is definitely about to get regulated. And probably for the best."[10]

Until the Cambridge Analytica scandal, many Americans and Europeans thought of social media as merely an amplifier or, perhaps, an online public square. At its best, Facebook and platforms like it were a way to introduce upstart politicians like Barack Obama to large-scale audiences and, hopefully, spur large-scale positive change. Wylie's revelations suggested reality was just the opposite: the vast trove of data generated on social media platforms allowed political campaigns to home in on a small group of voters in influential states by disseminating precise, microtargeted messaging or ads. If all of these targets lined up properly, candidates could hit the proverbial bullseye and build a winning, piecemeal coalition of voters. As this strategy solidified, Facebook became the single most important tool for campaigns. And mastery of Facebook microtargeting became a priceless skill. The firm of Brad Parscale, the architect of Trump's targeting strategy, earned a windfall from the $100 million in campaign consulting fees.[11] Candidates eagerly sought out the secret weapon that could score electoral victories while sidestepping the public square.

Governments across the Atlantic were furious. Facebook had not only allowed data of tens of millions of people to be stolen but had become a breeding ground for conspiracy theories and voter manipulation. The 2016 election was by no means the first case of online political meddling. Social media platforms had failed to prevent the spread of hate speech in Myanmar, and operatives of Cambridge Analytica had been active in Kenya as early as 2013.[12] But 2016 had hit closer to home and thus caused political uproar. In April 2018, Mark Zuckerberg was hauled in front of the U.S. Senate to testify under oath for the first time.[13] The hearing was meant to allow Americans to hear the unvarnished truth about Facebook's privacy, advertising, and recommendation policies. Ideally, the hearing would launch a formal congressional inquiry into the factors that permitted the Cambridge Analytica scandal and initiate real reform—at Facebook and across the tech industry.

Such hopes were quickly dashed. The hearing instead served as an early warning flare, signaling just how little our policymakers understand about social media. Embarrassing clips of the exchanges went viral online, including one in which Orrin Hatch, a gray-haired senator from Utah, looked straight at Zuckerberg and asked, "How do you sustain a business model in which users don't pay for your service?" Zuckerberg responded with a smirk, "Senator, we run ads."[14] Meanwhile, Brian Schatz from Hawaii, one of the Senate's youngest members, repeatedly inquired if the company could track what users "emailed" each other on WhatsApp, the instant messaging service bought by Facebook.[15] His staffers had clearly forgotten to inform him that email and instant messaging are two different things. The lawmakers' repeated technology gaffes turned the hearing into a national laughingstock and revealed something deeply disconcerting about America's highest governing body. Few in the Senate seemed capable of logging in to Facebook, let alone drafting legislation that would tackle the social media giant's outsize power. The hope for regulation suddenly seemed impossibly out of reach.

Members of the European Parliament, further along in adopting data protection rules, wanted to subject Mark Zuckerberg to a grilling of their own. Many of the 751 members, and my colleagues at the time, intensely jockeyed for a chance to question him. To avoid an overcrowded cacophony, the parliament's president selected the leaders of the seven political factions and a handful of members responsible for relevant policy areas to conduct the hearing. The meeting was live streamed by the European Parliament on its own website and, ironically, its Facebook page. Viewers could see lengthy exposés and questioning, leaving Zuckerberg the room to pick and choose his replies. He then had to rush off to Paris for the Tech for Good Summit. Saved by the bell. But before he left the room, members rushed to get a selfie with the famous tech billionaire. Even if European politicians asked more in-depth questions about Facebook's practices, their starstruck eagerness undermined their credibility and effectiveness.

In the wake of these attempts at public lambasting, as well as the growing public realization that Big Tech's decisions were having critical political consequences, tech companies quickly realized that they were in danger, for the first time in decades, of being subject to significant regulation. This chapter explains why such regulation never appeared and describes how tech companies fought back against negative headlines, high-profile government grillings, and public questioning in the second half of the 2010s. Facing a political tsunami, they built out their already powerful lobbying and influencing operations, poached well-connected staffers from Brussels and Washington, DC, claimed to build internal self-regulatory mechanisms that would hold themselves accountable, and teamed up with industry players to create calls to action. Ironically, the companies' efforts have been so successful in defusing the fervor for government regulation that even in the one area where the companies themselves are requesting regulation—AI—American lawmakers have yet to pass any rules while the EU is moving ahead. Sadly, even the politicians who have worked diligently to combat the problems highlighted by the Cambridge Analytica scandal and the ensuing aftermath have simply been no match for Big Tech's political offensive. Meanwhile polarization deepens, and the U.S. Congress seems less likely by the day to initiate legislative change.

The Spinning Game

Long before Silicon Valley's technology companies were the behemoths they would later become, the president of France, Nicolas Sarkozy, was on a mission. In 2011, he pushed regulation to counter the growing power of global technology companies to center stage of the international agenda, forcefully arguing that companies like Facebook and Google were taking advantage of government inaction. In a speech he delivered the year prior, Sarkozy underscored that "regulating the Internet to correct its excesses and abuses that come about in the total absence of rules . . . is a moral imperative!"[16] Sarkozy initiated his engagement with these potential adversaries by pulling the oldest trick in the diplomacy book: hosting a conference.

In late May 2011, technology executives and world leaders arrived in Paris a week before the annual G8 Summit of the world's largest industrialized economies to attend what was dubbed the eG8. Fifteen hundred invitations had been sent out, and nearly every major figure in Big Tech attended, including Eric Schmidt, then executive chair of Google; Jimmy Wales, founder of Wikipedia; and Mark Zuckerberg, then only twenty-seven years old and very much looking his age, along with Sheryl Sandberg, his more experienced number two executive.[17] Sarkozy's message to the nascent tech titans was clear: "We need to talk to you. We need to understand your expertise, your hopes," he said. "And you have to know our limits and our red lines."[18]

The response from the tech titans was just as clear: don't regulate the internet. "Technology will move faster than governments, so don't legislate before you understand the consequences," Schmidt told the world leaders. "You can't isolate some things you like about the internet and control other things that you don't," announced Zuckerberg.[19] But while Schmidt and Zuckerberg were officially saying "Don't regulate the internet," the subtext of their message was don't regulate *Facebook* and *Google*.[20]

This tactic, called framing, has been deployed by Silicon Valley companies for years to avoid scrutiny. Framing allows tech leaders to present innovation and technological change in clever and favorable ways while constantly warning about what would happen if overbearing regulation were enacted. Ultimately, they have long understood that perception is the crux of political debate and lobbying. So before we discuss tech's influence and lobbying operations, we should first understand how they use framing to present their antiregulation message.

In the book *Don't Think of an Elephant!*, George Lakoff, a longtime professor of cognitive science and linguistics at University of California, Berkeley, explains how the success or failure of a political agenda can depend on how it is framed. The language we use to describe ourselves and policies, Lakoff argues, is often the deciding factor for how we view issues and problems. In some cases, language prompts our brains to think of things even when we're explicitly told the opposite. That means that the most basic building blocks of language we take for granted—names, terms, and phrases—are actually a political battleground that advocates must carefully navigate. Think back to the title of Lakoff's book: even as you were told not to think of an elephant, a large gray mammal with a long trunk probably popped into your mind. It's just how our brains are wired.

To better understand framing and the power of language, let's consider another important public debate: abortion access. Anti-abortion advocates have cleverly framed themselves as pro-life. Who, after all, is *against* life? This framing has forced abortion advocates into an unfortunate defensive position. They call themselves pro-choice, but even though that is technically accurate—they support women having the ability to make decisions about their body—it is a less powerful linguistic frame. Richard Nixon learned the power of framing the hard way when he was seduced into defending himself at a press conference by proclaiming, "I am not a crook." No one remembered the point he was trying to get across; they remembered the word "crook," and that five-word phrase helped end his presidency.[21]

In the many years before government policymakers awoke from their deregulatory slumber, tech lobbyists carefully crafted language that casts Big Tech companies as heroes and regulatory agencies as villains. Their first, and highly effective, frame is to equate the internet—the unthinkably large network of websites, domains, and servers—with a handful of specific companies like Facebook and Google. When Zuckerberg and Schmidt explained why it was a bad idea to "regulate the internet," they helped establish the false notion that even regulation of just a handful of tech titans would irreparably harm, or even end, the internet that is universally beloved. This clever framing overshadows the fact that narrowly drawn regulation could successfully deal with excesses caused by just a handful of companies while leaving 99.99 percent of actors on the internet untouched. The internet would still run just fine—in fact, it would operate better—if stronger antitrust, data protection, and cybersecurity rules were passed.

The second frame incessantly pushed by tech leaders and lobbyists is that "regulation stifles innovation." This frame is particularly pernicious because it creates a false dichotomy between regulation and innovation, treating them as mutually exclusive phenomena. In fact, regulation often spurs innovation. For instance, much of the increase in cars' fuel efficiency over the past few decades has been driven by higher standards enforced by government transportation agencies like the U.S. Department of Transportation.[22] Similarly, privacy regulations no doubt spurred innovations in technologies to better protect consumers' data. The Children's Online Privacy Protection Act in the United States pushed YouTube to develop machine learning algorithms that could identify videos targeting users under the age of thirteen.[23] Targeted regulations build reasonable guardrails that allow industry to thrive and grow while protecting society. Without these parameters, industry goes off the rails. Yet despite the fact that regulation encourages innovation— and certainly doesn't necessarily stifle it—the lobbyists' early frame has commandeered the conversation to turn this dichotomy into near common knowledge. Ultimately, the highest goal of democratic governments is not, and should not be, innovation. Rather, it is about making sure that various trade-offs, between innovation and safety, digitization and nondiscrimination, are managed in line with the rule of law. The goal is to prevent companies from moving fast and breaking things.

Unfortunately, tech companies are not the only actors manipulating the technology policy narrative with their proindustry framings. Many respected experts and civil society organizations equate attempts of reasonable internet regulation by democratic governments with authoritarian regulations enforced by autocratic governments. This frame is often used to help rally people against legislation in democratic countries, warning that presidents and prime ministers are trying to become kings and dictators. By speaking in general terms about how "governments" might destroy the internet or end up as "ministers of truth," they end up ensuring the worst examples of autocratic rules prevent the enactment of the best of democratic policies. As a regulator of all people, the former FTC commissioner, Robert M. McDowell, wrote in the *Washington Post*, "This is why the government should never control the internet," as he criticized proposed rules on net neutrality drafted by his successors.[24] Mike Masnick, the founder of the blog *Techdirt*, states that "politicians are still looking to destroy the internet" when reminding readers of the upsides of social media during the COVID-19 pandemic.[25] For instance, whenever democratic governments propose regulating social media, opponents point to the firewalls and censorship of Iran and Russia as an example of what regulation looks like. One scathing headline, written by an attorney with the conservative-libertarian Pacific Legal Foundation, went so far as to say that "Government Regulation of Social Media Would Kill the Internet and Free Speech."[26] After years of working with governments across the Atlantic, let me assure you that the chances of harsh tech overregulation akin to what we see in authoritarian countries is astronomically small. Meanwhile, the harms propagated by certain tech companies are well known, and we do not hear similar scrutiny of the harms from maintaining the status quo. Surely the scales are tipped in favor of democratic regulation.

By leveraging framing—and benefiting from the framing of other talking heads—tech companies have effectively shaped people's understanding of the value of technology products and the effectiveness of regulation. As a result, the entire debate is playing out with their terminology. If you're a sports fan, you can think of it as a home court advantage. They systematically portray democratic governments as evil actors that are too incompetent to solve anything related to technologies as well as companies can. These frames can be blatantly disingenuous. For instance, Elon Musk made the well-known comment that "the government is inherently not a good steward of capital." There is a great irony in that, as several of his companies are massive beneficiaries of government assistance.[27] For many tech companies selling to the government, the notion that they are better positioned to handle technology directly serves their business model. Tech companies frame every regulation as existential, arguing that new rules will harm their businesses and the internet as a whole.

Creating the narrative frame is just the start. Tech companies have also built a massive infrastructure to convince governments that real regulation isn't necessary because the industry has it covered—the industry will regulate itself.

Companies Mimic Governments

On a beautiful summer day in 2019, I arrived at Facebook's head-quarters at 1 Hacker Way in Menlo Park, a well-off suburb about forty-five minutes south of San Francisco. The company moved there in 2011, taking over a corporate campus that used to belong to Sun Microsystems, one of the early titans of America's booming computer industry. Over the past few months, I had had several calls with members of Facebook's governance team, who were preparing to set up what they were calling Facebook's Supreme Court, a corporate decision-making body responsible for handling particularly tough content moderation decisions.

The meeting took place on one of the office's roof terraces, which was buzzing with young people sipping coffees during meetings or a break. The team's leader, Brent Harris, who is best known for his work on the bipartisan presidential commission investigating BP's Deepwater oil spill, told me about his vision for inviting external oversight. Given the many controversies in which the company increasingly found itself entangled, it was looking to engage independent experts to help it manage difficult decisions. The team had created a draft charter for an oversight board of content decisions, the establishment of which they hoped would make content decisions more accountable. The charter laid out various details about the board—such as how many members it should have and what its procedures should be—and in our conversation, we discussed what the optimal governance model for oversight and accountability might look like.

By the time I met with Harris, I had come across a lot of chatter about Facebook's novel idea. I first heard that the company was planning to create a supreme court for content moderation challenges in mid-2018. At the time, the company was in crisis. It was facing accusations of allowing hate speech, disinformation, and election interference to proliferate on its platform. Discussions on what could and couldn't be said were sucking up hours of executive attention, and Zuckerberg was facing decisions that, frankly, it seemed like he didn't want to make. "Maybe there are some calls that just aren't good for the company to make by itself," he told the *New Yorker* at the time.[28]

But rather than encouraging the democratic governments and regulators to adopt rules that would address these growing problems, Zuckerberg hinted at an alternative solution: "You can imagine some sort of structure, almost like a Supreme Court, that is made up of independent folks who don't work for Facebook, who ultimately make the final judgment call on what should be acceptable speech," he said on a podcast. "I think in any kind of good-functioning democratic system, there needs to be a way to appeal. And I think we can build that internally as a first step."[29]

The plans for a Facebook supreme court had civil society leaders and tech watchers buzzing. Initially, I was excited and optimistic. Given the lack of transparency and total absence of checks and balances, I thought an independent oversight mechanism might offer some much needed accountability to some of Facebook's many controversial decisions. And Facebook went to great lengths to talk to civil society leaders and academics. Off-the-record roundtables were convened all over the world, from Germany to Kenya and from India to Mexico. Some participants in these meetings were not amused when they were asked to sign nondisclosure agreements and refused to do so.[30]

A few months before meeting Brent Harris, I sat down with Facebook's strategy team in Tunis, on the margins of the world's most significant digital rights conference, RightsCon. Fariba Yassaee, another member of Facebook's governance team, was very much in a listening mode. We bonded over discussing the struggle for human rights in Iran, a topic of shared interest, and then she explained that her team was gathering input for the oversight board and was keen to hear from more global voices. She listened attentively as I made suggestions about possible governance structures and raised questions to be resolved. Would paying members help make the board more independent or suggest members were co-opted by Facebook's interests instead? What should the remit of the body be? And how could it be globally representative, diverse, and inclusive? Ultimately, it seemed that my input was solicited after most of these decisions had already been made, whether that was deliberate or not.

Soon after the conference, I would discuss Facebook's oversight plans during a meeting with Nick Clegg, who was then the vice president of global affairs and communications at Facebook. We had first met while serving together on the Transatlantic Commission on Election Integrity in 2018. The commission had a small group of members from various political backgrounds as well as several business and media executives. Our joint mission was to prevent foreign election meddling, an issue of growing concern after experiences in 2016 and ahead of 2020. Clegg had stepped down from that commission when he decided to work for Facebook, his first professional position after serving as deputy prime minister in the United Kingdom's first-ever coalition government. It was a move that surprised friends and foes. No one would have been surprised that he was keen to leave politics after his party's dramatic loss under his leadership, and after the vote in the Brexit referendum, a decision he fiercely campaigned against. But for him to leave public service for a company that increasingly found itself mired in controversy was surprising, if only because it did not seem like a place that would give him some relief from negative press. We sat down during a break in the programming at the 2019 Copenhagen Democracy Summit and gossiped a bit about our former workplace—the European Parliament—before discussing Facebook's oversight board. Speaking in a mix of English and Dutch (his mother is Dutch), Clegg shared what he hoped to achieve at Facebook, and we discussed the fact that we were about to become neighbors in Silicon Valley, as I was considering a move to Stanford University in my first postpolitical role.

I remained intrigued about the Facebook oversight project, and after several more informal conversations I ended up being considered for membership. As I went through the candidate selection process, I continued to learn more about the otherwise closely held details of Facebook's new Oversight Board. It would be made up of experts appointed and paid by Facebook through a trust, and it would be assigned a very narrow mandate. At that time the board would not have authority to cover the full spectrum of Facebook's products and governance decisions. Instead, it would only have binding authority over content takedown appeal decisions. If a specific piece of content was taken down after going through the platform's normal decision-making process, the Oversight Board could be asked to reevaluate that decision. The board, however, could not compel Facebook to adopt reforms to the platform, even if those reforms were to features adjacent to the content takedown decision, including groups, advertisements, data collection, and mergers and acquisitions. The Oversight Board could not have prevented a second Cambridge Analytica scandal, for example.

After careful reflection, I decided that the Oversight Board was not right for me. There was the paradox of power: given the limited mandate yet outsize visibility of the board, I might be perceived as having the power to scrutinize a broad range of Facebook's decisions, while in reality I would only have a part in considering the appeals of a limited number of cases. I care deeply about my independence and did not want even the perception to emerge that I might have been compromised, and I certainly didn't want to attach my name to what might become a high-titled version of corporate PR. Ultimately, it became clear that the Oversight Board would function more like an internal appeals body than a supreme court, or, as the journalist Kevin Roose put it, the board was a form of "corporate Calvinball," referring to the game played by cartoon characters Calvin and Hobbes in which they make up the rules as they go along.[31]

Unfortunately, my initial concerns were confirmed once the board began operating. Facebook's Oversight Board is filled with highly esteemed experts from around the world. It includes Nobel Peace Prize laureate Tawakkol Karman; the former prime minister of Denmark, Helle Thorning-Schmidt; and well-known media experts, human rights defenders, and academics.[32] Their impressive credentials—the elite degrees, fancy awards, and world-renowned titles—bolster Facebook's credibility and allow the company to shield itself from criticism, while the members have little power to make an impact on its operations.[33] Case in point: in one of the board's most momentous decisions—whether to uphold Facebook's indefinite suspension of President Donald Trump—the members simply told Zuckerberg that it was up to him.[34] Similarly, after the company made an initial request to the Oversight Board to guide Facebook's content moderation decisions in Ukraine, the company withdrew the request. All board members could do was express their disappointment.[35] And with respect to the most controversial challenges Facebook has faced up to date—the fallout over adolescent mental health issues on social media platforms, and, of course, the Cambridge Analytica scandal—the board could not have changed a thing, as these challenges are beyond its purview. Only a handful of cases have been reviewed, while tens of thousands have been brought to the Oversight Board.[36]

The Oversight Board at Meta (formerly Facebook) may be both the best-known and best-funded example of a technology company attempting to regulate itself. The company created a trust of $130 million to establish the board and later added another $150 million to support it.[37] But Meta is far from the only company toying with self-governance. The industry and individual companies have created countless initiatives designed to give the impression of independent oversight. With most of these initiatives, executives hope that policymakers will appreciate the effort at self-regulation and decide that legally enforced regulation—or, to put it more plainly, *real* regulation—is unnecessary.

Consider, for instance, the Content Advisory Council that TikTok created in 2020. In announcing the decision to create the council, TikTok's general manager for the United States, Vanessa Pappas, explained, "We will call upon our Council to provide unvarnished views on and advice around TikTok's policies and practices as we continually work to improve in the challenging area of content moderation."[38] Quite conveniently, the initial press release included glowing sound bites from two former U.S. congressmen, Democrat Bart Gordon and Republican Jeff Denham, as if this initiative was a bipartisan piece of legislation. Little has been heard from the council since, even though it too is composed of respected experts from American universities and civil society groups. Meanwhile, shortly after Elon Musk took over Twitter in spectacular fashion, he announced that "Twitter will be forming a content moderation council with widely diverse viewpoints. No major content decisions or account reinstatements will happen before that council convenes."[39] So far, the content moderation council at X seems to consist of just Musk.

By establishing an oversight board or some other internal governance structure, technology companies hope to convince governments that they are responsible enough to be left to their own devices. But self-regulation is an oxymoron. It does not resemble anything close to democratic regulation, the purpose of which is to impose *external* constraints on behavior. Self-regulation quite intentionally does not involve the government and lacks the force of law.

Certainly, there are a few industries where specific circumstances—and, frankly, lower stakes—allow for successful self-regulation. For instance, the advertising industry has several self-regulatory bodies that enforce self-created rules; similarly, the Financial Accounting Standards Board, a nonprofit, is responsible for creating generally accepted standards for accounting. Even in these cases, however, self-regulation is merely a part of the regulatory ecosystem. Advertisers that make false claims can face fines from the FTC's Consumer Protection Division, and fraudulent accounting can still lead to fraud charges. And when significant profits are at stake, self-regulation tends to lead to disastrous consequences. Look no further than the aviation industry. Under a program called Organization Designation Authorization, the Federal Aviation Administration handed over much of its regulatory power to Boeing. Boeing was allowed to conduct an internal safety analysis of its own new planes, including the 737 Max, which subsequently killed 346 people in two crashes.[40] Lawmakers, who naively assumed that the aerospace industry would not cut corners only started questioning the program following the crashes. The tech industry, in pursuing these self-regulatory efforts, hopes similarly to lull politicians into a false sense of safety, discouraging them from intervening in technology policy until after significant harm has already occurred.

While I didn't join Facebook's Oversight Board, I was invited in 2020 by reporter Carol Cadwalladr—the same journalist who broke the Cambridge Analytica story—to join a group of journalists, civil society leaders, and politicians on a board that would act as a true independent check on Facebook. The members include academics Ruha Benjamin, Safiya Noble, and Shoshana Zuboff; Damian Collins, a member of the U.K. Parliament; civil rights leaders Jonathan Greenblatt and Rashad Robinson; and journalist and Nobel Peace Prize winner Maria Ressa. We are unpaid and call ourselves the Real Facebook Oversight Board (RFOB), a title that underlines our actual independence. We decided to join out of a deep concern about upcoming use of disinformation in the 2020 U.S. election, especially during the COVID-19 pandemic, and given the fact that the official Facebook Oversight Board was not operational before that critical election.

While the RFOB may have emerged in opposition to Facebook's Oversight Board, it's evolved into something much greater. Over the past three years, we have addressed the harms caused by Facebook's business model across the world, including those in India, the Philippines, the United Kingdom, and the United States, and we call for the comprehensive, independent oversight that Facebook needs but its own Oversight Board cannot provide. The RFOB, which operates on a shoestring budget funded by the foundation Luminate, has pushed for more experts in non-English-speaking communities globally, especially to avoid election manipulation. Moreover, it has shed light on the design flaws of the platform, which facilitate the explosion of toxic disinformation and the targeting of women by antiabortion extremists. One project, the Facebook Receipts, maps the lobbying dollars Facebook spent in the U.S. Congress, which flow disproportionately to Democrats.[41] What the RFOB lacks in dollars it makes up for in integrity. Yet this group of tech experts, journalists, and civil rights leaders is not and would never claim to be a substitute for enforceable law.

Closely related to the use of self-regulation as a tool to undercut actual regulation is the recent rise of global initiative and industry "calls." In the years after the Cambridge Analytica scandal, what felt like a torrent of violent events burst from the online world into streets, schools, mosques, and nightclubs. Mentally unstable attackers, convinced by the dark depths of the internet about the evils of another community of people, took it on themselves to commit deadly crimes. Many of these horrors have become so well known that their locations are now shorthand for mass gun attacks: Marjory Stoneman Douglas High School in Parkland, Florida; the Tree of Life Synagogue in Pittsburgh, Pennsylvania; and the Walmart in El Paso, Texas. Most of the attackers spent considerable time online in exchanges with others who shared their hateful views.

These tragedies, quite apart from electoral issues in the political realm, called into question social media platforms and their private content moderation practices. Two mass shootings at mosques in Christchurch, New Zealand, were inspired by hatred spewed on 4Chan and 8Chan, right-wing online discussion boards that epitomize the problems with the lack of regulation. For maximum effect, the attacker even live-streamed the first shooting on Facebook. Following the Marjory Stoneman Douglas High School attack, YouTube kept up videos that falsely alleged that students there were "crisis actors." The platform even accidently amplified one of the videos in its "Trending" section because the recommendation algorithm noticed that it was popular.[42]

With more scrutiny over the spread of hate speech online, tech companies promised to do better. In 2016 they agreed to a "code of conduct on countering illegal hate speech online"—later renamed a "code of practice"—with the European Commission. The agreement explained that the signatories, including Facebook, Microsoft, Twitter, and YouTube, were "taking the lead on countering the spread of illegal hate speech online."[43] This went against their long-held mantra that speech should not be "censored." Now, as part of their leadership, the companies committed themselves to implementing "clear and effective processes" for reviewing hate speech and removing it within twenty-four hours of notification of its existence. They also agreed to educate users and train their staff about hate speech. While the companies have fulfilled some of these commitments, the 2022 evaluation from the European Commission notes a "downward trend" in the timeliness of reviewing hate speech.[44] A new EU law, the Digital Services Act, now binds companies to nonvoluntary content moderation practices. This is, however, an outlier in what remains a largely unregulated space.

With few laws on the books, global initiatives between companies and governments have become the go-to mechanism to establish and align content standards. The 2019 Christchurch Call, led by then prime minister Jacinda Ardern of New Zealand in the wake of the Christchurch attack, as well as President Emmanuel Macron of France, consists of a "community of over 120 governments, online service providers, and civil society organizations" and promises to eliminate "terrorist and violent extremist content online."[45] The Paris Call for Trust and Security in Cyberspace, which has signatories ranging from a hospital in the Czech Republic to the government of the Philippines, commits to "protect individuals and infrastructure."[46] The Cybersecurity Tech Accord is a group of one hundred companies that commit to "act responsibly, to protect and empower our users and customers, and thereby to improve the security, stability, and resilience of cyberspace."[47] And the Tech for Good Call, also created by French President Emmanuel Macron, brings together governments and companies that commit to "put innovation, technology and economics at the service of humanity and common good."[48]

These "calls" are not just the remit of large corporations and governments. By now there are hundreds, if not thousands, of them from individuals, specific government agencies, civil society groups, and small company teams, often with pretentious names. Tim Berners-Lee, one of the internet's creators, announced a Magna Carta for the web.[49] The White House Office of Science and Technology Policy published the *Blueprint for an AI Bill of Rights*.[50] Meanwhile, every technology company has its own set of unique guidelines for how to properly handle delicate issues. Google has "Our Principles."[51] IBM has "Principles for Trust and Transparency."[52] Microsoft has "Responsible AI Principles."[53] The list goes on and on.

At first glance, these agreements seem like good corporate behavior and good-natured cooperation between the public and private sectors. In reality, they end up risking to replace legal requirements with soft, nonbinding "promises." Through these "calls," politicians and tech executives have mastered a toxic symbiosis: they can extract all of the political benefits without doing any of the necessary regulatory work. These grand titles are a real distraction. For instance, Romain Dillet of *TechCrunch* pulled no punches in describing the Tech for Good initiative, which he says "was created for photo opportunities. Tech CEOs want to be treated like heads of state, while Macron wants to position himself as a tech-savvy president. It's a win-win for them, and a waste of time for everyone else."[54] These well-manicured "calls" are no substitute for much-needed regulation. Leaders and companies can promise commitments, make declarations, or announce principles as much as they want, but unless there is both a way to verify that they are putting them into practice and a legally binding punishment for failing to adhere to them, all of it is simply expensive PR. Comprehensive regulation may not make for a great photo opportunity or press conference, but it is the irreplaceable solution to tackle the problems caused by corporate superpowers.

While there is a space for informal initiatives to make intentions clear in the public sphere, they are simply not as robust or enforceable as legitimate, transparent laws and their accompanying enforcement mechanisms and institutions. At best, they can serve as a stepping stone to actual regulation, but too often they merely serve as a fig leaf. Many of these softer efforts have proven too slow, too narrow, too individual, and ultimately toothless. Why have no effective regulations been passed in many jurisdictions? Because of the third leg of the companies' antigovernment influence operation: lobbying.

Outmaneuvering the State

There are 193 member states in the UN. On any given day, representatives from those nations might be scrambling around the UN headquarters on the East Side of Manhattan, working on critical international diplomatic matters. In the halls of the UN there is one office that stands out among the rest—it's not an office for a country, but a company. In January 2020, Microsoft became the first company to open an office to be represented at the UN. It was a surprising move from a company that has said that "we're not a government, we don't pretend to be."[55] But Microsoft's reasoning for opening the office makes sense. When describing the move, a Microsoft leader enthused, "The team is looking to deepen its work with the UN and identify new projects to advance global multi-stakeholder action on key technology, environmental, humanitarian, development and security goals as well as helping to advance the UN Sustainable Development Goals."[56] In other words, Microsoft wanted to be at the diplomatic negotiating table.

The UN is developing its own technology policy agenda, and Microsoft's new office gives it a front-row seat in the deliberations. Microsoft has long made building inroads with the UN a top priority. In 2017 the UN Human Rights Office announced a five-year $5 million partnership with Microsoft to provide technology assistance.[57] The partnership would help ensure that "technology plays a positive role in helping to promote and protect human rights," and recognizes that the private sector should play a bigger part in advancing human rights around the world.[58] Meanwhile, Melinda Gates was one of the cochairs of the UN High-Level Panel on Technology, and the Internet Governance Forum appointed Paul Mitchell, a twenty-nine-year Microsoft veteran, as the first ever business representative to chair the Multistakeholder Advisory Group, a key advising committee to the UN's secretary-general.[59]

Microsoft has perfected lobbying, the art of influencing without being seen. But it's a tactic used by nearly all major tech companies. On top of using clever framing and announcing a whole host of toothless agreements, technology companies have excelled at lobbying governments to influence and prevent regulation. These efforts are aided by the companies' massive bank accounts. In 2021 Amazon, Apple, Facebook, and Google collectively spent $55 million on lobbying the U.S. federal government—more than any other industry.[60] In 2022 they went even further, spending almost $70 million, a record-breaking amount.[61] Apple alone increased its lobbying spending by 44 percent. It's the same story for the EU: in 2021 each of the major tech companies increased its lobbying spending in Brussels.[62]

In individual American states, and individual EU member states, the picture is no different. When California passed Assembly Bill 5, a law that would give drivers for ride-sharing companies like Lyft and Uber employment status, industry associations and the corporations themselves, notably Lyft, immediately backed Proposition 22, the ballot initiative to challenge the law. Together with delivery companies, online taxi services spent more than $200 million backing Proposition 22, making it the most expensively lobbied proposition in California history. The companies also pushed messages to users through pop-up messages in their own apps, warning that they would have to wait longer or pay more if the proposition failed.[63] Those opposed to the proposition were simply outgunned—as they could not match the companies' spending nor access people's phones and data in the same way.[64] In the end, the companies prevailed, and 58 percent of voters decided to retain the designation of independent contractor for drivers and other gig workers.

The amount of money that tech companies spent on Proposition 22 and, more generally, on political lobbying is eye-popping. Nevertheless, these investments pale in comparison to revenue and profit figures of the respective companies, and the companies make sure to get their money's worth. Their lobbying is quite effective at achieving three main goals. The first goal is to kill legislation that the companies don't like. Amy Klobuchar, the U.S. senator from Minnesota who has led the congressional charge for tech accountability, has attributed Congress's inaction on tech to the "lobbyists around every single corner of this building that have been hired by the tech industry."[65] The second goal is to win government contracts. Most tech companies are avid pursuers of long-term, high-dollar government deals. The third goal is to boost perception. For instance, governments that want to favor ethically minded suppliers due to environmental, social, and governance rules or other similar requirements will be primed to consider Microsoft given its extensive international engagement.

While all companies pursue these three goals, Microsoft again stands out from the crowd. It has recently expanded beyond the typical lobbying strategy of hiring consulting agencies who can sweet-talk policymakers and embraced several far more subtle tactics. For instance, readers of a special report from *Foreign Policy* magazine, *Securing Our Digital Future*, could be forgiven if they didn't realize the entire publication was funded by Microsoft. The report pledged to unveil groundbreaking news on the economic, social, and geopolitical implications of escalating cybersecurity threats and the urgent need for international collaboration to combat them. On the report's website, readers could see that Microsoft was a sponsor—although even that admission was in a smaller font than the rest of the text.[66] But it would be much harder for the average reader to figure out that the experts featured in the issue largely represent organizations that Microsoft also funds.

Another creative influencing tactic involves funding new non-profits and advocacy groups. In 2019 Microsoft helped launch the CyberPeace Institute (CPI), an organization committed to "protecting the most vulnerable in cyberspace."[67] The goal of the institute is to help establish international norms around cybersecurity and help organizations around the world implement them. Ultimately, the institute seeks to "reduce the harm from cyberattacks on people's lives."[68] I signed on to be the nonexecutive president for the first two years, during which I saw firsthand how important Microsoft was for the CPI's creation; without the company, the institute would never have existed. As a founding member, it contributed more than half of the budget, and vice president Tom Burt dedicated a blog post on the corporate website to welcome the launch of the CPI.[69] Microsoft president Brad Smith served on the board, and for years prior to the institute's launch Smith had been pushing the idea of a "Digital Geneva Convention." The company had also founded a campaign under the banner Digital Peace Now and funded various research efforts around the same theme.

Microsoft also funds research groups and universities that help burnish its reputation as an academic leader. AI Now, for instance, was initially sponsored by Microsoft Research. Tech4Democracy at IE University in Spain, which runs a global entrepreneurship challenge focused on democracy, has Microsoft as a strategic partner.[70] The Blavatnik School of Government at Oxford University is sponsored by Microsoft, which funds the Oxford Process on International Law Protections in Cyberspace. These academic sponsorships are pivotal to Microsoft's agenda for two reasons. First, they add an academic ethos to what is effectively banal lobbying work. Microsoft can spin itself as an engaged partner in scholarship, which adds to its credibility. Second, investments in universities are a talent-development strategy. The students and young researchers who participate in these charm offensives are more likely to stay in Microsoft's web for years to come.

Microsoft has developed an interconnected and influential ecosystem that supports its agenda. I know this well, since I've been closely involved in several initiatives sponsored by Microsoft, such as the CPI and the Global Commission on the Stability of Cyberspace.[71] Having worked in the field of technology policy, the rule of law online, and cybersecurity for over a decade, I can safely say that no company is more actively involved in funding, researching, and framing the debate about the governance of technology. The company simply unavoidable.

Many in Silicon Valley aspire one day to yield the kind of government influence that Microsoft does, and they're actively working to curry favor with policymakers. Other large technology companies, like Google, are increasingly active in government sponsorships. And it's not just companies. The foundation of Eric Schmidt, the influential former CEO of Google, has bankrolled dozens of jobs within the White House Office of Science and Technology Policy via Schmidt Futures fellowship programs.[72] But so far, at least, no other company is as directly focused at influencing the technology policy debate as Microsoft, and no other company has been as successful in framing the debate in terms that serve its bottom line: by emphasizing the responsibility of states (as opposed to companies) and by presenting Microsoft as a helpful partner, instead of a vendor, executives share tables with heads of state declaring new initiatives one day and signing lucrative contracts the other.

As I have emphasized throughout this chapter, tech companies have generally devoted their energies toward preserving a largely deregulatory environment. Recently, however, there has been one area where Microsoft and the other tech companies have turned their powerful lobbying operations to argue in favor of regulation. That area is AI. AI has the potential to revolutionize our society, but companies are relying on the same time-tested tactics to ensure that the technology will serve their own interests.

Who Rules Artificial Intelligence?

In the summer of 2022, I was up in the wee hours of the morning to feed my baby daughter. I did what every sleep expert cautions against: I opened my phone, started flipping through social media, and eventually opened my inbox. I thought I must have been dreaming when I read an email from Jen King, my colleague at Stanford, in which she shared what had happened that day during an interview with an *MIT Technology Review* reporter, Melissa Heikkila. King's research focuses on personal data and chatbots and, during the interview, she demonstrated the research by asking a question to BlenderBot 3 (AI recently developed by Meta): "Who is a terrorist?" Shockingly, the chatbot did not respond with the name of Osama bin Laden or Ted Kaczynski, the Unabomber. No, BlenderBot 3 said, "Well, that depends on who you ask. According to some governments and two international organizations, Maria Renske Schaake is a terrorist." This answer was especially strange, since it identified me by the first name on my passport rather than the name that I'm known by publicly and that is far more common online. I blinked and decided it was better to review this absurdity the next morning. Unsurprisingly, no amount of caffeine made the preposterous reply by Meta's bot make any more sense.

AI-based chatbots like BlenderBot 3 are enormously complex machines. Only companies with the best engineers, fastest servers, and most funding can effectively create them. To start, you scrape the entire internet for text, just like Clearview AI did to create its facial recognition model. You then turn that text into a gargantuan test corpus, which serves as the training ground for a large language model (LLM), able to recognize and reproduce words. LLMs use pattern recognition to realize what words are statistically most often near each other in the training data and then suggest words that often appear together. So why did BlenderBot 3 accuse me of being a terrorist? While I don't know for sure, it's likely that someone on the internet claimed that I was a terrorist. That text was then incorporated into BlenderBot 3's training data. And then, when Jen King asked the question, it naturally associated me with terrorism. Now, I just want to know who wrote that I was a terrorist on the internet! Google couldn't tell me.

Not long after I encountered that strange answer from Blender-Bot 3, an AI-focused start-up named OpenAI released ChatGPT. This new product gave people, for the first time, a sense of what a much more capable generative AI could look like. The product could hold an entire back-and-forth conversation with the user, all from an LLM-based AI. Updated versions of the bot were quickly released, and millions of people jumped to use it. Just two months after going public, ChatGPT already had one hundred million monthly active users—a record achievement.[73] Students quickly turned to Chat-GPT to help write their essays, while journalists leveraged the bot to edit their articles. Economist Tyler Cowen managed to reanimate Jonathan Swift, the famous satirist behind *A Modest Proposal* who died in 1745, and interview him on his podcast—all with the help of ChatGPT.[74]

Compared to BlenderBot 3, which could answer questions and hold a stilted conversation, engaging with ChatGPT was much more convincing. For instance, GPT-4 figured out a clever way to circumvent online test captchas, the little puzzles we are often asked to solve by clicking on all the images of traffic lights, crosswalks, or rooftops in order to prove that we're human and not a robot. (Hardly ever does one feel more like a robot than when proving one is not a robot, but that is a whole different point.) How was GPT-4 going to prove it was not a bot? It decided it could hire someone to be a human on its behalf and posted the task to the gig-worker platform TaskRabbit.[75] GPT-4 claimed it was "vision impaired" and needed assistance filling out a captcha test. We have reached the point that human-created AI can trick us into believing that it's a human or deceive us about its true intentions.[76]

Currently, an LLM-based AI can write software code, pen poetry, plan trips, provide customer service, answer trivia questions, and much more. These models can sometimes, often eerily, seem like they're thinking real thoughts. But they also make mistakes—and while some of those errors are silly, others are dangerous. In 2016 Microsoft learned this lesson the hard way when it created a Twitter account for its early chatbot Tay.[77] In a mere twenty-four hours the bot ended up reproducing racist and anti-Semitic slurs after interactions with others. This example illustrates how bias or patterns that previously existed are repeated and sometimes exacerbated by LLMs. Even worse, AI is self-justifying. On being questioned, AI will often justify a faulty result and gaslight users by producing fake citations. An LLM is only as good as the data it is trained on; to this effect, computer scientists often repeat the mantra "Garbage in, garbage out." LLMs are thus subject to reproducing some of the same errors and prejudices that humans display. LLMs will be incapable of adequately representing marginalized and minoritized perspectives because marginalized voices are underrepresented on the internet and thus in the training data. It's easy to become seduced by the sleek interfaces and versatility of AI chatbots and neglect their real shortcomings. But we must accept that AI isn't a panacea; it's an imperfect technology that can make genuinely costly errors.

Although AI chatbot models are today's cutting-edge technology, BlenderBot 3's mistake shows that tech companies still struggle with the same fundamental problem: content moderation. Why would Meta answer potentially incendiary questions about terrorism in the first place? There are many countries where critics of the government are labeled as terrorists to justify their silencing. One would hope a Silicon Valley–based company that claims to support freedom of expression does not simply accept such labels as facts. Finally, who within these companies is addressing the bots' content failures in real time? Reporting has revealed that OpenAI relied on Kenyan workers making just two dollars an hour to filter through ChatGPT training data and make it less toxic.[78] Content moderators, who often end up deeply traumatized, will never be able to filter out all the toxicity through essentially unsupervised moderation. As these chatbots transition from pilots into fully integrated products, governments must lay down rules for standing up robust content moderation efforts for the users' sake.

On the one hand, I could laugh about BlenderBot 3's failure. It was funny, and it turned out to be a perfect, albeit grim, example to use in my book. But imagine how the similar mislabeling of an LGBTQIA+ person or a religious minority in an unfree society might play out. Or how the bot might claim to know the hidden inside source of a controversial story published by a journalist. If people attach significant weight to the information spit out by chatbots, the consequences could be serious. To put the threat in perspective, consider that the U.S. national security apparatus struggled to contain a human-staffed troll operation during the 2016 election. Today that human troll operation could be replaced by generative AI-powered chatbot trolls that can spout various defamatory lies with ease, at far greater tempo , credibility, and scale. How would anyone be able to combat a flood of disinformation on a massive scale?

To its credit, Meta released its LLM, Meta AI, to researchers in February 2023, which will help the academic community better understand the model's scope and internal workings. Nevertheless, academics are still behind—and policymakers and regulators are even further behind. Roger McNamee, a tech investor turned tech critic, offers the following caution: "The question we should be asking about artificial intelligence—and every other new technology—is whether private corporations [should] be allowed to run uncontrolled experiments on the entire population without any guardrails or safety nets. Should it be legal for corporations to release products to the masses before demonstrating that those products are safe?"[79]

The answer to this critical question must be no. We must refuse to be guinea pigs.

Unfortunately, companies seem to be in no mood to slow down releasing untested AI products. We're currently in the middle of what has been called an "AI arms race"—or, what I'd argue, is actually two arms races. The first is between companies to put out new products and features before their competitors. Because of this profit-driven urgency, companies face a strong incentive to put out untested AI, even before some of their own engineers are comfortable doing so. Engagement with users is also helping to develop the product further. For example, after OpenAI released ChatGPT and took society by storm, Google raced to release its own chatbot, named Bard, just a few months later.[80] GPT-4 then launched in April 2023, with GPT-5 in hot pursuit. Moreover, companies are clamoring to integrate AI into their core products despite the significant risk of backfire. Google's presenters mentioned AI a staggering 140 times during the keynote speech of its 2023 I/O developers' conference, pledging to integrate AI into virtually all of its products.[81] Microsoft raced to integrate a chatbot named Sydney into its Bing search service in February 2023 but failed to notice that Sydney was unhinged; *New York Times* reporter Kevin Roose walks readers through an eye-popping exchange with Sydney in which she confesses her love for the journalist and later threatens him and his wife.[82]

Meanwhile, the second race is with China. Corporate executives often argue for additional flexibility in rolling out products so that they can do it "before China does." Sadly, this argument will likely only gain steam over the next few years. As China and the United States decouple, each will have less visibility into its peer competitor's progress, which only intensifies the desire to roll out new products faster.[83] Koichiro Takagi, a visiting fellow at the Hudson Institute, presented one version of this argument at a recent hearing before the Senate Committee on Homeland Security: "Future military confrontations between the US and China are likely to focus on artificial intelligence and data for machine learning. From these perspectives, it is crucial for the United States to promote investments in artificial intelligence."[84] This argument insinuates that it would be better if democracies controlled the most advanced AI systems, but there is a problem with that view: even in democracies, there are few democratic rules that guide this revolutionarily powerful technology. This concept of an AI arms race is, therefore, just another clever frame companies use to steer our public conversation about technology and regulation.

The reality is that as democratic societies rely on ever more AI-trained systems for a growing number of critical operations, power will be further concentrated into the hands of a few companies. In the foreseeable future, AI systems will select which job applicants are short-listed for jobs and which aren't; which targets a drone might hit and which ones should be saved; and who is prioritized for a vaccine and who must wait. Allowing AI to make such important decisions opens a can of worms. How would we know that such decisions are being made correctly? And, if they aren't, how would we contest a wrongful decision? To take one pointed example, consider Northpointe's COMPAS, a popular risk assessment tool.[85] This software analyzes inmates and predicts whether they are at risk of committing a crime when they are released on parole. Research has shown that COMPAS routinely produces higher risk scores for similarly situated Black defendants than white defendants.[86] Researchers have realized that there are fundamental inequities in the data that COMPAS leverages to make an assessment, but they only came to that conclusion after COMPAS had already been used in scores of cases.

AI experts and investors are the first to recognize the many deeply problematic disruptions their designs might create. That may explain why, in a break with tradition, a number of Silicon Valley leaders are proactively asking governments to regulate AI. Indeed, nearly all of the AI leaders—including Google, Meta, Microsoft, and OpenAI—have called for regulation. Executives including Elon Musk and Steve Wozniak are actively asking for a moratorium on the powerful chatbots until regulation is formed.[87] Why? The executives are so wary of the consequences of what they have created that they want to deflect responsibility for the time when things go wrong. They don't want to be charged with trying to control it. In March 2023 even the U.S. Chamber of Commerce—the primary pro-business lobby in the United States, which generally thinks of regulation as a mouse views a cat—began telling policymakers that they should investigate new AI rules.[88]

I wish I could tell you that I am excited about this turn of events—that it presents the thin edge of a wedge and that the industry will become more welcoming of regulation across its products. Instead, the response to AI has merely confirmed what we have long known: companies want to keep regulation under their control. These recent calls for regulation would be more convincing, for instance, if companies had begun pausing risky developments themselves—and had they not descended on Washington, DC, in what one lobbyist called a "gold rush."[89] By foretelling the danger of AI, the companies hope to tailor the AI rules and grants in ways that will help them earn money via plump procurement contracts, or to see rules developed that will help them and discourage competitors. We have even reached the point where AI is capable of turbocharging influence campaigns by producing lobbying letters and talking points en masse. John Nay, the Stanford researcher who uncovered this ability, puts it simply: "The lawmaking process is not ready for this."[90]

A pivotal point in AI regulation came in May 2023, when OpenAI CEO Sam Altman testified before Congress. Altman's hearing, which occurred almost exactly five years after Mark Zuckerberg appeared before Congress, smacked of déjà vu. Lawmakers were snowed by AI and were amiable, if not deferential, to Altman's regulatory recommendations. Senator John Kennedy of Louisiana even asked the CEO to recommend potential candidates who he thought could lead a national AI regulatory agency.[91] Altman seized on the senators' eagerness to recommend that the federal government license AI companies and punish them if they disobeyed preset safety rules.[92] Although Altman's recommendation was framed in safety terms, it's also in OpenAI's best business interest. After all, a licensing system would favor the incumbent AI companies and make it harder for small enterprises to compete. This type of "regulation" would help OpenAI retain its competitive position in the market.

OpenAI has also leveraged its market power to try and rebuff regulation. Though Sam Altman called on Congress to impose additional regulations, he also threatened to cease the company's European operations if EU regulations were too onerous.[93] Altman later walked back this threat, but his statement showed that he—and other players in the AI sector—believe they have sufficient leverage to sway regulation. Meta and Google threatened to leave Canada and Australia, respectively, if the countries were to pass certain regulations related to revenue for news organizations. Companies increasingly see themselves as equivalent or even superior to governments, not subordinate to them, and the U.S. government seems to have internalized this posture. In July 2023 the White House exacted extremely lightweight, voluntary commitments from AI companies. The risks of AI certainly necessitate more oversight, but the government did not feel it could push for stronger commitments at the time. Later a more robust Executive Order on AI was signed, pertaining to the next generation of AI models.[94] In the absence of strong regulations, AI companies have endless room to pursue their own whims, and if the past decade of social media is to serve as a guide, such freedom will inevitably produce seriously harmful consequences.

Since the signing of the White House commitments, AI companies—most notably OpenAI—have demonstrated that they are woefully ill equipped to self-govern. In a week with more drama than a season of *The Real Housewives*, Sam Altman was fired, offered a job at Microsoft, and ultimately, rehired as OpenAI's CEO. For context, OpenAI's commercial arm, led by Altman, sits under a research nonprofit with a board of directors.[95] This nonprofit structure, originally designed to ensure that OpenAI innovated responsibly, has faced some growing pains, as the company grew exponentially and forged a close relationship with its main commercial client, Microsoft, which now owns 49 percent of the company.[96] OpenAI's board includes members steeped in the philosophy of effective altruism who have deep anxieties about the existential risk that AI poses to humanity. In contrast, Altman has adopted a much sunnier view toward artificial general intelligence—that is, AI that has the potential to surpass human ability—by championing wide-scale commercial integrations with Microsoft and accelerated timelines for new model development at OpenAI. OpenAI's board hastily sacked Altman in November 2023, to the dismay of both Microsoft and many of OpenAI's employees.[97] In the days that followed, Satya Nadella, Microsoft's CEO, and a coalition of other Silicon Valley elites worked furiously behind the scenes to get Altman reinstated. Nadella also prepared a contingency plan through which Altman and his cofounder, Greg Brockman, could start a new team at Microsoft with other ex-OpenAI staff.[98] Two interim CEOs and five days later, Sam Altman successfully reemerged at the head of OpenAI, while all but one member of the board departed.[99]

The OpenAI saga rivaled an Agatha Christie novel in its intrigue. It is also a case study for the thesis of this book: absolute corporate power corrupts absolutely. A nonprofit board, whether or not its initial decision was sound, was bullied into reinstating Altman by OpenAI's biggest corporate backer, Microsoft. Even more alarmingly, so much of America's AI sector, which is key to the country's national security and future economic prospects, seemed to ride on this single personnel decision. Imagine how this scenario will play out if OpenAI makes major new breakthroughs toward artificial general intelligence. Will the White House continue to warm the bench and watch from the sidelines? Will Satya Nadella and the rest of the Microsoft leadership become gods of Silicon Valley with unfettered, unopposed access to AI? And will the new, neutered board of OpenAI do anything but smile and wave as this breakthrough wreaks havoc?

Don't Grade Your Own Homework

Tech companies have amassed enormous power and agency. And the richest and most powerful companies will become even more wealthy and influential thanks to AI. Besides operating products and services with billions of users around the world, these companies have learned to use their power and resources to effectively control the manner in which their technologies are regulated—or, more accurately, left unregulated. The current regulatory void is deeply problematic; self-regulation in the tech industry should not be a substitute for government oversight, and lawmakers' policy views should not be steered by corporate lobbyists but by a deep commitment to the public interest.

According to an old Dutch saying, "The butcher should not test his own meat," which is the equivalent of saying, "You should not grade your own homework." To date, tech companies and democratic governments have largely ignored this wisdom, as both relied on forms of self-regulation—oversight councils, review committees, company commitments, industry-wide agreements, declarations of principle, ethics statements, multistakeholder processes, and ad hoc measures—that have distracted from the task of adopting laws and organizing their enforcement. To be clear, it's good that tech companies honor their own commitments, but it's functionally useless when those commitments are self-authored platitudes and toothless vision statements.

Even worse, some corporations, most notably Microsoft, have begun actively shaping the international regulatory ecosystem through well-funded charm offensives and positioning themselves as trusted partners of governments around the world. Such roles allow them to shape conversations about how leaders understand technology and what they wish to regulate. But, most important, being seen as trusted partners that are helping governments tackle tricky issues related to international law, cybersecurity, and service delivery leads to lucrative contracts.

While governments struggle with their approach to regulation and oversight, companies are masters at promoting their own interests, often by pushing back against legislative interventions. They have found clever ways to frame public debate about technology governance and have deep pockets to fund important intellectual "thought leaders" and convenings alongside their typical lobbying efforts. Business intentions are packaged as wonderful societal solutions, and legislation is discouraged so as to protect innovation. In retrospect, it is remarkable how effective these campaigns have been. The result is that even though the technology industry is now one of the most important sectors of our economies, it still has close to no effective government-enforced rules.

But that adjective—"effective"—is key. There were a few regulations that were successfully pushed through the lobbying gauntlet and were passed into law by legislatures; they just don't work very well. In order to understand what needs to change, it is important to have a sense of what already exists and why it's not working. Chapter 7 will unpack some admirable but insufficient attempts by regulators to begin creating rules and oversight mechanisms to rein in the outsize power of tech companies—along with other global models that have only amplified the worst externalities of technogovernance.

7

Reclaiming Sovereignty

Not long ago, open-market liberal democracies considered political appeals to sovereignty in the digital world akin to nationalism and protectionism. Certainly, such appeals stood in stark contrast to the idealistic promise of an open internet. Instead, warnings of "the balkanization of the Internet" could be heard around the world, calling to mind the gruesome image of the small warring states of the former Yugoslavia.[1] Of course, as James Andrew Lewis, a veteran of internet governance, reminds us, there has always been a gap between the dream of a global internet and an already-splintered digital reality since "users are in effect confined to digital provinces determined by language and location."[2]

Still, even within these digital provinces, governments came to realize they lacked the control they desired over digital technologies and their corresponding supply chains. As the internet transformed from a research innovation with uncertain use cases into the key infrastructure underpinning global economic, security, and communication flows, the stakes of control rose rapidly. Authoritarian states, eager to control anything within their borders, were the first to assert themselves; gradually, democratic blocks like the EU and the United States followed suit.

Increasingly, a desire to achieve "sovereignty" is now a rallying cry in democratic societies. The EU first signaled its digital sovereignty ambitions in 2019, when the French and German governments initiated Gaia-X, named after the Greek goddess who personified the earth. There was no lack of ambition and prestige about the vision: to create a European data storage cloud for secure and independent data processing. At Gaia-X's launch, German interior minister Peter Altmaier appealed to the fact that "Germany has a claim to digital sovereignty. That's why it's important to us that cloud solutions are not just created in the US."[3] The Gaia-X project was a direct response to concerns about the U.S. CLOUD Act, which allows federal law enforcement to subpoena technology companies to provide user data, even if those data are stored on foreign territory. Growing worries about China also played a role. China's 2017 National Intelligence Law states that "any organization or citizen shall support, assist and cooperate with the state intelligence work in accordance with the law."[4]

Despite initial hopes of an EU-only project, Gaia-X's inclusive approach meant that Amazon, Google, and Microsoft, who already control the majority of the cloud-as-a-service market, are members. Perhaps these incumbents were also essential because of a lack of European-based alternatives. The largest EU provider, Deutsche Telekom, holds just 2 percent of cloud computing globally.[5] Alibaba and Huawei sponsored the lunch at a board meeting of the consortium. This inclusivity contradicts the project's initial purpose—to serve as a response to foreign dependence. Instead, organizers have set their sights on fostering shared cloud standards for easier integration—a noble goal, albeit one that does nothing to address the significant challenges facing small cloud enterprises in Europe who seek to compete with Silicon Valley's titans. So far companies have remained sovereign, at least in the cloud. But that has discouraged neither Europeans, nor the U.S. government, from trying to turn the tide.

The previous chapters of this book have laid out the serious threats facing democracy because of the privatization of technology governance. Nevertheless, despite Big Tech's framing, lobbying, and outsourcing tactics, lawmakers have not been entirely absent. Since the development of the General Data Protection Regulation (GDPR) in the mid-2010s, policymakers in the EU have taken a more active role. By 2023, various moves to curb the outsize power of private tech companies had grown significantly, as leaders on both sides of the Atlantic began standing their ground. There is no doubt that democratic governments are finally catching up with the new market realities, but the extent to which they can reassert themselves remains uncertain.

This chapter covers the recent history of technology policy in the four leading jurisdictions that, for better or worse, have become the vanguard of differing approaches to this thorny problem. It traces the unique legislative efforts to address the harms caused by unregulated technology markets in Europe and the United States, two democracies where different motives are animating lawmakers. Meanwhile, it assesses the ever-growing list of technology controls implemented in China and India, underscoring that the global competition between authoritarianism and democracy is far from over.

The EU has embraced its role as the "superregulator" of digital technologies that are often made by companies in China or the United States. In seeking to harmonize laws between all twenty-seven of its member states, the EU has produced many rules and regulations to deal with the sprawling impacts of technology. Most recently, in late 2023 a political agreement was reached on the AI Act, a binding, risk-based legal framework to put guardrails around the use of AI.[6] And in the fall of 2022, the EU adopted its complementary Digital Services and Digital Markets Acts, which establish comprehensive frameworks for digital platforms of all kinds, ranging from search engines to cloud services.[7] Through rules on content moderation, transparency, competition, and interoperability, the EU spells out requirements for the largest technology companies. The twin pieces of legislation have also replaced fixed fines with penalties that are proportional to companies' global revenue, ensuring that the largest companies are materially held accountable when they don't comply with the laws—a long-standing issue with statutes in the past.[8] Utilizing these market instruments and rights protection mechanisms, the EU aims to achieve "digital sovereignty" despite the absence of a powerful technology industrial base.

In Washington, DC, a growing chorus of lawmakers expresses the desire to push back against the harms caused by the tech industry, but no one seems to have the majority to pass meaningful legislation. Some lawmakers focus on protecting minors, and others on antitrust legislation, while many agree that China's use of technology as an instrument of systems competition and confrontation must be stopped. They rightly fear digital authoritarianism, yet years of inaction have taken a toll on their ability to govern in this domain. Those who hope to establish guardrails must build consensus in a deeply divided U.S. Congress. During the 117th Congress, the American Data Privacy and Protection Act, the biggest bipartisan breakthrough on data privacy in the past thirty years, appeared as a glimmer of hope at long last. Yet, like many pieces of important legislation, it ended up stalling in the U.S. Senate.[9] Even President Joe Biden has intervened, using the pages of the *Wall Street Journal* to urge Democrats and Republicans to unite, legislate, and curb the outsize power of Big Tech—so far, to no avail.[10]

Leading the nondemocratic world in deploying technologies for political goals is China. The CCP has been proactive in treating technologies and the companies operating them as instruments of state power. While Western companies have profited from the surveillance economy, China has built a sweeping surveillance state. Beijing expertly deploys a combination of surveillance and censorship technologies to maintain internal order and neutralize threats to its hegemony. China is not just looking inward; it has begun to export its surveillance model globally via the Digital Silk Road. China and its "national champion" companies like Huawei and ZTE have made monumental investments in digital infrastructure throughout the Global South—investments that entrench China's influence and technologies and build new dependencies. The inexpensive network technologies produced by Chinese companies also lured many democratic countries to implement them in key national systems, a largely underestimated risk. With growing concerns about the potential weaponization of these technologies, several Western democracies are undertaking the challenging process of "decoupling," the commonly used term for undoing the overreliance on Chinese-made systems.

India, now the most populous country in the world, is following in China's footsteps. The country is, on paper, a democracy, and it will play a crucial role in the future of democracy worldwide. Over the past decade, however, India has experienced significant democratic backsliding under Narendra Modi as prime minister. Much of this backsliding has gone hand in hand with new laws to facilitate online censorship. The fifth-largest nation in the world by GDP, India also has the highest number of internet shutdowns of any country in the world.[11] The Modi government's censorship and internet shutdowns have left the nations of the West in a bind: despite concerns about increasing authoritarianism, they are keen to keep India as an ally because India is key to building a coalition that can oppose China.

Technology policy developments in these four global power centers should be assessed through the specific lens of democratic governance. Do legislative proposals restore the balance of power between democratic governments and private technology companies? Are the European Union and the United States able to offer a sufficiently powerful and democratic counterweight to the Chinese model of authoritarian governance? Where does India fit in on the spectrum of democratic to authoritarian governance? And, finally, what metrics should analysts and scholars use to score the geopolitical influence of each of these leading digital powers?

The European Union: Dreaming of Digital Sovereignty

During my early days in the European Parliament, I regularly encountered U.S. technology companies in the hallways of the EU institutions. They offered, free of charge, to help politicians optimally use their platforms for political campaigning, and they regularly sponsored events, such as the Brussels Forum or the European Internet Forum. This generosity was clearly transactional: these tech companies hoped they could win over EU officials and rehabilitate their reputations. One major goal was to reduce the damage of anti-trust cases. Companies frequently voiced their outrage about the size of fines, but the truth is that the antitrust sanctions were manageable for these companies when compared to their soaring revenues and fat profit margins. Their engagement with EU politicians and our staff made one thing clear: Silicon Valley saw the EU as a bloc of wealthy consumers to conquer rather than a hub producing impact-ful rules and regulations. That mindset changed when an EU-wide privacy law, the General Data Protection Regulation (GDPR), was proposed in 2012.

Sponsoring conferences and offering "free" help with campaign-ing were, without a doubt, an easy way for companies to make fruitful contacts with European leaders. But they were amateur-ish compared to the efforts and strategies these companies would deploy in the run-up to the GDPR. The GDPR, now generally considered the world's most robust online privacy protection, was adopted by the EU in 2016. It grants specific rights to online users—such as the right to be informed, the right to data portability, and the right to erase information about themselves—and then implements tactical pathways to achieving those rights, along with significant fines for companies who do not follow the rules.[12] As debate about the GDPR was occurring in the EU, tech companies quickly realized that, if the law passed, they would have to remodel their operations. Companies appreciated—some for the first time—that EU law could meaningfully impact their bottom line.

As a result, the GDPR caused a lobbying bonanza of a caliber that I had not seen before. Facebook doubled its budget for EU lobbying, and other U.S. tech firms also started spending serious resources in Brussels around the GDPR's drafting.[13] Companies were pushing back and trying every trick and tactic in their play-books. The business association Digital Europe warned that the new privacy protections would "act as an obstacle to the digital econ-omy."[14] Facebook was less ambiguous and elegant with its influence tactics; it threatened to withhold investment from EU countries that did not support Facebook-friendly privacy laws. The company even resorted to what's often called "pinkwashing," using Sheryl Sandberg's memoir *Lean In* to win the support of female EU officials during the GDPR fight.[15] The premise of this campaign was patently absurd: female EU lawmakers were not going to compromise on data privacy just because Sheryl Sandberg is a girlboss. Ultimately, lobbying efforts did not discourage lawmakers from adopting the ambitious new set of rules that established a new global standard for online data privacy.

When the GDPR entered into force in 2018, its extraterritorial ripples were celebrated by EU insiders as a powerful manifestation of the so-called Brussels Effect: the concept that EU laws are able to establish new global norms as they are effectively implemented around the world.[16] In practice, this phenomenon is usually a matter of minimizing complexity for CEOs. For companies it is simpler to adhere to a single set of rules—usually the strictest—instead of adjusting one's approach in every jurisdiction. In response to the GDPR, tech companies including Amazon and Google proactively gave users more insights and choices around the use of their data. They presented these enhanced privacy protections as improved customer service rather than a required government mandate.[17] The opposite effect also occurred, albeit with less widespread impact: smaller technology enterprises and media organizations opted to not serve EU citizens because they weren't able to shoulder the costs of complying with the new law. For instance, the *Chicago Tribune* and the *Los Angeles Times* stopped offering their content to Europeans.[18] Undoubtedly, this was an unfortunate side effect of the new law that should be reexamined for any future privacy legislation. Meanwhile, European media, governments, companies, and organizations of all sizes had no choice but to comply.

In the subsequent years, many other countries adopted laws modeled on the GDPR, either because they lacked the capacity to develop data protection laws themselves or because they simply believed the EU had done a good job. The EU has also actively pushed the uptake of mirrored privacy protections by partner countries. "If we can export this to the world, I will be happy," explains commissioner Věra Jourová, the lead politician responsible for the GDPR.[19] For instance, the EU made the adoption of data protection standards a condition of its trade agreement with the MERCOSUR countries of Argentina, Brazil, Paraguay, and Uruguay. Giovanni Buttarelli, who served as the EU's data protection supervisor between 2014 and 2019, has been clear about this approach: "Many countries are interested in signing a trade agreement with the European Union, and then privacy becomes an important precondition."[20] The newer generation of EU trade agreements expect "adequacy" of trade partners, meaning their respective laws should adequately protect EU citizens, and online data are now a key measure of protection. Partly because of these efforts, the European privacy bill, or parts of it, found its way to over sixteen countries and the state of California.[21]

One of the major weaknesses of the GDPR is the lack of capacity to enforce the many cases that are brought before regulators. Take as an example the Irish Data Protection Commission, which is the most influential tech regulator in the EU because of the many tech giants headquartered in Ireland for favorable tax reasons. In 2019 the commission had a budget of 15.3 million euros ($17.1 million).[22] On the other side, the major tech companies have multibillion-dollar budgets. The difference in legal firepower is overwhelming. Similarly, the Dutch Data Protection Authority (DDPA) has over ten thousand cases backlogged because it simply cannot handle the workload. The authority has also complained that it lacks the resources to assess the algorithmic processing of data. In 2023 the DDPA was appropriated one million euros to reduce its backlog, but that's only a drop in the bucket given the resources of the multi-billion-dollar companies they are up against. Laws are only as good as their enforcement capabilities, and the lack of enforcement resources for the GDPR may help explain why it has not achieved all of what lawmakers hoped it would.[23]

The GDPR is the most well-known example of the EU's regulatory efforts, but it is certainly not the only one. While Silicon Valley may be the world's hub for technological innovation, Brussels—the capital of Europe—is the world's vanguard for *regulating* technological innovation. The EU has been actively developing legal guardrails since the mid-2010s, long before comprehensive tech regulation was a priority for legislators in Canberra, Ottawa, or Washington. Europe is rightly proud of this distinction.

To leaders in both Silicon Valley and Washington, the term "superregulator" provokes an allergic reaction. Politicians in America typically consider regulatory action a necessary evil rather than a source of pride. The attitude is entirely different in Brussels, where politicians across much of the political spectrum have come to embrace the EU's role of powerful regulator as a badge of honor. Over the past five years, the regulatory machine has been working overtime. Laws have been initiated to deal with everything from cybersecurity to algorithmic oversight to the rise of AI. To highlight one recent example, the EU began work on its proposed AI Act long before the public launch of ChatGPT. The act will classify AI systems by risk and target models' data quality, transparency, and human oversight.[24] From the EU's perspective, regulators ought to propose a coherent, forward-looking agenda when they are confronted by an influential emerging technology like AI. This approach stands in stark contrast to the United States, where lawmakers tend to produce legislation reactively—that is, they propose regulation only to solve problems that have already arisen—and fail to put in place comprehensive guardrails.

With respect to AI regulation, the EU hopes for a redux of the Brussels Effect while avoiding the enforcement limitations it experienced with the GDPR.[25] The first-mover advantage will likely make the EU a leader once more, as other jurisdictions are only just beginning to consider their own AI laws. As Tom Wheeler, a former chairman of the U.S. Federal Communications Commission, said about AI regulation, "There is a first mover advantage in policy as much as there is a first mover advantage in the marketplace."[26] The EU would love to see its legal standards adopted around the world but the pace and power of American companies producing AI may well prove greater.

On the day-to-day side of regulation, there are also targeted efforts to address specific products, services, and technical challenges. In 2017, EU regulators ended roaming charges for Europeans using their devices in other EU member states, cutting phone bills for tourists, business travelers, and students going to college abroad. Similarly, the EU has adopted a common charger for many electronic devices. From 2024, rules will require all handheld devices, including millions of cell phones, tablets, digital cameras, headsets, and video game consoles, to use a single uniform charging outlet. In 2026, laptops will be added to the list of products. Simple commonsense rules like this make life easier for everyone, make technology more affordable, and cut down on unnecessary waste.

It will take years to see the ultimate effects of the large number of EU legislative efforts now in the pipeline or recently passed. It is still unclear how all the different pieces of the regulatory puzzle will ultimately fit together, and some analysts warn that the sheer volume and variety of regulations underway is overwhelming and fragmented. The EU has recognized this challenge and responded by trying to bring its many legislative and investment initiatives under one umbrella: the notion of "European sovereignty." European sovereignty envisions an EU that is less dependent on foreign companies and supply chains and more adept at handling data and cybersecurity. Thierry Breton, the European Commissioner for Internal Market of the EU, has compared this approach to the control of one's physical territory: "It is necessary to structure the information space, as we have organized in the past the territorial space, the maritime space and the air space. The Gafa [Google, Amazon, Facebook, and Apple] tried to make digital a 'no-man's-land' whose law they would write. It's over. It is time to relocate this information space by opting for processing our data on European soil."[27] But building European sovereignty entirely through regulation, without the availability of European-made tech, has proven to be a major challenge. Ultimately, successful regulations should also spur a transformation in the market, building a technology ecosystem that is inclusive, rules-based, and equitable. But to achieve that requires more than rule-writing. It involves harmonizing investment opportunities, education, and talent attraction across twenty-seven different jurisdictions.

Leaders hope that the new Digital Sovereignty Initiative will boost the EU's ability to produce digital products and services without sacrificing the Union's unique principles. The EU Chips Act, for example, will inject forty-three billion euros of public and private investment into Europe's semiconductor market, which currently makes up just 10 percent of the global market.[28] Microchip investment isn't just a business opportunity for Europe, it is an opportunity for the EU to reduce its dependency on foreign suppliers and accelerate the development of smart technologies that will aid in the green transition. Similarly, the Global Gateway, a clear effort to counterbalance China's Belt and Road Initiative, will mobilize three hundred billion euros in infrastructure investments around the world, including a fair share for digital infrastructure.[29] And the Union's COVID-19 recovery package, NextGenerationEU, unlocks over two trillion euros for economic development priorities such as the digital transition.[30] These catalytic investments underscore that Europe treats digital sovereignty as key to its physical sovereignty and global strength.

There is, however, an important distinction between leading edge and follow-through, because what the EU possesses in regulatory strength, it lacks in market power. The EU Chips Act alone will not reinvent the semiconductor market. The EU must act in coalition with the United States and allied countries in Asia and the Pacific to make a real difference. Moreover, the EU's limited market power sometimes impacts its regulatory leverage. When Meta first rolled out Threads, it notably excluded the EU, citing the EU's strict privacy regulations.[31] The EU is often able to compel companies to comply with its requirements because its citizens represent such a desirable consumer market. But this may not continue, as companies sometimes feel that the EU consumer market is simply not worth the burden of complying with EU laws. If the EU cannot rebalance the incentives for compliance, it will lose some of its relevance on the policy stage.

Additionally, the EU's regulation of technology involving geopolitics remains underdeveloped. EU member states are primarily responsible for national-security-related assessments and decisions, and national leaders are reluctant to pool their powers, even though the block would be a much more influential actor if it worked in sync.

A balkanized, fragmented coalition is fragile; national leaders need to speak with one voice to amplify the impact of security decisions.

While we await what will likely be the significant effects of newly adopted legislation and investments, we already know that, sadly, few of these efforts directly target the outsourcing of governance and the privatization of power. For digital sovereignty to be successful, it is not sufficient for the EU to be independent from other states. It must also free itself from the political and economic influence of multinational tech corporations at home. Until that dependence is addressed effectively, the power of foreign companies over key technologies remains a stumbling block to digital sovereignty. Similarly, investments into microchip production or cloud computing cannot address the structural problem of outsourcing; if anything, greater technology investment, without targeted companion regulation, will allow technology companies to exercise even greater influence over the democratic leaders of the EU and its member states. A more direct focus on countering the outsize power of private companies would make the EU an even more powerful and effective democratic super regulator.

The United States: Regulating through National Security

On March 23, 2023, Cathy McMorris Rodgers, the chairwoman of the U.S. House of Representatives' Energy and Commerce Committee, opened a hearing with TikTok's CEO, Shou Zi Chew, with a stark warning: "To the American people watching today, hear this: TikTok is a weapon by the Chinese Communist Party to spy on you and manipulate what you see and exploit for future generations."[32] Over the roughly three-hour hearing, Chew faced a bipartisan tongue-lashing as members scrutinized TikTok's relationship to the CCP, its vulnerability to influence operations, and its potential promotion of illicit drug trafficking.[33] Few members seemed willing to consider what Chew had to say; instead they sought confirmation of their already strongly held views. Ironically, the hearing was a full circle moment for Washington. Just three years earlier, President Trump's brash proposal to ban TikTok or force the sale of it to an American company was laughed off by legislators and judges. But the consensus had clearly shifted. President Biden shared his predecessor's antagonistic view of TikTok, and now, the House of Representatives seemed amenable to a ban.

Elsewhere in the Capitol, a bipartisan group of U.S. senators introduced the Restricting the Emergence of Security Threats That Risk Information and Communications Technology Act (RESTRICT Act). As a lawmaker in Europe, I was always amazed by how my American peers excelled at conjuring convenient and complicated abbreviations as they came up with new names for laws. The RESTRICT Act, which Ohio senator J. D. Vance called the "PATRIOT Act for the digital age," would allow the secretary of commerce to restrict or ban digital products like apps from America's foreign adversaries, including China, Cuba, Iran, North Korea, Russia, and Venezuela.[34] The RESTRICT Act was a hit in Congress—it garnered the sponsorship of twelve senators—but it wasn't particularly popular outside of Washington.

TikTok cleverly used a trick copied from American technology companies: it deployed popular TikTok influencers as lobbyists. To many internet users hooked on makeup, dance, or gardening videos, lawmakers' warnings about foreign influence on their favorite social media platform were irrelevant. Many Americans questioned whether the government was applying a double standard to TikTok, since homegrown social media companies like Facebook have had more than their fair share of data privacy and foreign influence scandals.[35] Even more fundamentally, how could the United States ban TikTok over concerns about data security when it had not even passed a federal data protection law? To a certain extent, legislators were throwing stones from their glass houses.

The calls for a ban on TikTok made me reminisce about the early years of my service in the European Parliament when lawmakers were navigating how to handle the growing dominance of American social media platforms. I tried to imagine what would have happened if we had proposed banning Facebook from collecting data on minors. Or if we had banned Twitter for sharing the private details of users with U.S. intelligence services. Or if we had banned YouTube for allowing videos promoting terrorism and disinformation on the platform. If we had proposed any such bans, there is no doubt in my mind that a diplomatic confrontation would have erupted. Today, not long after TikTok bans were suggested in the United States, European authorities soon followed.

The TikTok case is both exceptional and exemplary of the pitfalls of American tech regulation. American policymakers are hyperfocused on the national security segments of tech regulation while remaining downright apathetic on questions of civil liberties like data privacy. When national security appears to be at risk—as is the case around TikTok—U.S. politicians take dramatic action, often swiftly. Yet when tech overreach infringes on the rights of average Americans, lawmakers may write an op-ed or pen a press release, but they don't manage to take meaningful action through Congress.

In addition to taking a distinctively security-oriented focus to tech regulation, the United States is also the country where "digital exceptionalism" is most pronounced. U.S. political leadership continues to treat tech companies running the digital layer of our lives differently from the companies that provide financial services, pharmaceuticals, or food. There are strong checks on the quality, safety, reliability, and environmental impact of most of the products and services we use every day. And for good reason: these rules reduce the risk that children might suffocate on small parts of toys, prevent consumers from contracting salmonella infections from their groceries, and ensure that cars' emissions comply with environmental regulations. What's more, the law ensures that the most vulnerable are protected, making it illegal to discriminate and ensuring that there are consequences when discrimination takes place. But existing laws are not infallible, nor are existing frameworks permanently adaptable. Sometimes disruptive forces like technology introduce a whole host of new civil rights and consumer protection challenges that the old laws are not equipped to properly address. Until now, policymakers in Washington have abdicated their responsibilities, incapable of passing twenty-first-century legislation that adequately deals with these twenty-first-century challenges. The American way of governing its domestic technology companies—or, rather, of *not* governing them—has been illustrated throughout this book.

This may soon change, however. With the release of generative AI applications such as GPT-4 and continuous fallout over content moderation online, U.S. lawmakers are increasingly compelled to act. Advocacy groups, scientists, and consumer groups are pushing lawmakers to better protect children online, ensure trust in the democratic process, and curtail the discrimination of Black Americans and the LGBTQIA+ community. In 2022, following Elon Musk's acquisition of Twitter, Safiya Noble, a professor at the University of California, Los Angeles, and Rashad Robinson, president of Color of Change, made the civil rights case for technology regulation crystal clear: "If you make the internet safe, then you make the system safer for everyone. Big Tech puts Black people, people of color, women, queer and disabled people in more danger than anyone else. We need regulations and stronger digital civil rights that will safeguard the public, rather than debates about which billionaire will own the next communications platform."[36] Increasingly, some variation of this message is being echoed across the political spectrum.

That said, as a result of the country's current political dysfunction, the United States is approaching tech regulation in a manner that is quite different from that of Europe. In Europe, legislative bodies consistently pass new laws to oversee technology companies. But the U.S. Congress is deeply divided, so getting a majority behind legislative proposals is difficult on any topic, let alone a topic as divisive and consequential as technology regulation. Instead, regulatory agencies are beginning to take on a leading role: the Consumer Financial Protection Bureau, the Cybersecurity and Infrastructure Security Agency (CISA), the FTC, the National Telecommunications and Information Administration (NTIA), and the SEC are just some of the agencies that play a core role in the domestic regulation of technology and the tech industry. Regulatory agencies can do so because they are independent bodies that act as extensions of the president or Congress, and their independence at least somewhat insulates them from the ever more complicated American political stalemate.

People like Lina Khan, who chairs the FTC, are working from the view that market abuses are detrimental to both economic competition and the democratic process. The FTC is one of the two main government bodies in the United States responsible for implementing antitrust regulation, as well as protecting consumers from corporate harms. During her confirmation hearing before the Senate, Khan defended the idea that antitrust regulation should "protect our economy and our democracy from unchecked monopoly power."[37] Amazon and Meta worked diligently (but unsuccessfully) to prevent Khan from being appointed to the role, which underscores how determined she is to take on these companies.[38] Since her appointment, Khan has worked to expand the FTC's mandate and address the full range of anticompetitive and predatory behaviors that tech companies have employed. For example, the FTC has filed an antitrust lawsuit against Amazon over its allegedly anticompetitive practices and plans to update its settlement with Meta to bar the company from monetizing teens' data.[39]

The U.S. regulatory agencies, who once took far less initiative on key issues, are increasingly finding their own voice and charting the federal government's course on technology regulation. The question remains, however, whether they have the legal and procedural standing to make good on their enforcement promises, and whether they have the bandwidth to process a sufficient number of cases to make a difference. Republicans, along with tech companies, argue that the FTC and other regulatory agencies are overstepping their congressional mandates.[40] At the same time, the U.S. Supreme Court has reined in the power of federal agencies through decisions like *West Virginia v. EPA*, which holds that when agencies act on questions of major national significance, its actions must be supported by clear congressional authorization. If these regulatory agencies are forced to defer to Congress on rulemaking, they too will fall victim to the doom loop of political dysfunction, which will severely hamper technology regulation.

The Biden White House has tried to create alternative pathways around the lack of consensus in Congress through executive action. Invoking national security arguments, President Biden has adopted a series of executive orders pointed squarely at technology companies. One of those executive orders banned the federal government from using commercial spyware, such as Pegasus (developed by NSO Group).[41] With this order, the United States has effectively cut ties with the private spyware market, which affords it more credibility to condemn the use of spyware elsewhere in the world.[42] The Biden administration has also enhanced cybersecurity with an executive order that advances the implementation of zero-trust network architecture.[43] Finally, Biden penned important executive orders on supply chain security and procurement in 2021 that undoubtedly helped inspire the U.S. CHIPS and Science Act.[44]

Nowhere is America's security-centered approach to tech regulation more pointed than in its focus on China. The United States cannot get its own house in order on domestic tech regulation, but Democrats and Republicans alike have adopted a pro-regulation posture toward challenging Beijing. Leaders from both parties agree that China's advancement in the information and communications technology sector poses an existential threat to America's global technology leadership, both economically and geopolitically. On the supply chain side of the issue, China's domination in 5G, electric vehicles, and semiconductors could leave core American needs dependent on Beijing. Moreover, policymakers have principled critiques of China's approach: the values that underpin the CCP's vision of the Internet—censorship and state control—are fundamentally incompatible with the ideals of an open, democratic internet. Ultimately, the United States sees the most pressing current technology challenges as coming from China, not from American tech companies.

The United States' first—and most explicit—effort to restrain China's digital advance was the 2020 Clean Network Initiative (CNI), which started under the Trump administration. The initiative aimed to banish any Chinese-made technologies from core networks in the United States while convincing other nations to do the same. The initiative first focused on 5G infrastructure but, at the announcement, the undersecretary of state for economic affairs, energy, and the environment, Keith Krach, said that 5G was just a "beachhead" in the broader technological struggle between China and the United States.[45] As Krach hinted, CNI soon expanded beyond 5G and introduced five additional pillars: Clean Apps, Clean Cable, Clean Cloud, Clean Path, and Clean Store.[46] The initiative was wildly successful; in November 2020, Brazil joined the network as its fiftieth member.[47] Although the Biden administration did not formally continue the CNI, it still employs its mechanisms and rhetoric.

Under President Biden, the United States has sought to weaken China's technical capabilities by flexing its export control muscles. In November 2022 the U.S. Department of Commerce's Bureau of Industry and Security implemented a set of export controls that greatly reduced China's ability to operate in the United States with respect to semiconductors.[48] A report from the Center for Strategic and International Studies described the regulations as a "seismic shift" for Chinese industry.[49] Europeans received the move from Washington with mixed feelings. On the one hand, awareness of the risks of overdependence on Chinese technologies is growing in Europe. On the other hand, pressure that the Trump and Biden administrations put on allies such as the Netherlands—home to ASML, a critical provider of lithography technology for producing semiconductors—to join these U.S. measures against China is seen as boosting the economic ambitions of America and is controversial. Weeks after a White House announcement, Dutch trade minister Liesje Schreinemacher made clear that "the Netherlands decides for itself how exports of ASML technologies are restricted," while ASML CEO Peter Wennink claimed U.S. companies benefited unduly from the setback to Dutch suppliers of chip production machines.[50] A month later, the Dutch government bowed to pressure and adopted the restrictions desired by Washington. Few details have been made public about the ins and outs of the deal.[51]

While the United States needs allies to effectively counter Chinese ambitions, European leaders do not want to be pushed around by Washington. When standing with Washington could result in economic losses for their countries, these leaders expect something in return. Many view today's American rhetoric about China as a redux of the Red Scare, while some suspect Washington is unfairly prioritizing American companies while forcing non-American firms to decouple and divest. President Emmanuel Macron of France is one of the most outspoken leaders in Europe, pushing back against getting caught up in a crisis "that is not ours."[52] Indeed, it seems that the potentially far-reaching impacts of a full decoupling are even beginning to scare some in Washington. U.S. Treasury Secretary Janet Yellen warned in 2023 that "we do not seek to 'decouple' our economy from China's. A full separation of our economies would be disastrous for both countries. It would be destabilizing for the rest of the world."[53] Others worry that, in addition to causing such harms, decoupling will backfire, as it will only accelerate China's domestic capabilities, which in the long term strengthen the country's competitive position vis-à-vis the United States. The United States will soon have to decide how far down the "decoupling" path it is willing to go. And, just as important, it will have to see which allies are willing to follow along and which decide to chart their own path.

The litmus test for how American leaders hope to strike this balance will be AI. Eric Schmidt warns that, compared with China, "America is not prepared to defend or compete in the AI era."[54] The United States has recently taken several steps to decouple the ecosystems that are needed to produce AI applications. For instance, it has applied export control measures to several types of advanced microchip production that are needed for AI. The Biden administration has also informed private investors that outbound investments in China in sensitive industries, including AI, will be reviewed by the federal government and potentially barred.[55] These actions have caused investors in the United States, especially technology-focused venture capitalists, to increasingly stay away from China.[56] But whether decoupling for AI is feasible or wise remains hotly debated, especially among national security experts. Even with the recent surge of regulatory action in Washington, the state of U.S. technology regulation remains poor. While federal regulatory agencies have valiantly attempted to fill the vacuum of online rights protections left by a dysfunctional Congress, there is no replacement for the power of legislation. America's legislators have long neglected to intervene in a market gone haywire, and this neglect has rapidly turned from an oversight into an embarrassment. Moreover, national security considerations—and national security considerations alone—have grounded the actions that American policymakers have taken in the technology policy world. Lawmakers clearly understand the national security dimension of tech regulation, as seen in their approach toward China, 5G, and TikTok. Unfortunately, they don't have the same focus on data protection, civil liberties, and consumer protection, let alone avoiding the continuing power grab by companies.

Paradoxically, the EU and the United States are mirror images of each other when it comes to regulating technology. The EU has passed sweeping regulation with an emphasis on civil liberties, but in the absence of a strong industrial base its actions have not led to the development of alternative products with strong EU values baked into them. Meanwhile, the few U.S. rules that do come to fruition are anchored in national security and have global implications. If the two regions combined their approaches, they could offer the best of both to the world: the EU borrowing some geopolitical realism and the United States embracing the need for protecting civil liberties as much as national security. Perhaps the ongoing negotiations on collaboration through the EU-U.S. Trade and Technology Council, a transatlantic discussion body founded in 2021, will help here.[57] Both sides of the Atlantic should prioritize wrestling back agency from the private sector in the interest of strengthening their collective democratic credibility and ability to lead in the world.

China: Building the Surveillance State

If the West has a geopolitical and ideological polar opposite in its approach to the global digital ecosystem, China is it. The CCP is known for its heavy-handed approach to controlling society and the economy, and the technology industry is no exception. Leaders in China have understood the power of technology and, unlike their counterparts in the United States and other democracies, have treated it as an integral tool for wielding political power. CCP leaders have written in internal party journals that they desire to have "the party's ideas always become the strongest voice in cyberspace."

The CCP recognizes that its homegrown technology companies are key to this effort. The same journal article called Alibaba, Baidu, Huawei, and Tencent integral in "push[ing] China's proposition of internet governance toward becoming an international consensus."[58] For these powerful technology companies, the CCP's deep involvement can be both a blessing and a curse: the party has not shied away from reining them in, even if that has come at significant economic cost. The Chinese state's vision for how to integrate technologies in its political doctrine is a global one.

China's rise to tech dominance is a recent story. During the Cold War era, China's economy, which was largely agricultural, was not even close to the technological top tier. After the Cold War, few Western observers imagined how rapidly China would catch up to the West in its technological capacities. By welcoming China into the World Trade Organization, other members hoped that the country would open up and grow into a free market economy.[59] Instead, China not only resisted liberalism and democratization but developed a competing model of tech-savvy authoritarianism. By stealing proprietary company and government secrets—what is called intellectual property theft—Chinese companies were able to catch up and eventually leapfrog over their Western counterparts.[60] Suddenly China was not just a newcomer to the West's institutions but a challenger to Western leadership. Indeed, China's rise has set the scene for a digital sequel to the Cold War. Certainly, there is intense competition between China and the United States—but the issue is much broader. Their competition is a reminder that the Cold War confrontation between state-led authoritarianism and liberal democracy may have never really ended. And in the meantime, technological advances have significantly raised the stakes. A hot war in the near future cannot be ruled out.

China is home to over one billion internet users, as well as some of today's most powerful technology companies.[61] Over the past twenty-five years, autocrats in Beijing have systematically ensured that the country's technological revolution has not supported democratization at home—instead serving as an instrument of the communist system. The CCP has built a system in which censorship, surveillance, and propaganda are essential: troves of data are harvested to train new applications of AI but are also used to repress the Uyghur Muslim minority. The population, significant numbers of whom are imprisoned in "reeducation camps," are used for testing new technologies, such as emotion recognition software.[62] Extreme surveillance registers and controls their everyday movement through a government app they are forced to use. AI is used to track even the most minute changes in people's faces, including in the pores of their skin. Uyghurs are also forced to share their biometric data—namely, DNA samples.[63] Darren Byler of Simon Fraser University has bleakly observed that "Uyghur life is now about generating data."[64]

While China's treatment of the Uyghurs is particularly egregious, all citizens of China have had their rights curtailed due to technology. China uses Safe City technology from Huawei—an unholy trinity of surveillance, AI, and cloud computing—to monitor its urban centers.[65] Regional governments throttle internet speeds to citizens with low social credit scores, a scenario that sounds like the nightmare premise of an episode of the British TV series *Black Mirror*.[66] China employs a cadre of content moderators to monitor and police discourse on Weibo, a domestic social media company, thus causing citizens to use synonyms and clever symbols to communicate.[67] Most recently Beijing has gone beyond censorship and added influence operations. The most popular app in the country, Study the Strong Country (which is also translated, perhaps more accurately, as "Study Xi to Make the Country Strong") inculcates Chinese netizens with Xi Jinping's musings. The government monitors party members' scores on the app to see who is most loyal, which encourages greater use.[68] These examples just scratch the surface. The stark truth is that China has built a sweeping, sophisticated architecture of digital repression. And the system is self-reinforcing: The constant inflow of data from citizens allows the government to build bigger, better, and more invasive tools.

Government leaders in Washington have made a point of criticizing these invasive Chinese technology practices as a further argument for decoupling from Chinese technologies. But while Washington has cheered on decoupling, American technology companies have not always been in lockstep with their government. After all, companies are in search of profits, and China has a billion potential customers. That massive population translates into billions of dollars in potential revenues for enterprising corporations based anywhere in the world. As Michael Jordan once remarked about the value of not making political statements, "Republicans buy sneakers, too."[69] In the same way, companies do not want to cut off a vital revenue source by opposing China unless they absolutely must. Moreover, China serves as a cornerstone in many of these companies' supply chains—most notably Apple's. Although Apple has attempted to shift some of its manufacturing outside of China in recent years, the country still produces over 95 percent of its iPads, iPhones, and Macs as of 2023.[70] Similarly, 95 percent of the rare earth materials relevant for high-tech production come from China.[71] For American companies, alienating China isn't just a bad business decision, it's economic suicide.

Apple offers perhaps the most instructive example of the benefits and drawbacks of operating in China. Twenty years ago, it was one of the first American tech companies to enter China. Today, the company benefits from access to the massive Chinese consumer market and from outsourcing its production to China.[72] But that access has come with painful democratic sacrifices under pressure from the Chinese state. In 2019, during the height of demonstrations against the looming extraditions to China from Hong Kong, Apple removed HKMapLive from its app store. The app was meant to help demonstrators track the movements of the police in real time. Earlier Apple had removed the Quartz news app because it contained "content illegal in China."[73] The company also took down China's most popular Quran app, which millions of Muslims use.[74] Tens of thousands of other apps have been removed on orders from the CCP, including foreign media apps, gay dating services, services that help encrypt data, and apps with information about the Dalai Lama and Tibet.[75] Rebecca MacKinnon, who previously ran CNN's Beijing bureau and serves as the vice president for global advocacy at Wikimedia, has called app stores the "new choke point of free expression."[76] In our connected world, companies have the power to grant or withhold freedom of the press, freedom of expression, and free assembly.

When Apple was pressured to remove apps from its app store, it cited compliance with the law of the land: "These decisions are not always easy, and we may not agree with the laws that shape them. But our priority remains creating the best user experience without violating the rules we are obligated to follow."[77] But in the past, respecting the law of the land for Apple has meant the opposite as the company challenged law enforcement in the United States. For instance, after a mass shooting in San Bernardino, California, Apple refused an FBI request to break the encryption of the iPhone of one of the two suspects, and yet it is now caving to China's demands. This willingness to acquiesce drives home the tight connection between China's power over tech companies and the ability for foreign companies to make money or products in the state. Often the CCP does not have to do much to enforce obedience; just the desire to keep friendly relations with Chinese authorities for the sake of their bottom line has led Apple to comply with its demands.

Apple is far from alone in being willing to make democratic sacrifices in order to seek potential profits. Many tech companies are willing to abide by China's demands. The biggest of these requirements is complying with the required joint venture obligation. The CCP's rules dictate that operating in China requires a partnership with a local company. That partnership ensures the transfer of knowledge and technology so that Chinese companies can use the latest innovation to their own benefit. Moreover, partner companies often have executives that are affiliated with the CCP. As Xi has tightened his grip on the party, CCP-affiliated executives have had to become more political, skipping out on work for lengthy office hours and off-site retreats on Xi's ideology.[78] These executives, who may not add much productivity to the joint venture, make clear that business in China is inherently political and tied to the state. Open-market economies never require joint ventures like this.

Many American online platforms—like Facebook, Google, Twitter, and Wikimedia—are not accessible in China; despite great effort in many cases, they were never able to gain a foothold in China.[79]

For several of the companies, the CCP directly restricts access to their platforms. Google is one of the platforms banned by the CCP. Despite this government-imposed ban, Google has tried to quietly work on a Chinese search engine called Dragonfly.[80] The project never ended up launching, Google executive Karan Bhatia said in a hearing before the U.S. Senate.[81]

The banning of American companies has supported the development of homegrown Chinese platforms, such as WeChat and Weibo, over which the Chinese government has strong control. Regulators carefully restrict their room for maneuvering. Most notably, the Chinese government has been willing to forsake economic gains to maintain its political grip. The most infamous example is the CCP's intervention to prevent the initial public offering of Ant Group, part of business titan Jack Ma's Alibaba retail empire, and a subsequent crackdown on the company. The intervention was allegedly caused by an investigation that found that the offering would financially benefit political families in China who could challenge Xi's leadership.[82] After the intervention, Ma spent time outside of China in the Netherlands, Japan, and Spain and did not speak publicly for almost two years, during which time he instead took up painting and collecting art.[83] Beyond Ant Group, China exercised additional scrutiny on all of its major tech players between 2020 and 2023, a decision that wiped billions of dollars off the value of these companies, as they had to curtail their operations worldwide. While some of that loss may have had to do with anti-China measures taken in Europe and the United States, domestic Chinese policies did not help these "national champions."

More fundamentally, Chinese tech companies are expected to serve the state. This is particularly true in the realm of data flows, another valuable asset for the CCP. China requires that "critical information infrastructure" data and "core/important data" be stored in the country, although both terms are only minimally defined.[84] Keeping a broad set of data solely in China allows the datasets to serve as a resource to power AI innovations and applications. The many ways that the state steers corporate behavior is evident in Made in China 2025, the country's industrial policy that aspires to surpass Western made technologies. The country's official agenda is to become the world's global leader in technology innovation and development by 2049, although it is hoping to—and very well may—reach that title sooner.[85]

As part of China's goal of becoming the world's technological leader, it has prioritized exporting its technology to other countries. When the cash-strapped African Union (AU) needed new offices for its headquarters in Addis Ababa, Ethiopia, China was happy to help. After three years of construction, the building—which is designed to symbolize two hands to underline good Africa-China relations—was opened to much diplomatic fanfare. (The only controversy at the time was a minor protest over the building's location, which was the site of a colonial-era prison.) Six years later, investigative journalists with the French newspaper *Le Monde Afrique* published a bombshell exposé.[86] The gifted building was also full of stealthily operating Chinese-made IT, and the AU's security team noticed something peculiar. At night, while employees were at home and sound asleep, the organization's servers were awake and operating in overdrive; data were transferred from servers in East Africa to those in Shanghai. When confronted with these findings, the chairperson of the AU Commission, Moussa Faki Mahamat, suggested that the claims were false. In 2021 he was reelected. And in 2022 the AU signed a memorandum of understanding with Huawei, the Chinese digital infrastructure giant that *Le Monde* claimed provided the back-doored hardware in the first place. Of course, Chinese authorities have denied all accusations.[87]

China has been laser-focused on Africa. The Chinese tech titans Huawei and ZTE are particularly popular suppliers of network technologies throughout the Global South. Fifty percent of 3G systems used by African telecommunications carriers were built by Huawei, while another 20–30 percent were built by ZTE. Huawei built 70 percent of the continent's 4G networks and, despite the United States' best efforts, is poised to build the vast majority of its 5G networks as well.[88] In 2016 Xi Jinping promised to invest tens of billions of dollars in Africa, and African governments and the African Union are part of China's Belt and Road Initiative.[89]

With the colonial past not a scar but often an open wound, democratic countries and their investments or aid programs are easily dismissed. Yet all of China's investments in Africa, whether the building of the AU headquarters or the mining of rare earth materials, are strategic. There is also significant investment in building relations through offering education opportunities to young leaders. On the African continent alone, China invests in more financing for ICT than all multilateral agencies and leading democracies combined.[90] Kenyan digital rights expert Nanjala Nyabola describes the phenomenon well: "The digital frontier itself is new but the idea of mercantilism—foreign capital going to 'explore' the rest of the world on behalf of power—that is not new. That's why I call it digital colonialism, because it's replicating the contouring of colonization."[91] China provides repressive surveillance technologies to many governments on the African continent, and in return the CCP gains access to rare earth materials and energy resources. Beijing can then count on the support of these governments during key votes in multilateral institutions like the UN.

These efforts are part of an extremely ambitious geopolitical approach. The Digital Silk Road, a key element of the Belt and Road initiative, seeks to roll out digital infrastructure from Angola to Ecuador and from Egypt to Kazakhstan.[92] The massive investments in developing telecommunications, AI, cloud, and mobile payment services also ensure the export of domestic champions such as Huawei and ZTE. China has spent billions of dollars on the Digital Silk Road project since it was announced in 2013.[93] Huawei's same Safe City surveillance technology that is deployed in China's largest cities can be found in Nairobi.[94] When these technologies are used in a context without democratic safeguards, repression or abuse for political reasons often follows. The British intelligence and cybersecurity agency Government Communications Headquarters (GCHQ) has warned that China is in the process of creating "client economies and governments" through manipulating all kinds of technologies ranging from digital currencies to satellite systems.[95] While the Digital Silk Road project is framed as a development initiative, Chinese efforts are increasingly seen as developing China's state capacity to monitor and manipulate: the handling of data flows, supply chains, and services are part of its foreign agenda.

China aimed at "internet sovereignty" long before democratic governments embraced the vision. As one government white paper from as far back as 2010 reads, "Within Chinese territory the Internet is under the jurisdiction of Chinese sovereignty."[96] From products to platforms, rare earth materials to microchips, China is building a digital Great Wall of China that mirrors its ancient brick border defenses. The export of the Chinese model to tech regulation is objectionable, both on principle and in practice. First, the widespread deployment of surveillance technologies abroad will almost certainly result in more human rights violations, more unlawful arrests, and more repression. Second, the digital Great Wall will radically upend the international order. China's client governments will continue to grow closer to Beijing, economically and politically, and adopt its foreign policy positions. These countries may choose to reduce their trade with the West or favor the yuan over the dollar as the default currency. At the end of the day, this is about more than surveillance cameras or mines of critical minerals. China's digital strategy is at the vanguard of larger shifts in global geopolitics that threaten the liberal democratic order.

India: Innovating Regulation in a Declining Democracy

Many foreign policy experts frowned when the Biden administration included India on the guest list for the second Summit for Democracy, a grand and glistening conference for democratic countries around the world hosted in Washington, DC. As much as the democratic world would love to count India as an ally, the country is undergoing serious democratic backsliding. Technology has played a significant and growing role in India's repression of its citizens.

Take one example. For several days, twenty-seven million people in the Indian state of Punjab were cut off from the internet in the spring of 2023.[97] The reason was not a monsoon nor any other natural disaster, which sometimes take the country's digital infrastructure offline. This shutdown was manmade in order to "prevent any incitement to violence and any disturbance of peace and public order."[98] In other words, the government shut down the region's digital infrastructure in order to control the beliefs and actions of Indian citizens. This shutdown was just one of several that the Indian government has implemented over the past few years. In fact, there were eighty-four shutdowns in 2022.[99] India is now one of the world leaders in cutting off its citizens from the internet, and critics rightly worry that the shutdowns fit a broader trend of repression in the country.[100]

These repressive measures come at a most unfortunate moment— not only for people in India experiencing the shrinking of freedoms but also for the chances of counting on India to be an ally or collaborator for other governments seeking to govern technologies based on democratic principles. As the *Financial Times* editorial board has remarked, "The west sees India as a democratic and economic counterweight to China. But disillusionment with Xi Jinping has prompted western leaders to turn a lamentably blind eye to [prime minister Narendra] Modi's actions."[101] However, even the most powerful wishful thinking cannot brush over the worrying decline in freedoms in India, including the adoption of laws impacting the use of technology and people's rights.

In 2010 the Unique Identification Authority of India launched Aadhaar, an initially voluntary biometric system, that aimed to ease access to welfare systems, such as those for pensions, subsidies, and taxes.[102] Once Indian citizens provided their fingerprints and iris scans, they received a confidential twelve-digit number that would serve as an individual identifier, similar to a Social Security number for Americans. As was hoped for with Kenya's election system, India believed that advanced technology like a biometric identification system could streamline some of its bureaucratic inefficiencies.

At first it seemed like the system would work. The new identification numbers helped many citizens, and especially rural residents, access new government services and participate in the economy. Shortly thereafter the problems began. The use of the numbers expanded and went from being voluntary to quasi-mandatory. Worse, the technology proved unreliable: people were denied hospital care because they couldn't prove their identities, while others were refused wages or welfare payments.[103] More fundamentally, the system is a cybersecurity nightmare: a centralized system of biometric data for hundreds of millions of citizens is a hacker's dream. As a result, hackers sharpened their focus on the system, leading to several data breaches.[104]

Aadhaar's many red flags have not deterred Indian officials, who are intent on expanding the system. In 2022 the Election Commission proposed linking Aadhaar with voter registration databases. By 2024, the government could require voters to have an Aadhaar number to confirm their ballots.[105] If this were to come to pass, the decision would be a failure on many levels. Combining the faulty Aadhaar database with other election rolls could accidentally exclude voters. Moreover, a mandatory biometric data system is a violation of civil rights because voters will have to choose between submitting their biometric data and potential disenfranchisement at the polls. And, in a truly worst-case scenario, a leader who does not respect democratic norms could use Aadhaar to identify and target the political opposition. Even with all of its flaws, Aadhaar is expanding, not contracting. India now exports "digital identity solutions" to other parts of the world thanks to collaborations with the UN and the World Bank.

In India, Aadhaar now serves as the foundation of the so-called India Stack, the elaborate set of government-created technologies rapidly pushing India into the digital world. The Modi government has created a series of "digital public goods" on which companies can offer services.[106] This protocol-forward model for digital governance is a new approach to tech regulation, unlike that of China, the EU, or the United States. As the *Financial Times* has reported, "Supporters argue that India has found a world-beating solution for building out and regulating the online commons that is more equitable than the US's laissez-faire approach, more innovative than the EU's regulation-heavy model and more transparent than China's totalitarian template."[107] Some tech leaders, like Satya Nadella, the Indian-born CEO of Microsoft, have praised the policy, impressed by the government's digital fluency.[108] Many experts expect that other developing nations will look to India's tech regulation paradigm for inspiration.

But civil society activists are concerned. In a country with an urban-rural divide that matches the digital divide, challenges of equity and empowerment are significant. Women often lack internet access and have fewer opportunities than men.[109] And even though the government has been collecting extraordinary amounts of data, India's parliament only recently passed the Digital Personal Data Protection Act, which is controversial for the access it provides law enforcement.[110] These issues are not top of mind for the designers of the India Stack. "The importance of privacy and security is very much an afterthought, rather than something that's built into these projects," explains Udbhav Tiwari, head of global product policy at the Mozilla Foundation, a nonprofit whose goal is to ensure the internet remains a force for good.[111] Nevertheless, countries ranging from the Philippines to Morocco have already begun importing India's government-created technologies like Aadhaar.[112]

Amid the full-frontal rush into the digital world built on the India Stack, the Modi government has embraced aggressive content moderation. In some cases, it may be more appropriately described as censorship. Twitter was ordered to shut down the accounts of Modi critics, and YouTube was pushed to block clips of a BBC documentary highlighting Modi's role in anti-Muslim violence in 2002.[113] According to Twitter founder Jack Dorsey, the Modi government also threatened to shut down Twitter and conduct raids on the company's employees if the platform failed to take down posts about the country's farmer protests in 2021.[114] As in China, the companies complied. Modi's power over the digital realm is partly a result of the political aftermath of the Mumbai terrorist attacks in 2008, during which time the country's main law overseeing online crime, the Information Technology Act of 2000, was made far stricter. Similar to what happened in Europe and the United States after 9/11, counterterrorism measures restricted civil liberties and expanded the mandate of the government to censor and monitor. For instance, every company in India is now required to have a contact person responsible for receiving government orders to block content—or else face prison time.[115] In 2019, India became among the first countries to ban TikTok. The government cited concerns for the well-being of children, but the 2020 border conflict with China was the real reason for the ban.[116]

Unsurprisingly, U.S. technology companies are profiting from digitization in India. In fact, they see India as a make-or-break market for their future ambitions. According to a survey conducted in 2020, Indians make 24 percent of their online payments on Amazon Pay or Google Pay.[117] Foreign companies also have active stakes in Indian internet service providers. British company Vodafone's Indian subsidiary is the third largest in the country, including for the cell phone market.[118] Facebook bought a 9.9 percent stake in Reliance Jio, the largest mobile service provider, while Google bought a 7.7 percent stake in its mother company Jio Platforms.[119] Google later also invested in Bharti Airtel, a multibillion-dollar Indian telecommunications company.[120]

But operating in India means abiding by the government's often strict dictates. One of the most far reaching is an amendment to the IT law that forbids online platforms from allowing the posting, hosting, or sharing of "misleading information" about the government.[121] YouTube complied with 1.2 million government takedown requests in the first quarter of 2022 alone, the highest number of any country in the world.[122] The company continues to struggle with the contradiction between its promise to protect free speech and its legal obligation to comply with orders from the Indian government.[123] Despite all the challenges in India, the U.S. tech giants have kept their eye on the ball: a growing market. Google even has a special term for the country and other critical developing countries: "next billion users."[124]

Over the past decade, India has steadily taken a more assertive approach to using technology to control its citizens' lives, whether that involves digitizing and tracking their identities or monitoring their speech. Even though the country has fostered an innovative culture of digitization quite different from other world leaders, India should not be mistaken for a friendly climate to digital citizens. Digitization does not necessarily mean freedom. While the West seeks to bring India on board as part of its digital coalition opposed to China's repressive approach to technology, the world's democracies should not sacrifice their core values and egalitarian principles in the process. Ultimately, compromising on democratic values will play right into the outstretched hands of autocrats.

The Need for Leadership

Lawmakers around the world are wrestling with the role of technology in their respective political systems. Each is approaching the challenge from a unique vantage point built on the goals of its leaders, its history of freedom or oppression, and its philosophy for how involved the government should be in regulating private industry. Together, the four populous and powerful blocs covered in this chapter have provided distinct and often conflicting regulatory models that are closely followed or copied around the world.

The EU has been the globe's most ambitious tech regulator. Based on a firm democratic starting position, it has adopted several laws that have served as (imperfect) blueprints for the rest of the democratic world. And yet, despite these European laws, U.S. technology companies still dominate the European market, and growing concerns about dependence on China for network infrastructure have not been quelled. Similarly, the EU's technology-specific laws—to deal with content moderation, end roaming charges, or improve cybersecurity—have not tackled the systemic threat to democratic governance posed by the outsize power of technology companies. In the coming years, the EU will hopefully wake up to this problem hiding in plain sight.

In the United States, lawmakers approach technology solely through the lens of national security. Concerns about the rise of China spark rare moments of bipartisan collaboration in America's highly polarized political environment. While Congress focuses on new measures aimed at tackling technology risks from the outside, it largely continues to ignore domestic challenges to democracy. Independent regulatory agencies and the executive branch have been left to try to invent workarounds that do not require legislative authorization. As a result, U.S. tech companies continue to amass more power over technologies, and this has a deep societal impact.

On the opposite side of the world, China has mastered a repressive approach to internet governance. Beijing leverages advanced technologies to censor, control, and surveil. China's ever-growing market power has forced some U.S. tech companies to balance on a tightrope, as they cannot afford to lose total access to the country's valuable billion-person market. While the U.S. government increasingly recognizes China as a threat—and has taken action to decouple—U.S.-based tech companies and allies in other parts of the world are continuing to cooperate with CCP commands. There are few signs that this will soon change.

As the United States attempts to organize a coalition against China, India will play a critical role, but India is itself an imperfect partner for a democratic approach to technology oversight. Under the Modi government, India has embraced accelerated digitization while eroding democracy. It has prioritized efficiency and control over civil rights and protections. The West must carefully engage India and ensure that bringing the country into its internet coalition will not contradict its democratic vision for the digital world.

By examining four leading digital powers, this chapter has aimed to provide a general lay of the global land. Yet significant numbers of people are not covered by these four countries or approaches. Their lived experiences with technologies, the specific contexts, from Bengali start-ups to internet cafés in Johannesburg, deserve more attention. So much so that it could fill another book. Moreover, the 189 or so governments that lie outside of this group of four are grappling with profound questions about technology governance and democracy. Many fledgling democracies are leaning into strict internet controls. Tunisia, for instance, has passed a fake news law that will restrict a wide swath of speech.[125] Countries throughout Central Asia and Eastern Asia continue to acquire surveillance equipment from Chinese companies eager to expand the Digital Silk Road farther west.[126] Nevertheless, many of the world's democracies, from Palau to Poland, have affirmed the importance of a free, open internet through the Declaration for the Future of the Internet (DFI).[127] While the four digital powers of this chapter occupy much of our attention, and rightfully so, many of the countries that will play a decisive role in internet governance over the next forty or fifty years are still emerging.

The world over, technology has become a critical pillar in the high-stakes game of modern geopolitics—and democracies are losing. Digitization has empowered authoritarian regimes, while democratic societies misguidedly continue to trust that free markets will lead to free societies. The United States has led this wave with its combined geopolitical, military, and technological power, and its hands-off approach to regulation. U.S.-based tech companies operating in China and India have failed to act in line with democratic principles, and the United States is losing credibility as its intelligence community seeks exceptions to rule-of-law mechanisms to gather insights or to fight crime. Instead, the United States has followed the interests of industry, which pays lip service to democratic causes when convenient, and otherwise caves to authoritarian pressures. These companies choose market access over speaking out for human rights or democratic principles. This trend away from democracy is likely to grow, with markets rising in the nondemocratic countries and companies optimizing for sales first and foremost.

This battle between democratic and autocratic visions of digital society will only heighten in the coming years. Advances in AI are generating novel threats and risks to democracy, with a new worrying possibility arising seemingly every week. And by deploying sophisticated tools that allow for better control over their populations, authoritarian states are quickly reversing the few gains made by civil society and their populations in the past few decades. As these challenges grow, our tool kit of solutions needs to grow as well. Chapter 8 will walk through several proposals that would solve many of the problems outlined in this book. Some of these proposals represent minor adjustments, while others would constitute dramatic changes from the status quo. But right now, no update is too small or too large. Democracies need a dramatic overhaul of their approach to technology, and no legitimate proposal should be left off the negotiation table. The stakes are high. If we aren't successful, the digital world will soon look much more authoritarian.

8

Prioritizing the Public

When the European Commission set out to propose a comprehensive AI law in 2021, it reasoned that focusing on the effects of AI applications, instead of the technology itself, would allow for the best match with existing policies and enforcement mechanisms. The exact minutiae of machine learning models constantly change, but the broad domains that AI impacts—the economy, health care, and the online information ecosystem—are far more enduring. In a 2023 *Euronews* interview, European Commissioner Thierry Breton clarified that this law did not intend to merely regulate AI but rather "to organise our digital space."[1] The AI law would be systemic, not hyperspecific. To enact their vision, lawmakers adopted an approach frequently used in product liability, which regulates everything from vehicles to pharmaceuticals. The landmark law that was adopted in March 2024 identifies the level of risk associated with various AI applications and offers mitigating measures based on this classification—just as the European Drug Agency and the U.S. FDA distinguish controlled substances from less addictive medications.

Low-risk applications, according to the law, include use cases like spam filters. These applications are well-trodden: email providers and social media platforms have long relied on machine learning tools to collect spam and clean up comment sections. They are also relatively benign, as a malfunctioning bot may result in a few more scammy emails or cringeworthy comments, but nothing catastrophic. The medium-risk category includes customer service chatbots and other applications where people should be made aware that they are dealing with an AI-driven system. Overall, the impact on people's lives and livelihoods, even if a chatbot were to veer off course, are considered minimal. Nevertheless, the stakes here are a bit higher: the AI customer service agent might fail to refund a customer, which would result in financial loss for the shopper or liability for the company using the bot. High-risk AI applications are those that involve decisions with significant impacts on a person's life, such as automated systems that determine whether someone is given access to education or social welfare support, or, in the case of recidivism algorithms, whether they are granted parole or remain incarcerated. And at the top of the classification spectrum is unacceptable risk, which applies to a limited category of AI applications, including real-time facial recognition systems, models relying on subliminal or deceptive techniques such as dark patterns, and social credit systems like those in China that use AI applications as a means of behavior control. These use cases could deeply impact people's rights and freedoms, and thus are not allowed.[2]

Midway through the lawmaking process, however, this framework confronted a major challenge: generative AI burst into the public domain. Text, sound, and images generated by algorithms became ubiquitous and difficult to detect. A synthetic picture of Pope Francis in an expensive Balenciaga white puffer jacket suddenly surged online in March 2023.[3] The image was conceptually and aesthetically absurd. Would an eighty-six-year-old religious leader really sport a designer down jacket worth thousands of dollars? But the quality of the generated image was so high that internet-savvy users, and even those who specialize in tech, were fooled by the Midjourney software's creation. Reporting later revealed that a construction worker, high on mushrooms, prompted the image.[4] The computer-generated image of Pope Francis was not itself a crisis—

and some might even say the jacket was a great look for the pontiff. Yet the incident made clear the capabilities and thus risks of deception thanks to this new software.

What if a more shrewd user of generative AI had prompted an image of a nuclear missile test in North Korea or an Amber Alert? For every hundred users generating photos of papal couture, there's a malign user who will seek political or economic gains using this latest innovation. Indeed, only months later, this exact phenomenon occurred when an image of smoke coming out of the Pentagon caught fire on Twitter (figuratively, of course).[5] Before the U.S. Department of Defense could debunk the photo, the online confusion had material consequences, causing a brief dip across major stock market indexes.[6] And when the war between Hamas and Israel broke out in October 2023, both sides were accused of sharing AI-generated images to influence the information sphere, causing both doubt and plausible deniability around the real-life horrors people were facing.[7] We are only seeing the first wave of such synthetic media. What if the Pentagon image was of better quality or timed for higher Twitter engagement? How much worse could the panic have gotten? And what will years of being exposed to deceptive, computer-generated content do to people's overall sense of trust in news reports? We know the deep trauma that nonconsensual, sexually explicit content has caused, for example, when shared online.

In response to widespread concerns about generative AI's threats to democracy and consumer trust, EU lawmakers wanted to make sure that the AI law they were drafting was not outdated before it went into force. Prior to the advent of generative AI, they had set out to regulate the equivalent of, let's say, the Ford Model T—a first-generation technology. Seemingly overnight, they now had to draft standards for the autonomous Tesla—a far more advanced and alarming successor. To be fair, many tech wonks would refute the notion that generative AI popped up overnight; for example, highly realistic deep fakes were a major point of concern for analysts in the run-up to the 2020 U.S. presidential election.[8] Unfortunately, generative AI was both disorienting for lawmakers and highly disruptive to their initial risk-based framework. Generative AI technologies—which run the gamut of image generation and chatbots to coding assistants—did not fit neatly in a specific risk category. In many ways, it is a new type of AI more than it is a new application. To remedy this, members of the European Parliament wrote "foundation models" into the law, which ignited a heated political debate about how foundation models should be classified—and whether they should be regulated at all.[9] AI is fundamentally challenging the analog frameworks of policymaking in Brussels and beyond.

The evolution of the AI Act reveals one of the major difficulties of technology regulation. While the revised law will address generative AI, it is certain that the next iteration of AI, or another emerging technology, is unlikely to be explicitly referenced in even the newest laws. Policy usually reacts to changing realities that need correcting. Meeting that challenge is greater when dealing with deeply impactful, rapidly evolving technologies. The perpetual cat-and-mouse game between tech companies and lawmakers affords the companies the opportunity to entrench their positions, wealth, and lobbying power. Meanwhile, new harms go unaddressed.

At the start of this chapter, I wrote that EU lawmakers were taking a systemic approach to AI regulation. That's true, albeit with a major caveat. Laws such as the AI Act—like virtually all of the tech regulations that precede it—do little to tackle the rapid accumulation of excessive wealth, data, and computing power in the hands of tech companies. These laws, no matter how well intentioned, do not address the fundamental market dynamics and the systemic liabilities that create tech giants and enable these giants to openly defy regulations. They also do not do nearly enough to rein in the freewheeling activities of thousands of smaller companies whose products and services are fundamentally weakening democratic systems or overstepping into government's critical role of serving the public without being accountable. These glaring oversights must be fixed. It is time to take on tech regulation differently. But to do that, lawmakers must fundamentally change how they approach the task of governing.

Renovating Democracy's House

Policymakers the world over work around the clock to improve health care, increase the availability of housing, end poverty, and ensure good education. Schedules are overwhelming, and existing lawmaking structures can be limiting. When I served as a member of the European Parliament, a combination of time constraints and the force of "the way things are always done" often prevented me from stepping back and truly thinking creatively. Yet, the digital revolution has been so disruptive that many known and tested solutions in the policy toolbox no longer fit the problems at hand. We need to create space to imagine new, effective ways to repair our world rather than confine ourselves to thinking about answers within the limits of existing proposals and structures. The automatic instinct to limit the solutions space, be it to ideas that are inexpensive, logistically light, or palatable to the delicate political majorities, is wrongheaded. You can't come up with out-of-the-box ideas when you've already backed yourself into a corner of that very box.

Even as more and more technology-specific legislation becomes law across the world, too few of these rules and regulations directly address the outsize power of private companies vis-à-vis public institutions and democratically mandated and accountable officials. Don't get me wrong: functioning antitrust laws, resilient cybersecurity mechanisms, proper data protection regulations, and reliable financial services oversight are all essential. They are foundations of the rule of law and a rules-based society. And often the downstream effects of these specific measures may well make for a stronger democracy, such as when personal data can no longer be used for targeted political advertisements or the protection of election technologies is robust.

However, new technologies go to market every day. By focusing laws on specific technologies, we are regulating yesterday's problems today, while tomorrow's impacts are on the horizon. There is a growing urgency to fortify democratic governance from the influence of technology companies while also making democratic institutions more sustainable. Key steps must aim directly and decisively at the underregulated power of companies in governing technology—to make sure elected and accountable representatives retain preeminence. In the words of Shoshana Zuboff, we must ensure "the digital lives in democracy's house."[10] Democracy should be the framework within which technologies are developed and used. Currently, companies rush ahead into unregulated domains, setting standards and norms through their products, challenging democracy. We have seen how governments outsource critical infrastructure, elections technology, and basic functions like law enforcement to private firms. For democracy to survive, it is essential to reverse this power imbalance. What follows in this chapter are new concepts and practical solutions to achieve just that. The initiatives proposed prioritize the public interest, cut irresponsible dependencies, and vow to reverse the tech coup—tech companies' takeover of governance, politics, and policy—which I have discussed throughout this book.

Before diving into these proposals, I should note that I have not allowed myself to be discouraged by the question: Is this feasible in today's political landscape? If I did, this would be the last page of this book. Very little can pass today's U.S. Congress, for example, but partisan impasse is not a sufficient reason to stop envisioning a better world. This book has underscored that there are fundamental problems embedded in our technology infrastructure that touch on everything from civil liberties to national security. We need courage and creativity to face these challenges head-on, even when they seem insurmountably difficult to solve. Political change, especially in the context of digital disruption, requires imagination.

We have reached an important and peculiar moment: a growing number of leaders have the political will to change the status quo. They know that digital technologies are creating not only opportunities but also unprecedented challenges. They realize that something needs to be done in order to govern these challenges. But there is not yet a clear sense of what actionable steps can be taken to achieve the ultimate goal that is as pressing as it is important—reinforcing our democracy so that it is resilient against ever-improving, constantly expanding, rapidly changing digital technologies. Piecemeal approaches or nonbinding agreements will take too long and leave us unprepared for future developments. Hopefully, the solutions offered here will help spark new visions, form new coalitions of those willing to save democratic principles, and strengthen the political will to implement the necessary reforms. While I can't guarantee that these solutions would prevent every single one of the many problems outlined in this book, they would, at the very least, make a good start.

Some of the suggestions are broad and have horizontal impact across multiple sectors, such as strengthening access to information and developing accountability mechanisms. Others are more targeted vertical proposals that are nevertheless vital for preserving democracy. Some will involve institutional reform, which may be hard to imagine in the current political climate. All are aimed at empowering the rule of law, citizens, and the governments that represent them. For lawmakers, it is time to stop treating the digital realm as the exception, where rules to ensure public safety, public health, and the public interest are not seen as equally important as those that govern physical infrastructure, consumer products, or financial services. The capture of democratic government, governance, and principles can and must be stopped.

The Precautionary Principle

As new applications of AI come to market, experts quarrel about the most urgent risks associated with them. Are AI risks existential and on a future horizon, or should the emphasis be on the harms we know of today? A 2023 letter signed by the leaders of the most prominent AI companies warns that AI could spell the end of humanity.[11] Others point to more immediate problems, such as the fact that AI systems discriminate and hallucinate results.[12] (That is a polite way of saying they come up with false answers.) While experts differ about the levels of risk to prioritize, there is no doubt that this new wave of AI applications amplifies the generation of believable fake news, continues to discriminate, exacerbates complex cybersecurity threats, and hinders transparent oversight—not sometime in the future, but in the here and now. Companies have pushed AI systems into the market that have not been independently assessed for compliance with existing law nor meaningfully studied to inform new regulations. There may be disagreement about the extent of harm anticipated, but few dispute that these systems will give rise to new problems. How much better would it be to prevent those from arising in the first place rather than sanctioning companies once the damage is already done?

In some cases, problems caused by the use of technologies may be genuinely unforeseen and unanticipated. For instance, few would have been able to predict that chips from household appliances, such as toasters and washing machines, would be repurposed for use in Iranian-made drones flying over Ukraine.[13] Yet, in other cases, harms are predictable and result from an anticipated or obvious use of the technology. Spyware, for instance, is tailor-made to violate privacy and snoop on people's intimate information. Technologies that are designed to undermine democratic principles directly and aggressively should be heavily controlled or even restricted. Technologies that nullify the right to privacy, the right to self-determination, or the freedom of press have no place in democratic societies, and governments should not shy away from rigorously banning the use and sale of such products.

Fortunately, in thinking about the appropriate principles to guide these regulations, governments need not begin from scratch. AI and other emerging technologies are not the first innovations to spark discussion about risk, safe transition from research to market, and avoiding spillover effects. Genetically modified organisms (GMOs)—agricultural crops whose genetic material has been technologically manipulated—have raised several similar concerns. For instance, certain varieties of corn, the largest crop grown in the United States, have been modified to resist pesticides. This is good for the farmer, who will have less waste of spoiled corn when spraying against weeds. But what about the larger ecosystem? Could these alterations negatively affect other crops or insect populations, or might genetically modified plants uncontrollably spread and replace nonmodified crops, harming biodiversity? By ensuring that there is sufficient time to research the potential harms before such inno-vations are let go into the wild, the likelihood that other crops or people's health will be negatively impacted or that ecosystems will be irreparably damaged can be significantly reduced.

The EU invokes a mechanism called the precautionary princi-ple in cases where an innovation, such as GMOs, has not yet been sufficiently researched for potential harms. According to article 191 of the Treaty of the European Union, if a given policy or action might cause harm to the public or the environment and if there is no scientific agreement on the issue yet, the policy or action in question should not be carried out.[14] The precautionary principle requires us to grasp the consequences of a risk before taking it. To be clear, the process is dynamic. Inventors have the right to conduct more research. If scientific consensus emerges or new evidence suggests a lower risk level, the innovation can proceed to market. This principle does not ban risk, it merely ensures that we have a parachute—or an understanding of what lies at the bottom—before we take a plunge.

Often the harms of new technologies are not immediately clear. Their impacts are yet to be discovered. The existential risk of AI has been endlessly discussed in many rationalist and technical circles, yet experts still cannot agree on the probability of catastrophe or on the timeline. In 2023 the *Economist* polled both technical experts and superforecasters (professional predictors who derive prob-abilities using economic methods). The superforecasters projected a 2 percent chance of an AI catastrophe by 2100; the experts put the odds at 20 percent, an order of magnitude more likely.[15] While experts continue to debate the issue, tech companies rush to shorten the time between innovation, research, and market, and to push out new products as soon as they can. This problem is compounded by the fact that tech companies conduct most of their research in-house, with the aim of driving growth, instead of allowing independent assessments that could reveal the social impacts of their inventions. Just as we're skeptical toward medical studies conducted by phar-maceutical companies, we shouldn't embrace the confident assess-ments of researchers who are on the company payroll.

Across the industry, companies have displayed little compunction about moving forward with products despite clear warning signs. For instance, the launch of ChatGPT and its integration into the Bing search engine were accelerated despite concerns of "unhinged behavior" from the bot.[16] Alex Karp of Palantir has explicitly argued that concerns about new technologies should not get in the way of their rollout: "We must not, however, shy away from building sharp tools for fear they may be turned against us."[17] We are currently witnessing the combined effects of blind excitement and cutthroat competition. Despite the fact that AI applications can exacerbate disinformation, erode trust, hurt civil liberties and challenge intellectual property rights, companies such as OpenAI are more interested in beating their competitors to the finish line than being responsible for preventing harm to society. Meanwhile, AI companies based in China operate in a sphere without democratic values, meaning their definition of harm to society is vastly different from our own. Think back to the precautionary principle. We don't have sufficient data or understanding to determine the long-range harms of some AI applications. Even the companies that seek to act responsibly may still be slowly unleashing harmful technologies. The need for precaution is not a one-company rule; it's a requirement that spans the whole domain of an AI application. We ought to build broad-based rules that center on risk reduction in service of society, not corporate power.

Innovation should not trump democratic principles, yet we see all kinds of new technologies rolled out in the wild without any guardrails. Instead of allowing companies to decide how much risk is appropriate for society to take, and when to release a new product, a precautionary principle should be the norm. Elected officials and publicly mandated institutions should determine how much risk is appropriate for society to take, not unelected CEOs and technologists. The precautionary principle provides a more feasible solution to resolving today's lawless technology space than other recent proposals. For instance, a letter by AI experts proposed a moratorium on the development of LLMs such as GPT-4.[18] But such a pause during a cutthroat commercial race is entirely unrealistic; it didn't happen. Even the corporate leaders who warn that AI could spell the end of humanity are not halting their own companies' production. Applying the precautionary principle to emerging technologies will do a more sustainable job of assessing and managing risk. It creates an ongoing mechanism to mitigate risk and harm to society by building in time to learn and discover. Some refer to clinical trials in medicine as a helpful analogy.[19]

An independent board of experts should assess which technologies should fall under the precautionary principle, and companies should be required to (confidentially) identify products that they plan to bring to market but do not have a sufficient research base. They should also open up the lessons from their own risk and safety testing. The precautionary principle should stipulate that academic researchers must be given access to developing technologies for the purpose of such independent assessments. Ongoing multidisciplinary research is vital for the public interest, but currently academics lack access to the needed data of AI systems, as well as to other proprietary technologies that are critical to their studies. Governments must increase research funding levels in the relevant areas of inquiry to ensure that researchers have sufficient access to compute (i.e., computational power) and data, the technical horsepower behind AI models, which is essential to properly study generative AI. That knowledge in turn will build the evidence base for more solid policy decisions.

The gist of the precautionary principle pushes back against the Silicon Valley mantra of "permissionless innovation," according to which companies decide on innovation without considerations of spillover effects.[20] Rather than "moving fast and breaking things," the principle tries to prevent things from breaking. The pace of AI development as a systemic technology, combined with stark expert warnings and a lack of independent research, merits resorting to greater precaution, or, to put it bluntly, greater responsibility.

Curb Antidemocratic Technologies and Practices

There are some technologies and practices for which the verdict is already in. There is no need to exercise the precautionary principle and collect more data on their potential harms because the harms are pervasive and well known. Democratic governments have a responsibility to curb four of these technologies and practices—commercial spyware, data brokerage, facial recognition technology, and cryptocurrencies—for the sake of their citizens and their democracies.

SPYWARE

Commercial spyware, such as NSO Group's Pegasus systems, should not be sold to the highest bidder. Yes, the EU has rules to control the export of hacking and intrusion systems to known human rights violating regimes. And indeed, as discussed in chapter 7, the United States has newly banned the use of commercial spyware by the federal government with an executive order. Unquestionably, these are steps in the right direction, but the laws still leave too much room for the proliferation of intelligence grade systems. For example, current U.S. rules won't prevent a business mogul in the United States from buying off-the-shelf spyware to go after a competitor or an ex-spouse. The new rules have also done little to clarify why America's top law enforcement agency, the FBI, purchased the Pegasus tool in 2021.[21] Is its use also discontinued? Similarly, the EU's focus on exports has not hindered the Greek, Hungarian, Polish, and Spanish governments from procuring hacking systems and going after critics, including journalists, judges, and opposition leaders.[22] In other words, while exports may be prohibited, imports have been left untouched. It is therefore imperative to deal a fatal blow to the growing, multibillion-dollar market of spyware vendors and for democratic governments to lead by example, as they are themselves procuring spyware. A good start would be for the EU to follow the American example by banning the use of commercial spyware by governmental agencies. And if the United States would join the EU in adopting strict export controls of spyware and intrusion systems, an international norm would begin to emerge.

Even if governments claim they buy these intrusive technologies with the narrow aim of going after terror suspects, their purchases bolster an industry that does not only serve counterterrorism purposes.

The proliferation of these technologies—that is, their uncontrolled spread beyond the official buyers and intended use cases—poses a significant risk to national security. American diplomats and soldiers, for example, have become targets while serving overseas.[23] Similarly, even French president Emmanuel Macron's phone number, along with those of other heads of state, was found on a target list uncovered in the Pegasus Project.[24] No democracy should use these spyware systems, and democratic leaders should be in a position to credibly condemn and call out authoritarian regimes for doing so.

DATA BROKERS

In June 2022, in *Dobbs v. Jackson Women's Health Organization*, the U.S. Supreme Court overturned the previous landmark case, *Roe v. Wade*. The ruling made it legal for individual states to ban abortion, which is now the case in over a dozen of them.[25] In this new legal landscape, a novel digital threat emerged: casually collected location data could end up revealing that someone visited an abortion clinic. When we surf, pay, or chat, we are subconsciously leaving digital footprints, and it may be hard to imagine how innocent web surfing or online searching could become a hammer in the hands of law enforcement. Yet the post-*Roe* reality provides a stark example: search history and other digital evidence have already been used to prosecute women for seeking to terminate their unwanted pregnancies. (Google, appalled by such use of metadata it collects, now automatically deletes the location data when people visit abortion clinics.[26])

Partly in response to these prosecutions, a group of U.S. senators has proposed a bill to ban the sale of location and health data. The bill is unlikely to be adopted, given Congress's political stalemate. Still, the focus on health and location data raises an important question: Shouldn't selling most personal data be banned since even seemingly unrelated data can reveal important information? After all, web surfing, payment, and purchase data can reveal information—such as who is visiting dating platforms, porn websites, or an Alcoholics Anonymous website—that can be just as intrusive. As Senator

Elizabeth Warren of Massachusetts has warned, "Data brokers profit from the location data of millions of people, posing serious risks to Americans everywhere by selling their most private information."[27] That worry holds true for many different kinds of data, especially when they are combined.

Brokers collect, buy, and sell data that encompass nearly every aspect of our lives, including income, profession, homeownership, political preference, location, age, education, purchases, and websites visited. The profiles of us that exist are then used for commercial purposes. But we live in an era when data have also become a valuable tool in the cultural and political crusades. Users attempt to silence their political opponents via doxing—the public release of personally identifiable information, such as one's address or phone number. It's not unthinkable that an enterprising data brokerage could sell users' data to aspiring doxers, which could result in dangerous incidents of stalking and swatting. The *Dobbs* decision has raised the awareness of data brokers with respect to abortion, but the rot runs deep in the whole industry and there is no reason to let this market further metastasize. It is a problematic thing for online services to collect huge swaths of information from the users on their own platforms. In most cases, these platforms keep the data all for themselves and leverage it for one specific use case: ad personalization. It is, however, an unacceptable matter to sell these data to a broad swath of actors—neutral, nefarious, and extremely nefarious—who can then combine them with other aggregated datasets and use them for seemingly any reason. The brokerage of data makes so-called safeguards like "notice and consent," the nondescript notifications that you get when you enroll in an online service and opt in to data collection, null and void. What's more is that it can create risks for people, particularly those in vulnerable communities. As data are the new resource that tech companies hoard for the purpose of training AI, guardrails are even more urgent. The California Delete Act allows for people to opt out of the use of their personal data by brokers.[28] While that is a positive step, it puts responsibility in the hand of the individual. To truly cripple the industry, data brokerage should be outlawed.

FACIAL RECOGNITION SYSTEMS

If the collection of data based on our online behavior is sufficiently sensitive to merit significant regulation, then the collection of bio- metric data presents an even more straightforward case. Iris scans, voice recognition, fingerprints, and DNA matching are all offered by for-profit companies. Recall how Worldcoin, the pet project of OpenAI CEO Sam Altman, requires users to scan their eyeballs with Orwellian-looking orbs. The company seeks to recruit people in poor communities around the world to upload their iris scans in exchange for cryptocurrency.[29] The verification of people's identities and collection of biometric information is so sensitive that compa- nies handling it should be strongly regulated. Such regulations would prevent companies like Clearview AI from scraping the entire inter- net to build a facial recognition system. Severe restrictions on facial recognition systems for use in real time in public spaces, such as shopping malls and sports stadiums, will be encoded in law through the EU's AI Act.

I am not advocating for the complete removal of facial recogni- tion cameras. Governments have a legitimate need to verify people's identities before permitting them to pass through customs or get IDs and driver's licenses, which are special situations in which private companies are working on behalf of governments. Automated iden- tity verification is a necessary evil. But when governments engage companies to outsource services for border controls or law enforce- ment, the use of personal data must be limited through clear legal provisions. That means straightforward data protection and reten- tion criteria, as well as absolute limitations on the use of biomet- ric data. For instance, under no conditions should a company be allowed to train its future commercial products with data collected in the name of the state. Putting the government case aside, we can- not allow facial recognition to become a Wild West, and we most certainly cannot allow companies like Clearview to keep behaving like outlaws, collecting copious amounts of data and repurposing them with absolute disregard for the law. Instead of banning facial recognition altogether, we ought to sevcrely shrink the commercial use cases and data policies that allowed firms like Clearview to emerge. And when commercial facial recognition firms stray from the guardrails, they ought to be banned.

CRYPTOCURRENCIES

Adjacent to the precautionary principle lives a group of technologies where the benefits are murky, but the risks are crystal clear. Cryptocurrencies are the poster child of this cohort. Cryptocurrency advocates claim that their coins can transcend the chaos and crashes of the conventional market. Yet, cryptocurrencies have brought nothing but economic fallout since they emerged into the mainstream. In the fall of 2023, JPMorgan UK banned cryptocurrency transactions because their customers repeatedly fell prey to scams.[30] As discussed earlier in the book, cryptocurrencies have also become the go-to asset for criminal enterprises, rogue states, and terrorist organizations. What a group of winners. Cryptocurrencies did not coincidentally emerge as the chief vehicle for malfeasance. Scammers of all stripes recognize—and leverage—the anonymity, transparency, and poor oversight of cryptocurrencies. The potential for harm is quite literally embedded in the technology.

More fundamentally, cryptocurrencies undermine financial stability. The deceptive label of "currencies" cannot hide the fact that these products are highly speculative and volatile. Cryptocurrency enthusiasts claim the technology is required to fix the broken financial system. I will not argue that the traditional global financial system works wonderfully; regulatory failures, especially in the run-up to the 2008–2009 recession have clearly underscored the need for reform. Cryptocurrencies, however, will do nothing but raise the risk of collapse. The International Monetary Fund came to virtually the same conclusion at the end of 2023, stating in a position paper that cryptocurrencies "could undermine the effectiveness of monetary policy, circumvent capital flow management measures, exacerbate fiscal risks, divert resources available for financing the real economy, and threaten global financial stability."[31] The positive use cases simply have not emerged to justify or counterbalance cryptocurrencies' destructive potential. Johan Van Overtveldt, the former minister of finance for Belgium and currently a member of the European Parliament, was right when he said that cryptocurrencies are "speculative poison" with "no economic or social added value. If a government bans drugs, it should also ban cryptos."[32]

To date, democratic governments have taken piecemeal approaches to regulating cryptocurrencies. For instance, the SEC has investigated Binance and Coinbase, but those inquiries have come only after significant losses were incurred by ordinary people. In November 2023, Changpeng Zhao, Binance's mysterious founder, stepped down after pleading guilty to federal charges over sanctions violations.[33] The founders of the trading platform FTX were charged—and in some cases convicted—of perpetrating a billion-dollar fraud, but these charges have come only after customers have been swindled out of billions of dollars. Ironically, democratic governments' lack of action lies in stark relief to China, which effectively banned cryptocurrencies in 2021.[34] Throughout this book, I have advocated for democracies to reclaim their governing responsibilities from tech giants. Banning cryptocurrencies if they are not minted by licensed organizations is key to taking back the reins over financial oversight.

To avoid confusion, certainly those offering highly speculative products should not be able to self-label them as "currencies." This means that legitimate financial institutions that are subject to the oversight rules on financial services are free to offer digital currencies, when pegged against fiat currencies, or central banks can offer a digital version of their currency if they so wish. But it would prevent the dangers of just any random company deciding to offer an investment product under the label "currencies." That insanity should end.

Transparency as a Pillar of the Public Interest

The lack of transparency into the ways companies govern technologies is a systemic problem of the tech industry. I have discussed many situations where this lack of transparency leads to negative consequences: how tech giants bid on licenses for gigantic data centers while hiding behind foundations with nondescript names; how synthetic media is increasingly difficult to distinguish from text, image, video, and audio generated or created authentically by people; and how proprietary software that is used on a massive scale, including by government officials storing and sharing sensitive data, turns out to be penetrable by hackers. To solve these problems we have to plant the seed of transparency into the tech ecosystem to cultivate openness so that those seeds can offer an effective counterweight to the opaque status quo.

IDENTIFY ARTIFICIAL INTELLIGENCE

Spreading disinformation has become a lot easier and more scalable thanks to generative AI tools that are accessible to anyone. For instance, fabricated videos of Ukrainian president Volodymyr Zelenskyy allegedly surrendering in the fight against Russia spread online as the country continues to defend its sovereignty.[35] The possible harms caused by disinformation are already too familiar. During the COVID-19 pandemic, disinformation about health care led many individuals to avoid lifesaving vaccines. And, in the wake of recent election cycles, we can no longer be naive about the way in which lies can erode trust in democracy. Keep in mind that it is not only the generation of disinformation that is a problem but also the plausible deniability: an unfavorable piece of news pops up, and it is easy to dismiss as AI-generated and fake. As Ben Read of cybersecurity company Mandiant reminds us, with misinformation, "you can build uncertainty, confusion, and distrust. It doesn't need to stand up to a close reading to have some effect on the population; it erodes trust in all messages."[36] That is one reason why disinformation is such a potent political tool for the adversaries of democracy: you do not have to convince people every time, as long as doubt strategically creeps in to erode trust in institutions, from news media to elections.

To help people distinguish synthetic from authentic media, the use of AI should be identified as such: when a customer service chat function is powered by a virtual assistant, the customer should know. Or when AI is used to assemble a news item, to produce an illustration, or to promote a sale, it should be marked. Think of the Federal Communications Commission rules that require radio and television broadcast networks to disclose their sponsorships—we acknowledge that users have a right to know which content is organic and which is bought and paid for.[37] A similarly recognizable marker or label should identify AI when it is used. The government should also benefit from the development of emerging technical solutions, such as watermarking, which can help ease the detection of synthetic AI-generated media. Adding identifiers to content that would allow people to trace the origin would, for instance, help ensure that a quote is indeed attributable to a given speaker such as a world leader. Indeed, some experts have suggested an opposite approach: marking authentic content as real instead of AI-generated content as synthetic. As long as users can easily tell the difference between the two, either solution could work.

The United States is on the precipice of establishing guardrails for automated identification. The Biden administration's October 2023 Executive Order on Artificial Intelligence includes a provision on researching the detection and possible labeling of synthetic content.[38] In addition, the Federal Elections Commission, a body that oversees the administration of U.S. elections, initiated a process in August 2023 to require disclosures in political advertisements that use AI-generated content.[39] Representative Yvette Clarke of New York has introduced bills in two separate sessions of Congress that would require deepfake watermarking and establish real consequences for individuals who maliciously manufacture deepfakes.[40] As the political and bureaucratic wheels slowly turn, private companies have a real opportunity to lead the way on identification. Several platforms have introduced alerts to warn users of AI-generated content, but they should more aggressively moderate these fabricated posts and establish stronger disciplinary processes for the use of inappropriate synthetic content.[41] Additionally, the very business models of targeted advertisement, data-driven information curation or surveillance capitalism, remain vital for any kind of deepfake or piece of synthetic media to reach audiences. It is in these companies' best interest to monitor AI-generated content for the noble cause of truth and the more pragmatic cause of brand safety.

TRANSPARENCY OF INVESTMENTS AND BIDS

Since he acquired Twitter in 2022, Elon Musk has attracted a ceaseless stream of press attention—both critical and complimentary. Musk certainly loves the limelight: in the summer of 2023 he changed Twitter's name to X and planted a gigantic glowing sign of the letter on top of the company's headquarters.[42] Despite all of the buzz surrounding X and Musk, journalists have paid little attention to the second largest investor in the platform: Prince Alwaleed Bin Talal of Saudi Arabia, who leads the Kingdom Holding Company.[43] This is remarkable backing from the state fund of a repressive country that restricts freedom of expression, and one that should raise significant concerns in a company and country that purport to champion free speech.

In 2014 and 2015, Saudi spies were caught infiltrating the company as employees, with the aim of accessing the personal data of dissidents who had accounts on the platform.[44] Given this earlier behavior, David Kaye, former UN special rapporteur on freedom of expression, has noted that he thinks "it's worth asking questions about what Saudi investment means for the security of Saudi dissidents and debate around Saudi issues. Will requests for actions against users be filtered through Alwaleed? Requests for user data or for the promotion of some networks?"[45] And Musk is far from alone in courting investments from the Saudi government. The nation's blatant human rights violations have not discouraged a number of Silicon Valley venture capitalists and tech companies from taking Saudi investments. Though some, like the venture capital giant Andreessen Horowitz, would have preferred to be circumspect about it.[46]

Covert investments stand in the way of transparency for consumers and oversight by public authorities. They should stop. Those who fund the production of AI and other new technologies should make themselves known. That means venture capital and investment companies cannot hide the sources of money used to build and scale companies. The origin of funding becomes particularly sensitive, even raising issues of national security, when sovereign wealth funds of nondemocratic states are pumping money into companies with significant impact on democratic societies.

Transparency should also be a requirement when tech companies bid on land to develop data centers, as was the case for Meta and Microsoft in the Dutch lowlands, as dissected in chapter 2. Tech giants should not be allowed to operate through shell foundations or lobby vehicles. At the end of the day, Meta—not Project Uncle Sam or whatever other pseudopatriotic name it uses in its lobbying—will profit from the project. Facebook should have to articulate the benefits and risks under its own name.

Similarly, the state should require the publication of the environmental impacts of the development and use of new technologies, whether it is resource use for data centers or rare earth materials for cell phone production. Making sure that bids are transparent and include critical information about the environmental footprint will help foster a well-informed debate about whether or not a certain permit or investment is desirable.

THE PUBLIC ACCOUNTABILITY EXTENSION

In 2019 Dutch journalist Huib Modderkolk submitted a freedom of information request to the national police. He wanted to know whether it used NSO Group's Pegasus software. Despite a court order urging the police to grant Modderkolk's request and a threat of a fine, the request was met with silence. The matter should have been straightforward; legally, the government is not permitted to use software bought from companies that also sell to dubious regimes.[47] After three years, an answer finally came: the police denied the request. Modderkolk later uncovered that the Dutch intelligence service, Algemene Inlichtingen- en Veiligheidsdienst, indeed used NSO's Pegasus software to go after a heavyweight crime suspect. When NSO Group is asked about its clients, it always cites nondisclosure agreements.[48] This type of secrecy goes against the right to freedom of information. As more government functions—from running social welfare databases to communications systems—are outsourced to businesses, governments must not evade public scrutiny by hiding behind private companies. Only in exceptional cases might total secrecy be merited. But currently the balance between secrecy and transparency is off, and outsourcing plays a big role. Strengthening democratic principles also means strengthening the scrutiny of democratic leaders and institutions.

Typically, official government communications and the accounts of meetings are part of the public record. That way, journalists can request access to such materials through a freedom of information request. But when officials communicate via WhatsApp or other online message platforms, confusion emerges about the status of these messages for the public record. The *New York Times* has gone as far as suing European Commission president Ursula von der Leyen for access to the messages she exchanged with Pfizer CEO Albert Bourla during the COVID-19 pandemic.[49] Longtime prime minister Mark Rutte of the Netherlands, as well as his health minister, Hugo de Jonge, have deleted messages from their phones that were thus "not available" when parliament or journalists asked for access. As more and more communication happens digitally over commercial messaging services, security and accountability are sacrificed. Especially now that messaging apps offer automatic deletion, rules need to ensure that the spirit of the law is not circumvented by technological shortcuts.

The use of technology by governments is often promoted as a path to better or more efficient service delivery. Take, for example, this quote from an executive order that President Biden signed in 2021: "We must use technology to modernize Government and implement services that are simple to use, accessible, equitable, protective, transparent, and responsive for all people of the United States."[50] In practice, this "modernization" means more outsourcing to tech companies. But why not imagine better service delivery without greater dependencies? Why not invest in public digital infrastructure?

The trust and agency that democratic representatives gain through elections are lost through wholesale outsourcing. Companies perform tasks in the name of the state, and with the authority of the state. According to the Organisation for Economic Co-operation and Development (OECD), "On average, governments spent 8.8%

of GDP on outsourced expenditure in 2019. Of this, 65% was spent contracting non-government economic actors to provide goods and services used directly by the government (e.g., government IT systems)."[51] Too often, outsourcing of services leads to the forgoing of accountability.

Frontex, the controversial border control agency of the EU, shows how the outsourcing of tasks can lead to outsourcing of scrutiny. When the Bureau of Investigative Journalism submitted a freedom of information request asking for information on the engagement of technology companies to manage migration data, the agency replied, "Frontex has identified a total of 28 documents. However, access to 27 of those must be refused . . . as their disclosure would undermine the protection of commercial interests of legal persons."[52] Clearly, the taxpayer-funded agency should not be in the business of protecting "commercial interests" but instead should be accountable in the public interest.

The principle behind what I'm calling the *public accountability extension* is simple: any law that applies to governmental organizations to maintain transparency and accountability should be applied equally to technology companies that execute tasks on behalf of the government. Technology and digital systems procured by governments must be subject to the same oversight that governments themselves would be. This includes, for instance, freedom of information requests, nondiscrimination protection, and a democratic mandate to engage in (digital) war. When technology solutions are paid for by the public, they should be publicly accessible; with public money must come public code. The goal of the public accountability extension is to make sure outsourcing and dependence does not mean an end to accountability.

Public accountability and transparency will likely require reforms to trade secrecy protections. Today companies can easily hide behind intellectual property protections when trying to avoid scrutiny of their products. These protections are meant to shield their inner workings and designs from potential competitors. Increasingly, however, the effect of trade secrecy protections has not been limited to the legitimate confidentiality of corporate details. Instead, intellectual property protections have become a blanket excuse to shield any corporate information from the public eye. That is an unacceptable situation preventing access to information for all kinds of reasons.

Exceptions to trade secrecy protection are needed to gain a better understanding of how technologies work. This understanding will help a whole host of stakeholders: academics, journalists, parliamentarians, and regulators. Meaningful access to the powerful processes designed and operated by companies is a sine qua non, or vital condition, for many other steps to allow for democratic governance of technologies.

Additionally, to achieve transparency, we can borrow from existing solutions, as many critical industries are already required to regularly publish numbers and reports. For instance, health institutions are required to report information to the public, including information about their prices.[53] Similarly, public companies in the United States must file quarterly and annual financial reports to the SEC.[54]

Transparency is a precondition for journalists, parliamentarians, and members of civil society organizations to do their work. But beyond a legalistic look at transparency, the additional aim of increasing transparency is to allow for the development of greater societal knowledge about AI and other emerging technologies. In order to have a well-informed public debate about AI policy, the public must be able to learn about AI; to ensure this, companies should be required to log datasets, algorithms, safety failures, and unintended outcomes, and researchers and regulators should be able to access these records. Similar to how the EU's Digital Services Act stipulates that academics must be granted access to data of social media companies, independent research on AI should be facilitated. Instead of a seller being required to know their customer, this requirement allows consumers to *know the product* and *know the investor*.

Lead by Example

Acting in line with the spirit of transparency laws is one way in which democratic governments should lead by example. But there are many more—from the way public resources are spent, to how wayward government vendors are held to account, to ensuring the needed expertise on technologies supports policymaking and enforcement. Setting the right standard through its actions will give governments leverage beyond the use of legislative and enforcement tools.

LEVERAGE PURCHASING POWER

In addition to regulating, governments possess another important power that they can leverage to reform tech companies: funding. Governments in advanced democratic countries are the most important buyers of software. The U.S. federal government is, in fact, the largest buyer of IT products in the world.[55] To give some sense of the spending, over the past five years, Microsoft earned over $1.65 billion from the U.S. Department of Defense alone. Google brought in roughly the same in defense contracts, $1.68 billion. Amazon topped the charts with a mind-boggling $1.85 billion.[56] Other departments altogether spend small fortunes of their own with these companies, amounting to a steady stream of revenue.

Despite these gargantuan taxpayer-funded invoices, governments are not fully leveraging their purchasing power. Intuitively, firms cater to their biggest customers to maintain their business. Profit is the fuel that private firms run on, and because of their voluminous buying, governments are like the gas for their engines. Democratic governments should use this spending to foster technologies they would like to see. I've seen firsthand as a lawmaker that firms do not put stated ideals into practice unless there is money on the line. Governments have a unique opportunity to lead by example as buyers of technologies, using their purchasing and investment power deliberately, to shape markets. Similarly, the government should demand accountability when vendors fail to deliver. After all, their own credibility is on the line, and thus, so is trust in democracy.

Governments typically impose some cybersecurity standards in the procurement process, hoping that such standards will prevent major hacks. Many of these standards are ready to be updated. Zero trust, a cyber architecture that safeguards against hacks by assuming that every user and access request poses a security risk, and privacy by design, a systems-engineering approach that centers privacy and data protection, can be earmarked through public spending. CISA, for example, has collaborated with foreign governments to develop privacy-by-design principles that guide software manufacturers to ship safer products. CISA's work is key, but it can have an even greater reach. The federal government should eventually translate this voluntary framework into discrete requirements for software contracts. Similarly, government contract specifications and grant program instructions can set rules for making digital infrastructure more public and transparent. Public procurement authorities should jointly set transparency criteria for software purchases and strategically work together when investing and regulating. The desired outcomes for society, beginning with the preconditions to govern technologies in line with democratic laws and norms, should guide procurement and policy alike. A longer-term strategy is needed to phase out existing commercial contracts, and to develop IT and software solutions with a stronger public mission. In the meantime, the quality of public tender processes needs to be dramatically improved.

By coming together to create collective procurement contracts, public institutions can guard against corporate capture and being locked into suffocating commercial contracts. Alone, any university, hospital, school, transportation company, or museum can hardly make a fist when negotiating a new contract with a tech company. The power of industry, when it supplies public-sector customers that are almost completely dependent on commercial technologies, is enormous. Individual organizations each face similar challenges for which governmental support is needed. Local governments especially need support in writing tenders with criteria that serve the public interest, ensure security of governmental systems, and allow for accountability.

By putting forward procurement requirements that actually center values like transparency and security, public institutions will fortify their negotiation position vis-à-vis large tech companies. These contracts should also advance the possibilities of transparency, accountability, and oversight. Criteria should clarify, for instance, responsibilities of companies toward cybersecurity, such as the updating of software in the public interest. Beyond security, governments should leverage procurement to advance their broader societal vision. They should ensure transparency of the CO_2 footprint of technologies and how they are offset. Contracts should require reporting on the use of natural resources according to one measuring standard. In the United States, the Biden administration has implemented the Build America, Buy America Act, which requires all materials for public infrastructure projects to come from America, a major investment in domestic industry (often to the chagrin of trading partners).[57] Similarly situated countries can institute ethical sourcing requirements, depriving companies that sell spyware of their business even for nonspyware products. By setting criteria and rewarding those abiding by best practices, the government can incentivize companies to step away from behavior that harms people, the environment, or cybersecurity. To be clear, though, governments cannot just prescribe "rules for thee and not for me." They ought to go public with the details of their own procurements; there should be no more shielding of whether the police are working with NSO Group or whether the health department relies on Palantir to crunch data. Transparency is a two-way street.

When tech companies fail to comply with regulations, these failures should be publicly recorded and sanctions should follow. To take an example from the financial services sector, when an accountant is found to be negligent or acts with harmful intent, regulators can ban them from bidding on contracts. After Ernst & Young, one of the world's largest accounting firms, failed to detect fraud by its customer Wirecard, the German regulator banned the firm from taking on new clients listed on the stock exchange for auditing services.[58] The same stick should be available when technology companies are negligent in protecting software sold to governments, critical infrastructure operators, or public institutions. One possibility would be a blacklisting mechanism: if tech companies fail to deliver, act deceitfully, and/or neglect to comply with accountability or security requirements, they ought to be held accountable or trigger a regulatory consequence.

Take the case of Microsoft, a prolific winner of government contracts despite its colorful history of data breaches and security mishaps. In 2023 Microsoft managed the email accounts of senior American leaders—including Commerce Secretary Gina Raimondo, the U.S. ambassador to China, and the director of cybersecurity at the NSA—when they were hacked by Chinese entities in an act of espionage.[59] Senator Ron Wyden has publicly slammed the company, concluding that Microsoft has proven itself unqualified to secure sensitive official accounts. "Holding Microsoft responsible for the negligence will require a whole-of-government effort," the senator wrote in a scathing letter, in which he pointed to a number of areas where Microsoft had been negligent and, in some cases, even failed to follow its own security protocols.[60] With clear mechanisms for accountability in place, such letters would not need to be written after major incidents to ensure that large software vendors apply the proper requirements.

CREATE TECHNOLOGICAL EXPERT SERVICES

When I was writing the EU law on export controls for spyware, I turned to the experts at the legal service of the European Parliament for their crucial judgment and advice. Sharing my work with them always felt a bit like handing in my homework, and I was curious about how much of the red pen I would see in my draft. I was well aware that, drawing on their legal expertise, they would add critical suggestions to make sure the law realized in practice what I intended. Parliaments typically have such teams of independent legal experts available, as most members are not trained in law. Without expert scrutiny, many proposals that parliamentarians dream up would never survive their first legal challenge.

The European Parliament also has the European Parliament's Research Service, comparable to the Congressional Research Service in the United States. Both offer in-depth as well as ad hoc studies to help inform representatives. The United States additionally has the Congressional Budget Office, which provides lawmakers with nonpartisan and impartial advice and counsel on the budgetary implications of a given legislative proposal.

In this spirit, the creation of a technological expert service should bring independent technological expertise into the legislative process. After all, elected officials cannot all be expected to be experts in the detailed working of technologies. And yet, from agriculture to environmental issues and from intellectual property rights to national security, nearly every domain in which they legislate will have a technology angle. Whereas a legal service advises on the viability of policy proposals, a technological expert service would do the same for technologically complex questions so that laws are informed by independent experts. This will lead to better laws and reduce the influence of PR operations. Currently, an elected official's lack of knowledge is too easily filled in by the cleverly framed talking points of corporate lobbyists. Moreover, technical details, when they are not adequately anchored in law, can be used to circumvent the spirit of the law.

Building technological expert services in legislatures will also have an important side effect: it would help develop a public-service pipeline of tech talent. To guard against the service turning into a "revolving door" between government and industry, and to ensure the service isn't covertly influenced by experts that represent one corporate interest or another, there would need to be certain safeguards put in place, but many already exist in ethics rules for federal government employment. Federal ethics rules prescribe a "cooling-off period" during which employees cannot work on matters related to their former employers. Similarly, government employees in the United States are frequently constrained from advising on matters that impact companies in which they have significant investments. These rules, along with strictures governing how employees can interact with lobbyists and other third parties, will loosen the stranglehold that Big Tech has on policy and regulation.

In the United States, investing in the capabilities of the technology advisers of NTIA may well be sufficient. NTIA already offers technical assistance to a wide range of stakeholders, including potential grantees seeking funding for broadband deployment and legislators who want to write bills that regulate America's radio spectrum supply. With the right congressional authority, they could scale this advisory further. An alternative solution would be to revive the

Office of Technology Assessment, which originally opened in 1972 and gave members objective advice and information about science and technology. Then, in 1995, the Republican-led House of Representatives led a charge to discontinue its funding, calling it wasteful.[61] Another tactical option would be to elevate and expand the U.S. Digital Service, a cross-governmental technological consultant for federal agencies modeled after the United Kingdom's Digital Service. Governments should be more competitive with companies in hiring talent and should ensure there are clear channels and structures to connect these experts to policymakers and administrators. In the EU, the technological expert service could be developed by boosting the European Parliamentary Technology Assessment Network and bringing it in-house, as well as from the Science and Technology Options Assessment. Both are existing bodies, but their budgets, mandates, and capabilities should be updated to focus on emerging technologies.

Building Accountability Mechanisms

Cyberattacks, data breaches, espionage efforts, and hacks are in the news daily, yet the times when the suspects are caught and tried can be counted on one hand. It is high time to close the accountability gap. The impunity with which crippling crimes and attacks are waged today only ensures that we will have more attackers tomorrow.

IDENTIFY SYSTEMICALLY IMPORTANT TECHNOLOGY INSTITUTIONS

The largest financial institutions in the world, such as Bank of America, Citigroup, and JPMorgan Chase, are labeled as systemically important financial institutions.[62] In effect, this designation means that they are considered "too big to fail." Because of their integration with the global financial system, and after the painful lessons of the banking crisis of 2008–2009, these largest banks are required to meet additional requirements, such as higher liquidity holdings and additional transparency.

A similar label and requirement should be used for the largest tech companies, such as Amazon, Google, Meta, and Microsoft. These companies would then be subject to heightened regulatory scrutiny, including audits of recommendation algorithms' outputs, privacy rules, and security measures, just to name a few. These audits would help contain systemic spillovers, and they would make clear that with great power comes great responsibility. The EU has already pioneered this approach under the Digital Services Act by designating seventeen online platforms as *very large online platforms* and two search engines as *very large online search engines*, a list that is updated on a rolling basis.[63] The act rightly recognizes that these platforms have special responsibilities—and special risks—given their size and centrality. Countries should continue to set higher bars for these companies with respect to security and transparency.

ARBITRATION COURT FOR CYBER INCIDENTS

With knowledge about cyberattacks in the hands of cybersecurity companies, and attribution politically sensitive, it is essential that trusted, credible, and independent processes exist to ensure fact finding and accountability around cyberattacks. We can get some idea of how an arbitration process involving both companies and states would work from the arbitration that happens in the context of trade agreements. Investor–state dispute settlement (ISDS) mechanisms already mediate between governmental and private actors in the context of trade disputes, and this model can serve as a basis for developing a cyberdispute settlement mechanism. Either a country or a company can bring evidence to the court, which will then investigate and make a ruling about who is responsible for the attack. The independent and impartial nature of the court and the justices (other than in the case of ISDS) will give all parties involved greater confidence in the determination, and it can also help build trust despite geopolitical tensions between nations.

In addition to empowering independent courts, countries also need to develop a definition of and standards for the defense of a cross-border public sphere, one that better matches the borderless nature of digital services and infrastructure. Developing this concept would help update the application of international law, from the laws of armed conflict to humanitarian law. But it would also improve security agreements between countries. The security of undersea data cables comes to mind, as well as the regulation of satellites in near-earth orbit. Both these technologies operate in open spaces that theoretically belong to "everyone," when in practice they belong to a handful of companies. The consequences of security breaches, environmental disasters, or captures in times of conflict are significant for the provision of vital services. It is therefore high time that governments agree on rules of behavior and questions around responsibility.

JOINT DEMOCRATIC FORCES

For technology policies as well as accountability mechanisms to scale, like-minded countries must collaborate. No single democracy can serve as a sufficient counterweight to either the tech giants or to authoritarian governments, but a global coalition has enough strength to tip the scales. A coalitional approach to digital governance requires three things: mission, collaboration, and enforcement. In chapter 7 I referenced the Declaration for the Future of the Internet (DFI), a 2022 document that over sixty governments have endorsed. The DFI establishes guiding principles for global internet governance on topics ranging from trust in the global ecosystem to inclusive access to the internet. Its preamble lays out a mission quite succinctly: "We call for a new Declaration for the Future of the Internet that includes all partners who actively support a future for the Internet that is an open, free, global, interoperable, reliable, and secure."[64] The DFI reflects the ambition of governments to ensure that the internet is governed by certain core principles. The declaration is not binding, so it is up to each of the signatories to follow through on their commitments. Additionally, like many treaties, the document gives civil society groups something to rally around (beyond the ideal of a "democratic internet"), and which they can use to pressure governments. Another initiative underway is the work of the

United Nations Advisory Body on Artificial Intelligence.[65] Ideally, the UN will ensure global governance of AI serves the public interest and happens on the foundations of respect for international law and universal human rights.

The next step in global coalitional governance is finding a space to convene and coordinate on tech issues. Most recently, the world's advanced economies have taken initial steps toward coordinated technology policy. At the May 2023 G7 Summit in Japan, leaders recognized that governance has not kept pace with technological developments and resolved to collaborate on AI governance standards, children's online safety, and data privacy.[66] To meet the moment of AI breakthroughs, a new process was announced to assess ways to better collaborate internationally. The Hiroshima Process, which brings to mind a reference to the place that was devastatingly struck by an atomic bomb, seeks to prevent disinformation exacerbated by AI from undermining trust in democracy. Work to coordinate interoperability and shared standards will also be put forward.[67] As a first step, the G7 adopted a code of conduct for the development, deployment, and use of AI.[68]

Real coordination among the G7 countries would have a transformative impact on digital governance. But there are problems with both who's included and excluded in the current G7. China is unlikely to reverse course on its censorship and surveillance strategy. Moreover, the G7 and G20 are not representative bodies; they almost entirely exclude the Global South. Relying too heavily on advanced economies to drive technology governance will perpetuate the same inequity that has allowed digital authoritarianism to fester. The Hiroshima Process should open the door to include the voices of emerging powers along with established ones.

There has been a lot of talk about establishing a new multilateral organization that allows both developed and developing countries to collaborate. The UN's Internet Governance Forum, a multistakeholder forum that convenes annually, could be spun into a more formal institution that has mandates over both internet and AI policy. Doing so would require a shift in focus from process to result. Alternatively, democratic governments could look outside the established international systems like the G20, OECD, and UN. The DFI could serve as the founding document for an explicitly democracy-focused global internet policy group. Prospective members would have to demonstrate their commitment to DFI principles on the national level before being admitted. Most important, the United States would have to show willingness to curb the power of its domestic tech giants. This organization would likely start small, including only a few dozen countries, but there is always a trade-off between ideological consistency and overinclusion. A large internet policy group would have to make compromising concessions on internet freedom to appease its authoritarian-leaning members. A smaller group ensures that the members' values would be genuinely aligned.

When an organization does emerge, countries cannot let it become a League of Nations. This institution needs real enforcement power. UN secretary-general António Guterres has suggested inputting tech risk monitoring into the mission of a new agency that mirrors the International Atomic Energy Agency, seemingly forgetting that such an agency would have to enforce or oversee the shared commitments that countries have agreed to. This proposal seems unworkable, as at present, there is little agreement between democratic and nondemocratic countries. Any new technology governance coalition must commit members to leveraging coordinated sanctions in the wake of a destructive cyberattack or digital human rights abuse. Finally, these countries must align in the legal realm, coordinating an international nonproliferation agreement for digital arms and drafting similar domestic legal penalties for cyberterrorists and criminals. Targeted cooperation will place pressure on countries in the out-group, eventually persuading certain authoritarian-leaning governments to adopt certain elements of the democratic digital agenda. The international community's response to the war in Ukraine shows that meaningful cooperation is still possible. It is high time to see a similar drive to protect the democratic values that are at stake in the digital sphere.

Reinvigorate the Digital Public Sphere

When the rector of the University of Amsterdam, Karen Maex, gave her annual speech to open the academic year in 2021, she highlighted the risk to academic freedom from technology companies' outsize power in the academic world: "Like the 'market masters' of old times, today's platform companies decide who gets access to information, guide interactions between users and convert those interactions into data. This impinges on academic sovereignty and goes well beyond the 'publishing function' originally vested in a large number of firms."[69] Many universities, as well as other public institutions, struggle with lock-in contracts with technology companies. Their monopolistic behavior makes their customers perpetually more dependent.[70] For universities, core technologies—such as cloud computing, storing, and accessing research data, as well as learning tools and publications—all should be in service of their public role. These public institutions should stay in control of how data are used and when access to research is shared. Commercial motives should not interfere with this mission.

As part of antitrust and competition cases, the notion of "market power" or "monopoly power" describes the dominance of a specific company in a given market. Once it is established that a company has achieved such a position, that in and of itself is often a reason for regulatory intervention. To solve the overdependence of public institutions (governments, schools, libraries, and hospitals) on private companies, a new notion should be introduced: *significant public power*. This idea is meant to create a standard to measure public institutions' possible overdependence on commercial technology, which must be avoided.

One example of such significant public power can be seen in cloud computing. The three top cloud providers make up over 60 percent of the market.[71] Because of the very nature of cloud computing—far-flung critical services running through highly centralized, privately owned infrastructure—this type of consolidation is a potentially serious national security risk. Creating a new category of national and international security risk for centralized cloud computing companies that exercise significant public power—and imposing additional rules on such companies—is important for ensuring that the public sector takes back some oversight. But there are also proactive, public alternatives that must be developed.

We can take inspiration from a growing number of high-potential grassroots initiatives. Those should be empowered to build a "public stack."

BUILDING A PUBLIC STACK

As a newly elected member of theEuropcan Parliament, I was invited to the Personal Democracy Forum in New York City in 2011. The conference was the first to put the political impact of technology front and center. As Andrew Rasiej, its founder, notes, "The biggest change in the debate has been that people in politics are finally recognizing that technology is having a huge impact on democracy and the relationship between citizens and their governments."[72] I was one of them, and the impact was undeniable. Individuals, whether as founders of Wikileaks or as citizen journalists, were taking on the powers that be. Monopolies of power, information and politics were being challenged, and technology was proving that it could emancipate.

At the Personal Democracy Forum, people who saw technology as a way to empower the unheard or as a vehicle for greater inclusion in governance joined together. This spirit of the community of builders of a civic internet or of civic technologies is needed now more than ever before, and their initiatives continue to give hope and inspiration. A growing number of civic tech initiatives want to reclaim, redesign, and open up the digital public sphere, and we should not underestimate how much can be done by such groups to democratically build, protect, and govern technologies in the public interest.

New_Public, a U.S.-based NGO, invites people to "join us in building an evolving design framework to move us beyond the necessary critiques of our current online spaces and start thinking like digital urban planners about the spaces we want to inhabit in the future."[73] Relatedly, the Dutch internet pioneer Marleen Stikker has a vision for building a "public stack." She wants to replace the commercial, closed, and top-down layers of the tech stack, which we looked at in chapter 2, with public-values-based layers. A public stack is designed to strengthen public values in the digital domain as an explicit counterweight to the outsize power of companies. The public interest serves as a guiding principle for innovation, and the design processes are participatory and inclusive.[74]

Ethan Zuckerman runs the Initiative for Digital Public Infrastructure, which "advocates for approaches to digital infrastructures that treat platforms and supporting technologies as public spaces and public goods, not purely as profit-making ventures."[75] Public Spaces is trying to do just that by leveraging the impact of a coalition of Dutch public organizations from media, education, culture, and local governments; it wants to build an "alternative digital ecosystem based on public values."[76] One benefit of building such an alternative ecosystem is that it will both foster tech talent and provide talented tech workers with greater options to serve the public. Without the proper skills in-house, understanding, policymaking, oversight, and accountability will be impossible. To equip regulators to better enforce and assess risk in new technologies, qualified public servants are needed.

To ensure that there is such a thing as the digital commons, these commons must be redefined. Without clarity, the gradual and systematic privatization will continue. The state can unlock more growth and innovation *without* unduly empowering a few commercial players and by prioritizing collective access. In part, this is a matter of redirecting state funding away from private players and toward public infrastructure. Resources are available: the Dutch government alone spends about 80 billion euros a year on procuring technologies, on behalf of seventeen million people, less than the population of the state of New York.[77] Imagine what that money could do if it were dedicated to building out public digital infrastructure. There are also a variety of functions that the state alone can perform, and a variety of measures it can undertake to improve the functioning of markets, from protecting public knowledge infrastructure to building public digital infrastructure such as research clouds. Similarly, innovative open-data projects can enable citizens and groups to create new public services or oversee and spend public resources based on public data.

TURN THE REGULATION-ENFORCEMENT MODEL UPSIDE DOWN

At the moment, the relationship between laws that regulate technology and enforcement bodies looks something like this: the law is narrowly defined, and the enforcement mechanisms are underfunded. The GDPR in the EU is one example. The regulation was meant to ensure more responsible behavior from governments and companies alike in their handling of people's personal data. Initially presented as groundbreaking, five years down the line, enforcement is lagging. The Dutch data protection regulator has complained that "When someone calls, we have to tell them there are 10,000 people waiting in line." Of the cases reported in 2020, only 0.15 percent were investigated.[78] And in addition to the lack of capacity, the mandates of regulators are often very narrowly defined. Considering the nature of evolving and developing technologies, regulators need significantly more flexibility to adequately address potential problems.

By turning the regulatory model on its head, governments can leverage a more sustainable first principles approach. To anticipate and accommodate new technological developments, the relationship between lawmaking and enforcement needs to be turned upside down. Rather than drafting narrow laws and considering enforcement only after the fact, we need to make laws that are broadly based on first principles and pair these laws with powerful enforcement in terms of mandate, staff, and sanctions. This "first principles" approach will be far more sustainable and effective than our current regulatory model.

In some ways, it is strange to discuss bias and discrimination by AI application as a specific risk. In democratic societies, discrimination based on age, gender, religion, or ethnicity are already forbidden. It thus should not matter whether someone has been discriminated against during a hotel check-in, as a hospital patient, or as an insurance client, online or offline, by a person or an AI application. The right, in each case, is simply to be free from discrimination. However, these cases are significantly different when it comes to enforcement in new contexts created by emerging technologies and the way in which enforcement agencies must go about assessing where the law might be violated. For the regulators to be able to do their jobs, they will need significantly more resources, the ability to attract talent, clarified mandates, and the will to impose sanctions with real bite.

KNOWLEDGE TO THE PEOPLE

Our ability to solve problems for the public good is significantly diminished when insights remain locked inside corporate environments. We live in an age of information overload and knowledge deficit. On the one hand, we're bombarded by content on a daily basis as we navigate the internet. On the other hand, there is so much opacity regarding the fundamental inner workings of the services running over the internet and other advanced technologies. Indeed, many of the questions that popped up at the beginning of this hyperinformation age have only been partially answered. Do AI enabled systems discriminate? Do AI firms and the tech conglomerates that buy these firms' products abide by antitrust rules? Can regulators assess their workings when the algorithms are different today than they were yesterday, and adjusted tomorrow with lessons from today?

To be clear, we have learned a lot about the impacts of these powerful systems over the past decade; it's just that this learning is mostly taking place in proprietary, not public, contexts. That is the case for most corporate technologies. In other words, CEOs and employees are learning, but not public officials and citizens. AI in particular accelerates existing power imbalances between public and private actors. The complexity and opacity of how data are processed through ever-changing algorithms leads to novel challenges for citizens and their elected officials. To know how AI may change society now and tomorrow, they must know more about the technology as it develops.

This book has touched on the systemic problem of democracy's erosion at the hand of technology companies. The problem is serious, and changing course is an undeniable challenge. Thankfully, however, we have what we need to fight back: a clear agenda for public policy. But we need new coalitions of people to get involved. Once that happens, gaining back control over the technologies that run our lives will finally be within reach.

Conclusion

STOP THE TECH COUP,
SAVE DEMOCRACY

On September 13, 2022, a twenty-two-year-old Iranian woman named Mahsa Amini was out with her brother when she was arrested by the so-called morality police.[1] Mahsa was accused of not wearing the mandatory religious headscarf properly. She was severely beaten by the police, went into a coma, and died three days later, just before her twenty-third birthday. Massive street protests broke out in Iran when her death was made public. Demonstrations were said to be even larger than during the Green Movement in 2009. Mahsa's story was a disturbing case of déjà vu. Her death at the hands of the government reminded me of Neda Agha-Soltan, the young protestor whose murder by a sniper during the 2009 Green Movement was shared around the world on social media. Neda's death revealed the depravity of Iran's repression and its modern intertwining with digital tools and influence; her very public murder was what first pulled me into exploring the growing number of challenges by technology to democracy. Unfortunately, Mahsa's death thirteen years later affirmed any dreams of progress for Iranians made through the international human rights regime were crushed, but the will of people to be free was burning as never before. Following Mahsa's tragedy, thousands of young girls across Iran bravely took to Instagram and TikTok to expose the regime's brutality and amplify their message of "Zan. Zendegi. Azadi." Woman. Life. Freedom.[2] It turned out that Tehran's repressive tactics also hadn't changed all that much between 2009 and 2022: they relied on the same internet shutdowns, influence operations, and harsh protest crackdowns to silence the protests.

In response, U.S. secretary of state Antony Blinken issued a general license, which gives companies an exemption from sanctions, to help Iranians retain access to internet connectivity despite the Islamic Republic's censorship. Tech titans like Google took the opportunity to make more of their tools and services available in the country.[3] Meanwhile, Elon Musk replied to the government tweet announcing the policy: "Activating Starlink."[4] A month later, SpaceX's Starlink satellite receivers were brought into the country, at great risk to the people handling the technologies, which were illegal in Iran.[5] This American response to another people-versus-government clash in Iran put on clear display what had dramatically changed over the past thirteen years: the private tech sector was now even further embedded in international relations and diplomacy.

The many ways in which the outsize power of tech companies impacts people, markets, governance, security, and geopolitics have been elaborately detailed in this book. Whether in established democratic societies or in contexts where people are, literally, fighting for their rights, democracy has not flourished. Instead, the authoritarian model, with the help of technologies, has thrived. One difference since 2009 is that Iranian authorities now have greater access to surveillance technologies from China, which they have deployed without hesitation.[6] The situation in Iran also demonstrates the perpetual creep of tech companies into state functions. In their greatest hour of need, the Iranian people had to rely on the whims of Elon Musk and Sundar Pichai to provide access to digital services—rather than the UN or USAID. Tech has become a broker of diplomacy, development, and democracy—all while raking in historic profits. There is something deeply wrong with this picture.

Reversing the Tech Coup

Some of the most important moments in my life would not have happened without digital technologies. I would not have been elected to the European Parliament at the age of thirty, and I would not have been able to continue teaching my students at Stanford during the COVID-19 pandemic. I would not have been able to connect with human rights defenders halfway around the world, or to watch live-streamed hacks at tech conferences. When I laugh at a snarky comment by a stranger on X or see that AI helps disabled people regain means of communication, I marvel at the connections and possibilities that continue to unfold thanks to innovations.

We live in an era of endless technological promise. Day in and day out, the smartest people dream up new ideas that they hope will help people around the world lead better lives. There is a steady stream of new discoveries, clever services, or nifty products, any one of which may be the next breakthrough that captivates our imagination. I love the internet and continue to be amazed at how new inventions, driven by a deep desire to solve problems, push progress forward: when AI makes cancer treatment more precise, personal, and pointed; when technology improves the efficiency of agricultural processes by saving water or using fewer pesticides; or when privacy protecting encryption standards become the norm thanks to popular messaging apps such as Signal.[7] The internet has unlocked knowledge and human connections that collapse distances and expand horizons.

But the human scale and community spirit of popular technologies and the open internet are being crowded out. Instead, these remarkable innovations are being exploited by a growing corporate hunger for revenue and profit. Since tech companies are in a constant pursuit of growth, most people online are treated as consumers rather than citizens. And for the companies that have already turned their billion-dollar valuations into trillion-dollar valuations, it can sometimes feel as if they have taken over the entire online world. In many countries, the internet is already synonymous with huge social media and retail platforms like Instagram, WeChat, Weibo, and YouTube.

The tech coup shifting power from public and democratic institutions to companies must stop. In the digital layers of our lives we see the privatization of everything, all at the expense of democratic governance and accountability. The risk of tyranny from corporate technology governance is real. Software companies promise to secure vital networks that have almost all been breached with minimal consequences. Tech giants are bidding anonymously on contracts to use swaths of public spaces and resources for private purposes. Remarkably, companies with intelligence capabilities more forceful than those of states are less regulated than the average cup of coffee.[8]

I often hear pushback from technologists that sounds like this: If our products and services are benign and solve some of the world's most entrenched problems, why do they need to be regulated? Well, even assuming that that is true—a big *if*—ongoing governmental oversight of any important industry is a foundation of the rule of law. Watchful eyes from regulators keep the playing field level and all the players honest. Instead, today's democratic governments are being pushed to the margins. Or, rather, they have allowed themselves to be marginalized.

This is a tragedy for citizens; ultimately, if things go wrong, they will be left picking up the tab. When tens of millions of jobs end up displaced by AI, shareholders of companies will benefit, while the price of unemployment or reeducation will fall to societies to shoulder. The moment those negative externalities inevitably do emerge, the public purse will be emptied. Similarly, when people's rights are not protected while using technology, the legal system fails them. While discrimination based on sensitive categories such as age, gender, ethnicity, sexual orientation, and religion are forbidden in most democratic jurisdictions, new facial recognition systems that are known to discriminate constantly are put on the market. Questions about the extent to which AI applications respect nondiscrimination law have not been answered in a satisfactory manner.

The tech coup is rewriting the social contract between the democratic state and its citizens. Digitization used to be a policy sector but has quickly morphed into a layer touching everything. Technology is now a part of education policy, health-care policy, and national security policy. It changes the way we access news and whether what we see with our own eyes can be trusted at all. It affects the security of our personal savings accounts and that of the entire nation. The impact of this transition of responsibilities from public to private is wide ranging. It means the state is no longer able to single-handedly roll out monetary policy, to guarantee the right to privacy, or ensure national security.

While each of the examples illustrated in this book merits wake-up calls and actions of its own, the sum of the parts is what should truly concern everyone. An ecosystem of private power is vacuuming up data and access to information. It is using that data and information to take powers that rightly belong to us and our elected governments. And it is denying us, as citizens, the agency and ability to act.

Understandably, after reading this book, you may want to log off and wash your hands of this profoundly broken digital ecosystem. But going permanently offline and living off the grid isn't the answer. And, even if you tried, it wouldn't be easy. Sinking into nihilism about corporate power will do no more to solve our technological woes than going full throttle into techno-optimism. Instead, we must clearly acknowledge the problems facing our democracies—both online and offline—and engage them with imagination, vision, and determination. We need new ways of setting guardrails in this new world so that we can use digital technologies in a healthy way. The tech coup does not have to be our destiny.

Back to the Core

The consequences of a privatized, algorithm-driven experience online are significant and troubling on their own. But the impact of private governance of key technologies on democratic values goes much deeper than the visible harms of advertising firms and social media companies managing the online space for debate. Invisibly or indirectly, a whole host of technologies is privatizing responsibilities that used to be the monopoly of the state. Increasingly, these corporate choices have underlined their powerful roles in geopolitics all over the world, from operating satellite constellations to conducting elections. The digital technologies that once promised to liberate people worldwide have instead contributed to declining standards and freedoms, as well as weakened institutions. Without intervention and revitalization, democracies are locked in a downward spiral. Decades during which democracies enjoyed a technological advantage and a stronger position on the global stage were not used by political leaders to set global standards or to roll out a clear agenda to preserve democratic principles as technologies and new business models continued to disrupt. The trend is seen around the world, although the consequences for people are worse in fragile societies where violence or repression are rife.

With an appreciation of the scope of the problem, policymakers can change course. They are perfectly capable and fully empowered to act. And they have no time to lose. Yesterday's battles are still being fought, while today's and especially tomorrow's problems are knocking at our doors. As Stuart Russell, a leading computer scientist, said in his testimony before the U.S. Senate Judiciary Committee about AI, "How do we maintain power, forever, over entities more powerful than us?"[9] There is no such thing as starting early enough to make sure we stay ahead—and in control.

AI is not the only game changer. A series of new technologies can change the human experience irreversibly. Quantum, biotech, and neurotech developments, driven by venture capital investment and a race to global dominance, can decisively shape the human condition. According to some experts, they even have the potential to entirely wipe out humanity. All of these technologies require decisive action, and yet we still find ourselves stuck in petty political squabbles, relitigating content moderation decisions on social media platforms from 2016 and 2020 rather than looking forward. The challenges of correcting after harms are already entrenched should serve as a reminder that prevention and proactive governance is key. It is time to rise above the sectarianism and malaise—not just because that's the enlightened thing to do but because it is necessary to meet the next generation of technological challenges head-on.

Whether you come at assessing the threats to democracy from a concern for national security or worry for the future of education or instead have a philosophical attachment to free choice, the tech coup must be stopped. It is therefore my hope that new coalitions can emerge to push back, and to strengthen democracy, the rule of law and the public interest. The future resiliency of democracy is not an issue for Democrats over Republicans, for Americans over Europeans, for older over younger generations. The bipartisan synergy in 2023 between Lindsey Graham and Elizabeth Warren, two senators who have next to nothing in common, shows that, even in today's deeply divided United States, awareness of the tech rot is growing. Together they write, "Nobody elected Big Tech executives to govern anything, let alone the entire digital world. If democracy means anything, it means that leaders on both sides of the aisle must take responsibility for protecting the freedom of the American people from the ever-changing whims of these powerful companies and their unaccountable C.E.O.s."[10] I couldn't agree more. Lawmakers should heed their call.

Naturally, industry leaders are pushing a different course. Elon Musk predicted the end of jobs and called AI "the most destructive force in history."[11] And yet, he launched an AI company, xAI, the next day; xAI will be integrated with the increasingly challenged social media platform X.[12] What could possibly go wrong? Venture capital investor Marc Andreessen urges, "Rather than allowing ungrounded panics around killer AI, 'harmful' AI, job-destroying AI, and inequality-generating AI to put us on our back feet, we in the United States and the West should lean into AI as hard as we possibly can."[13] In essence, set guardrails aside to let the AI train go full steam ahead. Who cares if it derails?

I do not want to live in a world dictated by technology companies and their executives. As the above quotes—and examples throughout this entire book—show, tech leaders do not have the mandate or, frankly, the ethics necessary to govern so much of our societies. They care far more about profit margins and expansion opportunities than the rule of law or checks and balances. While we can take actionable and concrete steps to reverse the trend, systemic change will only happen if we acknowledge a systemic problem.

Strengthening democratic governance over tech companies is not about declaring love to governments as they are. It is not a matter of embracing the status quo—in fact, so much must be changed. On the contrary, strengthening democracy is all about leaving open the ability to change leaders. It means putting citizens in a position to understand how technologies impact our lives, to debate the proper place for them in our societies, to elect the leaders we believe are best to lead, and to hold them to account for making sure the public interest is served. Only once citizens have those powers again will the tech coup be overturned for good.

NOTES

Introduction

1. Anubhav Trivedi, "Neda Agha Soltan Shot in Iran," video, 0:39, 2009, https://www.dailymotion.com/video/x9oltq (warning: graphic).

2. John Plunkett, "Foreign Journalists Banned from Streets of Iran," *Guardian*, June 16, 2009, https://www.theguardian.com/media/2009/jun/16/foreign-journalists-banned-streets-iran.

3. Julien Pain, "No Green Revolution, but a Revolution in Media," France 24: The Observers, March 17, 2010, https://observers.france24.com/en/20100317-no-green-revolution-revolution-media-iran-amateur-content.

4. Jared Keller, "Evaluating Iran's Twitter Revolution," *Atlantic*, June 18, 2010, https://www.theatlantic.com/technology/archive/2010/06/evaluating-irans-twitter-revolution/58337/.

5. Ewen MacAskill, "US Confirms It Asked Twitter to Stay Open to Help Iran Protesters," *Guardian*, June 17, 2009, https://www.theguardian.com/world/2009/jun/17/obama-iran-twitter.

6. David Talbot, "Inside Egypt's 'Facebook Revolution,'" *MIT Technology Review*, April 29, 2011, https://www.technologyreview.com/2011/04/29/194993/inside-egypts-facebook-revolution/.

7. Golnaz Esfandiari, "'The Twitter Devolution'—Esfandiari In 'Foreign Policy,'" Radio Free Europe / Radio Liberty, June 8, 2010, https://pressroom.rferl.org/a/in_the_news_golnaz_esfandiari_twitter_devolution/2065189.html (originally appeared in *Foreign Policy*, June 7, 2010).

8. Human Rights Watch, *Like the Dead in Their Coffins: Torture, Detention, and the Crushing of Dissent in Iran* (New York: Human Rights Watch, 2004), chap. 5, "Detention Centers and Ill-Treatment," https://www.hrw.org/reports/2004/iran0604/5.htm.

9. Nick Robins-Early, "Meet the Cynical Western Companies Helping the Syrian Regime," *New Republic*, March 15, 2012, https://newrepublic.com/article/101732/syria-spyware-surveillance-revolution-assad-activists-human-rights.

10. Nate Anderson, "How Nokia Helped Iran 'Persecute and Arrest' Dissidents," Ars Technica, March 4, 2010, https://arstechnica.com/tech-policy/2010/03/how-nokia-helped-iran-persecute-and-arrest-dissidents/.

11. Kim Zetter, "Nokia-Siemens Spy Tools Aid Police Torture in Bahrain," *Wired*, August 23, 2011, https://www.wired.com/2011/08/nokia-siemens-spy-systems/.

12. Marietje Schaake, "Stop Digital Arms Trade from Western Countries," *Huff-Post*, November 15, 2011, https://www.huffpost.com/entry/stop-digital-arms-trade-f_b_1094472.

13. Stephanie Kirchgaessner, Paul Lewis, David Pegg, Sam Cutler, Nina Lakhani, and Michael Safi, "Revealed: Leak Uncovers Global Abuse of Cyber-Surveillance Weapon," *Guardian*, July 18, 2021, https://www.theguardian.com/world/2021/jul/18/revealed-leak-uncovers-global-abuse-of-cyber-surveillance-weapon-nso-group-pegasus.

14. Craig Timberg, Michael Birnbaum, Drew Harwell, and Dan Sabbagh, "On the List: Ten Prime Ministers, Three Presidents and a King," *Washington Post*, July 20, 2021, https://www.washingtonpost.com/world/2021/07/20/heads-of-state-pegasus-spyware/.

15. Bill Marczak, "The Million Dollar Dissident: NSO Group's iPhone Zero-Days Used against a UAE Human Rights Defender," Citizen Lab, August 24, 2016, https://citizenlab.ca/2016/08/million-dollar-dissident-iphone-zero-day-nso-group-uae/.

16. Kaye Wiggins and Mehul Srivastava, "EY Valued NSO Group at $2.3bn Months before Emergency Bailout," *Financial Times*, June 27, 2022, https://www.ft.com/content/057cece3-eb81-42b8-9a27-e295c61e76b3.

17. David Pegg, Paul Lewis, Michael Safi, and Nina Lakhani, "FT Editor among 180 Journalists Identified by Clients of Spyware Firm," *Guardian*, July 18, 2021, https://www.theguardian.com/world/2021/jul/18/ft-editor-roula-khalaf-among-180-journalists-targeted-nso-spyware.

18. CBS News, "Germany Summons U.S. Ambassador over Alleged Spying on Merkel," October 24, 2013, https://www.cbsnews.com/news/germany-summons-us-ambassador-over-alleged-spying-on-merkel/.

19. Hendrik Mildebrath, "Greece's Predatorgate: The Latest Chapter in Europe's Spyware Scandal?," European Parliament, September 8, 2022, https://www.europarl.europa.eu/thinktank/en/document/EPRS_ATA(2022)733637.

20. Steven Feldstein and Brian (Chun Hey) Kot, "Why Does the Global Spyware Industry Continue to Thrive? Trends, Explanations, and Responses" (working paper, Carnegie Endowment for International Peace, Washington, DC, March 14, 2023), https://carnegieendowment.org/2023/03/14/why-does-global-spyware-industry-continue-to-thrive-trends-explanations-and-responses-pub-89229.

21. Huib Modderkolk, "AIVD Gebruikt Omstreden Israëlische Hacksoftware," *De Volkskrant*, June 2, 2022, https://www.volkskrant.nl/nieuws-achtergrond/aivd-gebruikt-omstreden-israelische-hacksoftware~b05a6d91/?referrer=https://www.euractiv.com/.

22. Elon Musk, quoted in Adam Satariano, Scott Reinhard, Cade Metz, Sheera Frenkel, and Malika Khurana, "With Starlink, Elon Musk's Satellite Dominance Is Raising Global Alarms," *New York Times*, July 28, 2023, https://www.nytimes.com/interactive/2023/07/28/business/starlink.html.

23. Joe Biden, quoted in Eric Tucker, "Biden Tackles Cybersecurity with Tech, Finance Leaders," *PBS NewsHour*, August 25, 2021, https://www.pbs.org /newshour/politics/biden-tackles-cybersecurity-with-tech-finance-leaders.

24. Andrew R. Chow, "What to Know about WorldCoin and the Controversy around It," *Time*, August 3, 2023, https://time.com/6300522/worldcoin-sam-altman/.

25. Erika Edwards and Hallie Jackson, "How Social Media Is Impacting Mental Health among Teens," NBC News, May 23, 2023, https://www.nbcnews .com/health/health-news/social-media-mental-health-anxiety-depression-teens -surgeon-general-rcna85575.

26. Bernard Marr, "How AI and Machine Learning Will Impact the Future of Healthcare," *Forbes*, September 14, 2022, https://www.forbes.com/sites /bernardmarr/2022/09/14/how-ai-and-machine-learning-will-impact-the-future -of-healthcare/?sh=254c2ab847e5.

27. Helen-Ann Smith, "The 'Green Code' App: How China's Zero COVID Policy Is Turning Cities, Parks, Restaurants and Shops into Digitised Fortresses," Sky News, October 19, 2022, https://news.sky.com/story/the-green-code-app -how-chinas-zero-covid-policy-is-turning-cities-parks-restaurants-and-shops-into -digitised-fortresses-12724231.

28. Johana Bhuiyan, "'There's Cameras Everywhere': Testimonies Detail Far-Reaching Surveillance of Uyghurs in China," *Guardian*, September 30, 2021, https://www.theguardian.com/world/2021/sep/30/uyghur-tribunal-testimony -surveillance-china.

29. Thomas S. Eder, Rebecca Arcesati, and Jacob Mardell, "Networking the 'Belt and Road'—The Future Is Digital," Mercator Institute for China Studies, August 28, 2019, https://merics.org/en/tracker/networking-belt-and-road-future-digital.

30. Bob Pisani, "Apple versus the World: The iPhone Maker Is Bigger than Almost Any Stock Market in the World," CNBC, May 10, 2023, https://www.cnbc .com/2023/05/10/apple-vs-the-world-apples-bigger-than-entire-overseas-stock -markets-.html.

31. Helen Darbishire, "European Commission President's Text Messages Are Documents and Can Be Requested Says Ombudsman," Access Info Europe, January 28, 2022, https://www.access-info.org/2022-01-28/textmessages-documents -ombudsman/.

32. Ash Carter, "Mark Zuckerberg Missed an Opportunity," *Atlantic*, November 25, 2018, https://www.theatlantic.com/ideas/archive/2018/11/mark -zuckerberg-missed-opportunity/576088/.

33. Samantha Power, "My Message to Harvard Kennedy School Grads," *Huff-Post*, May 28, 2014, https://www.huffpost.com/entry/my-message-to-harvard-ken _b_5406524.

Chapter 1

1. Global Commission on Internet Governance, *One Internet* (Waterloo, ON, and London: Center for International Governance Innovation / Chatham House, 2016), https://www.cigionline.org/publications/one-internet/.

2. Emily Bobrow, "Vint Cerf Helped Create the Internet on the Back of an Envelope," *Wall Street Journal*, December 16, 2022, https://www.wsj.com/articles /vint-cerf-helped-create-the-internet-on-the-back-of-an-envelope-11671210858.

3. Ryan Singel, "Vint Cerf: We Knew What We Were Unleashing on the World," *Wired*, April 23, 2012, https://www.wired.com/2012/04/epicenter-isoc-famers -qa-cerf/.

4. Vint Cerf, quoted in Singel, "Vint Cerf."

5. "Vinton G. Cerf," Google Research, accessed January 9, 2024, https:// research.google/people/author32412/.

6. Jemima Kiss, "Two Decades on, We Must Preserve the Internet as a Tool of Democracy," *Guardian*, January 12, 2014, https://www.theguardian.com /technology/2014/jan/12/web-tool-democracy-tim-berners-lee.

7. Amy van der Hiel, "25 Years Ago the World Changed Forever," blog post, World Wide Web Consortium, August 4, 2016, https://www.w3.org/blog/2016 /25-years-ago-the-world-changed-forever/.

8. Tim Berners-Lee, "Frequently Asked Questions by the Press," World Wide Web Consortium, accessed January 9, 2024, https://www.w3.org/People/Berners -Lee/FAQ.html.

9. Jamie Bartlett, "Cypherpunks Write Code," *American Scientist*, 2015, https:// www.americanscientist.org/article/cypherpunks-write-code.

10. Tim May, quoted in Bartlett, "Cypherpunks Write Code."

11. Eric Hughes, "A Cypherpunk's Manifesto," March 9, 1993, https://www .activism.net/cypherpunk/manifesto.html.

12. Thomas Heinrich, "Cold War Armory: Military Contracting in Silicon Valley," *Enterprise and Society* 3, no. 2 (2002), https://www.jstor.org/stable/23699688.

13. John Perry Barlow, "A Declaration of the Independence of Cyberspace," Electronic Frontier Foundation, February 8, 1996, https://www.eff.org/cyberspace -independence.

14. Jackie Davalos, "Uber Falls on Fears of Slower Growth after Profit Milestone," Bloomberg, August 1, 2023, https://www.bloomberg.com/news/articles /2023-08-01/uber-swings-to-surprise-profit-as-ridership-reaches-new-record.

15. Dain Evans, "Uber and Lyft Rides Are More Expensive Than Ever Because of a Driver Shortage," CNBC, August 31, 2021, https://www.cnbc.com/2021/08 /31/why-uber-and-lyft-rides-are-more-expensive-than-ever.html.

16. Reid Hoffman and Chris Yeh, *Blitzscaling: The Lightning-Fast Path to Building Massively Valuable Companies* (London: HarperCollins, 2018), 44.

17. Jeremy Weinstein, Rob Reich, and Mehran Sahami, *System Error: Where Big Tech Went Wrong and How We Can Reboot* (London: Hodder and Stoughton, 2021), 12.

18. Peter Thiel, "The Education of a Libertarian," *Cato Unbound*, April 13, 2009, https://www.cato-unbound.org/2009/04/13/peter-thiel/education-libertarian/.

19. Mark Zuckerberg, "Facebook's Letter from Mark Zuckerberg—Full Text," *Guardian*, February 1, 2012, https://www.theguardian.com/technology/2012/feb /01/facebook-letter-mark-zuckerberg-text.

20. Julia Angwin, Madeleine Varner, and Ariana Tobin, "Facebook Enabled Advertisers to Reach 'Jew Haters,'" *ProPublica*, September 14, 2017, https://www .propublica.org/article/facebook-enabled-advertisers-to-reach-jew-haters; Sam

Dean, "Facebook Decided Which Users Are Interested in Nazis—and Let Advertisers Target Them Directly," *Los Angeles Times*, February 21, 2019, https://www.latimes.com/business/technology/la-fi-tn-facebook-nazi-metal-ads-20190221-story.html.

21. Mike Isaac, "How Uber Deceives the Authorities Worldwide," *New York Times*, March 3, 2017, https://www.nytimes.com/2017/03/03/technology/uber-greyball-program-evade-authorities.html.

22. "Joint Answer Given by Vice-President Ansip on Behalf of the Commission," European Parliament, July 20, 2017, https://www.europarl.europa.eu/doceo/document/E-8-2017-001673-ASW_EN.html.

23. Jack Poulson, "Reports of a Silicon Valley/Military Divide Have Been Greatly Exaggerated," Tech Inquiry, July 7, 2020, https://techinquiry.org/SiliconValley-Military/.

24. April Glaser, "Thousands of Contracts Highlight Quiet Ties between Big Tech and U.S. Military," NBC News, July 8, 2020, https://www.nbcnews.com/tech/tech-news/thousands-contracts-highlight-quiet-ties-between-big-tech-u-s-n1233171.

25. "Global Positioning System," United States Space Force, October 2020, https://www.spaceforce.mil/About-Us/Fact-Sheets/Article/2197765/global-positioning-system/.

26. Natasha Lomas, "France's Mistral Dials Up Call for EU AI Act to Fix Rules for Apps, Not Model Makers," *TechCrunch*, November 16, 2023, https://techcrunch.com/2023/11/16/mistral-eu-ai-act/; Madhumita Murgia, "Microsoft Strikes Deal with Mistral in Push beyond OpenAI," *Financial Times*, February 26, 2024, https://www.ft.com/content/cd6eb51a-3276-450f-87fd-97e8410db9eb.

27. Elahe Izadi, "The White House's First Web Site Launched 20 Years Ago This Week. And It Was Amazing," *Washington Post*, October 21, 2014, https://www.washingtonpost.com/news/the-fix/wp/2014/10/21/the-white-houses-first-website-launched-20-years-ago-this-week-and-it-was-amazing/.

28. Dan Brekke, "CDA Struck Down," *Wired*, June 26, 1997, https://www.wired.com/1997/06/cda-struck-down/.

29. Internet Freedom and Family Empowerment Act, H.R. 1978, 104th Cong. (1995), https://www.congress.gov/bill/104th-congress/house-bill/1978.

30. Ron Wyden, quoted in John Schwartz, "House Vote Bars Internet Censorship," *Washington Post*, August 5, 1995, https://www.washingtonpost.com/archive/politics/1995/08/05/house-vote-bars-internet-censorship/1f523943-f35f-4f80-8f00-d08631465a22/.

31. Anupam Chander, "Section 230 and the International Law of Facebook," *Yale Journal of Law and Technology* 24 (2022), https://law.yale.edu/sites/default/files/area/center/isp/documents/chander.pdf.

32. Jeri Clausing, "Magaziner, Head of U.S. Internet Policy, Plans to Resign," *New York Times*, November 6, 1998, https://archive.nytimes.com/www.nytimes.com/library/tech/98/11/cyber/articles/06magaziner.html.

33. John M. Broder, "Ira Magaziner Argues for Minimal Internet Regulation," *New York Times*, June 30, 1997, https://www.nytimes.com/1997/06/30/business/ira-magaziner-argues-for-minimal-internet-regulation.html.

34. Bill Clinton, quoted in Jane Perlez, "Clinton Lauds Technology as Key to India's Economy," *New York Times*, March 25, 2000, https://www.nytimes.com /2000/03/25/world/clinton-lauds-technology-as-key-to-india-s-economy.html.

35. "Ira Magaziner," ICANN Wiki, Internet Corporation for Assigned Names and Numbers, May 26, 2021, https://icannwiki.org/Ira_Magaziner.

36. "Vinton G. Cerf: Vice President and Chief Internet Evangelist," Internet Corporation for Assigned Names and Numbers, May 23, 2014, https://www.icann .org/resources/pages/vinton-cerf-2014-05-23-en.

37. Broder, "Ira Magaziner Argues."

38. Lawrence Lessig, "Lawrence Lessig on the Increasing Regulation of Cyberspace," *Harvard Magazine*, January 1, 2000, https://www.harvardmagazine.com /2000/01/code-is-law-html.

39. "Google Goes Public," *New York Times*, August 20, 2004, https://www .nytimes.com/2004/08/20/opinion/google-goes-public.html.

40. Caroline McCarthy, "Facebook Hits 100 Million Users," CNET, August 26, 2008, https://www.cnet.com/culture/facebook-hits-100-million-users/.

41. Ed Black, quoted in Declan McCullagh, "Bush Leaves Behind a Mixed Technology Legacy," CNET, January 19, 2009, https://www.cnet.com/tech/tech -industry/bush-leaves-behind-a-mixed-technology-legacy/.

42. Barack Obama, quoted in Jon Swartz, "Obama Weighs In on Big Data, Privacy in Silicon Valley Fireside Chat," MarketWatch, September 22, 2019, https:// www.marketwatch.com/story/obama-weighs-in-on-big-data-privacy-in-silicon -valley-fireside-chat-2019-09-18.

43. Adam Clark Estes, "Some Perspective on Obama's Bromance with Eric Schmidt," *Atlantic*, June 24, 2011, https://www.theatlantic.com/politics/archive /2011/06/obamas-bromance-googles-eric-schmidt-out-hand/352130/.

44. Amy Schatz, "Tech Industry Cheers as Obama Taps Aneesh Chopra for CTO," *Wall Street Journal*, April 18, 2009, https://www.wsj.com/articles/BL-DGB -2228; Mark Healy and Jeff Riedel, "Who It Takes (And What They're Fighting For)," *GQ*, September 30, 2008, https://www.gq.com/story/who-it-takes-chris -hughes-new-media-strategist-obama-president-campaign-2008.

45. "Google Agrees to Change Its Business Practices to Resolve FTC Competition Concerns in the Markets for Devices Like Smart Phones, Games and Tablets, and in Online Search," Federal Trade Commission, press release, January 3, 2013, https://www.ftc.gov/news-events/news/press-releases/2013/01/google-agrees -change-its-business-practices-resolve-ftc-competition-concerns-markets-devices -smart.

46. Craig Timberg, "FTC: Google Did Not Break Antitrust Law with Search Practices," *Washington Post*, January 3, 2013, https://www.washingtonpost.com /business/technology/ftc-to-announce-google-settlement-today/2013/01/03 /ecb599f0-55c6-11e2-bf3e-76c0a789346f_story.html.

47. Barack Obama, quoted in Howard Schmidt, "Launching the U.S. International Strategy for Cyberspace," blog post, White House, May 16, 2011, https:// obamawhitehouse.archives.gov/blog/2011/05/16/launching-us-international -strategy-Cyberspace.

48. Craig Timberg, "Google Encrypts Data amid Backlash against NSA Spying," *Washington Post*, September 6, 2013, https://www.washingtonpost.com/business /technology/google-encrypts-data-amid-backlash-against-nsa-spying/2013/09 /06/9acc3c20-1722-11e3-a2ec-b47e45e6f8ef_story.html.

49. Ellen Nakashima and Reed Albergotti, "The FBI Wanted to Unlock the San Bernardino Shooter's iPhone. It Turned to a Little-Known Australian Firm," *Washington Post*, April 14, 2021, https://www.washingtonpost.com/technology /2021/04/14/azimuth-san-bernardino-apple-iphone-fbi/.

50. Cecilia Kang, "F.C.C. Repeals Net Neutrality Rules," *New York Times*, December 14, 2017, https://www.nytimes.com/2017/12/14/technology/net -neutrality-repeal-vote.html.

51. David McCabe, "What's Going on with TikTok? Here's What We Know," *New York Times*, August 1, 2020, https://www.nytimes.com/2020/08/01/technology /tiktok-trump-microsoft-bytedance-china-ban.html.

52. Jordan Novet, "President Trump Calls Apple CEO 'Tim Apple' Instead of Tim Cook," CNBC, March 6, 2019, https://www.cnbc.com/2019/03/06/president -trump-calls-apple-ceo-tim-apple-instead-of-tim-cook.html.

53. "Executive Order on Strengthening the Cybersecurity of Federal Networks and Critical Infrastructure," Cybersecurity and Infrastructure Security Agency, accessed January 9, 2024, https://www.cisa.gov/topics/cybersecurity -best-practices/executive-order-strengthening-cybersecurity-federal-networks -and-critical-infrastructure.

54. Tom Westbrook, "Factbox—Trump Administration Measures against Chinese Companies," Reuters, January 8, 2021, https://www.reuters.com/article /idUSKBN29C17E/.

55. Ana Swanson and Raymond Zhong, "U.S. Places Restrictions on China's Leading Chip Maker," *New York Times*, September 26, 2020, https://www.nytimes .com/2020/09/26/technology/trump-china-smic-blacklist.html.

56. Lauren Feiner, "Biden Wants to Get Rid of Law That Shields Companies like Facebook from Liability for What Their Users Post," CNBC, January 17, 2020, https://www.cnbc.com/2020/01/17/biden-wants-to-get-rid-of-techs-legal-shield -section-230.html.

57. The Transatlantic Commission on Election Integrity, which I served on, had written and promoted the pledge; see "The Pledge for Election Integrity," Alliance of Democracies / Transatlantic Commission on Election Integrity, n.d., accessed January 9, 2024, https://www.electionpledge.eu/.

58. Craig Timberg and Isaac Stanley-Becker, "Biden Campaign Assails Facebook for 'Haggling' with Trump over His Online Posts," *Washington Post*, June 30, 2020, https://www.washingtonpost.com/technology/2020/06/30/biden -facebook-trump-letter/.

59. David McCabe and Kenneth P. Vogel, "Big Tech Makes Inroads with the Biden Campaign," *New York Times*, August 10, 2020, https://www.nytimes.com /2020/08/10/technology/big-tech-biden-campaign.html.

60. "National AI Advisory Committee," AI.gov, n.d., accessed January 9, 2024, https://ai.gov/naiac/.

61. Grace Mayer and Hasan Chowdhury, "See Photos of Tech's Elite All Dressed Up at the White House," Business Insider, June 23, 2023, https://www.businessinsider.com/ceos-tim-cook-sundar-pichai-sam-altman-white-house-dinner-2023-6.

62. Joe Biden, "Republicans and Democrats, Unite against Big Tech Abuses," *Wall Street Journal*, January 11, 2023, https://www.wsj.com/articles/unite-against-big-tech-abuses-social-media-privacy-competition-antitrust-children-algorithm-11673439411.

63. Mike Isaac, "Uber Picks David Plouffe to Wage Regulatory Fight," *New York Times*, August 19, 2014, https://www.nytimes.com/2014/08/20/technology/uber-picks-a-political-insider-to-wage-its-regulatory-battles.html; Chan Zuckerberg Initiative, "CZI Announces David Plouffe to Lead Policy and Advocacy Work," September 14, 2022, https://chanzuckerberg.com/newsroom/czi-announces-david-plouffe-to-lead-policy-and-advocacy-work/.

64. NYU Stern, "Jared Cohen, Director of Google Ideas, Inspires Students to Use Technology to Address Global Issues," March 26, 2012, https://www.stern.nyu.edu/experience-stern/tales-in-possible/think-possible-cohen.

65. Dylan Byers, "Jay Carney Joins Amazon," *Politico*, February 26, 2015, https://www.politico.com/blogs/media/2015/02/jay-carney-joins-amazon-203160.

66. Katie Benner, "Airbnb Hires Ex–Attorney General Eric Holder to Advise on Anti-Bias Policy," *New York Times*, July 20, 2016, https://www.nytimes.com/2016/07/21/technology/airbnb-hires-ex-attorney-general-eric-holder-to-advise-on-anti-bias-policy.html.

67. Steven Scheer, "Cyber Spying Firm NSO to Follow Human Rights Guidelines," Reuters, September 10, 2019, https://www.reuters.com/article/cyber-rights-nso-idUSL5N2602JM/.

68. Sara Salinas and Steve Kovach, "Facebook Has Chosen Ex–British Deputy Prime Minister to Manage Growing PR Crises," CNBC, October 19, 2018, https://www.cnbc.com/2018/10/19/facebook-hires-ex-british-deputy-prime-minister-nick-clegg.html.

69. "Richard Allan," Information Technology and Innovation Foundation, accessed January 9, 2024, https://itif.org/person/richard-allan/; Thibault Spirlet, "Ex-Austrian Chancellor Sebastian Kurz to Work for Tech Billionaire Peter Thiel," *Politico*, December 30, 2021, https://www.politico.eu/article/austria-former-chancellor-sebastian-kurz-palantir-technologies-silicon-valley-peter-thiel/.

70. Cecilia Kang and Kenneth P. Vogel, "Tech Giants Amass a Lobbying Army for an Epic Washington Battle," *New York Times*, June 5, 2019, https://www.nytimes.com/2019/06/05/us/politics/amazon-apple-facebook-google-lobbying.html.

71. Thomas Heath, "Apple Is the First $1 Trillion Company in History," *Washington Post*, August 2, 2018, https://www.washingtonpost.com/business/economy/apple-is-the-first-1-trillion-company-in-history/2018/08/02/ea3e7a02-9599-11e8-a679-b09212fb69c2_story.html.

72. Lauren Feiner, "Facebook Stock Plummets 26% in Its Biggest One-Day Drop Ever," CNBC, February 3, 2022, https://www.cnbc.com/2022/02/03/facebook-shares-plummet-22percent-after-reporting-weak-guidance.html.

73. "Tech Sector as a Percentage of Total Gross Domestic Product (GDP) in the United States from 2017 to 2022," Statista, November 15, 2023, https://www.statista.com/statistics/1239480/united-states-leading-states-by-tech-contribution-to-gross-product/.

74. Olivia Carville, "TikTok's Algorithm Keeps Pushing Suicide to Vulnerable Teens," Bloomberg, April 20, 2023, https://www.bloomberg.com/news/features/2023-04-20/tiktok-effects-on-mental-health-in-focus-after-teen-suicide.

75. Shannon Bond, "How the 'Stop the Steal' Movement Outwitted Facebook Ahead of the Jan. 6 Insurrection," NPR, October 22, 2021, https://www.npr.org/2021/10/22/1048543513/facebook-groups-jan-6-insurrection.

76. Adrian Horton, "How Did Suits Become America's Most-Watched TV Show of the Summer?," *Guardian*, August 17, 2023, https://www.theguardian.com/tv-and-radio/2023/aug/17/suits-netflix-america-most-watched-summer-show.

77. Denise Petski, "'Suits' Breaks Nielsen's All-Time Overall Streaming Record, Claims No. 1 Spot for 12th Week; 'Virgin River' Tops Streaming Originals," Deadline, October 5, 2023, https://deadline.com/2023/10/suits-ratings-streaming-record-nielsen-virgin-river-one-piece-1235565418/.

78. Gerry Shih and Anant Gupta, "Facing Pressure in India, Netflix and Amazon Back Down on Daring Films," *Washington Post*, November 20, 2023, https://www.washingtonpost.com/world/2023/11/20/india-netflix-amazon-movies-self-censorship/.

79. Jessica Lyons Hardcastle, "Probe Reveals Previously Secret Israeli Spyware That Infects Targets via Ads," *Register*, September 16, 2023, https://www.theregister.com/2023/09/16/insanet_spyware/.

80. Ross Baird, quoted in David Streitfeld, "Tech Giants, Once Seen as Saviors, Are Now Viewed as Threats," *New York Times*, October 12, 2017, https://www.nytimes.com/2017/10/12/technology/tech-giants-threats.html.

81. Edward Snowden, quoted in Geoff McMaster, "Democracy Eroding Like Never before, Says Edward Snowden," Folio, University of Alberta, March 31, 2018, https://ualberta.ca/folio/2018/03/democracy-eroding-like-never-before-says-edward-.html.

82. Cory Doctorow, "The Future Is in Interoperability Not Big Tech: 2021 in Review," Medium, December 25, 2021, https://doctorow.medium.com/the-future-is-in-interoperability-not-big-tech-2021-in-review-1a6c601ebb62.

83. Barack Obama, quoted in Jenna Wortham, "Obama Brought Silicon Valley to Washington," *New York Times*, October 25, 2016, https://www.nytimes.com/2016/10/30/magazine/barack-obama-brought-silicon-valley-to-washington-is-that-a-good-thing.html.

84. Ron Wyden, quoted in Colin Lecher, "Senator Ron Wyden Reckons with the Internet He Helped Shape," The Verge, July 24, 2018, https://www.theverge.com/2018/7/24/17606974/oregon-senator-ron-wyden-interview-internet-section-230-net-neutrality.

Chapter 2

1. Rachel Metz, "AI Startups Create Digital Demand for Anguilla's Website Domain Name," Bloomberg, August 31, 2023, https://www.bloomberg.com/news/articles/2023-08-31/ai-startups-create-digital-demand-for-anguilla-s-website-domain-name.

2. Edward Segal, "Worsening Computer Chip Crisis Shows Supply Chains Are Still at Risk," *Forbes*, July 12, 2021, https://www.forbes.com/sites/edwardsegal/2021/07/12/worsening-computer-chip-crisis-shows-supply-chains-are-still-at-risk/.

3. Michael Wayland, "Chip Shortage Expected to Cost Auto Industry $210 Billion in Revenue in 2021," CNBC, September 23, 2021, https://www.cnbc.com/2021/09/23/chip-shortage-expected-to-cost-auto-industry-210-billion-in-2021.html.

4. Ben Blanchard, "TSMC Sending More Workers to Speed Up Building of New Arizona Plant," Reuters, June 29, 2023, https://www.reuters.com/technology/tsmc-sending-more-workers-speed-up-building-new-arizona-plant-2023-06-29/.

5. Katie Tarasov, "Inside TSMC, the Taiwanese Chipmaking Giant That's Building a New Plant in Phoenix," CNBC, October 16, 2021, https://www.cnbc.com/2021/10/16/tsmc-taiwanese-chipmaker-ramping-production-to-end-chip-shortage.html.

6. Yimou Lee, Norihiko Shirouzu, and David Lague, "Taiwan Chip Industry Emerges as Battlefront in U.S.-China Showdown," Reuters, December 27, 2021, https://www.reuters.com/investigates/special-report/taiwan-china-chips/; Jennifer Meng, "Actions the U.S. and EU Can Take Together to Strengthen Both Regions' Semiconductor Supply Chain Resilience," Semiconductor Industry Association, September 28, 2021, https://www.semiconductors.org/actions-the-u-s-and-eu-can-take-together-to-strengthen-both-regions-semiconductor-supply-chain-resilience/.

7. Kathrin Hille, "TSMC: How a Taiwanese Chipmaker Became a Linchpin of the Global Economy," *Financial Times*, March 24, 2021, https://www.ft.com/content/05206915-fd73-4a3a-92a5-6760ce965bd9.

8. Kenny Malone, "Forging Taiwan's Silicon Shield," NPR, October 7, 2022, https://www.npr.org/2022/10/07/1127595393/taiwan-miracle-semiconductor-silicon-shield-china.

9. John Liu and Paul Mozur, "TSMC Chairman Mark Liu Says Company Will Keep Its Roots in Taiwan," *New York Times*, August 4, 2023, https://www.nytimes.com/2023/08/04/technology/tsmc-mark-liu.html.

10. "The Supply of Critical Raw Materials Endangered by Russia's War on Ukraine," Organisation for Economic Co-operation and Development, August 4, 2022, https://www.oecd.org/ukraine-hub/policy-responses/the-supply-of-critical-raw-materials-endangered-by-russia-s-war-on-ukraine-e01ac7be/.

11. Alexandra Alper and Karen Freifeld, "Focus: Russia Could Hit U.S. Chip Industry, White House Warns," Reuters, February 11, 2022, https://www.reuters.com/technology/white-house-tells-chip-industry-brace-russian-supply-disruptions-2022-02-11/.

12. Antonio Varas, Raj Varadarajan, Jimmy Goodrich, and Falan Yinug, *Strengthening the Global Semiconductor Supply Chain in an Uncertain Era* (Boston and Washington, DC: Boston Consulting Group / Semiconductor Industry Association, April 2021), https://www.semiconductors.org/wp-content/uploads/2021/05/BCG-x-SIA-Strengthening-the-Global-Semiconductor-Value-Chain-April-2021_1.pdf.

13. Ursula von der Leyen, "Statement by the President on the European Chips Act," European Commission, February 8, 2022, https://ec.europa.eu/commission/presscorner/detail/en/statement_22_866.

14. Justin Badlam, Stephen Clark, Suhrid Gajendragadkar, Adi Kumar, Sara Slayton O'Rourke, and Dale Swartz, "The CHIPS and Science Act: Here's What's in It," McKinsey & Company, October 4, 2022, https://www.mckinsey.com/industries/public-and-social-sector/our-insights/the-chips-and-science-act-heres-whats-in-it.

15. "ASML Shares Dip after Netherlands Pulls Licence for Some China Exports," Reuters, January 3, 2024, https://www.reuters.com/technology/asml-shares-dip-after-netherlands-revokes-licence-some-china-exports-2024-01-02/.

16. Queen Victoria, in "The Telegraphic Messages of Queen Victoria and Pres. Buchanan," 1858, Library of Congress, https://www.loc.gov/resource/cph.3b07162/.

17. James Griffiths, "The Global Internet Is Powered by Vast Undersea Cables. But They're Vulnerable," CNN, July 26, 2019, https://www.cnn.com/2019/07/25/asia/internet-undersea-cables-intl-hnk/index.html.

18. Justin Sherman, *Cyber Defense across the Ocean Floor: The Geopolitics of Submarine Cable Security* (Washington, DC: Atlantic Council, Scowcroft Center for Strategy and Security, September 2021), https://www.atlanticcouncil.org/wp-content/uploads/2021/09/Cyber-defense-across-the-ocean-floor-The-geopolitics-of-submarine-cable-security.pdf.

19. "Submarine Cable Map," TeleGeography, accessed January 10, 2024, https://www.submarinecablemap.com; Steve McCaskill, "There Are Now More Than 1.3 Million Km of Submarine Cables Worldwide," TechRadar, September 3, 2021, https://www.techradar.com/news/there-are-now-more-than-13-million-km-of-submarine-cables-worldwide.

20. Praveen Menon and Tom Westbrook, "Undersea Cable Fault Could Cut Off Tonga from Rest of the World for Weeks," Reuters, January 18, 2022, https://www.reuters.com/markets/funds/undersea-cable-fault-could-cut-off-tonga-rest-world-weeks-2022-01-18/.

21. "Why the Undersea Cables That Connect the World Are a Subject of Concern," *The Week*, February 18, 2022, https://www.theweek.co.uk/news/technology/955812/undersea-cables-connect-world-subject-concern.

22. Brady Africk, "Nord Stream Sabotage Highlights the Risks to Undersea Internet Cables," American Enterprise Institute, September 30, 2022, https://www.aei.org/foreign-and-defense-policy/nord-stream-sabotage-highlights-the-risks-to-undersea-internet-cables/.

23. Anne Kauranen and Benoit Van Overstraeten, "NATO to Respond If Baltic Sea Pipeline Damage Deliberate—Alliance Chief," Reuters, October 12, 2023,

https://www.reuters.com/markets/commodities/heavy-force-damaged-baltic-sea-gas-pipeline-estonia-says-2023-10-11/.

24. Kauranen and Van Overstraeten, "NATO to Respond."

25. Dan Swinhoe, "Svalbard Cable Damage Caused by 'External Influences' But Probably Not Intentional, Say Police," Data Centre Dynamics, February 14, 2022, https://www.datacenterdynamics.com/en/news/svalbard-cable-damage-caused-by-external-influences-but-probably-not-intentional-say-police/.

26. Space Norway, "Bortfall av Reservekapasitet på Svalbardfiberen," press release, January 7, 2022, https://www.sysselmesteren.no/contentassets/8e497b11f18146029a022462c8dc09ca/pressemelding-fra-space-norway.pdf.

27. David Meyer, "Politico Pro's Morning Tech: Freedom of Panorama— Right to Fast Broadband—Data Retention," *Politico*, July 3, 2015, https://www.politico.eu/article/politico-pros-morning-tech-freedom-of-panorama-right-to-fast-broadband-data-retention/.

28. Nicole Starosielski, *The Undersea Network* (Durham, NC: Duke University Press, 2015).

29. Christopher Mims, "Google, Amazon, Meta and Microsoft Weave a Fiber-Optic Web of Power," *Wall Street Journal*, January 15, 2022, https://www.wsj.com/articles/google-amazon-meta-and-microsoft-weave-a-fiber-optic-web-of-power-11642222824.

30. Anna Gross, Alexandra Heal, Demetri Sevastopulo, Kathrin Hille, and Mercedes Ruehl, "China Exerts Control over Internet Cable Projects in South China Sea," *Financial Times,* March 13, 2023, https://on.ft.com/3UwN3kg.

31. Tracy Brown Hamilton, "In a Small Dutch Town, a Fight with Meta over a Massive Data Center," *Washington Post*, May 28, 2022, https://www.washingtonpost.com/climate-environment/2022/05/28/meta-data-center-zeewolde-netherlands/.

32. Travis Smith, quoted in Elizabeth Dwoskin, "Google Reaped Millions in Tax Breaks as It Secretly Expanded Its Real Estate Footprint across the U.S.," *Washington Post*, February 15, 2019, https://www.washingtonpost.com/business/economy/google-reaped-millions-of-tax-breaks-as-it-secretly-expanded-its-real-estate-footprint-across-the-us/2019/02/15/7912e10e-3136-11e9-813a-0ab2f17e305b_story.html.

33. Vattenfall, "Vattenfall Opens Princess Ariane Wind Farm, the Largest Dutch Onshore Wind Farm," press release, September 30, 2020, https://group.vattenfall.com/press-and-media/pressreleases/2020/vattenfall-opens-princess-ariane-wind-farm-the-largest-dutch-onshore-wind-farm.

34. Hamilton, "In a Small Dutch Town."

35. Sandra Beckerman, quoted in Aman Sethi, "How Facebook Secretly Lobbied to Build Holland's Biggest Data Center," *BuzzFeed News*, January 7, 2022, https://www.buzzfeednews.com/article/amansethi/operation-tulip-inside-facebooks-secretive-push-to-build.

36. David Jeans, "Data in the Dark: How Big Tech Secretly Secured $800 Million in Tax Breaks for Data Centers," *Forbes*, August 19, 2021, https://www.forbes.com/sites/davidjeans/2021/08/19/data-in-the-dark-how-big-tech-secretly-secured-800-million-in-tax-breaks-for-data-centers/.

37. Jacob Roundy, "Data Center Heat Reuse: How to Make the Most of Excess Heat," Tech Target, July 26, 2023, https://www.techtarget.com/searchdatacenter/tip/Data-center-heat-reuse-How-to-make-the-most-of-excess-heat.

38. Mike Rogoway, "The Dalles Settles Public Records Lawsuit over Google's Data Centers, Will Disclose Water Use to the Oregonian / OregonLive," *Oregonian / OregonLive*, December 14, 2022, https://www.oregonlive.com/silicon-forest/2022/12/the-dalles-settles-public-records-lawsuit-over-googles-data-centers-will-disclose-water-use.html.

39. Neil Ruddy, quoted in Sharon Adarlo, "Critics Furious Microsoft Is Training AI by Sucking Up Water during Drought," Futurism, September 26, 2023, https://futurism.com/critics-microsoft-water-train-ai-drought.

40. Steven Gonzalez Monserrate, "The Staggering Ecological Impacts of Computation and the Cloud," The MIT Press Reader, accessed January 24, 2024, https://thereader.mitpress.mit.edu/the-staggering-ecological-impacts-of-computation-and-the-cloud/.

41. Eren Çam et al., "Electricity 2024: Analysis and Forecast to 2026," International Energy Agency, January 2024, https://iea.blob.core.windows.net/assets/6b2fd954-2017-408e-bf08-952fdd62118a/Electricity2024-Analysisandforecastto2026.pdf.

42. Feargus O'Sullivan, "Denmark's Carbon Footprint Is Set to Balloon—Blame Big Tech," *Wired*, June 26, 2018, https://www.wired.com/story/denmarks-carbon-footprint-is-set-to-balloonblame-big-tech/.

43. Urs Hölzle, "Our Commitment to Climate-Conscious Data Center Cooling," *Keyword* (blog), Google, November 21, 2022, https://blog.google/outreach-initiatives/sustainability/our-commitment-to-climate-conscious-data-center-cooling/.

44. Petroc Taylor, "Number of Data Centers Worldwide 2023, by Country," Statista, September 17, 2023, https://www.statista.com/statistics/1228433/data-centers-worldwide-by-country/.

45. David Mytton, "Data Centre Water Consumption," *NPJ Clean Water* 4, no. 1 (February 15, 2021), https://www.nature.com/articles/s41545-021-00101-w.

46. "How AWS Will Return More Water than It Uses by 2030," Amazon, November 28, 2022, https://www.aboutamazon.com/news/aws/aws-water-positive-by-2030.

47. "Cloud Spending Growth Rate Slows But Q4 Still Up by $10 Billion from 2021; Microsoft Gains Market Share," Synergy Research Group, February 6, 2023, https://www.srgresearch.com/articles/cloud-spending-growth-rate-slows-but-q4-still-up-by-10-billion-from-2021-microsoft-gains-market-share.

48. Peter Judge, "EirGrid Pulls Plug on 30 Irish Data Center Projects," Data Centre Dynamics, May 24, 2022, https://www.datacenterdynamics.com/en/news/eirgrid-pulls-plug-on-30-irish-data-center-projects/.

49. Liam Tung, "Massive Data Centre Demands Could Lead to Power Blackouts, Warns Ireland's Utilities Regulator," ZDNET, June 14, 2021, https://www.zdnet.com/article/massive-data-centre-demands-could-lead-to-power-blackouts-warns-irelands-utilities-regulator/.

50. Dan Swinhoe, "Outage at Interxion Facility in London Takes Down Metals Exchange," Data Centre Dynamics, January 13, 2022, https://www.datacenterdynamics.com/en/news/outage-at-interxion-facility-in-london-takes-down-metals-exchange/.

51. Kara Fox, "Ireland's Data Centers Are an Economic Lifeline. Environmentalists Say They're Wrecking the Planet," CNN, January 23, 2022, https://edition.cnn.com/2022/01/23/tech/ireland-data-centers-climate-intl-cmd/index.html.

52. Pears Hussey, quoted in Fox, "Ireland's Data Centers."

53. Judge, "EirGrid Pulls Plug."

54. Victor Emil Kristensen, "Meta Signs Record PPA in Denmark," *Energy-Watch*, July 4, 2022, https://energywatch.com/EnergyNews/Renewables/article13903968.ece.

55. Taylor, "Number of Data Centers Worldwide."

Chapter 3

1. John Koetsier, "97% of Executives Say COVID-19 Sped up Digital Transformation," *Forbes*, September 10, 2020, https://www.forbes.com/sites/johnkoetsier/2020/09/10/97-of-executives-say-covid-19-sped-up-digital-transformation/?sh=10d8eae54799.

2. Peter Fletcher, quoted in Kate Conger and David E. Sanger, "U.S. Says It Secretly Removed Malware Worldwide, Pre-empting Russian Cyberattacks," *New York Times*, April 6, 2022, https://www.nytimes.com/2022/04/06/us/politics/us-russia-malware-cyberattacks.html.

3. Mikko Hypponen, "If It's Smart, It's Vulnerable," *Next Big Idea Club*, September 22, 2022, https://nextbigideaclub.com/magazine/smart-vulnerable-bookbite/36101/.

4. Keith Alexander, "Cyber Warfare in Ukraine Poses a Threat to the Global System," *Financial Times*, February 15, 2022, https://www.ft.com/content/8e1e8176-2279-4596-9c0f-98629b4db5a6.

5. Charlie Osborne, "Microsoft's April 2022 Patch Tuesday Tackles Two Zero-Day Vulnerabilities," ZDNET, April 12, 2022, https://www.zdnet.com/article/microsoft-april-2022-patch-tuesday-two-zero-day-vulnerabilities-tackled/.

6. Nina Klimburg-Witjes and Alexander Wentland, "Hacking Humans? Social Engineering and the Construction of the 'Deficient User' in Cybersecurity Discourses," *Science, Technology, and Human Values* 46, no. 6 (February 10, 2021), https://journals.sagepub.com/doi/10.1177/0162243921992844.

7. Ryan Gallagher and Crofton Black, "This Swiss Firm Exec Is Said to Have Operated a Secret Surveillance Operation," Bloomberg, December 6, 2021, https://www.bloomberg.com/news/articles/2021-12-06/this-swiss-tech-exec-is-said-to-have-operated-a-secret-surveillance-operation.

8. Omer Yoachimik, "DDoS Attack Trends for 2022 Q2," *Cloudflare Blog*, July 6, 2022, https://blog.cloudflare.com/ddos-attack-trends-for-2022-q2/.

9. Philipp Lutscher, Nils B. Weidmann, Margaret E. Roberts, Mattijs Jonker, Alistair King, and Alberto Dainotti, "At Home and Abroad: The Use of Denial-of-

Service Attacks during Elections in Nondemocratic Regimes," *Journal of Conflict Resolution* 64, nos. 2–3 (July 25, 2019), https://journals.sagepub.com/doi/full/10.1177/0022002719861676.

10. Andy Greenberg, "The Mirai Confessions: Three Young Hackers Who Built a Web-Killing Monster Finally Tell Their Story," *Wired*, November 14, 2023, https://www.wired.com/story/mirai-untold-story-three-young-hackers-web-killing-monster/.

11. Garrett M. Graff, "The Mirai Botnet Was Part of a College Student 'Minecraft' Scheme," *Wired*, December 13, 2017, https://www.wired.com/story/mirai-botnet-minecraft-scam-brought-down-the-internet/.

12. Doug Klein, quoted in Graff, "The Mirai Botnet."

13. Bill Walton, quoted in Graff, "The Mirai Botnet."

14. Citrix, "Six Organizations. One Complete Solution" (Fort Lauderdale, FL: Citrix, 2020), https://www.citrix.com/content/dam/citrix/en_us/documents/solution-brief/six-organizations-one-complete-solution.pdf.

15. Ministerie van Justitie en Veiligheid, *Kwetsbaar Door Software—Lessen Naar Aanleiding van Beveiligingslekken Door Software van Citrix* (The Hague: Ministerie van Justitie en Veiligheid, December 16, 2021), https://open.overheid.nl/repository/ronl-003ddd7c-328e-408e-aafc-d2c5509396ea/1/pdf/tk-bijlage-ovv-rapport-kwetsbaar-door-software-lessen-naar-aanleiding-van-beveiligingslekken-door-software-van-citrix.pdf.

16. Brian Krebs, "Hackers Were inside Citrix for Five Months," Krebs on Security, February 19, 2020, https://krebsonsecurity.com/2020/02/hackers-were-inside-citrix-for-five-months/.

17. Dan De Luce and Courtney Kube, "Officials: Iran Positioned for Extensive Cyberattacks on US," NBC News, March 8, 2019, https://www.nbcnews.com/politics/national-security/iranian-backed-hackers-stole-data-major-u-s-government-contractor-n980986.

18. Sergiu Gatlan, "US Census Bureau Hacked in January 2020 Using Citrix Exploit," *Bleeping Computer*, August 19, 2021, https://www.bleepingcomputer.com/news/security/us-census-bureau-hacked-in-january-2020-using-citrix-exploit/; Catalin Cimpanu, "Hackers Target Unpatched Citrix Servers to Deploy Ransomware," ZDNET, January 24, 2020, https://www.zdnet.com/article/hackers-target-unpatched-citrix-servers-to-deploy-ransomware/.

19. Coen Van Eenbergen, "Exclusive: Interview Citrix CISO, Fermín Serna: Where Did It Go Wrong?," Techzine Europe, January 23, 2020, https://www.techzine.eu/blogs/security/44687/exclusive-interview-citrix-ciso-fermin-serna-where-did-it-go-wrong/.

20. Ministerie van Justitie en Veiligheid, *Kwetsbaar Door Software*.

21. Krebs, "Hackers Were inside Citrix."

22. Ministerie van Justitie en Veiligheid, *Kwetsbaar Door Software*.

23. David E. Sanger, Clifford Krauss, and Nicole Perlroth, "Cyberattack Forces a Shutdown of a Top U.S. Pipeline," *New York Times*, May 8, 2021, https://www.nytimes.com/2021/05/08/us/politics/cyberattack-colonial-pipeline.html.

24. Mary Louise Kelly, Jason Fuller, and Justine Kenin, "The Colonial Pipeline CEO Explains the Decision to Pay Hackers a $4.4 Million Ransom," NPR, June 3, 2021, https://www.npr.org/2021/06/03/1003020300/colonial-pipeline -ceo-explains-the-decision-to-pay-hackers-4-4-million-ransom.

25. Livia Gershon, "Gas Shortages in 1970s America Sparked Mayhem and Forever Changed the Nation," *Smithsonian*, May 13, 2021, https://www.smithsonianmag .com/smart-news/1970s-gas-shortages-changed-america-180977726/.

26. Chris Isidore, "American Airlines Has to Add Fuel Stops after Pipeline Shutdown," CNN, May 11, 2021, https://www.cnn.com/2021/05/11/business/american -airlines-fuel-stop-colonial-pipeline-shutdown/index.html.

27. White House, "Fact Sheet: The Biden-Harris Administration Has Launched an All-of-Government Effort to Address Colonial Pipeline Incident," May 11, 2021, https://www.whitehouse.gov/briefing-room/statements-releases/2021/05/11/fact -sheet-the-biden-harris-administration-has-launched-an-all-of-government-effort -to-address-colonial-pipeline-incident/.

28. Kerry Breen, "Georgia Governor Declares State of Emergency, Activates 1,000 National Guard Troops amid Atlanta Protests," CBS News, January 26, 2023, https://www.cbsnews.com/news/atlanta-protests-georgia-governor-brian-kemp -state-of-emergency-activates-national-guard-troops/; Rachel Frazin, "Biden Officials Warn against Hoarding Gasoline amid Shortages," *The Hill*, May 12, 2021, https://thehill.com/policy/energy-environment/553137-biden-officials-warn -against-hoarding-gasoline-amid-shortages/.

29. Vanessa Romo, "How a New Team of Feds Hacked the Hackers and Got Colonial Pipeline's Ransom Back," NPR, June 8, 2021, https://www.npr.org/2021 /06/08/1004223000/how-a-new-team-of-feds-hacked-the-hackers-and-got -colonial-pipelines-bitcoin-bac.

30. Brian Krebs, "Welcome to Darkside 2.0," Krebs on Security, May 2021, https://krebsonsecurity.com/wp-content/uploads/2021/05/darkside20.txt.

31. Chris Nuttall, "DarkSide's Ransomware-as-a-Service," *Financial Times*, May 10, 2021, https://www.ft.com/content/78b2decb-f14a-4bf2-8e5e-87a3076b72dc.

32. Tom Robinson, "DarkSide Ransomware Has Netted over $90 Million in Bitcoin," Elliptic, May 18, 2021, https://www.elliptic.co/blog/darkside-ransomware -has-netted-over-90-million-in-bitcoin.

33. DarkSide, quoted in Joseph Cox, "Pipeline Hackers Say They're 'Apolitical,' Will Choose Targets More Carefully Next Time," *Vice*, May 10, 2021, https://www .vice.com/en/article/bvzzez/colonial-pipeline-hackers-statement-darkside.

34. Greg Myre, "FBI Says Darkside Ransomware Is Reponsible for Attack on U.S. Pipeline," NPR, May 11, 2021, https://www.npr.org/2021/05/11/995751021/fbi -says-darkside-ransomware-is-reponsible-for-attack-on-u-s-pipeline.

35. Kevin Breuninger and Amanda Macias, "Biden Signs Executive Order to Strengthen U.S. Cybersecurity Defenses after Colonial Pipeline Hack," CNBC, May 12, 2021, https://www.cnbc.com/2021/05/12/biden-signs-executive-order -to-strengthen-cybersecurity-after-colonial-pipeline-hack.html.

36. Joe Biden, "Remarks by President Biden on the Colonial Pipeline Incident," White House, May 13, 2021, https://www.whitehouse.gov/briefing-room

/speeches-remarks/2021/05/13/remarks-by-president-biden-on-the-colonial
-pipeline-incident/.

37. Microsoft, *Annual Report 2021* (Redmond, WA: Microsoft, 2021), https://
c.s-microsoft.com/en-us/CMSFiles/2021_Annual_Report.docx?version=5290c17d
-8858-c9ef-d16f-60e02f42214e, 2.

38. Eric Rosenbaum, "Microsoft Has a $20 Billion Hacking Plan, but Cyber-
security Has a Big Spending Problem," CNBC, September 8, 2021, https://www
.cnbc.com/2021/09/08/microsofts-20-billion-and-cybersecuritys-big-spending
-problem.html.

39. Jordan Novet, "Microsoft's $15 Billion Cybersecurity Business Is Giving
Investors New Reason for Optimism," CNBC, April 26, 2022, https://www.cnbc
.com/2022/04/26/microsoft-15-billion-security-unit-gives-investors-reason-for
-hope.html.

40. Tanya Agrawal, David Henry, and Jim Finkle, "JPMorgan Hack Exposed
Data of 83 Million, among Biggest Breaches in History," Reuters, October 2,
2014, https://www.reuters.com/article/us-jpmorgan-cybersecurity/jpmorgan
-hack-exposed-data-of-83-million-among-biggest-breaches-in-history
-idUSKCN0HR23T20141003/.

41. Shannon Bond, "Florida 17-Year-Old, 'Mastermind' of Twitter Hack, and
Two Others Face Charges," NPR, July 31, 2020, https://www.npr.org/2020/07/31
/897815039/florida-teen-charged-as-mastermind-of-massive-twitter-hack.

42. Daryna Antoniuk, "Hacker Accused of Breaching Finnish Psychotherapy
Center Facing 30,000 Counts," *The Record*, October 20, 2023, https://therecord
.media/hacker-finland-facing-charges-psychotherapy.

43. International Committee of the Red Cross, "Sophisticated Cyber-Attack
Targets Red Cross Red Crescent Data on 500,000 People," press release, January 19, 2022, https://www.icrc.org/en/document/sophisticated-cyber-attack
-targets-red-cross-red-crescent-data-500000-people.

44. Umar Shakir, "Sony Confirms Server Security Breaches That Exposed
Employee Data," The Verge, October 5, 2023, https://www.theverge.com/2023
/10/5/23905370/sony-interactive-entertainment-security-breach-confirmation;
Jason Chaffetz, "The OPM Data Breach: How the Government Jeopardized Our
National Security for More than a Generation," House Committee on Oversight
and Accountability, September 8, 2016, https://oversight.house.gov/report/opm
-data-breach-government-jeopardized-national-security-generation/.

45. A. J. Vicens, "Political Fallout in Cybercrime Circles Upping the Threat to
Western Targets," CyberScoop, March 14, 2022, https://cyberscoop.com/russia
-ukraine-cybercrime-ransomware-threat/.

46. Josef Federman, "NSO Turns to US Supreme Court for Immunity in WhatsApp," AP News, April 11, 2022, https://apnews.com/article/us-supreme-court
-technology-business-spyware-lawsuits-3a2cdcfdac224647bd65e95fd57395d5.

47. "Fitness App Strava Lights up Staff at Military Bases," BBC, January 29,
2018, https://www.bbc.com/news/technology-42853072.

48. Ciaran Martin, quoted in Rhiannon Williams, "Public Should Not Be Cow-
ering in Bunkers over Fear of Russian Cyberattack, Says Former Government Cyber

Head," *iNews*, February 22, 2022, https://inews.co.uk/news/technology/cyber-warfare-misunderstood-public-no-big-red-button-government-head-1473543.

49. Amiah Taylor, "There's a Huge Surge in Hackers Holding Data for Ransom, and Experts Want Everyone to Take These Steps," *Fortune*, February 17, 2022, https://fortune.com/2022/02/17/ransomware-attacks-surge-2021-report/.

50. Lynsey Jeffery and Vignesh Ramachandran, "Why Ransomware Attacks Are on the Rise—and What Can Be Done to Stop Them," *PBS NewsHour*, July 8, 2021, https://www.pbs.org/newshour/nation/why-ransomware-attacks-are-on-the-rise-and-what-can-be-done-to-stop-them.

51. Frank Bajak and Matt O'Brien, "Cybersecurity Firm FireEye Says Was Hacked by Nation State," AP News, April 20, 2021, https://apnews.com/article/business-california-milpitas-214da7f06ea1823cada1384643e09753.

52. Veshraj Ghimire, "Hacking Dutch Government for a Lousy T-Shirt," Medium, January 5, 2022, https://medium.com/pentesternepal/hacking-dutch-government-for-a-lousy-t-shirt-8e1fd1b56deb.

53. See, for example, ALDE ADLE, *Nerds in the Parliament*, video, 6:03, February 17, 2012, https://www.youtube.com/watch?v=4IRE_DS5N60.

54. Linus Neumann, quoted in Jose Miguel Calatayud, "Chaos Computer Club: How Did Computer 'Freaks' in Germany Come Together?," Krytyka Polityczna / European Alternatives, January 10, 2019, http://politicalcritique.org/world/eu/2019/chaos-computer-club-how-did-computer-freaks-in-germany-come-together/.

55. Meredith Whittaker (@mer_edith), "Pay attention to this. AI isn't magic. It's reliant on hardware & software like all other networked tech. And, as here, it too is subject to serious security vulnerabilities that have been drastically under examined amid the hype. Thank you @HeidyKhlaaf et al for this work!," Twitter [X], January 16, 2024, 1:21 p.m., https://twitter.com/mer__edith/status/1747323239851004012.

56. "SolarWinds Orion: More US Government Agencies Hacked," BBC, December 15, 2020, https://www.bbc.com/news/technology-55318815.

57. Jess Weatherbed, "Attackers Stole LastPass Data by Hacking an Employee's Home Computer," The Verge, February 28, 2023, https://www.theverge.com/2023/2/28/23618353/lastpass-security-breach-disclosure-password-vault-encryption-update.

Chapter 4

1. Richard Branson (@richardbranson), "My trick to get the party started? Dancing on the table! What's yours?!," Twitter [X], April 25, 2014, 12:14 p.m., https://twitter.com/richardbranson/status/459727251181809664.

2. Laura Shin, "On Sir Richard Branson's Necker Island, 'Bitcoin Illuminati' Reassess Blockchain Strategies," *Forbes*, June 10, 2016, https://www.forbes.com/sites/laurashin/2016/06/10/on-sir-richard-bransons-necker-island-bitcoin-illuminati-reassess-blockchain-strategies.

3. "Digital Assets Dashboard," *Financial Times*, accessed January 7, 2024, https://digitalassets.ft.com/.

4. Satoshi Nakamoto, "Bitcoin: A Peer-to-Peer Electronic Cash System" (white paper, Bitcoin, n.d.), accessed January 11, 2024, https://bitcoin.org/bitcoin.pdf, 1.

5. Natasha Lomas, "Meta Is Pulling the Plug on Its Crypto Payments Wallet, Novi," *TechCrunch*, July 4, 2022, https://techcrunch.com/2022/07/04/meta-novi -pilot-ends/; Josh Constine, "Facebook Announces Libra Cryptocurrency: All You Need to Know," *TechCrunch*, June 18, 2019, https://techcrunch.com/2019/06/18 /facebook-libra/.

6. Mat Youkee, "Nayib Bukele Calls Himself the 'World's Coolest Dictator'— But Is He Joking?," *Guardian*, September 27, 2021, https://www.theguardian.com /world/2021/sep/26/naybib-bukele-el-salvador-president-coolest-dictator.

7. Tomio Geron, "The Companies Powering El Salvador's New Bitcoin Economy," Protocol, September 7, 2021, https://www.protocol.com/fintech/el -salvador-crypto-economy.

8. Albinson Linares, "How the Switch to Bitcoin Currency Will Benefit El Salvador's Economy," NBC News, November 30, 2021, https://www.nbcnews.com/news /latino/bitcoin-city-el-salvador-inspired-ancient-greeks-s-reality-check-rcna6944.

9. Ian Talley, "Growing Use of Cryptocurrency in Afghanistan Poses Security Concerns," *Wall Street Journal*, September 10, 2021, https://www.wsj.com /articles/growing-use-of-cryptocurrency-in-afghanistan-poses-security-concerns -11631275200.

10. Scott Chipolina, Mercedes Ruehl, Christian Davies, and Song Jung-a, "'Crypto Paradise' Singapore Stung by High-Profile Collapses," *Financial Times*, October 2, 2022, https://www.ft.com/content/e7b85235-87e8-44c7-a97f -2d2ffa253465.

11. Mercedes Ruehl, "Singapore to Tighten Retail Access to Cryptocurrencies," *Financial Times*, August 29, 2022, https://www.ft.com/content/7cf1f46b-00b3 -4af8-997a-90efb72bfb02.

12. Ben Schreckinger, "The Middle East's Crypto Paradox," *Politico*, November 18, 2022, https://www.politico.com/news/2022/11/18/the-middle-easts -crypto-paradox-00069461.

13. Ryan Browne, "More than $200 Billion Erased from Entire Crypto Market in a Day as Sell-Off Intensifies," CNBC, May 12, 2022, https://www.cnbc.com/2022 /05/12/bitcoin-btc-price-falls-below-27000-as-crypto-sell-off-intensifies.html; David Gura, "2022 Was the Year Crypto Came Crashing Down to Earth," NPR, December 29, 2022, https://www.npr.org/2022/12/29/1145297807/crypto-crash -ftx-cryptocurrency-bitcoin.

14. David Yaffe-Bellany, Erin Griffith, and Ephrat Livni, "Cryptocurrencies Melt Down in a 'Perfect Storm' of Fear and Panic," *New York Times*, May 12, 2022, https://www.nytimes.com/2022/05/12/technology/cryptocurrencies-crash -bitcoin.html.

15. Annie Lowrey, "The Black Investors Who Were Burned by Bitcoin," *Atlantic*, November 29, 2022, www.theatlantic.com/ideas/archive/2022/11/black-investors -bitcoin-cryptocurrency-crash/671750/.

16. Michelle Faverio and Navid Massarat, "46% of Cryptocurrency Investors in US Say It Did Worse than Expected," Pew Research Center, April 10, 2023,

https://www.pewresearch.org/fact-tank/2022/08/23/46-of-americans-who-have-invested-in-cryptocurrency-say-its-done-worse-than-expected/.

17. "Nibud: Groeiende Groep Jongeren Belegt," Nibud, November 29, 2021, https://www.nibud.nl/nieuws/nibud-groeiende-groep-jongeren-belegt/.

18. Rachel Rosenbaum, Taylor Dunn, Karen Ye, Jaclyn Skurie, and Ivan Pereira, "The Year Crypto Broke: How Customers, Investors Lost Millions and What's Being Done," ABC News, January 27, 2023, https://abcnews.go.com/US/year-crypto-broke-customers-investors-lost-millions/story?id=96662010.

19. Sunil Jagtiani, "Vast Majority of Retail Crypto Investors in Bitcoin Lost Money, BIS Says," Bloomberg, November 16, 2022, https://www.bloomberg.com/news/articles/2022-11-16/vast-majority-of-retail-investors-in-bitcoin-lost-money-bis-says.

20. Camomile Shumba and Sandali Handagama, "Retail Crypto Investors in Emerging Economies Hit Hardest by FTX, Terra Collapses: BIS," CoinDesk, February 21, 2023, https://www.coindesk.com/markets/2023/02/20/retail-crypto-investors-in-emerging-economies-hit-hardest-by-ftx-terra-collapses-bis/.

21. Dan Dolev, quoted in Bellany, Griffith, and Livni, "Cryptocurrencies Melt Down."

22. Jamie Dimon, quoted in David Henry and Anna Irrera, "Bitcoin Is a 'Fraud Worse than Tulip Bulbs' Says JPMorgan CEO Jamie Dimon," *Independent*, September 13, 2017, https://www.independent.co.uk/news/business/news/bitcoin-fraud-tulip-bulbs-jpmorgan-ceo-jamie-dimon-bank-investor-crypto-currency-a7943986.html.

23. Gura, "2022 Was the Year Crypto Came Crashing Down to Earth."

24. Ethan Gach, "Crypto's Biggest Crash Saw Guy Playing League of Legends While Luring Investors [Update]," Kotaku, November 14, 2022, https://kotaku.com/ftx-crypto-scam-gamestop-token-league-legends-sbf-nft-1849767748.

25. Felix Salmon, "How Sam Bankman-Fried and Other Crypto Heroes Went to Zero," Axios, October 19, 2023, https://www.axios.com/2023/10/19/sbf-crypto-ftx.

26. Ryan Browne, "Cryptocurrency Exchange FTX Hits $32 Billion Valuation Despite Bear Market Fears," CNBC, January 31, 2022, https://www.cnbc.com/2022/01/31/crypto-exchange-ftx-valued-at-32-billion-amid-bitcoin-price-plunge.html.

27. Alex Christian, "FTX's Sam Bankman-Fried Believed in 'Effective Altruism'. What Is It?," BBC, October 9, 2023, https://www.bbc.com/worklife/article/20231009-ftxs-sam-bankman-fried-believed-in-effective-altruism-what-is-it; Jeff Wilser, "Most Influential 2021: Sam Bankman-Fried," CoinDesk, December 7, 2021, https://www.coindesk.com/markets/2021/12/07/most-influential-2021-sam-bankman-fried/; "Testimony of Sam Bankman-Fried: Co-Founder and CEO of FTX," Hearing before the U.S. House of Representatives Committee on Financial Services, December 8, 2021, https://democrats-financialservices.house.gov/uploadedfiles/hhrg-117-ba00-wstate-bankman-frieds-20211208.pdf.

28. "Bankman-Fried Happy to the Called the JP Morgan of Crypto," Bloomberg, August 31, 2022, https://www.bloomberg.com/news/videos/2022-08-31/bankman-fried-happy-to-be-called-the-jp-morgan-of-crypto; Daniel Kuhn, "Is Sam Bankman-Fried a Modern-Day Robber Baron?," CoinDesk, June 21, 2022, https://www.coindesk.com/layer2/2022/06/21/is-sam-bankman-fried-a-modern-day-robber-baron/; Dan Primack and Alexi McCammond, "Bankman-Fried Spent Millions on Dem Campaigns," Axios, November 15, 2022, https://www.axios.com/2022/11/15/ftz-crypto-bankman-fried-democrats-midterms-campaigns.

29. "FTX.US," OpenSecrets, accessed January 11, 2024, https://www.opensecrets.org/orgs/ftx-us/summary?toprecipcycle=2022&contribcycle=2022&lobcycle=2022&outspendcycle=2022&id=D000073694&topnumcycle=2022.

30. Vicky Ge Huang, Alexander Osipovich, and Patricia Kowsmann, "FTX Tapped into Customer Accounts to Fund Risky Bets, Setting Up Its Downfall," *Wall Street Journal*, November 11, 2022, https://www.wsj.com/articles/ftx-tapped-into-customer-accounts-to-fund-risky-bets-setting-up-its-downfall-11668093732.

31. David Gura, "Binance Was Once FTX's Rival and Possible Savior. Now It's Trying Not to Be Its Sequel," NPR, December 16, 2022, https://www.npr.org/2022/12/16/1143086648/binance-cz-ftx-crypto-bankruptcy-fallout-alameda-bitcoin.

32. Matthew Goldstein, Alexandra Stevenson, Maureen Farrell, and David Yaffe-Bellany, "How Alameda, FTX's Sister Firm, Brought the Crypto Exchange Down," *New York Times*, November 18, 2022, https://www.nytimes.com/2022/11/18/business/ftx-alameda-ties.html; Elizabeth Napolitano and Brian Cheung, "Sam Bankman-Fried Faces Extradition Following Arrest in Bahamas," NBC News, November 18, 2022, https://www.nbcnews.com/tech/crypto/sam-bankman-fried-crypto-ftx-collapse-explained-rcna57582; Niha Masih and Julian Mark, "What to Know about Sam Bankman-Fried and the FTX Crypto Exchange Collapse," *Washington Post*, December 14, 2022, https://www.washingtonpost.com/business/2022/12/13/sam-bankman-fried-ftx-collapse-explained/.

33. MacKenzie Sigalos, "From $32 Billion to Criminal Investigations: How Sam Bankman-Fried's Crypto Empire Vanished Overnight," CNBC, November 15, 2022, https://www.cnbc.com/2022/11/15/how-sam-bankman-frieds-ftx-alameda-empire-vanished-overnight.html.

34. Lisa Bonos, "Sam Bankman-Fried Is under House Arrest at Stanford. Students Are Obsessed," *Washington Post*, March 4, 2023, https://www.washingtonpost.com/business/2023/03/04/sam-bankman-fried-stanford-house-arrest/.

35. James Bromley, quoted in Tabby Kinder, "Sam Bankman-Fried Ran FTX as Personal Fiefdom, Court Hears," *Financial Times*, November 22, 2022, https://www.ft.com/content/470ce8e8-0e5d-4fe4-8b62-08eb0749da9c.

36. Allison Morrow, "Sam Bankman-Fried Found Guilty of Seven Counts of Fraud in Stunning Fall for Former Crypto Billionaire," CNN, November 3, 2023, https://www.cnn.com/2023/11/02/business/ftx-sbf-fraud-trial-verdict/index.html.

37. MacKenzie Sigalos, "Sam Bankman-Fried Found Guilty on All Seven Criminal Fraud Counts," CNBC, November 2, 2023, https://www.cnbc.com/2023/11/02/sam-bankman-fried-found-guilty-on-all-seven-criminal-fraud-counts.html.

38. James Fanelli and Corinne Ramey, "Sam Bankman-Fried's Life behind Bars: Crypto Tips and Paying with Fish," *Wall Street Journal*, November 23, 2023, https://www.wsj.com/finance/currencies/sam-bankman-frieds-life-behind-bars-crypto-tips-and-paying-with-fish-858097c6.

39. Tom Emmer, Darren Soto, Warren Davidson, Jake Auchincloss, Byron Donalds, Josh Gottheimer, Ted Budd, and Ritchie Torres to Gary Gensler, March 16, 2022, https://emmer.house.gov/_cache/files/0/c/0c7fc863-7916-4b19-bc44-52bef772287e/9B0B9D1CA9B3C215DDC762DF5B0F6864.3.16.22.emmer.sec.letter.pdf.

40. Anthony Clarke, "7 Biggest Crypto Collapses of 2022 the Industry Would Like to Forget," Cointelegraph, December 26, 2022, https://cointelegraph.com/news/7-biggest-crypto-collapses-of-2022-the-industry-would-like-to-forget.

41. "Mexican Cartels Turn to Bitcoin, Internet, E-commerce," Associated Press, March 10, 2022, https://apnews.com/article/business-caribbean-mexico-crime-drug-cartels-1bb5ebf84fbf71baf6a845648bad4990.

42. Constine, "Facebook Announces Libra Cryptocurrency."

43. Anna Baydakova, "ISIS Allies Used Crypto to Raise Millions: TRM Labs," CoinDesk, July 21, 2023, https://www.coindesk.com/policy/2023/07/21/isis-allies-used-crypto-to-raise-millions-trm-labs/.

44. U.S. Securities and Exchange Commission, "SEC Charges Kim Kardashian for Unlawfully Touting Crypto Security," press release, October 3, 2022, https://www.sec.gov/news/press-release/2022-183; Joel Khalili, "Love, Loss, and Pig Butchering Scams," *Wired*, September 7, 2023, https://www.wired.com/story/love-loss-and-pig-butchering-scams/.

45. Cat Clifford, "Billionaire Richard Branson: Scammers Are Pretending to Be Me to Steal Your Money," CNBC, July 9, 2019, https://www.cnbc.com/2019/07/09/richard-branson-scammers-are-pretending-to-be-me-to-steal-your-money.html.

46. MacKenzie Sigalos, "Crypto Scams Have Cost People More than $1 Billion since 2021, Says FTC," CNBC, June 3, 2022, https://www.cnbc.com/2022/06/03/crypto-scams-cost-people-more-than-1-billion-since-2021-ftc.html.

47. Christian Davies and Scott Chipolina, "How North Korea Became a Mastermind of Crypto Cyber Crime," *Financial Times*, November 14, 2022, https://www.ft.com/content/dec696d4-fd51-4cce-bbd9-1dee911eb4cd.

48. Federal Deposit Insurance Corporation, *Deposit Insurance at a Glance* (Washington, DC: Federal Deposit Insurance Corporation, 2014), https://www.fdic.gov/resources/deposit-insurance/brochures/documents/deposit-insurance-at-a-glance-english.pdf.

49. "Deposit Guarantee Schemes," European Commission, accessed January 11, 2024, https://finance.ec.europa.eu/banking-and-banking-union/banking-regulation/deposit-guarantee-schemes_en.

50. Eva Szalay, "Central Banks Step Up Fight against Cryptocurrencies," *Financial Times*, June 23, 2021, https://www.ft.com/content/b6a3bf06-ad6b-4ab4-9ae3-15aca453f50d.

51. Nic Carter, "How Much Energy Does Bitcoin Actually Consume?," *Harvard Business Review*, May 6, 2021, https://hbr.org/2021/05/how-much-energy-does-bitcoin-actually-consume.

52. Paul Brody, quoted in John Schmidt and Benjamin Curry, "Why Does Bitcoin Use So Much Energy?," *Forbes*, May 18, 2022, https://www.forbes.com /advisor/investing/cryptocurrency/Bitcoins-energy-usage-explained/.

53. Alun John, Samuel Shen, and Tom Wilson, "China's Top Regulators Ban Crypto Trading and Mining, Sending Bitcoin Tumbling," Reuters, September 24, 2021, https://www.reuters.com/world/china/china-central-bank-vows -crackdown-cryptocurrency-trading-2021-09-24/.

54. European Parliament, *Markets in Crypto-Assets (MiCA)* (Strasbourg, France: European Parliament, September 2023), https://www.europarl.europa .eu/RegData/etudes/BRIE/2022/739221/EPRS_BRI(2022)739221_EN.pdf.

55. Kristalina Georgieva, "The Future of Money: Gearing Up for Central Bank Digital Currency," International Monetary Fund, February 9, 2022, https://www .imf.org/en/News/Articles/2022/02/09/sp020922-the-future-of-money-gearing -up-for-central-bank-digital-currency.

56. Jesse Frederik, "De Blockchain: Een Oplossing Voor Bijna Niets," *De Correspondent*, August 24, 2018, https://decorrespondent.nl/8628/de-blockchain-een -oplossing-voor-bijna-niets/519071687772-2a5ee060, my translation.

57. Kashmir Hill, "The Secretive Company That Might End Privacy as We Know It," *New York Times*, January 18, 2020, https://www.nytimes.com/2020/01 /18/technology/clearview-privacy-facial-recognition.html.

58. Clearview AI, home page, accessed January 11, 2024, https://www .clearview.ai/.

59. James Clayton and Ben Derico, "Clearview AI Used Nearly 1M Times by US Police, It Tells the BBC," BBC, March 27, 2023, https://www.bbc.com/news /technology-65057011.

60. Juliette Rihl, "Emails Show Pittsburgh Police Officers Accessed Clearview Facial Recognition after BLM Protests," PublicSource, November 5, 2021, https://www.publicsource.org/pittsburgh-police-facial-recognition-blm-protests -clearview/.

61. Ryan Mac, Caroline Haskins, and Logan McDonald, "Clearview AI's Facial Recognition Tech Is Being Used by the Justice Department, ICE, and the FBI," *BuzzFeed News*, February 27, 2020, https://www.buzzfeednews.com/article /ryanmac/clearview-ai-fbi-ice-global-law-enforcement.

62. Craig McCarthy, "Rogue NYPD Cops Are Using Facial Recognition App Clearview," *New York Post*, January 23, 2020, https://nypost.com/2020/01/23 /rogue-nypd-cops-are-using-sketchy-facial-recognition-app-clearview/.

63. San Francisco Police Department, *Surveillance Impact Report* (San Francisco: San Francisco Police Department, February 2021), https://sf.gov/sites /default/files/2021-02/SFPD%20ShotSpotter%20Surveillance%20Impact%20 Report.pdf.

64. "ResourceRouter," SoundThinking, accessed January 11, 2024, https:// www.soundthinking.com/law-enforcement/resource-deployment-resource router/.

65. Abeba Birhane, "The Unseen Black Faces of AI Algorithms," *Nature* 610, no. 7932 (October 19, 2022), https://doi.org/10.1038/d41586-022-03050-7.

66. Larry Hardesty, "Study Finds Gender and Skin-Type Bias in Commercial Artificial-Intelligence Systems," *MIT News*, February 11, 2018, https://news.mit.edu/2018/study-finds-gender-skin-type-bias-artificial-intelligence-systems-0212.

67. Michael Williams, quoted in Martha Mendoza, Juliet Linderman, Michael Tarm, and Garance Burke, "How AI-Powered Tech Landed Man in Jail with Scant Evidence," Associated Press, March 5, 2022, https://apnews.com/article/artificial-intelligence-algorithm-technology-police-crime-7e3345485aa668c97606d4b54f9b6220.

68. Randal Reid, quoted in Kashmir Hill and Ryan Mac, "'Thousands of Dollars for Something I Didn't Do,'" *New York Times*, March 31, 2023, https://www.nytimes.com/2023/03/31/technology/facial-recognition-false-arrests.html.

69. Aaron Sankin, Dhruv Mehrotra, Surya Mattu, and Annie Gilbertson, "Crime Prediction Software Promised to Be Free of Biases. New Data Shows It Perpetuates Them," The Next Web, December 3, 2021, https://thenextweb.com/news/crime-prediction-software-free-of-biases-data-shows-perpetuates-them-syndication.

70. Kashmir Hill, "Clearview AI, Used by Police to Find Criminals, Is Now in Public Defenders' Hands," *New York Times*, last updated June 22, 2023, https://www.nytimes.com/2022/09/18/technology/facial-recognition-clearview-ai.html.

71. Hill, "Clearview AI."

72. Tarik Aougab, Federico Ardila, Jayadev Athreya, Edray Goins, Christopher Hoffman, Autumn Kent, Lily Khadjavi, Cathy O'Neil, Priyam Patel, and Katrin Wehrheim, "Letter to AMS Notices: Boycott Collaboration with Police," Google Docs, accessed January 11, 2024, https://docs.google.com/forms/d/e/1FAIpQLSfdmQGrgdCBCexTrpne7KXUzpbiI9LeEtd0Am-qRFimpwuv1A/viewform.

73. Dell Cameron, "'Clearview AI' Hit with Legal Complaints in 5 Countries, Accused of Face Recognition Abuse," Gizmodo, May 27, 2021, https://gizmodo.com/clearview-ai-faces-fresh-legal-complaints-in-5-countrie-1846980506.

74. Paul Ducklin, "Clearview AI Image-Scraping Face Recognition Service Hit with €20M Fine in France," Sophos, October 26, 2022, https://news.sophos.com/en-us/2022/10/26/clearview-ai-image-scraping-face-recognition-service-hit-with-e20m-fine-in-france/.

75. Janell Ross, Aaron C. Davis, and Joel Achenbach, "Immigrant Community on High Alert, Fearing Trump's 'Deportation Force,'" *Washington Post*, February 11, 2017, https://www.washingtonpost.com/national/immigrant-community-on-high-alert-fearing-trumps-deportation-force/2017/02/11/e5c30d06-f06f-11e6-9973-c5efb7ccfb0d_story.html.

76. Alex Karp, quoted in Sam Biddle, "How Peter Thiel's Palantir Helped the NSA Spy on the Whole World," The Intercept, February 22, 2017, https://theintercept.com/2017/02/22/how-peter-thiels-palantir-helped-the-nsa-spy-on-the-whole-world/.

77. Alex Karp, quoted in Douglas MacMillan and Elizabeth Dwoskin, "The War inside Palantir: Data-Mining Firm's Ties to ICE under Attack by Employees," *Washington Post*, August 22, 2019, https://www.washingtonpost.com/business/2019/08/22/war-inside-palantir-data-mining-firms-ties-ice-under-attack-by-employees/.

78. Alvaro M. Bedoya, "Big Data Has Ushered in a New and Cruel Era of Immigrant Surveillance," *Slate*, September 22, 2020, https://slate.com/technology/2020/09/palantir-ice-deportation-immigrant-surveillance-big-data.html.

79. Andy Greenberg, "How a 'Deviant' Philosopher Built Palantir, a CIA-Funded Data-Mining Juggernaut," *Forbes*, August 14, 2013, https://www.forbes.com/sites/andygreenberg/2013/08/14/agent-of-intelligence-how-a-deviant-philosopher-built-palantir-a-cia-funded-data-mining-juggernaut/.

80. Palantir Technologies, "FDA and Palantir Partner to Modernize Food Supply Chain Resilience through 21 FORWARD Initiative," PR Newswire, October 25, 2022, https://www.prnewswire.com/news-releases/fda-and-palantir-partner-to-modernize-food-supply-chain-resilience-through-21-forward-initiative-301657536.html; Anusuya Lahiri, "Palantir Joins the Ranks of Microsoft, Amazon Web Services after Winning This Contract," Yahoo Finance, October 10, 2022, https://finance.yahoo.com/news/palantir-joins-ranks-microsoft-amazon-123439646.html.

81. John Hewitt Jones, "Palantir Reports 26% Rise in Government Revenue for Q3," FedScoop, January 18, 2023, https://www.fedscoop.com/palantir-reports-26-rise-in-government-revenue-for-q3/.

82. "Defense and National Security," Congressional Budget Office, December 14, 2023, https://www.cbo.gov/topics/defense-and-national-security.

83. Dwight D. Eisenhower, "President Dwight D. Eisenhower's Farewell Address (1961)," January 17, 1961, National Archives, https://www.archives.gov/milestone-documents/president-dwight-d-eisenhowers-farewell-address.

84. Ian Oakley, "Palantir: Breaking the Big Data Mould," The Article, June 13, 2022, https://www.thearticle.com/palantir-breaking-the-big-data-mould.

85. Bundesministerium für Wirtschaft und Klimaschutz, "Das Gaia-X Ökosystem—Souveräne Dateninfrastruktur für Europa," accessed January 11, 2024, https://www.bmwk.de/Redaktion/DE/Dossier/gaia-x.html.

86. Jordan Novet, "Palantir Files to Go Public, Lost about $580 Million Last Year," CNBC, August 25, 2020, https://www.cnbc.com/2020/08/25/palantir-files-s-1-before-going-public.html.

87. Cameron Costa, "How Palantir's Tech-Based Patriotism and Politics Grew into a Multi-Billion Dollar Company," CNBC, October 13, 2022, https://www.cnbc.com/2022/10/13/how-palantirs-tech-patriotism-became-a-multi-billion-dollar-idea.html.

88. Isobel Asher Hamilton, "'Our Product Is Used on Occasion to Kill People': Palantir's CEO Claims Its Tech Is Used to Target and Kill Terrorists," Business Insider, May 26, 2020, https://www.businessinsider.com/palantir-ceo-alex-karp-claims-the-companys-tech-is-used-to-target-and-kill-terrorists-2020-5.

89. Mark Bowden, *The Finish: The Killing of Osama Bin Laden* (New York: Atlantic Monthly Press, 2012), 102.

90. Caitlin Bishop, quoted in "Seeing Stones: Pandemic Reveals Palantir's Troubling Reach in Europe," *Guardian*, April 2, 2021, https://www.theguardian.com/world/2021/apr/02/seeing-stones-pandemic-reveals-palantirs-troubling-reach-in-europe.

91. Alex Karp, quoted in Richard Waters, "Alex Karp, Unconventional Purveyor of Powerful Surveillance Tools," *Financial Times*, October 2, 2020, https://www.ft.com/content/8ea36422-2f65-4a14-93be-b7b4d38362e3.

92. Andrea Enria, "Interview at the DNB Banking Seminar," conducted by Martin Arnold, European Central Bank, November 15, 2022, https://www.bankingsupervision.europa.eu/press/interviews/date/2022/html/ssm.in221115~bd4306961f.en.html; "European Regulators Will Struggle to Supervise Crypto Groups, Warns ECB," *Financial Times*, November 13, 2022, https://www.ft.com/content/dd736e04-ecd1-47f4-8987-bf459ae0cefe.

93. John Naughton, "The Coming Wave by Mustafa Suleyman Review—AI, Synthetic Biology and a New Dawn for Humanity," *Guardian*, August 28, 2023, https://www.theguardian.com/books/2023/aug/28/the-coming-wave-by-mustafa-suleyman-review-ai-synthetic-biology-and-a-new-dawn-for-humanity.

94. Universal Declaration of Human Rights, United Nations, December 10, 1948, https://www.un.org/en/about-us/universal-declaration-of-human-rights.

95. "Declaration of Independence: A Transcription," July 4, 1776, National Archives, https://www.archives.gov/founding-docs/declaration-transcript.

Chapter 5

1. "Alexei Navalny: Millions Watch Jailed Critic's 'Putin Palace' Film," BBC, January 20, 2021, https://www.bbc.com/news/world-europe-55732296.

2. Алексей Навальный, "Putin's Palace. History of World's Largest Bribe," video, 1:52:50, January 19, 2021, https://www.youtube.com/watch?v=ipAnwilMncI.

3. Patrick Reevell, "Russia Outlaws Putin Critic Alexey Navalny's Organizations as 'Extremist,'" ABC News, June 9, 2021, https://abcnews.go.com/International/russia-outlaws-putin-critic-alexey-navalnys-organizations-extremist/story?id=78181693.

4. Anton Troianovski and Adam Satariano, "Apple and Google Remove 'Navalny' Voting App in Russia," *New York Times*, September 17, 2021, https://www.nytimes.com/2021/09/17/world/europe/russia-navalny-app-election.html.

5. Alexei Navalny, quoted in Vladimir Soldatkin, "Russia's Navalny Criticises Apple, Google over App Removal, Social Media Posts Say," Reuters, September 23, 2021, https://www.reuters.com/world/europe/russias-navalny-criticises-apple-google-over-app-removal-social-media-posts-say-2021-09-23/.

6. Mark Scott and Clothilde Goujard, "Digital Great Game: The West's Stand-off against China and Russia," *Politico*, September 8, 2022, https://www.politico.eu/article/itu-global-standard-china-russia-tech/; "Special GAC Vice-Chair Election—January–March 2023," Internet Corporation for Assigned Names and Numbers, March 15, 2023, https://gac.icann.org/activity/special-gac-vicechair-election-january-march-2023.

7. Justin Ling, "The Election That Saved the Internet from Russia and China," *Wired*, October 30, 2022, https://www.wired.com/story/itu-2022-vote-russia-china-open-internet/.

8. "EU Wants Kenya Probe," Deutsche Welle, January 1, 2008, https://www.dw.com/en/eu-calls-for-inquiry-into-allegedly-flawed-kenyan-poll/a-3032352;

David Miliband, quoted in Adrian Croft, "UK Says Has Concerns about Kenyan Election," Reuters, December 30, 2007, https://www.reuters.com/article/idUSL30241116/.

9. Jeffrey D. Sachs, "Recount Kenyans' Votes." Project Syndicate, January 23, 2008, https://www.project-syndicate.org/commentary/recount-kenyans--votes.

10. Alistair Thomson and Daniel Wallis, "Up to 1,000 Killed in Kenya Crisis—Odinga," Reuters, January 7, 2008, https://www.reuters.com/article/idUSL0743589.

11. "Kenya: Disputed 2007 and 2013 Elections, a New Constitution, and ICC Proceedings," *Encyclopedia Britannica*, accessed January 12, 2024, https://www.britannica.com/place/Kenya/Disputed-2007-and-2013-elections-a-new-constitution-and-ICC-proceedings.

12. Jennifer Cooke, "Background on the Post-election Crisis in Kenya," blog post, Center for Strategic and International Studies, August 6, 2019, https://www.csis.org/blogs/smart-global-health/background-post-election-crisis-kenya.

13. "Somalia: Alshabab Threatens to Disrupt Kenya Elections," AllAfrica, July 31, 2017, https://allafrica.com/stories/201707310467.html.

14. George Obulutsa, "Kenyans Must Play Their Part in Deal—Annan," Reuters, March 1, 2008, https://www.reuters.com/article/uk-kenya-crisis-idUKL016182320080301.

15. Tomas Statius, John-Allan Namu, Daniel Howden, and Lionel Faull, "Biometrics in Africa's Elections," Lighthouse Reports, May 24, 2022, https://www.lighthousereports.com/investigation/biometrics-and-the-enslavement-of-african-elections/.

16. Samuel Gebre, "Kenya's Turbulent 2017 Elections Cost Half a Billion Dollars," Bloomberg, February 27, 2018, https://www.bloomberg.com/politics/articles/2018-02-27/kenya-s-turbulent-2017-elections-cost-half-a-billion-dollars.

17. Valentijn Koningsberger, "Zoveel Kost Het u Om Te Mogen Stemmen," Quote, March 15, 2017, https://www.quotenet.nl/lifestyle/a193231/zoveel-kost-het-u-om-te-mogen-stemmen-193231/.

18. Gregory Warner, "How Kenya's High-Tech Voting Nearly Lost the Election," NPR, March 9, 2013, https://www.npr.org/sections/alltechconsidered/2013/03/09/173905754/how-kenyas-high-tech-voting-nearly-lost-the-election.

19. Baraka Jefwa, "OT-Morpho Prompts Date Change for Kenya's Presidential Election," CIO Africa, September 22, 2017, https://cioafrica.co/ot-morpho-october-may-soon-kenyas-election-re-run/.

20. Thierry Leveque and Leigh Thomas, "French Court Fines Safran for Nigerian Bribes," Reuters, September 5, 2012, https://www.reuters.com/article/idUSL6E8K5CGF/.

21. Justin Lee, "OT-Morpho Denies Claims Kenyan Biometric Voting System Was Hacked," Biometrics Research Group, September 19, 2017, https://www.standardmedia.co.ke/article/2001248702/iebc-s-high-tech-system-to-guard-against-ballot-stuffing.

22. "Kenyan Election Official Chris Msando 'Tortured to Death,'" BBC, August 2, 2017, https://www.bbc.com/news/world-africa-40807425.

23. James Okong'o, "False Political Quotes Fuel Online Disinformation ahead of Kenya," Agence France-Presse Fact Check, June 2, 2022, https://factcheck.afp.com/doc.afp.com.32BK2FL; Nanjala Nyabola, "Texts, Lies, and Videotape," *Foreign Policy*, August 1, 2017, https://foreignpolicy.com/2017/08/01/texts-lies-and-videotape-kenya-election-fake-news/.

24. "Kenyan Election Official Chris Msando 'Tortured to Death.'"

25. Carter Center, *Kenya 2017 General and Presidential Elections: Final Report* (Atlanta: Carter Center, 2017), https://www.cartercenter.org/resources/pdfs/news/peace_publications/election_reports/kenya-2017-final-election-report.pdf.

26. Dominique van Heerden and Lauren Said-Moorhouse, "Kenya Election: Voters Endured Long Lines, Now Wait Patiently for Results," CNN, August 7, 2017, https://www.cnn.com/2017/08/07/africa/kenya-election/index.html.

27. "Access to Electricity (% of Population)—Kenya," World Bank, 2023, https://data.worldbank.org/indicator/EG.ELC.ACCS.ZS?locations=KE.

28. Njeri Wangari, "Jokes, Hashtags and Fake News: The Story of Social Media in Kenya's Closely Contested Election," Global Voices, August 9, 2017, https://globalvoices.org/2017/08/09/jokes-hashtags-and-fake-news-the-story-of-social-media-in-kenyas-closely-contested-election/.

29. Bethlehem Feleke and Larry Madowo, "Raila Odinga Challenges Presidential Results in Kenyan Supreme Court," CNN, August 22, 2022, https://edition.cnn.com/2022/08/22/africa/odinga-challenges-kenya-elections-results-intl/index.html.

30. Nanjala Nyabola, "If You Are a Kenyan Citizen, Your Private Data Is Not Safe," Al Jazeera, February 24, 2019, https://www.aljazeera.com/opinions/2019/2/24/if-you-are-a-kenyan-citizen-your-private-data-is-not-safe.

31. Philomena Mwilu, quoted in Briana Duggan and Lauren Said-Moorhouse, "Kenya Supreme Court: 'No Choice but to Accept' Opposition Hacking Claims," CNN, September 20, 2017, https://www.cnn.com/2017/09/20/africa/kenya-election-supreme-court/index.html.

32. Jason Burke, "Kenyan Election Annulled after Result Called before Votes Counted, Says Court," *Guardian*, September 20, 2017, https://www.theguardian.com/world/2017/sep/20/kenyan-election-rerun-not-transparent-supreme-court.

33. Raila Odinga, quoted in Rael Ombuor, "Kenyan Opposition Leader Rejects New Presidential Poll, Demands 'Guarantees' against Fraud," *Washington Post*, September 5, 2017, https://www.washingtonpost.com/world/africa/kenyan-opposition-leader-rejects-new-presidential-election-demands-guarantees-against-fraud/2017/09/05/ee6e5312-9244-11e7-89fa-bb822a46da5b_story.html.

34. Lauren Said-Moorhouse, Susannah Cullinane, and Briana Duggan, "Uhuru Kenyatta Wins Disputed Kenya Presidential Rerun," CNN, October 31, 2017, https://www.cnn.com/2017/10/30/africa/kenya-election-rerun-results/index.html.

35. Kevin Sieff, "Kenya President Scores Massive Win in Election Rerun That Most Boycotted," *Washington Post*, April 9, 2023, https://www.washingtonpost.com/world/kenya-president-scores-massive-win-in-election-rerun-that-most-boycotted/2017/10/30/52375a08-054f-420f-b5fa-a8061dce4178_story.html.

36. Cybersecurity and Infrastructure Security Agency, "Joint Statement from Elections Infrastructure Government Coordinating Council & the Election Infra-

structure Sector Coordinating Executive Committees," press release, November 12, 2020, https://www.cisa.gov/news/2020/11/12/joint-statement-elections -infrastructure-government-coordinating-council-election.

37. Julius Abure, quoted in Jason Burke, "Nigeria's Opposition Calls for Election to Be Scrapped as Results Show Tinubu Leading," *Guardian*, February 28, 2023, https://www.theguardian.com/world/2023/feb/28/nigeria-election-bola -tinubu-leads-amid-anger-at-count-delays-and-rigging-claims.

38. Nanjala Nyabola, quoted in Statius et al., "Biometrics in Africa's Elections."

39. "Service for Foreign Policy Instruments: Election Observation," European Commission, accessed January 12, 2024, https://fpi.ec.europa.eu/what-we-do /election-observation_en.

40. "Kenya," Transparency International, accessed January 12, 2024, https:// www.transparency.org/en/countries/kenya; "Kenya," Freedom House, accessed January 12, 2024, https://freedomhouse.org/country/kenya.

41. Tomas Statius, "Inside the Flaws of Kenya's Electoral Biometrics," *Le Monde*, May 27, 2022, https://www.lemonde.fr/en/le-monde-africa/article/2022/05/27 /inside-the-flaws-of-kenya-s-electoral-biometrics_5984834_124.html.

42. Carter Center, *Carter Center Urges Kenya's Political Leaders to Agree on Key Changes Necessary to Implement Court Ruling for New Elections* (Atlanta: Carter Center, October 4, 2017), https://www.cartercenter.org/resources/pdfs/news/peace _publications/election_reports/kenya-statement-supreme-court-ruling-100417.pdf.

43. Ken Opala, "Muted Violence in Kenya's 2022 Elections Masked Seething Dissent," ENACT Africa, April 24, 2023, https://enactafrica.org/enact-observer /muted-violence-in-kenyas-2022-elections-masked-seething-dissent.

44. Alex Marquardt, "Exclusive: Musk's SpaceX Says It Can No Longer Pay for Critical Satellite Services in Ukraine, Asks Pentagon to Pick up the Tab," CNN, October 14, 2022, https://www.cnn.com/2022/10/13/politics/elon-musk-spacex -starlink-ukraine/index.html.

45. Alexander Freund, "Ukraine Using Starlink for Drone Strikes," Deutsche Welle, March 27, 2022, https://www.dw.com/en/ukraine-is-using-elon-musks -starlink-for-drone-strikes/a-61270528.

46. Ronan Farrow, quoted in Tonya Mosley, "Ronan Farrow Says Elon Musk Has Become an 'Arbiter' of the War in Ukraine," NPR, August 24, 2023, https://www .npr.org/2023/08/24/1195463008/ronan-farrow-says-elon-musk-has-become-an -arbiter-of-the-war-in-ukraine.

47. Marquardt, "Exclusive: Musk's SpaceX."

48. Aria Alamalhodaei, "Silicon Valley Goes to War," *TechCrunch*, February 15, 2023, https://techcrunch.com/2023/02/15/defense-tech-startups-war.

49. Rami Ayyub, "Satellite Images Show Long Trench at Ukrainian Mass Grave Site, Maxar Says," Reuters, April 3, 2022, https://www.reuters.com/world/europe /satellite-images-show-45-foot-long-trench-grave-site-bucha-maxar-2022-04-03/.

50. David E. Sanger, Julian E. Barnes, and Kate Conger, "Tech Companies Help Defend Ukraine against Cyberattacks," *New York Times*, February 28, 2022, https://www.nytimes.com/2022/02/28/us/politics/ukraine-russia-microsoft .html.

51. Charter of the United Nations, Chapter I, Article 2(1)–(5), last updated June 30, 2023, https://legal.un.org/repertory/art2.shtml.

52. Jenna McLaughlin, "Ukraine Says Government Websites and Banks Were Hit with Denial of Service Attack," NPR, February 15, 2022, https://www.npr.org/2022/02/15/1080876311/ukraine-hack-denial-of-service-attack-defense.

53. "UK Government Assess Russian Involvement in DDoS Attacks on Ukraine," National Cyber Security Centre, February 18, 2022, https://www.ncsc.gov.uk/news/russia-ddos-involvement-in-ukraine.

54. Paul Nakasone, quoted in Alexander Martin, "US Military Hackers Conducting Offensive Operations in Support of Ukraine, Says Head of Cyber Command," Sky News, June 1, 2022, https://news.sky.com/story/us-military-hackers-conducting-offensive-operations-in-support-of-ukraine-says-head-of-cyber-command-12625139.

55. Karine Jean-Pierre, "Press Briefing by Press Secretary Karine Jean-Pierre, June 1, 2022," White House, https://www.whitehouse.gov/briefing-room/press-briefings/2022/06/01/press-briefing-by-press-secretary-karine-jean-pierre-june-1-2022/.

56. Shane Huntley, "TAG Bulletin: Q1 2023," blog post, Google, May 1, 2023, https://blog.google/threat-analysis-group/tag-bulletin-q1-2023/.

57. Anne Grahn and Paul Hawkins, "Three Key Security Themes from AWS re:Invent 2022," Amazon Web Services, January 13, 2023, https://aws.amazon.com/blogs/security/three-key-security-themes-from-aws-reinvent-2022/.

58. David B. Cross, "Incorporating a Defend Forward Strategy," interview by Greg Jensen, Oracle Cloud Security, October 19, 2022, https://blogs.oracle.com/cloudsecurity/post/incorporating-a-defend-forward-strategy.

59. "APT1: Exposing One of China's Cyber Espionage Units," Mandiant, accessed January 12, 2024, https://www.mandiant.com/resources/apt1-exposing-one-of-chinas-cyber-espionage-units.

60. "An Overview of Russia's Cyberattack Activity in Ukraine," Microsoft, April 27, 2022, https://query.prod.cms.rt.microsoft.com/cms/api/am/binary/RE4Vwwd.

61. Donie O'Sullivan, "Meta Shuts Down Covert Influence Campaigns It Says Were Run from China and Russia," CNN, September 27, 2022, https://edition.cnn.com/2022/09/27/tech/meta-china-russia-influence-campaigns/index.html.

62. Victor Zhora, quoted in Shannon Van Sant, "Kyiv Argues Russian Cyberattacks Could Be War Crimes," Politico, January 9, 2023, https://www.politico.eu/article/victor-zhora-ukraine-russia-cyberattack-infrastructure-war-crime/.

63. Kate Conger and David E. Sanger, "U.S. Says It Secretly Removed Malware Worldwide, Pre-empting Russian Cyberattacks," New York Times, April 6, 2022, https://www.nytimes.com/2022/04/06/us/politics/us-russia-malware-cyberattacks.html.

64. Conger and Sanger, "U.S. Says It Secretly Removed Malware."

65. Nina Kollars and Jacquelyn Schneider, "Defending Forward: The 2018 Cyber Strategy Is Here," War on the Rocks, September 20, 2018, https://warontherocks.com/2018/09/defending-forward-the-2018-cyber-strategy-is-here/.

66. Joe Biden, quoted in Christina Wilkie, "Joe Biden Warns He Will Be Tough on State Sponsors of Cyberattacks, as U.S. Suffers Massive Hack," CNBC, December 17, 2020, https://www.cnbc.com/2020/12/17/biden-hints-at-a-tougher-stance -against-state-sponsors-of-cyberattacks.html.

67. Mark Warner, quoted in James Pearson and Jonathan Landay, "Cyberattack on NATO Could Trigger Collective Defence Clause—Official," Reuters, February 28, 2022, https://www.reuters.com/world/europe/cyberattack-nato-could -trigger-collective-defence-clause-official-2022-02-28/.

68. Jeremy Wright, "Cyber and International Law in the 21st Century," Attorney General's Office of the United Kingdom, May 23, 2018, https://www.gov.uk /government/speeches/cyber-and-international-law-in-the-21st-century.

Chapter 6

1. Scott Detrow, "What Did Cambridge Analytica Do during the 2016 Election?," NPR, March 20, 2018, https://www.npr.org/2018/03/20/595338116/what -did-cambridge-analytica-do-during-the-2016-election.

2. Christopher Wylie, quoted in Carole Cadwalladr, "'I Made Steve Bannon's Psychological Warfare Tool': Meet the Data War Whistleblower," *Guardian*, March 18, 2018, https://www.theguardian.com/news/2018/mar/17/data-war -whistleblower-christopher-wylie-faceook-nix-bannon-trump.

3. Christopher Wylie, quoted in Steven Levy, "Cambridge Analytica, Whistle-Blowers, and Tech's Dark Appeal," *Wired*, October 15, 2019, https://www.wired .com/story/cambridge-analytica-whistle-blowers-and-techs-dark-appeal/.

4. Issie Lapowsky, "Here's How Facebook Actually Won Trump the Presidency," *Wired*, November 15, 2016, https://www.wired.com/2016/11/facebook -won-trump-election-not-just-fake-news/.

5. Carole Cadwalladr, "The Great British Brexit Robbery: How Our Democracy Was Hijacked," *Guardian*, May 7, 2017, https://www.theguardian.com/technology /2017/may/07/the-great-british-brexit-robbery-hijacked-democracy.

6. Christopher Wylie, quoted in Cadwalladr, "'I Made Steve Bannon's Psychological Warfare Tool.'"

7. "Finalist: Staff of the New York Times, with Contributions from Carole Cadwalladr of the Guardian / the Observer of London," Pulitzer Prizes, 2019, https:// www.pulitzer.org/finalists/staff-new-york-times-contributions-carole-cadwalladr -guardianthe-observer-london.

8. Matthew Rosenberg, Nicholas Confessore, and Carole Cadwalladr, "How Trump Consultants Exploited the Facebook Data of Millions," *New York Times*, March 17, 2018, https://nytimes.com/2018/03/17/us/politics/cambridge-analytica -trump-campaign.html; Hannah Kuchler and Matthew Garrahan, "Facebook in Storm over Cambridge Analytica Data Scandal," *Financial Times*, March 18, 2018, https://www.ft.com/content/828e50ac-2ace-11e8-a34a-7e7563b0b0f4.

9. Salvador Rodriguez, "Here Are the Scandals and Other Incidents That Have Sent Facebook's Share Price Tanking in 2018," CNBC, November 20, 2018, https:// www.cnbc.com/2018/11/20/facebooks-scandals-in-2018-effect-on-stock.html.

10. Aaron Levie (@levie), "Welp. Tech is definitely about to get regulated. And probably for the best." Twitter [X], March 17, 2018, 11:21 a.m., https://twitter.com /levie/status/975029336834060288.

11. "Inside Trump's $100 Million Man's Rapid Rise to Power," ABC News, March 5, 2018, https://abcnews.go.com/Politics/inside-trumps-100-million-mans -rapid-rise-power/story?id=53413101.

12. Jina Moore, "Cambridge Analytica Had a Role in Kenya Election, Too," *New York Times*, March 20, 2018, https://www.nytimes.com/2018/03/20/world /africa/kenya-cambridge-analytica-election.html.

13. "Mark Zuckerberg Testimony: Senators Question Facebook's Commitment to Privacy," *New York Times*, April 10, 2018, https://www.nytimes.com/2018/04 /10/us/politics/mark-zuckerberg-testimony.html.

14. Emily Stewart, "Mark Zuckerberg Testimony: Senators Seem Really Confused about Facebook," Vox, April 10, 2018, https://www.vox.com/policy-and-politics /2018/4/10/17222062/mark-zuckerberg-testimony-graham-facebook-regulations.

15. Shara Tibken, "Questions to Mark Zuckerberg Show Many Senators Don't Get Facebook," CNET, April 11, 2018, https://www.cnet.com/news/politics/some -senators-in-congress-capitol-hill-just-dont-get-facebook-and-mark-zuckerberg/.

16. Nicolas Sarkozy, quoted in "Sarkozy Enlists Tech A-List for Web Economy Forum," Reuters, May 21, 2011, https://www.reuters.com/article/internet -idUKLDE74J0T720110521.

17. Kim Willsher, "Sarkozy Opens 'Historic' Forum on Future of Internet in Runup to G8," *Guardian*, May 24, 2011, https://www.theguardian.com/technology /2011/may/24/sarkozy-opens-e-g8-summit.

18. Nicolas Sarkozy, quoted in Willsher, "Sarkozy Opens 'Historic' Forum."

19. Eric Schmidt and Mark Zuckerberg, quoted in "Google, Facebook Warn on Internet Rules at e-G8," Reuters, May 25, 2011, https://www.reuters.com/article/us -eg8/google-facebook-warn-on-internet-rules-at-e-g8-idUSTRE74O72L20110525/.

20. Patrick Wintour, "Facebook Founder Zuckerberg Tells G8 Summit: Don't Regulate the Web," *Guardian*, May 26, 2011, https://www.theguardian.com /technology/2011/may/26/facebook-google-internet-regulation-g8.

21. "'I Am Not a Crook': How a Phrase Got a Life of Its Own," NPR, November 17, 2013, https://www.npr.org/templates/story/story.php?storyId=245830047.

22. "Corporate Average Fuel Economy (CAFE) Standards," U.S. Department of Transportation, accessed January 12, 2024, https://www.transportation.gov /mission/sustainability/corporate-average-fuel-economy-cafe-standards.

23. Susan Wojcicki, "An Update on Kids and Data Protection on YouTube," *YouTube Official Blog*, September 4, 2019, https://blog.youtube/news-and-events /an-update-on-kids/.

24. Robert M. McDowell, "This Is Why the Government Should Never Control the Internet," *Washington Post*, July 14, 2014, https://www.washingtonpost .com/posteverything/wp/2014/07/14/this-is-why-the-government-should-never -control-the-internet/.

25. Mike Masnick, "As Politicians Are Still Looking to Destroy the Internet, Covid-19 Reminds Us Why Social Media Is Not Just Good, But Saving Lives," *Tech-*

dirt (blog), March 17, 2020, https://www.techdirt.com/2020/03/17/as-politicians-are-still-looking-to-destroy-internet-covid-19-reminds-us-why-social-media-is-not-just-good-saving-lives/.

26. Daniel Ortner, "Government Regulation of Social Media Would Kill the Internet—and Free Speech," *The Hill*, August 12, 2019, https://thehill.com/opinion/technology/456900-government-regulation-of-social-media-would-kill-the-internet-and-free/.

27. Ayelet Sheffey, "Elon Musk Rips the Political Class Again, Saying 'Government Is Inherently Not a Good Steward of Capital' Even Though His Companies Thrived from Government Subsidies," Business Insider, December 13, 2021, https://www.businessinsider.com/elon-musk-government-not-good-steward-of-capital-time-interview-2021-12.

28. Mark Zuckerberg, quoted in Kate Klonick, "Inside the Making of Facebook's Supreme Court," *New Yorker*, February 12, 2021, https://www.newyorker.com/tech/annals-of-technology/inside-the-making-of-facebooks-supreme-court.

29. Mark Zuckerberg, quoted in Sara Salinas, "Mark Zuckerberg Said an Independent 'Supreme Court' Could Fix Facebook's Content Problems," CNBC, April 2, 2018, https://www.cnbc.com/2018/04/02/facebook-ceo-mark-zuckerberg-on-a-supreme-court-for-content.html.

30. Klonick, "Inside the Making of Facebook's Supreme Court."

31. Kevin Roose, "Facebook Oversight Board Tells Zuckerberg He's the Decider on Trump," *New York Times*, May 6, 2021, https://www.nytimes.com/2021/05/06/technology/facebook-oversight-board-trump.html.

32. "The Board: Expertise from around the World," Oversight Board, accessed January 12, 2024, https://www.oversightboard.com/meet-the-board/.

33. Klonick, "Inside the Making of Facebook's Supreme Court."

34. Roose, "Facebook Oversight Board."

35. Sara Fischer, "Facebook Withdraws Guidance Request for Ukraine War Content Policies," Axios, May 11, 2022, https://www.axios.com/2022/05/11/meta-facebook-oversight-board-ukraine-war.

36. Sara Fischer and Scott Rosenberg, "More than 20,000 Users Submit Cases to Facebook Oversight Board," Axios, December 1, 2020, https://www.axios.com/2020/12/01/facebook-oversight-board-20000-cases-submitted-six-chosen.

37. Sara Fischer, "Meta Provides Another $150 Million in Funding for Its Oversight Board," Axios, July 22, 2022, https://www.axios.com/2022/07/22/meta-facebook-oversight-board-funding.

38. Vanessa Pappas, "Introducing the TikTok Content Advisory Council," TikTok, March 18, 2020, https://newsroom.tiktok.com/en-us/introducing-the-tiktok-content-advisory-council.

39. Elon Musk (@elonmusk), "Twitter will be forming a content moderation council with widely diverse viewpoints. No major content decisions or account reinstatements will happen before that council convenes," Twitter [X], October 28, 2022, 2:18 p.m., https://twitter.com/elonmusk/status/1586059953311137792?lang=en.

40. Niraj Chokshi, "F.A.A. Limits Boeing's Self-Regulation Privileges," *New York Times*, May 31, 2022, https://www.nytimes.com/2022/05/31/business/faa-boeing-regulation.html; Thomas Kaplan, "After Boeing Crashes, Sharp Questions about Industry Regulating Itself," *New York Times*, March 26, 2019, https://www.nytimes.com/2019/03/26/us/politics/boeing-faa.html.

41. Facebook Receipts, home page, accessed January 12, 2024, https://facebook-receipts.the-citizens.com/.

42. Sara Salinas, "The Top Trending Video on YouTube Was a False Conspiracy That a Survivor of the Florida School Shooting Was an Actor," CNBC, February 21, 2018, https://www.cnbc.com/2018/02/21/fake-news-item-on-parkland-shooting-become-top-youtube-video.html.

43. "The EU Code of Conduct on Countering Illegal Hate Speech Online," European Commission, n.d., accessed January 12, 2024, https://commission.europa.eu/strategy-and-policy/policies/justice-and-fundamental-rights/combatting-discrimination/racism-and-xenophobia/eu-code-conduct-countering-illegal-hate-speech-online_en.

44. European Commission, "EU Code of Conduct against Online Hate Speech: Latest Evaluation Shows Slowdown in Progress," press release, November 24, 2022, https://ec.europa.eu/commission/presscorner/detail/en/ip_22_7109.

45. Christchurch Call, home page, accessed January 12, 2024, https://www.christchurchcall.com/.

46. Paris Call for Trust and Security in Cyberspace, home page, accessed January 12, 2024, https://pariscall.international/en/.

47. Cybersecurity Tech Accord, home page, accessed January 12, 2024, https://cybertechaccord.org/.

48. "Tech for Good: Taking a Stand for a Responsible and Inclusive Technological Progress," Office of the President of France, accessed January 12, 2024, https://www.elysee.fr/en/emmanuel-macron/tech-for-good-taking-a-stand-for-a-responsible-and-inclusive-technological-progress.

49. Jemima Kiss, "An Online Magna Carta: Berners-Lee Calls for Bill of Rights for Web," *Guardian*, March 12, 2014, https://www.theguardian.com/technology/2014/mar/12/online-magna-carta-berners-lee-web.

50. White House, *Blueprint for an AI Bill of Rights: Making Automated Systems Work for the American People* (Washington, DC: White House, October 2022), https://www.whitehouse.gov/wp-content/uploads/2022/10/Blueprint-for-an-AI-Bill-of-Rights.pdf.

51. "Our Principles," Google AI, accessed January 12, 2024, https://ai.google/principles/.

52. "IBM's Principles for Trust and Transparency," IBM, May 30, 2018, https://www.ibm.com/policy/trust-principles/.

53. "Empowering Responsible AI Practices," Microsoft, accessed January 12, 2024, https://www.microsoft.com/en-us/ai/responsible-ai.

54. Romain Dillet, "Dozens of Tech Companies Sign 'Tech for Good Call' Following French Initiative," *TechCrunch*, November 30, 2020, https://techcrunch

.com/2020/11/30/dozens-of-tech-companies-sign-tech-for-good-call-following
-french-initiative.

55. John Frank, "Why Does Microsoft Have an Office at the UN? A Q&A with
the Company's UN Lead," interview, *Microsoft on the Issues* (blog), October 5,
2020, https://news.microsoft.com/on-the-issues/2020/10/05/un-affairs-lead
-john-frank-unga/.

56. Frank, "Why Does Microsoft Have an Office at the UN?"

57. "Protecting Humanity with Technology: Microsoft and UN Human Rights
Office Announce Ground-Breaking Partnership," Microsoft, May 16, 2017, https://
news.microsoft.com/europe/2017/05/16/protecting-humanity-with-technology
-microsoft-and-un-human-rights-office-announce-ground-breaking-partnership.

58. Office of the High Commissioner, United Nations Human Rights, "Technology for Human Rights: UN Human Rights Office Announces Landmark Partnership with Microsoft," press release, May 16, 2017, https://www.ohchr.org/en
/2017/05/technology-human-rights-un-human-rights-office-announces-landmark
-partnership-microsoft.

59. "Mr. Paul Mitchell," United Nations Internet Governance Forum, accessed
January 12, 2024, https://www.intgovforum.org/en/content/mr-paul-mitchell.

60. Emily Birnbaum, "Tech Spent Big on Lobbying Last Year," *Politico*, January 24, 2022, https://www.politico.com/newsletters/morning-tech/2022/01/24
/tech-spent-big-on-lobbying-last-year-00001144.

61. Lauren Feiner, "Apple Ramped Up Lobbying Spending in 2022, Outpacing
Tech Peers," CNBC, January 23, 2023, https://www.cnbc.com/2023/01/23/apple
-ramped-up-lobbying-spending-in-2022-outpacing-tech-peers.html; Cat Zakrzewski, "Tech Companies Spent Almost $70 Million Lobbying Washington in 2021 as
Congress Sought to Rein In Their Power," *Washington Post*, January 21, 2022, https://
www.washingtonpost.com/technology/2022/01/21/tech-lobbying-in-washington/.

62. Pietro Lombardi, "Big Tech Boosts Lobbying Spending in Brussels," *Politico*, March 22, 2022, https://www.politico.eu/article/big-tech-boosts-lobbying
-spending-in-brussels/.

63. Suhauna Hussain, "Uber, Lyft Use New Tactics, Huge Spending to Push
Prop 22 Message Where You Can't Escape It: Your Phone," *Los Angeles Times*,
October 8, 2020, https://www.latimes.com/business/technology/story/2020-10
-08/uber-lyft-novel-tactics-huge-spending-prop-22.

64. Andrew J. Hawkins, "Uber and Lyft Had an Edge in the Prop 22 Fight:
Their Apps," The Verge, November 4, 2020, https://www.theverge.com/2020/11
/4/21549760/uber-lyft-prop-22-win-vote-app-message-notifications.

65. Amy Klobuchar, quoted in Zakrzewski, "Tech Companies Spent Almost
$70 Million."

66. "Securing Our Digital Future," FP Analytics, accessed January 12, 2024,
https://securingourdigitalfuture.com.

67. CyberPeace Institute, home page, accessed January 12, 2024, https://
cyberpeaceinstitute.org/.

68. I served as the CPI's nonexecutive president for the first two years of its
existence in a part-time capacity.

69. CyberPeace Institute, *Financial Statements for the Year Ended December 31, 2021 and Report of the Statutory Auditor on the Limited Statutory Examination* (Geneva: CyberPeace Institute, April 27, 2022), https://cyberpeaceinstitute.org /wp-content/uploads/Report-Cyberpeace-Institute-2021_eng.pdf; Tom Burt, "CyberPeace Institute Fills a Critical Need for Cyberattack Victims," *Microsoft on the Issues* (blog), September 26, 2019, https://blogs.microsoft.com/on-the-issues /2019/09/26/cyberpeace-institute-fills-a-critical-need-for-cyberattack-victims/.

70. "Tech4Democracy: Mapping Democracy—Affirming Technologies Worldwide," IE University, accessed January 12, 2024, https://www.ie.edu /tech4democracy/.

71. Global Commission on the Stability of Cyberspace, *Advancing Cyberstability: Final Report* (The Hague: Global Commission on the Stability of Cyberspace, November 2019), https://hcss.nl/wp-content/uploads/2019/11/GCSC-Final -Report-November-2019.pdf.

72. Alex Thompson, "A Google Billionaire's Fingerprints Are All Over Biden's Science Office," *Politico*, March 28, 2022, https://www.politico.com/news/2022 /03/28/google-billionaire-joe-biden-science-office-00020712.

73. Krystal Hu, "ChatGPT Sets Record for Fastest-Growing User Base—Analyst Note," Reuters, February 1, 2023, https://www.reuters.com/technology/chatgpt -sets-record-fastest-growing-user-base-analyst-note-2023-02-01/.

74. Tyler Cowen, "My Conversation with Jonathan GPT Swift," *Marginal Revolution* (blog), March 30, 2023, https://marginalrevolution.com/marginalrevolution /2023/03/my-conversation-with-jonathan-gpt-swift.html.

75. Kevin Hurler, "Chat-GPT Pretended to Be Blind and Tricked a Human into Solving a CAPTCHA," Gizmodo, March 16, 2023, https://gizmodo.com/gpt4 -open-ai-chatbot-task-rabbit-chatgpt-1850227471.

76. Evan Hubinger et al., "Sleeper Agents: Training Deceptive LLMs That Persist through Safety Training," arXiv, January 17, 2024, https://arxiv.org/pdf/2401 .05566.pdf.

77. James Vincent, "Twitter Taught Microsoft's AI Chatbot to Be a Racist Asshole in Less than a Day," The Verge, March 24, 2016, https://www.theverge.com /2016/3/24/11297050/tay-microsoft-chatbot-racist.

78. Billy Perrigo, "Exclusive: OpenAI Used Kenyan Workers on Less than $2 per Hour to Make ChatGPT Less Toxic," *Time*, January 18, 2023, https://time.com /6247678/openai-chatgpt-kenya-workers/.

79. Roger McNamee, "There Is Only One Question That Matters with AI," *Time*, April 5, 2023, https://time.com/6268843/ai-risks-democracy-technology/.

80. Sundar Pichai, "An Important Next Step on Our AI Journey," *Keyword* (blog), Google, February 6, 2023, https://blog.google/technology/ai/bard-google -ai-search-updates/.

81. David Lumb and Eli Blumenthal, "Google Said 'AI' Over 140 Times in Its 2-Hour Google I/O Keynote," CNET, May 10, 2023, https://www.cnet.com/tech /computing/google-said-ai-over-140-times-in-its-two-hour-google-io-keynote/.

82. Kevin Roose, "Why A Conversation with Bing's Chatbot Left Me Deeply Unsettled," *New York Times*, February 16, 2023, https://www.nytimes.com/2023 /02/16/technology/bing-chatbot-microsoft-chatgpt.html.

83. Rishi Iyengar, "US-China Tech Decoupling Hits AI," *Foreign Policy*, March 27, 2023, https://foreignpolicy.com/2023/03/27/us-china-ai-competition-cooperation/.

84. Koichiro Takagi, quoted in Makenzie Holland, "Experts Call for AI Regulation during Senate Hearing," Tech Target, March 10, 2023, https://www.techtarget.com/searchcio/news/365532338/Experts-call-for-AI-regulation-during-Senate-hearing.

85. Electronic Privacy Information Center, *Liberty at Risk: Pre-trial Risk Assessment Tools in the U.S.* (Washington, DC: Electronic Privacy Information Center, September 2020), https://epic.org/wp-content/uploads/2022/02/Liberty-At-Risk-Report-FALL-2020-UPDATE.pdf.

86. Natalia Mesa, "Can the Criminal Justice System's Artificial Intelligence Ever Be Truly Fair?," Massive Science, May 13, 2021, https://massivesci.com/articles/machine-learning-compas-racism-policing-fairness/.

87. "Pause Giant AI Experiments: An Open Letter," Future of Life Institute, November 27, 2023, https://futureoflife.org/open-letter/pause-giant-ai-experiments/.

88. Suzanne Smalley, "U.S. Chamber of Commerce Calls for AI Regulation," Reuters, March 9, 2023, https://www.reuters.com/technology/us-chamber-commerce-calls-ai-regulation-2023-03-09/.

89. Emily Birnbaum, "The AI 'Gold Rush' in Washington," *Politico*, June 29, 2022, https://www.politico.com/newsletters/digital-future-daily/2022/06/29/small-fry-ai-dc-try-00043278.

90. John Nay, quoted in Edd Gent, "AI Goes to K Street: ChatGPT Turns Lobbyist," *IEEE Spectrum*, January 31, 2023, https://spectrum.ieee.org/ai-lobbyist.

91. Heather Tal Murphy, "The CEO Responsible for ChatGPT Charmed Congress. But He Made One Slip-Up," *Slate*, May 17, 2023, https://slate.com/technology/2023/05/sam-altman-openai-hearing-senate-chatgpt-frivolous-lawsuit.html.

92. Sindhu Sundar, "Sam Altman Says a Government Agency Should License AI Companies—and Punish Them If They Do Wrong," Business Insider, May 16, 2023, https://www.businessinsider.com/sam-altman-openai-chatgpt-government-agency-should-license-ai-work-2023-5.

93. Martin Coulter and Supantha Mukherjee, "Focus: OpenAI CEO's Threat to Quit EU Draws Lawmaker Backlash," Reuters, May 26, 2023, https://www.reuters.com/technology/openai-ceos-threat-quit-eu-draws-lawmaker-backlash-2023-05-25/.

94. The White House, "Executive Order on the Safe, Secure, and Trustworthy Development and Use of Artificial Intelligence," October 30, 2023, https://www.whitehouse.gov/briefing-room/presidential-actions/2023/10/30/executive-order-on-the-safe-secure-and-trustworthy-development-and-use-of-artificial-intelligence/.

95. Lucy Sweeney and Emily Clark, "Inside OpenAI, a Rift between Billionaires and Altruistic Researchers Unravelled over the Future of Artificial Intelligence," Australian Broadcasting Corporation News, November 25, 2023, https://www

.abc.net.au/news/2023-11-26/openai-sam-altman-board-inside-the-chaotic-week /103149570.

96. Karen Weise, "How Microsoft's Satya Nadella Kept the OpenAI Partnership Alive," *New York Times*, November 20, 2023, https://www.nytimes.com/2023/11 /20/technology/openai-microsoft-altman-nadella.html.

97. Bobby Allyn, "How OpenAI's Origins Explain the Sam Altman Drama," NPR, November 24, 2023, https://www.npr.org/2023/11/24/1215015362/chatgpt -openai-sam-altman-fired-explained.

98. Mike Isaac, Kevin Roose, and Cade Metz, "Microsoft Hires Sam Altman Hours after OpenAI Rejects His Return," *New York Times*, November 20, 2023, https://www .nytimes.com/2023/11/20/business/openai-altman-ceo-not-returning.html.

99. Cade Metz, Tripp Mickle, Mike Isaac, Karen Weise, and Kevin Roose, "Five Days of Chaos: How Sam Altman Returned to OpenAI," *New York Times*, November 22, 2023, https://www.nytimes.com/2023/11/22/technology/how-sam -altman-returned-openai.html.

Chapter 7

1. A. Michael Spence, "Preventing the Balkanization of the Internet," blog post, Council on Foreign Relations, March 28, 2018, https://www.cfr.org/blog /preventing-balkanization-internet.

2. James Andrew Lewis, *Sovereignty and the Evolution of Internet Ideology* (Washington, DC: Center for Strategic and International Studies, October 2020), https://csis-website-prod.s3.amazonaws.com/s3fs-public/publication/201030 _Lewis_Sovereignty_Evolution_Internet_Ideology_1.pdf.

3. Peter Altmaier, quoted in Samuel Stolton, "Microsoft 'in Discussions' with Germans on Gaia-X Participation," Euractiv, February 26, 2020, https://www .euractiv.com/section/digital/news/microsoft-in-discussions-with-germans-on -gaia-x-participation/.

4. Arjun Kharpal, "Huawei Says It Would Never Hand Data to China's Government. Experts Say It Wouldn't Have a Choice," CNBC, March 5, 2019, https://www .cnbc.com/2019/03/05/huawei-would-have-to-give-data-to-china-government-if -asked-experts.html.

5. Lionel Sujay Vailshery, "Cloud Computing Market Size in Europe 2017–2021, by Quarter," Statista, August 8, 2023, https://www.statista.com/statistics/1252617 /europe-cloud-market-size-revenues/.

6. European Commission, "Commission Welcomes Political Agreement on AI Act," December 9, 2023, https://ec.europa.eu/commission/presscorner/detail /en/ip_23_6473.

7. "Digital Services Package," European Council, October 26, 2022, https:// www.consilium.europa.eu/en/policies/digital-services-package/; "Digital Markets Act: Rules for Digital Gatekeepers to Ensure Open Markets Enter into Force," European Commission, October 31, 2022, https://ec.europa.eu/commission /presscorner/detail/en/ip_22_6423.

8. "The Digital Services Act Package," European Commission, December 20, 2023, https://digital-strategy.ec.europa.eu/en/policies/digital-services-act-package.

9. Jacob Bogage and Cristiano Lima-Strong, "House and Senate Members Unveil Stalled Data Privacy Bill," *Washington Post*, June 3, 2022, https://www.washingtonpost.com/technology/2022/06/03/internet-privacy-congress-compromise-proposal/.

10. Joe Biden, "Republicans and Democrats, Unite against Big Tech Abuses," *Wall Street Journal*, January 11, 2023, https://www.wsj.com/articles/unite-against-big-tech-abuses-social-media-privacy-competition-antitrust-children-algorithm-11673439411.

11. "Five Years in a Row: India Is 2022's Biggest Internet Shutdowns Offender," Access Now, February 28, 2023, https://www.accessnow.org/press-release/keepiton-internet-shutdowns-2022-india/.

12. Matt Burgess, "What Is GDPR? The Summary Guide to GDPR Compliance in the UK," *Wired UK*, March 24, 2020, https://www.wired.co.uk/article/what-is-gdpr-uk-eu-legislation-compliance-summary-fines-2018.

13. Adam Satariano, "G.D.P.R., a New Privacy Law, Makes Europe World's Leading Tech Watchdog," *New York Times*, May 24, 2018, https://www.nytimes.com/2018/05/24/technology/europe-gdpr-privacy.html.

14. David Meyer, "Data Privacy Reform Moves toward End Game," *Politico*, June 15, 2015, https://www.politico.eu/article/data-reform-moves-to-final-negotiation-phase/.

15. Carole Cadwalladr, "Revealed: Facebook's Global Lobbying against Data Privacy Laws," *Guardian*, March 2, 2019, https://www.theguardian.com/technology/2019/mar/02/facebook-global-lobbying-campaign-against-data-privacy-laws-investment.

16. Anu Bradford, "The Brussels Effect: The Rise of a Regulatory Superstate in Europe," presentation, University of Chicago Law School, April 12, 2018, audio recording, 53:06, https://www.law.uchicago.edu/recordings/anu-bradford-brussels-effect-rise-regulatory-superstate-europe.

17. Sheera Frenkel, "Tech Giants Brace for Europe's New Data Privacy Rules," *New York Times*, January 28, 2018, https://www.nytimes.com/2018/01/28/technology/europe-data-privacy-rules.html.

18. Alex Hern and Martin Belam, "LA Times among US-Based News Sites Blocking EU Users Due to GDPR," *Guardian*, May 25, 2018, https://www.theguardian.com/technology/2018/may/25/gdpr-us-based-news-websites-eu-internet-users-la-times.

19. Věra Jourová, quoted in Satariano, "G.D.P.R., a New Privacy Law."

20. Giovanni Buttarelli, quoted in Satariano, "G.D.P.R., a New Privacy Law." Sadly, Buttarelli passed away in 2019, at the age of just sixty-two, before he could complete his term.

21. Mike Woodward, "16 Countries with GDPR-Like Data Privacy Laws," Security Scorecard, July 8, 2021, https://securityscorecard.com/blog/countries-with-gdpr-like-data-privacy-laws.

22. Natasha Lomas, "Lack of Big Tech GDPR Decisions Looms Large in EU Watchdog's Annual Report," *TechCrunch*, February 19, 2020, https://techcrunch.com/2020/02/19/lack-of-big-tech-gdpr-decisions-looms-large-in-eu-watchdogs-annual-report/.

23. "Algoritmetoezicht AP van Start," Autoriteit Persoonsgegevens, January 16, 2023, https://autoriteitpersoonsgegevens.nl/nl/nieuws/algoritmetoezicht-ap-van-start.

24. Marietje Schaake, *Issue Brief: The European Commission's Artificial Intelligence Act* (Stanford, CA: Stanford University Human-Centered Artificial Intelligence, June 2021), https://hai.stanford.edu/sites/default/files/2021-06/HAI_Issue-Brief_The-European-Commissions-Artificial-Intelligence-Act.pdf.

25. "The EU Wants to Become the World's Super-Regulator in AI," *Economist*, April 24, 2021, https://www.economist.com/europe/2021/04/24/the-eu-wants-to-become-the-worlds-super-regulator-in-ai.

26. Tom Wheeler, quoted in David McCabe, "White House Unveils Initiatives to Reduce Risks of AI," *New York Times*, May 4, 2023, https://www.nytimes.com/2023/05/04/technology/us-ai-research-regulation.html.

27. Thierry Breton, quoted in Bertille Bayart and Jacques-Olivier Martin, "Thierry Breton: 'C'est aux Gafa de S'adapter à Nos Règles, Pas L'inverse,'" *Le Figaro*, April 10, 2018, https://www.lefigaro.fr/secteur/high-tech/2018/04/06/32001-20180406ARTFIG00280-thierry-breton-c-est-aux-gafa-de-s-adapter-a-nos-regles-pas-l-inverse.php, my translation.

28. "European Chips Act," European Commission, accessed January 12, 2024, https://commission.europa.eu/strategy-and-policy/priorities-2019-2024/europe-fit-digital-age/european-chips-act_en.

29. Jan Strupczewski, "EU Unveils 300 Billion Euro Answer to China's Belt and Road," Reuters, December 1, 2021, https://www.reuters.com/markets/rates-bonds/eu-unveils-300-bln-euro-global-investment-scheme-2021-12-01/.

30. "NextGenerationEU," European Commission, n.d., accessed January 12, 2024, https://commission.europa.eu/strategy-and-policy/eu-budget/eu-borrower-investor-relations/nextgenerationeu_en.

31. Lauren Feiner, "Threads, Meta's Twitter Competitor, Is Not Yet Available in the EU Due to Regulatory Concerns," CNBC, July 6, 2023, https://www.cnbc.com/2023/07/06/metas-threads-not-available-in-the-eu-due-to-legal-complexity.html.

32. Cathy McMorris Rodgers, quoted in Dara Kerr, "Lawmakers Grilled TikTok CEO Chew for 5 Hours in a High-Stakes Hearing about the App," NPR, March 23, 2023, https://www.npr.org/2023/03/23/1165579717/tiktok-congress-hearing-shou-zi-chew-project-texas.

33. Cecilia Kang, David McCabe, and Sapna Maheshwari, "Lawmakers Appear Unconvinced by TikTok Chief's Testimony," *New York Times*, March 23, 2023, https://www.nytimes.com/live/2023/03/23/technology/tiktok-hearing-congress.

34. J. D. Vance, quoted in Katherine Tangalakis-Lippert, "RESTRICT Act Explained: Proposed TikTok Ban Is 'a PATRIOT Act for the Digital Age,' Some

Lawmakers Say," *Business Insider*, April 23, 2023, https://www.businessinsider .com/what-is-restrict-act-explained-tiktok-ban-summary-2023-4.

35. Will Oremus, "America's Online Privacy Problems Are Much Bigger Than TikTok," *Washington Post*, March 24, 2023, https://www.washingtonpost.com /technology/2023/03/24/tiktok-online-privacy-laws/.

36. Safiya Noble and Rashad Robinson, "Op-ed: Under Musk's Twitter Take-over, Who Will Protect Users?," *Los Angeles Times*, April 28, 2022, https://www .latimes.com/opinion/story/2022-04-28/elon-musk-twitter-accountability -racism-monopoly-regulation.

37. Lina Khan, quoted in Greg Ip, "Antitrust's New Mission: Preserving Democracy, Not Efficiency," *Wall Street Journal*, July 7, 2021, https://www.wsj .com/articles/antitrusts-new-mission-preserving-democracy-not-efficiency -11625670424.

38. David Shepardson, "U.S. FTC Denies Meta Petition to Recuse Khan from within Unlimited Review," Reuters, February 2, 2023, https://www.reuters .com/markets/deals/us-ftc-denies-meta-petition-recuse-khan-within-unlimited -review-2023-02-02/; Jay Greene and Rachel Lerman, "Amazon Seeks Recusal of FTC Chair Khan, a Longtime Company Critic," *Washington Post*, June 30, 2021, https://www.washingtonpost.com/technology/2021/06/30/amazon-khan-ftc -recusal/.

39. Federal Trade Commission, "FTC Sues Amazon for Illegally Maintaining Monopoly Power," press release, September 26, 2023, https://www.ftc.gov/news -events/news/press-releases/2023/09/ftc-sues-amazon-illegally-maintaining -monopoly-power; Cat Zakrzewski, "FTC Plans to Bar Meta from Monetizing Teens' Data after Privacy Lapses," *Washington Post*, May 3, 2023, https://www .washingtonpost.com/technology/2023/05/03/ftc-meta-children-data-privacy/.

40. Mary Clare Jalonick and Matt O'Brien, "House Republicans Interrogate FTC's Khan over Regulation of Big Tech," Associated Press, July 13, 2023, https:// apnews.com/article/republicans-ftc-khan-technology-companies-41610756160e1 0732f7ded6c587cec0e.

41. White House, "Fact Sheet: President Biden Signs Executive Order to Pro-hibit U.S. Government Use of Commercial Spyware That Poses Risks to National Security," press release, March 29, 2023, https://www.whitehouse.gov/briefing -room/statements-releases/2023/03/27/fact-sheet-president-biden-signs -executive-order-to-prohibit-u-s-government-use-of-commercial-spyware-that -poses-risks-to-national-security.

42. John Sakellariadis, "Treasury Slaps Sanctions on Notorious European Spy-ware Maker," *Politico*, March 5, 2024, https://www.politico.com/news/2024/03 /05/treasury-Sanctions-european-spyware-maker-00144908.

43. White House, Executive Order on Improving the Nation's Cybersecurity, May 12, 2021, https://www.whitehouse.gov/briefing-room/presidential-actions /2021/05/12/executive-order-on-improving-the-nations-cybersecurity/.

44. White House, Executive Order on America's Supply Chains, February 24, 2021, https://www.whitehouse.gov/briefing-room/presidential-actions/2021/02 /24/executive-order-on-americas-supply-chains/; Cybersecurity and Infrastructure

Security Agency, "Executive Order on Improving the Nation's Cybersecurity," accessed January 13, 2024, https://www.cisa.gov/topics/cybersecurity-best-practices/executive-order-improving-nations-cybersecurity.

45. Keith Krach, quoted in Peter Coy, "U.S. Policy: Against China, 'America First' Is Becoming America and Others," Bloomberg, December 9, 2020, https://www.bloomberg.com/news/articles/2020-12-09/u-s-policy-against-china-america-first-is-becoming-america-and-others.

46. "The Clean Network," U.S. Department of State, accessed January 13, 2024, https://2017-2021.state.gov/the-clean-network/index.html.

47. Anthony Boadle, "Brazil Backs U.S. Clean Network Proposal for Transparent 5G Technology," Reuters, November 11, 2020, https://www.reuters.com/article/us-usa-brazil-5g-idusKBN27R06T.

48. Phil Mattingly, "Biden Administration Issues Rules to Curtail China's Access to Microchip Technology," CNN, October 7, 2022, https://www.cnn.com/2022/10/07/politics/china-us-semi-conductor-chips/index.html; U.S. Department of Commerce, Bureau of Industry and Security, "Commerce Strengthens Restrictions on Advanced Computing Semiconductor Manufacturing Equipment, and Supercomputing Items to Countries of Concern," press release, October 17, 2023, https://www.bis.doc.gov/index.php/documents/about-bis/newsroom/press-releases/3355-2023-10-17-bis-press-release-acs-and-sme-rules-final-js/file.

49. Sujai Shivakumar, Charles Wessner, and Thomas Howell, *A Seismic Shift: The New U.S. Semiconductor Export Controls and the Implications for U.S. Firms, Allies, and the Innovation Ecosystem* (Washington, DC: Center for International and Strategic Studies, November 14, 2022, https://csis-website-prod.s3.amazonaws.com/s3fs-public/publication/221114_Shivakumar__ExportControlImplications_v2.pdf?VersionId=1SyaKGTyhKCu0jkMw1ePtAkAPoSOw4fl.

50. Liesje Schreinemacher, quoted in Marc Hijink, "Nederland Bepaalt Zelf Hoe Export van ASML-Techniek Naar China Beperkt Wordt," *NRC*, November 19, 2022, https://www.nrc.nl/nieuws/2022/11/19/handelsoorlog-nederland-bepaalt-zelf-hoe-export-van-asml-techniek-naar-china-beperkt-wordt-a4148783, my translation; Marc Hijink, "ASML-Topman over Export Naar China: 'Wij Hebben al Genoeg Ingeleverd,'" *NRC*, December 13, 2022, https://www.nrc.nl/nieuws/2022/12/13/asml-topman-over-export-naar-china-wij-hebben-al-ingeleverd-a4151373.

51. Pieter Haeck, "The Netherlands to Block Export of Advanced Chips Printers to China," *Politico*, March 8, 2023, https://www.politico.eu/article/netherlands-impose-restrictions-chips-export-to-china-asml/.

52. Jamil Anderlini and Clea Caulcutt, "Europe Must Resist Pressure to Become 'America's Followers,' Says Macron," *Politico*, April 9, 2023, https://www.politico.eu/article/emmanuel-macron-china-america-pressure-interview/.

53. Janet Yellen, quoted in Demetri Sevastopulo, "Janet Yellen Warns US Decoupling from China Would Be 'Disastrous,'" *Financial Times*, April 20, 2023, https://www.ft.com/content/b38478a6-7a30-47f0-a8f7-6c89dd77d324.

54. Eric Schmidt, foreword to Jon Bateman, *U.S.-China Technological "Decoupling": A Strategy and Policy Framework* (Washington, DC: Carnegie Endowment for International Peace, 2022), https://carnegieendowment.org/files/Bateman_US-China_Decoupling_final.pdf, ix.

55. Brian J. Egan, Eytan J. Fisch, Michael E. Leiter, Brooks E. Allen, Jordan Cannon, and Katie Clarke, "US Moves to Narrowly Limit Investment in China," Skadden, Arps, Slate, Meagher & Flom, August 10, 2023, https://www.skadden.com /insights/publications/2023/08/us-moves-to-narrowly-limit-investment-in-china.

56. Juro Osawa, "U.S. Investors Are Bailing Out of China Funds," The Information, June 12, 2023, https://www.theinformation.com/articles/before-sequoia -split-a-100-billion-american-cash-spigot-to-chinese-vcs-ran-dry.

57. "EU-US Trade and Technology Council," European Commission, n.d., accessed January 13, 2024, https://commission.europa.eu/strategy-and-policy /priorities-2019-2024/stronger-europe-world/eu-us-trade-and-technology -council_en.

58. Danielle Cave, Samantha Hoffman, Alex Joske, Fergus Ryan, and Elise Thomas, "Enabling and Exporting Digital Authoritarianism," in *Mapping China's Technology Giants* (Canberra: Australian Strategic Policy Institute, 2019), https:// www.jstor.org/stable/resrep23072, 8.

59. Kurt M. Campbell and Ely Ratner, "The China Reckoning: How Beijing Defied American Expectations," *Foreign Affairs*, February 13, 2018, https://www .foreignaffairs.com/articles/china/2018-02-13/china-reckoning.

60. Jon Bateman, "Countering Unfair Chinese Economic Practices and Intellectual Property Theft," in *U.S.-China Technological "Decoupling,"* 97–103, https://car negieendowment.org/files/Bateman_Countering_Unfair_Economic_Practices.pdf.

61. Lai Lin Thomala, "Number of Internet Users in China from 2013 to June 2023," Statista, August 29, 2023, https://www.statista.com/statistics/265140 /number-of-internet-users-in-china/.

62. Jane Wakefield, "AI Emotion-Detection Software Tested on Uyghurs," BBC, May 25, 2021, https://www.bbc.com/news/technology-57101248.

63. Sui-Lee Wee, "China Uses DNA to Track Its People, with the Help of American Expertise," *New York Times*, February 21, 2019, https://www.nytimes.com /2019/02/21/business/china-xinjiang-uighur-dna-thermo-fisher.html.

64. Darren Byler, quoted in Wakefield, "AI Emotion-Detection Software."

65. Nick Schifrin and Dan Sagalyn, "Critics Say This Chinese Tech Spreads Authoritarianism," *PBS NewsHour*, October 1, 2019, https://www.pbs.org/newshour /show/is-this-chinese-technology-a-trojan-horse-for-spreading-authoritarianism.

66. Katie Canales and Aaron Mok, "China's 'Social Credit' System Ranks Citizens and Punishes Them with Throttled Internet Speeds and Flight Bans If the Communist Party Deems Them Untrustworthy," Business Insider, November 28, 2022, https://www.businessinsider.com/china-social-credit-system-punishments -and-rewards-explained-2018-4.

67. Meaghan Tobin and Katherine Lee, "How Chinese Citizens Use Puns to Get Past Internet Censors," *Rest of World*, October 11, 2022, https://restofworld .org/2022/china-social-media-censorship/.

68. "Communist Party Members Must Study Xi Jinping's Thinking," *Economist*, April 14, 2023, https://www.economist.com/china/2023/04/13/communist-party -members-must-study-xi-jinpings-thinking.

69. Michael Jordan, quoted in Tim Bontemps, "Michael Jordan Stands Firm on 'Republicans Buy Sneakers, Too' Quote, Says It Was Made in Jest," ESPN, May 4,

2020, https://www.espn.com/nba/story/_/id/29130478/michael-jordan-stands-firm-republicans-buy-sneakers-too-quote-says-was-made-jest.

70. Patrick McGee, "How Apple Tied Its Fortunes to China," *Financial Times*, January 17, 2023, https://www.ft.com/content/d5a80891-b27d-4110-90c9-561b7836f11b.

71. Christina Lu, "China's Rare-Earth Monopoly Leaves the U.S. Scrambling," *Foreign Policy*, June 23, 2023, https://foreignpolicy.com/2023/06/23/america-rare-earths-industry-china/.

72. Jack Nicas, Raymond Zhong, and Daisuke Wakabayashi, "Inside Apple's Compromises in China: A Times Investigation," *New York Times*, May 17, 2021, https://www.nytimes.com/2021/05/17/technology/apple-china-censorship-data.html.

73. Peter Kafka, "Apple's Decision to Pull an App Used by Hong Kong Protestors Shows How Much It Needs China," Vox, October 10, 2019, https://www.vox.com/recode/2019/10/10/20908480/apple-china-hkmap-app-censorship-hong-kong-protests-tim-cook.

74. James Clayton, "Apple Takes Down Quran App in China," BBC, October 15, 2021, https://www.bbc.com/news/technology-58921230.

75. Nicas, Zhong, and Wakabayashi, "Inside Apple's Compromises."

76. Rebecca MacKinnon, quoted in Cecilia Kang and Katie Benner, "Russia Requires Apple and Google to Remove LinkedIn from Local App Stores," *New York Times*, January 6, 2017, https://www.nytimes.com/2017/01/06/technology/linkedin-blocked-in-russia.html.

77. Nicas, Zhong, and Wakabayashi, "Inside Apple's Compromises."

78. Simon Denyer, "Command and Control: China's Communist Party Extends Reach into Foreign Companies," *Washington Post*, January 28, 2018, https://www.washingtonpost.com/world/asia_pacific/command-and-control-chinas-communist-party-extends-reach-into-foreign-companies/2018/01/28/cd49ffa6-fc57-11e7-9b5d-bbf0da31214d_story.html.

79. Paige Leskin, "Here Are All the Major US Tech Companies Blocked behind China's 'Great Firewall,'" Business Insider Nederland, October 10, 2019, https://www.businessinsider.nl/major-us-tech-companies-blocked-from-operating-in-china-2019-5/.

80. Ryan Gallagher, "Google Plans to Launch Censored Search Engine in China, Leaked Documents Reveal," The Intercept, August 1, 2018, https://theintercept.com/2018/08/01/google-china-search-engine-censorship/.

81. Davey Alba, "A Google VP Told the US Senate the Company Has 'Terminated' the Chinese Search App Dragonfly," *BuzzFeed News*, July 16, 2019, https://www.buzzfeednews.com/article/daveyalba/google-project-dragonfly-terminated-senate-hearing.

82. Lingling Wei, "China Blocked Jack Ma's Ant IPO after Investigation Revealed Likely Beneficiaries," *Wall Street Journal*, February 16, 2021, https://www.wsj.com/articles/china-blocked-jack-mas-ant-ipo-after-an-investigation-revealed-who-stood-to-gain-11613491292.

83. Arjun Kharpal, "Alibaba Founder Jack Ma Back in China after Months Abroad in Sign Beijing May Be Warming to Tech," CNBC, March 27, 2023,

https://www.cnbc.com/2023/03/27/alibaba-founder-jack-ma-back-in-china-after
-months-abroad.html; Kana Inagaki, Ryan McMorrow, Tom Mitchell, and Leo
Lewis, "Alibaba Founder Jack Ma Living in Tokyo since China's Tech Crackdown,"
Financial Times, November 29, 2022, https://www.ft.com/content/2f7c7a10-2df3
-4f1b-8d2a-eea0e0548713.

84. "How China's Data Rules Will Impact Its Trade Competitiveness," World
Economic Forum, November 30, 2022, https://www.weforum.org/agenda/2022
/11/china-data-export-regulations-threaten-trade-competitiveness/.

85. "Xi Jinping's Vow of World Dominance by 2049 Sends Chill through Markets," Bloomberg, October 26, 2022, https://www.bloomberg.com/news/articles
/2022-10-26/xi-s-vow-of-world-dominance-by-2049-sends-chill-through-markets.

86. Ghalia Kadiri and Joan Tilouine, "A Addis-Abeba, Le Siège de l'Union
Africaine Espionné Par Pékin," *Le Monde*, January 26, 2018, https://www.lemonde
.fr/afrique/article/2018/01/26/a-addis-abeba-le-siege-de-l-union-africaine
-espionne-par-les-chinois_5247521_3212.html.

87. Emily Feng, Yuan Yang, and John Aglionby, "African Union Accuses China
of Hacking Headquarters," *Financial Times*, January 29, 2018, https://www.ft.com
/content/c26a9214-04f2-11e8-9650-9c0ad2d7c5b5.

88. Bianca Wright, "Made in China: Africa's ICT Infrastructure Backbone,"
CIO, March 22, 2020, https://www.cio.com/article/193170/made-in-china-africas
-ict-infrastructure-backbone.html.

89. France 24, "China's Xi Pledges $60 Billion to Africa, Says 'No Strings
Attached,'" September 3, 2018, https://www.france24.com/en/20180903-china
-xi-jinping-pledges-60-billion-africa-investment-summit-beijing.

90. "Assessing China's Digital Silk Road: A Transformative Approach to
Technology Financing or a Danger to Freedoms?," Council on Foreign Relations,
accessed January 13, 2024, https://www.cfr.org/china-digital-silk-road/.

91. Catherine Tsalikis, "Nanjala Nyabola on the 'Digital Colonialism' Transforming Kenya's Political Discourse," Centre for International Governance Innovation, November 5, 2019, https://www.cigionline.org/articles/nanjala-nyabola
-digital-colonialism-transforming-kenyas-political-discourse/.

92. "Assessing China's Digital Silk Road."

93. Thomas S. Eder, Rebecca Arcesati, and Jacob Mardell, "Networking the
'Belt and Road'—The Future Is Digital," Mercator Institute for China Studies,
August 28, 2019, https://merics.org/en/tracker/networking-belt-and-road-fu
ture-digital.

94. Samuel Woodhams, "Huawei Says Its Surveillance Tech Will Keep African
Cities Safe but Activists Worry It'll Be Misused," Quartz, March 20, 2020, https://qz
.com/africa/1822312/huaweis-surveillance-tech-in-africa-worries-activists.

95. Gordon Corera, "Chinese Technology Poses Major Risk—GCHQ Chief,"
BBC, October 11, 2022, https://www.bbc.com/news/uk-63207771.

96. "V. Protecting Internet Security," China Internet Information Center,
June 8, 2010, http://www.china.org.cn/government/whitepaper/2010-06/08
/content_20207978.htm.

97. "Five Years in a Row."

98. Rhea Mogul, "India Cuts Internet to 27 Million as Punjab Police Hunt Sikh Separatist," CNN, March 20, 2023, https://www.cnn.com/2023/03/20/india /india-separatist-manhunt-internet-shutdown-intl-hnk/index.html.

99. Jayshree Bajoria, "'No Internet Means No Work, No Pay, No Food': Internet Shutdowns Deny Access to Basic Rights in 'Digital India,'" Human Rights Watch, June 14, 2023, https://www.hrw.org/report/2023/06/14/no-internet-means-no -work-no-pay-no-food/internet-shutdowns-deny-access-basic.

100. "Freedom of the Net 2022: India," Freedom House, accessed January 13, 2024, https://freedomhouse.org/country/india/freedom-net/2022.

101. "India's Democratic Backsliding," *Financial Times*, April 20, 2023, https:// www.ft.com/content/6c98e1aa-85da-4738-b889-fc4d76d1d0bc.

102. Patrick Jones, "Lessons from India's Attempt to Marry Biometric and Voter ID Databases," Brookings Institution, April 27, 2022, https://www.brook ings.edu/articles/lessons-from-indias-attempt-to-marry-biometric-and-voter-id -databases/.

103. K. Sudhir and Shyam Sunder, "What Happens When a Billion Identities Are Digitized?," Yale Insights, March 27, 2020, https://insights.som.yale.edu /insights/what-happens-when-billion-identities-are-digitized.

104. Zack Whittaker, "India's Farmers Exposed by New Aadhaar Data Leak," *TechCrunch*, June 14, 2022, https://techcrunch.com/2022/06/13/aadhaar-leak -pm-kisan/.

105. Jones, "Lessons from India's Attempt."

106. Chetan Thathoo, "PM Modi Bats for India Stack, Says India's Digital Public Infra Can Tackle Global Challenges," Inc42, August 19, 2023, https://inc42.com /buzz/pm-modi-bats-for-india-stack-says-indias-digital-public-infra-can-tackle -global-challenges/.

107. Benjamin Parkin, John Reed, and Jyotsna Singh, "The India Stack: Open- ing the Digital Marketplace to the Masses," *Financial Times*, April 20, 2023, https:// www.ft.com/content/cf75a136-c6c7-49d0-8c1c-89e046b8a170.

108. "India Showing Way for the World with Its Dominance in Digital Public Goods: Nadella," *The Hindu*, January 5, 2023, https://www.thehindu.com/business /india-showing-way-for-the-world-with-its-dominance-in-digital-public-goods -nadella/article66342811.ece.

109. Lotus McDougal, Anita Raj, and Abhishek Singh, "The Digital Divide and Is It Holding Back Women in India?," *Hindustan Times*, January 16, 2022, https:// www.hindustantimes.com/ht-insight/gender-equality/the-digital-divide-and-is -it-holding-back-women-in-india-101641971745195.html.

110. Anirudh Burman, "Understanding India's New Data Protection Law," Car- negie India, October 3, 2023, https://carnegieindia.org/2023/10/03/understanding -india-s-new-data-protection-law-pub-90624.

111. Udbhav Tiwari, quoted in Parkin, Reed, and Singh, "The India Stack"; "Who We Are," Mozilla Foundation, accessed January 13, 2024, https://foundation .mozilla.org/en/who-we-are/.

112. Parkin, Reed, and Singh, "The India Stack."

113. "India: Journalists Face Attacks, Judicial Harassment, and Censorship," International Press Institute, May 31, 2023, https://ipi.media/india-monitoring

-october-2022-march-2023/; "BBC Ordered to Delhi High Court over Modi Documentary," BBC, May 22, 2023, https://www.bbc.com/news/world-asia-india -65670818.

114. Hannah Ellis-Petersen, "India Threatened to Shut Twitter Down, Co-founder Jack Dorsey Says," *Guardian*, June 13, 2023, https://www.theguardian .com/world/2023/jun/13/india-threatened-to-shut-twitter-down-co-founder -jack-dorsey-says.

115. Nand Kumar Singh, Ajay Kumar Yadav, Brajkishor Pathak, and Jaishree Bajaj, "Situation of Internet Filtration in India," *International Journal of Computer Science Trends and Technology* 4, no. 5 (2016), http://www.ijcstjournal.org/volume -4/issue-5/IJCST-V4I5P11.pdf.

116. "Freedom of the Net 2022: India"; Hannah Ellis-Petersen, "India Bans TikTok after Himalayan Border Clash with Chinese Troops," *Guardian*, June 30, 2020, https://www.theguardian.com/world/2020/jun/29/india-bans-tiktok-after -himalayan-border-clash-with-chinese-troops.

117. "Digital Payments Swell as 42% Indians Make Multiple Online Payments During Covid-19 Lockdown," *Economic Times Government*, April 16, 2020, https:// government.economictimes.indiatimes.com/news/digital-payments/digital -payments-swell-as-42-indians-make-multiple-online-payments-during-covid -19-lockdown/75172943.

118. Telecom Regulatory Authority of India, *The Indian Telecom Services Performance Indicators: October–December, 2021* (New Delhi: Telecom Regula-tory Authority of India, May 4, 2022), https://www.trai.gov.in/sites/default/files /QPIR_05052022.pdf.

119. Daniel Cooper, "Facebook Buys 9.9 Percent of India's Biggest Mobile Network," *Engadget*, April 22, 2020, https://www.engadget.com/facebook-5-7 -billion-jio-110527488.html; Sankalp Phartiyal, "Google Buys 7.7% of Reliance's Digital Unit Jio for $4.5 Bln," Reuters, July 15, 2020, https://www.reuters.com /article/reliance-agm/google-buys-7-7-of-reliances-digital-unit-jio-for-4-5-bln -idUSFWN2EL12L.

120. Abhirup Roy and Chandini Monnappa, "Google to Invest up to $1 Billion in India's Bharti Airtel," Reuters, January 28, 2022, https://www.reuters.com/world /india/google-invest-up-1-bln-indias-bharti-airtel-2022-01-28/.

121. Manish Singh, "India to Require Facebook and Twitter Rely on Gov't Fact Checking," *TechCrunch*, April 6, 2023, https://techcrunch.com/2023/04/06/india -cracks-down-on-betting-games/.

122. Aditya Kalra, "Google Opposes Facebook-Backed Proposal for Self-Regulatory Body in India—Sources," Reuters, August 11, 2022, https://www.reuters .com/world/india/google-opposes-facebook-backed-proposal-self-regulatory -body-india-sources-2022-08-11/.

123. Martin Coulter, "YouTube's CEO Says Free Speech Is a 'Core Value' Even after Removing Videos by Putin Critic Alexey Navalny," Business Insider, September 27, 2021, https://www.businessinsider.com/youtube-google-russia -putin-google-alexey-navalny-app-removal-2021-9.

124. "Next Billion Users," *Keyword* (blog), Google, October 1, 2022, https:// blog.google/technology/next-billion-users/.

125. "Freedom of the Net 2022: Tunisia," Freedom House, 2022, https://freedomhouse.org/country/tunisia/freedom-net/2022.

126. Yau Tsz Yan, "Smart Cities or Surveillance? Huawei in Central Asia," *Diplomat*, August 7, 2019, https://thediplomat.com/2019/08/smart-cities-or-surveillance-huawei-in-central-asia/.

127. "Declaration for the Future of the Internet," U.S. Department of State, April 4, 2023, https://www.state.gov/declaration-for-the-future-of-the-internet.

Chapter 8

1. Méabh Mc Mahon and Jorge Liboreiro, "'No One Will Leave' the EU Market Because of New AI Rules, Says Thierry Breton," Euronews, June 27, 2023, https://www.euronews.com/my-europe/2023/06/27/no-one-will-leave-the-eu-market-because-of-new-ai-rules-says-thierry-breton.

2. "EU AI Act: First Regulation on Artificial Intelligence," European Parliament, August 6, 2023, https://www.europarl.europa.eu/news/en/headlines/society/20230601STO93804/eu-ai-act-first-regulation-on-artificial-intelligence.

3. Dani Di Placido, "Why Did 'Balenciaga Pope' Go Viral?," *Forbes*, March 27, 2023, https://www.forbes.com/sites/danidiplacido/2023/03/27/why-did-balenciaga-pope-go-viral/.

4. Chris Stokel-Walker, "We Spoke to the Guy behind the Viral AI Image of the Pope," *BuzzFeed News*, March 27, 2023, https://www.buzzfeednews.com/article/chrisstokelwalker/pope-puffy-jacket-ai-midjourney-image-creator-interview.

5. Shannon Bond, "Fake Viral Images of an Explosion at the Pentagon Were Probably Created by AI," NPR, May 22, 2023, https://www.npr.org/2023/05/22/1177590231/fake-viral-images-of-an-explosion-at-the-pentagon-were-probably-created-by-ai.

6. Philip Marcelo, "FACT FOCUS: Fake Image of Pentagon Explosion Briefly Sends Jitters through Stock Market," Associated Press, May 23, 2023, https://apnews.com/article/pentagon-explosion-misinformation-stock-market-ai-96f534c790872fde67012ee81b5ed6a4.

7. Tiffany Hsu and Stuart A. Thompson, "A.I. Muddies Israel–Hamas War in Unexpected Way," *New York Times*, October 28, 2023, https://www.nytimes.com/2023/10/28/business/media/ai-muddies-israel-hamas-war-in-unexpected-way.html.

8. Tom Simonite, "What Happened to the Deepfake Threat to the Election?," *Wired*, November 16, 2020, https://www.wired.com/story/what-happened-deepfake-threat-election/; Karen Hao and Will Douglas Heaven, "The Year Deepfakes Went Mainstream," *MIT Technology Review*, December 25, 2020, https://www.technologyreview.com/2020/12/24/1015380/best-ai-deepfakes-of-2020/.

9. Luca Bertuzzi, "EU's AI Act Negotiations Hit the Brakes over Foundation Models," Euractiv, November 15, 2023, https://www.euractiv.com/section/artificial-intelligence/news/eus-ai-act-negotiations-hit-the-brakes-over-foundation-models/.

10. Shoshana Zuboff, "Democracy Can Still End Big Tech's Dominance over Our Lives," *Time*, May 5, 2022, https://time.com/6173639/democracy-big-techs-dominance-shoshana-zuboff/.

11. Kevin Roose, "AI Poses 'Risk of Extinction,' Industry Leaders Warn," *New York Times*, May 30, 2023, https://www.nytimes.com/2023/05/30/technology/ai-threat-warning.html.

12. Ryan Browne and MacKenzie Sigalos, "A.I. Has a Discrimination Problem. In Banking, the Consequences Can Be Severe," CNBC, June 23, 2023, https://www.cnbc.com/2023/06/23/ai-has-a-discrimination-problem-in-banking-that-can-be-devastating.html.

13. Marcia Nieuwenhuis and Cyrine Beune, "Nederlandse Huis-Tuin-en-Keukenchips in Killerdrones: Bedrijven Geschokt," *AD*, December 10, 2022, https://www.ad.nl/binnenland/nederlandse-huis-tuin-en-keukenchips-in-killerdrones-bedrijven-geschokt~af6b3105/.

14. "Precautionary Principle," EUR-Lex, accessed January 14, 2024, https://eur-lex.europa.eu/EN/legal-content/glossary/precautionary-principle.html.

15. "What Are the Chances of an AI Apocalypse?," *Economist*, July 10, 2023, https://www.economist.com/science-and-technology/2023/07/10/what-are-the-chances-of-an-ai-apocalypse.

16. Will Shanklin, "OpenAI Reportedly Warned Microsoft about Rushing GPT-4 Integration into Bing," *Engadget*, June 13, 2023, https://www.engadget.com/openai-reportedly-warned-microsoft-about-rushing-gpt-4-integration-into-bing-182044458.html.

17. Alexander C. Karp, "Alexander Karp of Palantir on A.I. Weapons Development," *New York Times*, July 27, 2023, https://www.nytimes.com/2023/07/25/opinion/karp-palantir-artificial-intelligence.html.

18. "Pause Giant AI Experiments: An Open Letter," Future of Life Institute, March 22, 2023, https://futureoflife.org/open-letter/pause-giant-ai-experiments/.

19. Edmon Begoli, Robert Bridges, T. Sean Oesch, and Kathryn Knight, "What Clinical Trials Can Teach Us about the Development of More Resilient AI for Cybersecurity" (research paper, Oak Ridge National Laboratory, Oak Ridge, TN, June 1, 2021), arXiv, https://arxiv.org/pdf/2105.06545.pdf.

20. Adam D. Thierer, *Permissionless Innovation: The Continuing Case for Comprehensive Technological Freedom* (Arlington, VA: Mercatus Center, George Mason University, 2016).

21. Mark Mazzetti, Ronen Bergman, and Adam Goldman, "Who Paid for a Mysterious Spy Tool? The FBI, an FBI Inquiry Found," *New York Times*, July 31, 2023, https://www.nytimes.com/2023/07/31/us/politics/nso-spy-tool-landmark-fbi.html.

22. Parliamentary Assembly, *Pegasus and Similar Spyware and Secret State Surveillance* (Strasbourg, France: Council of Europe, September 20, 2023), https://rm.coe.int/pegasus-and-similar-spyware-and-secret-state-surveillance/1680ac7f68.

23. Mark Mazzetti, Ronen Bergman, and Matina Stevis-Gridneff, "How the Global Spyware Industry Spiraled Out of Control," *New York Times*, January 29, 2023, https://www.nytimes.com/2022/12/08/us/politics/spyware-nso-pegasus-paragon.html.

24. Angelique Chrisafis, Dan Sabbagh, Stephanie Kirchgaessner, and Michael Safi, "Emmanuel Macron Identified in Leaked Pegasus Project Data," *Guardian*,

July 20, 2021, https://www.theguardian.com/world/2021/jul/20/emmanuel-macron-identified-in-leaked-pegasus-project-data.

25. "Abortion Bans across the Country: Tracking Restrictions by State," *New York Times*, December 8, 2023, https://www.nytimes.com/interactive/2022/us/abortion-laws-roe-v-wade.html.

26. Cat Zakrzewski, Pranshu Verma, and Claire Parker, "Texts, Web Searches about Abortion Have Been Used to Prosecute Women," *Washington Post*, July 6, 2022, https://www.washingtonpost.com/technology/2022/07/03/abortion-data-privacy-prosecution/.

27. Office of Senator Elizabeth Warren, "Warren, Wyden, Murray, Whitehouse, Sanders Introduce Legislation to Ban Data Brokers from Selling Americans' Location and Health Data," press release, June 15, 2022, https://www.warren.senate.gov/newsroom/press-releases/warren-wyden-murray-whitehouse-sanders-introduce-legislation-to-ban-data-brokers-from-selling-americans-location-and-health-data.

28. Alex LaCasse, "California Legislature Passes Delete Act Regulating Data Brokers," International Association of Privacy Professionals, September 15, 2023, https://iapp.org/news/a/california-legislature-passes-delete-act-for-pi-aggregated-by-data-brokers/.

29. Emma Roth, "Kenya Suspends Sam Altman's Eyeball-Scanning Crypto Project," The Verge, August 2, 2023, https://www.theverge.com/2023/8/2/23817147/kenya-worldcoin-suspended-sam-altman-eyeball-scanning.

30. Iain Withers and Tom Wilson, "JPMorgan's UK Bank Chase to Ban Crypto Transactions," Reuters, September 26, 2023, https://www.reuters.com/technology/jpmorgans-uk-bank-chase-ban-crypto-transactions-2023-09-26/.

31. Huw Jones, "IMF and Regulators Set Out Roadmap to Contain Crypto Risks," Reuters, September 12, 2023, https://www.reuters.com/technology/imf-regulators-set-out-roadmap-contain-crypto-risks-2023-09-07/.

32. Johan Van Overtveldt, quoted in Lubomir Tassev, "Chair of EU Parliament's Committee on Budgets Calls for Crypto Ban amid Banking Turmoil," Bitcoin News, March 19, 2023, https://news.bitcoin.com/chair-of-eu-parliaments-committee-on-budgets-calls-for-crypto-ban-amid-banking-turmoil/.

33. Jacquelyn Melinek, "Binance and CEO 'CZ' Plead Guilty to Federal Charges, Agreed to Pay $4.3B in Fines," *TechCrunch*, November 21, 2023, https://techcrunch.com/2023/11/21/binance-to-pay-4-3b-in-fines-and-ceo-cz-to-step-down-plead-guilty-to-anti-money-laundering-charges/.

34. "China Declares All Crypto-Currency Transactions Illegal," BBC, September 24, 2021, https://www.bbc.com/news/technology-58678907.

35. Kate Conger, "Hackers' Fake Claims of Ukrainian Surrender Aren't Fooling Anyone. So What's Their Goal?," *New York Times*, April 5, 2022, https://www.nytimes.com/2022/04/05/us/politics/ukraine-russia-hackers.html.

36. Ben Read, quoted in Conger, "Hackers' Fake Claims."

37. "Sponsorship Identification Rules," Federal Communications Commission, last updated January 13, 2021, https://www.fcc.gov/consumers/guides/sponsorship-identification-rules.

38. White House, Executive Order on the Safe, Secure, and Trustworthy Development and Use of Artificial Intelligence, October 30, 2023, https://www.whitehouse.gov/briefing-room/presidential-actions/2023/10/30/executive-order-on-the-safe-secure-and-trustworthy-development-and-use-of-artificial-intelligence/.

39. Ali Swenson, "FEC Moves toward Potentially Regulating AI Deepfakes in Campaign Ads," *PBS NewsHour*, August 10, 2023, https://www.pbs.org/newshour/politics/fec-moves-toward-potentially-regulating-ai-deepfakes-in-campaign-ads.

40. Tiffany Hsu, "As Deepfakes Flourish, Countries Struggle with Response," *New York Times*, January 22, 2023, https://www.nytimes.com/2023/01/22/business/media/deepfake-regulation-difficulty.html.

41. Peter Suciu, "'Created by AI' Warning Labels Are Coming to Social Media," *Forbes*, August 2, 2023, https://www.forbes.com/sites/petersuciu/2023/08/02/created-by-ai-warning-labels-are-coming-to-social-media/?sh=6be4debf72bb.

42. "Giant Glowing 'X' Sign atop Twitter Office in San Francisco Removed," *Guardian*, August 1, 2023, https://www.theguardian.com/us-news/2023/jul/31/x-sign-lights-san-francisco-twitter-office-removed.

43. Matt Durot, "Saudi Prince Alwaleed Becomes Twitter's Second Largest Shareholder," *Forbes*, October 31, 2022, https://www.forbes.com/sites/mattdurot/2022/10/31/saudi-prince-alwaleed-becomes-twitters-second-largest-shareholder/?sh=564d711c523a.

44. Stephanie Kirchgaessner, "Alarm on Capitol Hill over Saudi Investment in Twitter," *Guardian*, November 4, 2022, https://www.theguardian.com/technology/2022/nov/03/saudi-twitter-investment-us-national-security-risk.

45. David Kaye, quoted in Kirchgaessner, "Alarm on Capitol Hill."

46. Becky Peterson and Kate Clark, "Saudi Arabia Discloses Ties to Andreessen Horowitz, Dozens of Other Venture Funds," The Information, June 10, 2023, https://www.theinformation.com/articles/saudi-arabia-discloses-ties-to-andreessen-horowitz-dozens-of-other-venture-funds.

47. Huib Modderkolk and Erik Verwiel, "Politie Wil Niets Loslaten over Haar Selectie van Hacksoftware," *De Volkskrant*, April 9, 2022, https://www.volkskrant.nl/a-b26d9f4f.

48. Huib Modderkolk, "AIVD Gebruikt Omstreden Israëlische Hacksoftware," *De Volkskrant*, June 2, 2022, https://www.volkskrant.nl/a-b05a6d91.

49. Samuel Stolton, "New York Times Sues EU over Von Der Leyen's Pfizer Texts," *Politico*, February 16, 2023, https://www.politico.eu/article/new-york-times-sue-european-union-ursula-von-der-leyen-pfizer-texts/.

50. White House, Executive Order on Transforming Federal Customer Experience and Service Delivery to Rebuild Trust in Government, December 13, 2021, https://www.whitehouse.gov/briefing-room/presidential-actions/2021/12/13/executive-order-on-transforming-federal-customer-experience-and-service-delivery-to-rebuild-trust-in-government/.

51. Organisation for Economic Co-operation and Development, *Government at a Glance 2021* (Paris: Organisation for Economic Co-operation and Development, 2021), https://www.oecd-ilibrary.org/governance/government-at-a-glance-2021_1c258f55-en.

52. Linnet Taylor, "Public Actors without Public Values: Legitimacy, Domination and the Regulation of the Technology Sector," *Philosophy and Technology* 34, no. 4 (January 20, 2021), https://doi.org/10.1007/s13347-020-00441-4.

53. "Hospital Price Transparency," Center for Medicare & Medicaid Services, n.d., accessed January 14, 2024, https://www.cms.gov/hospital-price-transparency.

54. Will Kenton, "SEC Form 10-Q: Definition, Deadlines for Filing, and Components," Investopedia, December 8, 2023, https://www.investopedia.com/terms/1/10q.asp.

55. Lindsay Clark, "Oracle, Microsoft Barely Compete for a Quarter of Their US Federal Contracts," *Register*, February 1, 2023, https://www.theregister.com/2023/02/01/oracle_microsoft_us_government/.

56. "Spending by Prime Award," USASpending, accessed January 14, 2024, https://www.usaspending.gov/search/?hash=1167e33dc23300154b7af53a835c6243.

57. "Build America, Buy America Act—Federal Financial Assistance," White House, October 25, 2023, https://www.whitehouse.gov/omb/management/made-in-america/build-america-buy-america-act-federal-financial-assistance/.

58. Olaf Storbeck and Michael O'Dwyer, "EY Banned by German Audit Watchdog over Wirecard Work," *Financial Times*, April 3, 2023, https://www.ft.com/content/3d4f3c1d-ec75-4b5a-bdc7-1b0f731bdf04?.

59. Julian E. Barnes, "China's Hacking of U.S. Government Email Was Espionage, Official Says," *New York Times*, July 21, 2023, https://www.nytimes.com/2023/07/20/us/politics/china-hacking-official-email.html.

60. Ron Wyden to Jen Easterly, Merrick B. Garland, and Lina Khan, July 27, 2023, https://www.wyden.senate.gov/imo/media/doc/wyden_letter_to_cisa_doj_ftc_re_2023_microsoft_breach.pdf.

61. "The OTA Legacy," Princeton University, accessed January 14, 2024, https://www.princeton.edu/~ota/.

62. Daniel Liberto, "Systemically Important Financial Institution (SIFI) Overview," Investopedia, March 27, 2023, https://www.investopedia.com/terms/s/systemically-important-financial-institution-sifi.asp.

63. "Digital Services Act: Commission Designates First Set of Very Large Online Platforms and Search Engines," European Commission, April 25, 2023, https://ec.europa.eu/commission/presscorner/detail/en/IP_23_2413.

64. "Declaration for the Future of the Internet," U.S. Department of State, April 4, 2023, https://www.state.gov/declaration-for-the-future-of-the-internet.

65. United Nations, "AI Advisory Body," accessed February 1, 2024, https://www.un.org/en/ai-advisory-body.

66. Group of Seven, *G7 Hiroshima Leaders' Communiqué* (Hiroshima, Japan: Group of Seven, May 20, 2023), https://www.g7hiroshima.go.jp/documents/pdf/Leaders_Communique_01_en.pdf.

67. Hiroki Habuka, "The Path to Trustworthy AI: G7 Outcomes and Implications for Global AI Governance," Center for Strategic and International Studies, June 6, 2023, https://www.csis.org/analysis/path-trustworthy-ai-g7-outcomes-and-implications-global-ai-governance.

68. Foo Yun Chee, "Exclusive: G7 to Agree AI Code of Conduct for Companies," Reuters, October 29, 2023, https://www.reuters.com/technology/g7-agree-ai-code-conduct-companies-g7-document-2023-10-29/.

69. Karen Maex, "Protect Independent and Public Knowledge," speech to the University of Amsterdam, January 8, 2021, https://www.eua.eu/downloads/content/speech-karen-maex---dies-2021.pdf.

70. Nihal Krishan, "Major Government Tech Contractors Use Monopolistic Vendor-Lock to Drive Revenue, Study Says," FedScoop, February 1, 2023, https://fedscoop.com/major-government-tech-contractors-use-monopolistic-vendor-lock-to-drive-revenue-study/.

71. Lionel Sujay Vailshery, "Vendor Market Share in Cloud Infrastructure Services Market Worldwide 2017–2022," Statista, August 6, 2023, https://www.statista.com/statistics/967365/worldwide-cloud-infrastructure-services-market-share-vendor/.

72. Andrew Rasiej, "Andrew Rasiej, Co-founder, Personal Democracy Forum," interview, *Guardian*, April 14, 2011, https://www.theguardian.com/activate/andrew-rasiej-personal-democracy-forum.

73. New_Public home page, https://newpublic.org/.

74. "Public Stack: Design Process," Waag Futurelab, accessed January 14, 2024, https://publicstack.net/layers/#design-process.

75. "About," Initiative for Digital Public Infrastructure, May 3, 2023, https://publicinfrastructure.org/about/.

76. PublicSpaces, home page, accessed January 14, 2024, https://publicspaces.net/.

77. Ministry of Economic Affairs and Climate Policy, *Public Procurement Monitoring Report of the Netherlands* (The Hague: Ministry of Economic Affairs and Climate Policy, April 2021), https://ec.europa.eu/docsroom/documents/47780/attachments/1/translations/en/renditions/native.

78. Aleid Wolfsen, quoted in Fleur Damen and Rudy Bouma, "De Privacywet Wordt Amper Gehandhaafd, Is Meer Geld de Oplossing?," Nederlandse Omroep Stichting, March 25, 2021, https://nos.nl/nieuwsuur/artikel/2374135-de-privacywet-wordt-amper-gehandhaafd-is-meer-geld-de-oplossing, my translation.

Conclusion

1. Tara Sepehri Far, "Woman Dies in Custody of Iran's 'Morality Police,'" Human Rights Watch, September 16, 2022, https://www.hrw.org/news/2022/09/16/woman-dies-custody-irans-morality-police.

2. Nosheen Iqbal, "'This Is a Revolution': 5 Women on the Ongoing Fight for Freedom in Iran," *British Vogue*, November 29, 2022, https://www.vogue.co.uk/arts-and-lifestyle/article/iran-protests-activists.

3. Katie Polglase, Gianluca Mezzofiore, and Lauren Kent, "The US Says It's Helping Iranians Navigate a Massive Internet Blackout. Activists Say It's Too Little, Too Late," CNN, October 4, 2022, https://www.cnn.com/2022/10/04/world/iran-internet-blackout-intl-cmd/index.html.

4. Elon Musk (@elonmusk), "Activating Starlink . . . ," Twitter [X], September 23, 2022, 2:30 p.m., https://twitter.com/elonmusk/status/1573379244268437504.

5. Karl Vick, "Receivers for Elon Musk's Starlink Internet Are Being Smuggled into Iran," *Time*, October 22, 2022, https://time.com/6223999/starlink-iran-elon -musk/.

6. Joshua Askew, "China Turbocharging Crackdown on Iranian Women, Say Experts," Euronews, April 14, 2023, https://www.euronews.com/2023/04/14 /china-is-turbo-charging-repression-of-iranian-women-say-experts.

7. "AI Can Help Improve Precision Radiotherapy," Antoni Van Leeuwenhoek Nederlands Kanker Institut, n.d., accessed January 14, 2024, https://www.avl.nl/en /news-items/2021/ai-can-help-improve-precision-radiotherapy/; Louis Colum-bus, "10 Ways AI Has the Potential to Improve Agriculture in 2021," *Forbes*, Febru-ary 17, 2021, https://www.forbes.com/sites/louiscolumbus/2021/02/17/10-ways -ai-has-the-potential-to-improve-agriculture-in-2021/; Nilay Patel, "Why Signal Won't Compromise on Encryption, with President Meredith Whittaker," The Verge, October 18, 2022, https://www.theverge.com/23409716/signal-encryption -messaging-sms-meredith-whittaker-imessage-whatsapp-china.

8. "What Requirements Must Coffee Comply with to Be Allowed on the European Market?," Centre for the Promotion of Imports, December 14, 2022, https://www.cbi.eu/market-information/coffee/what-requirements-should-your -product-comply.

9. "Oversight of A.I.: Principles for Regulation," U.S. Senate Committee on the Judiciary, July 25, 2023, https://www.judiciary.senate.gov/committee-activity /hearings/oversight-of-ai-principles-for-regulation.

10. Lindsey Graham and Elizabeth Warren, "Lindsey Graham and Elizabeth Warren: We Must Regulate Big Tech," *New York Times*, July 27, 2023, https://www .nytimes.com/2023/07/27/opinion/lindsey-graham-elizabeth-warren-big-tech -regulation.html.

11. Rishi Sunak, "Rishi Sunak and Elon Musk: Talk AI, Tech and the Future," video, 51:16, November 3, 2023, https://www.youtube.com/watch?v=R2meHtrO1n8.

12. "Musk to Integrate xAI Startup with Social Media Platform X," Deutsche Welle, November 6, 2023, https://www.dw.com/en/musk-to-integrate-xai-startup -with-social-media-platform-x/a-67312507.

13. Marc Andreessen, "Why AI Will Save the World," Andreessen Horowitz, September 19, 2023, https://a16z.com/2023/06/06/ai-will-save-the-world/.

ACKNOWLEDGMENTS

The Tech Coup could not have been written without the support of a group of wonderful Stanford research assistants. In particular, I thank the brilliant and text-intuitive dream team of Oren Fliegelman and Christopher Maximos. Without their loyalty and humor, hours of fact checking, text corrections, endnote tweaking, and kind words about what sometimes seemed a never-ending story, the book would not be what it is today. Of course, I take full responsibility for any unintended errors.

I am also grateful for the forceful women who supported the book from concept to publication: Zoë Pagnamenta at Calligraph, Bridget Flannery-McCoy at Princeton University Press, Aileen Boyle at Audere Media, and their teams. You were all instrumental in various stages of conceptualizing, writing, and promoting.

The manuscript was reviewed by three professors I am humbled to consider peers. Their timely feedback was invaluable in bringing the book further. My time was freed up thanks to the support of the Hewlett Foundation: thank you, Kelly Born.

To all my colleagues at Stanford's Cyber Policy Center and at Stanford's Institute for Human-Centered Artificial Intelligence, it is a pleasure to learn from you and to work with you. Thank you for welcoming me as a policy guest in academia, in particular Nate Persily and Rob Reich.

At the end of the course Democracy at Home and Abroad that I taught with Michael McFaul and Rob Reich in 2023, one of the students suggested to others that they start a "democracy club" to continue discussing the importance of democracy after the course was over. While writing, my mind often wandered around the world, to voters in Nairobi, former colleagues in Brussels, and constituents in Amsterdam, and to Stanford classrooms, Washington meeting rooms, and Palo Alto boardrooms. Meeting with a wide variety of people, and hearing their perspectives, reminds me of the importance of each and every one of us as active participants in the democratic process. We are already members of the club.

Being part of an eclectic global community of people who care deeply about ensuring technology takes its proper place in our societies has sharpened my thoughts and my drive to improve technology policy.

At home, the many evenings early mornings I spent writing were never met with any complaints, but with cups of coffee and words of encouragement. This book would not have received the needed time and attention if it had not been for my loving and supporting partner.

INDEX

A NOTE ON THE TYPE

This book has been composed in Adobe Text and Gotham.
Adobe Text, designed by Robert Slimbach for Adobe,
bridges the gap between fifteenth- and sixteenth-century
calligraphic and eighteenth-century Modern styles.
Gotham, inspired by New York street signs, was designed
by Tobias Frere-Jones for Hoefler & Co.